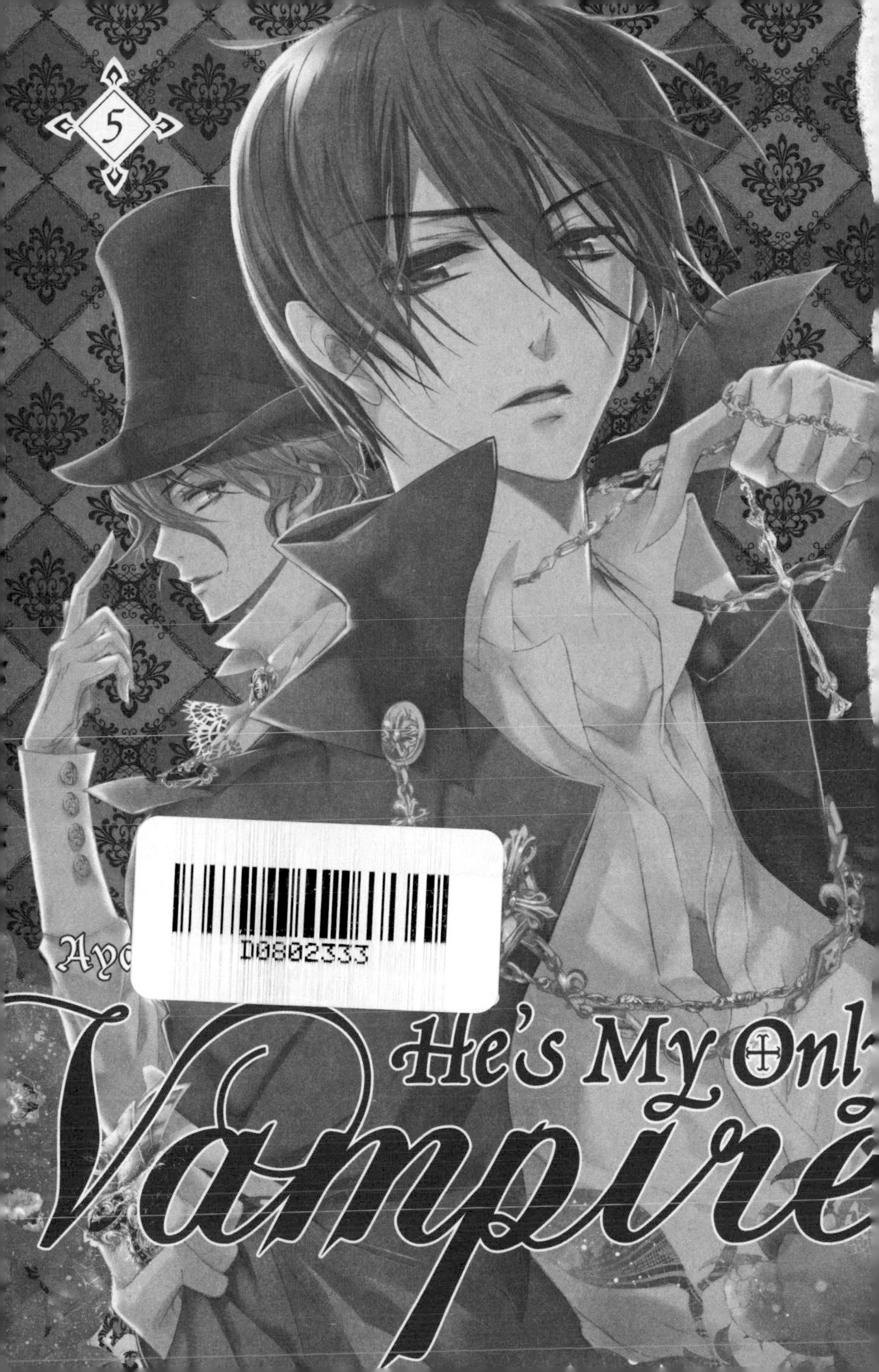
5
Ayo
He's My Onl
Vampire

Characters and Story

"Thrall"

**One who is ageless and deathless,
and shall surrender the entirety of their being to
their vampire master for all of eternity...**

THIS IS THE STORY OF THE VAMPIRE AKI AND HIS THRALL, KANA. AKI HAD COME TO THE TOWN IN WHICH KANA LIVES IN ORDER TO WIN THE GAME TO COLLECT THE SEVEN STIGMAS AND USE THEIR POWER TO WAKE HIS SLUMBERING BROTHER, ERIYA. AKI AND KANA, ALONG WITH THEIR FRIEND JIN, FORMED A SCHOOL CLUB CALLED THE "CURIOUS EVENTS CLUB" IN ORDER TO GATHER INFORMATION ON THE STIGMAS.

ONE DAY, THE DARK NOBILITY CATCHES UP TO AKI IN THE FORM OF A PERVERSE "SOIREE," DURING WHICH KANA AWAKENS AS A "TRUE THRALL." WHEN AKI IS WEAKENED AFTER OBTAINING HIS SECOND STIGMA, KANA USES HER NEW POWER TO PROTECT HIM FROM THE ANGELS ISUKA AND HITAKI. SOON AFTER, WHEN THE SERIAL KILLER "PHANTOM" BEGINS HUNTING AKI FOR HIS STIGMAS, KANA AND FRIENDS MANAGE TO TURN THE TABLES AND CAPTURE HIM INSTEAD, ALLOWING AKI TO SUCCESSFULLY GAIN HIS THIRD STIGMA. BUT UNBEKNOWNST TO THEM, SOMEONE WAS OBSERVING THE ENTIRE ENCOUNTER FROM THE SHADOWS...

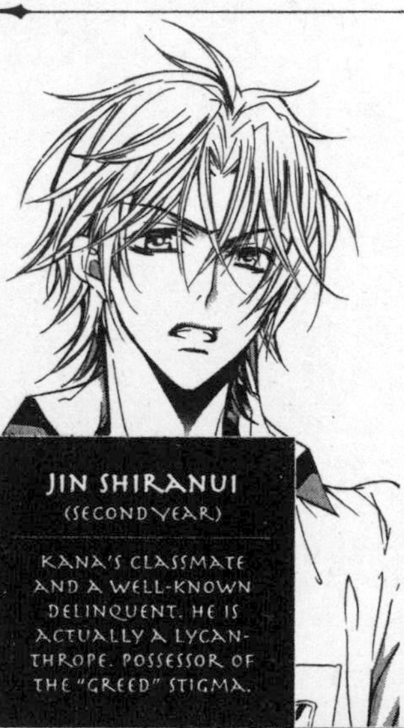

JIN SHIRANUI
(SECOND YEAR)

KANA'S CLASSMATE AND A WELL-KNOWN DELINQUENT. HE IS ACTUALLY A LYCANTHROPE. POSSESSOR OF THE "GREED" STIGMA.

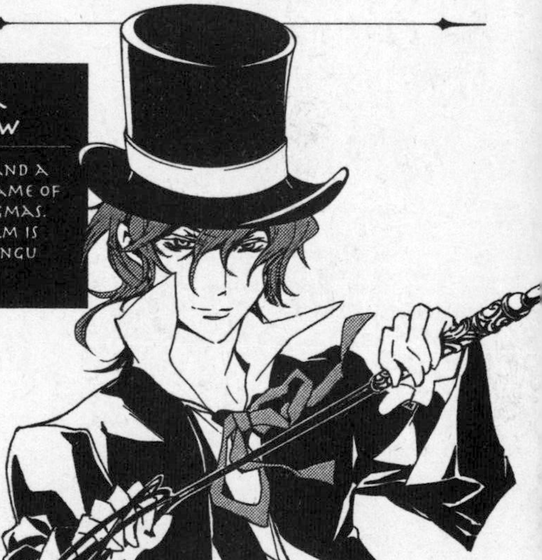

DEALER SWALLOW

AKI'S SENTRY AND A JUDGE IN THE GAME OF THE SEVEN STIGMAS. HIS TRUE FORM IS THAT OF A TENGU DEMON.

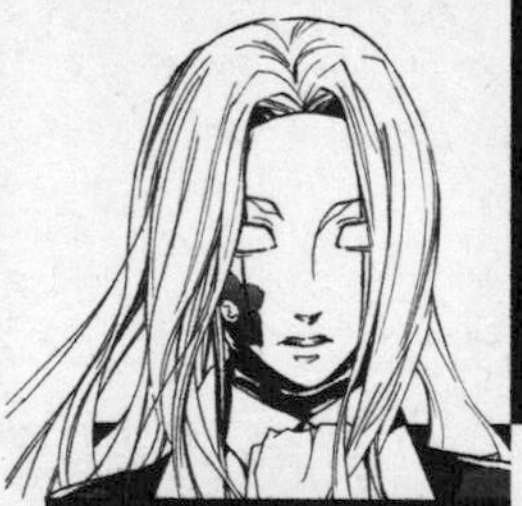

THE EMPEROR
(LORD TSUBAKIIN)

THE POWERFUL FIGURE WHO RULES THE HOUSE OF "TSUBAKIIN" FROM THE SHADOWS. RAISED AND EDUCATED AKI.

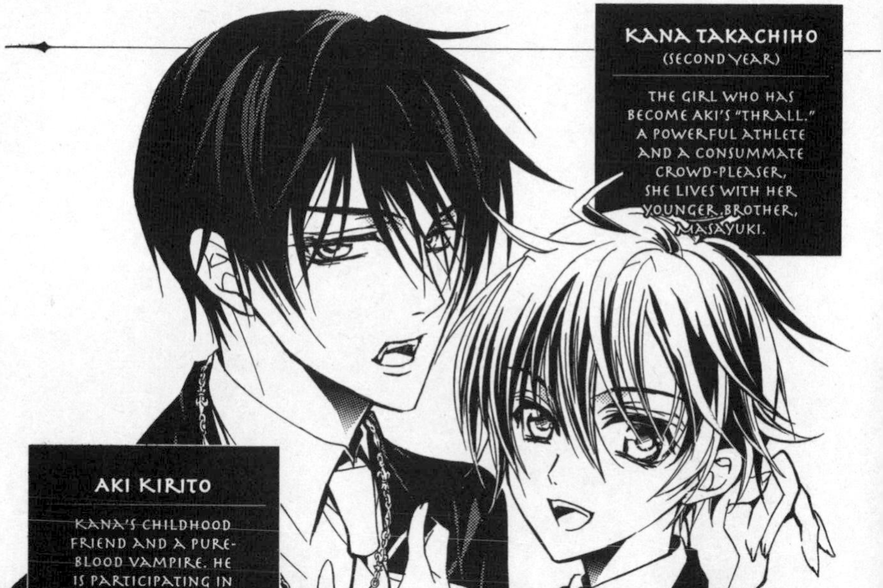

KANA TAKACHIHO
(SECOND YEAR)

THE GIRL WHO HAS BECOME AKI'S "THRALL." A POWERFUL ATHLETE AND A CONSUMMATE CROWD-PLEASER, SHE LIVES WITH HER YOUNGER BROTHER, MASAYUKI.

AKI KIRITO

KANA'S CHILDHOOD FRIEND AND A PURE-BLOOD VAMPIRE. HE IS PARTICIPATING IN THE GAME TO FIND THE SEVEN STIGMAS SO THAT HE CAN SAVE HIS BROTHER, ERIYA.

ISUKA BERNSTEIN
(THIRD YEAR)
HITAKI MIYAJIMA
(THIRD YEAR)

ST. AGATHA ACADEMY'S STUDENT COUNCIL PRESIDENT AND VICE PRESIDENT. IN TRUTH, THEY ARE ANGELS AND ARE KEEPING AN EYE ON AKI.

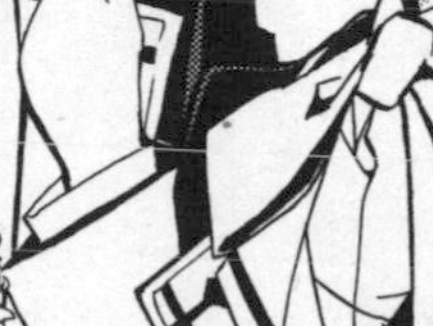

ERIYA

KANA'S CHILDHOOD FRIEND AND AKI'S YOUNGER TWIN BROTHER.

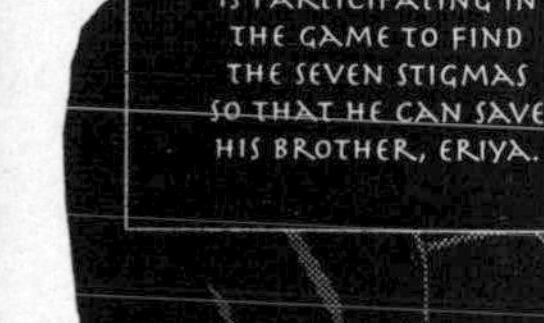

He's my only vampire
Aya Shouoto

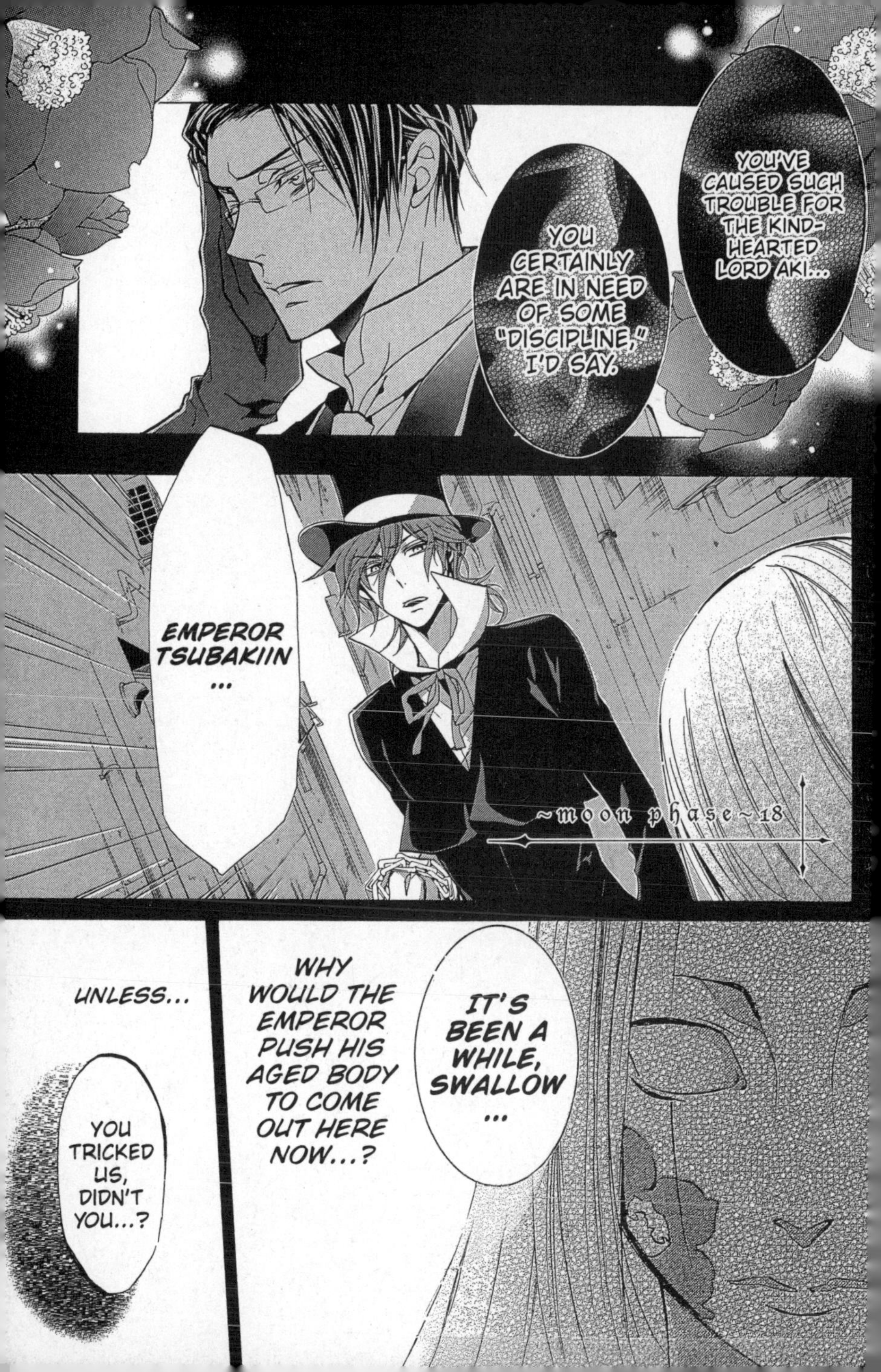
YOU'VE CAUSED SUCH TROUBLE FOR THE KIND-HEARTED LORD AKI...
YOU CERTAINLY ARE IN NEED OF SOME "DISCIPLINE," I'D SAY.
~moon phase~18
EMPEROR TSUBAKIIN ...
IT'S BEEN A WHILE, SWALLOW ...
WHY WOULD THE EMPEROR PUSH HIS AGED BODY TO COME OUT HERE NOW...?
UNLESS...
YOU TRICKED US, DIDN'T YOU...?

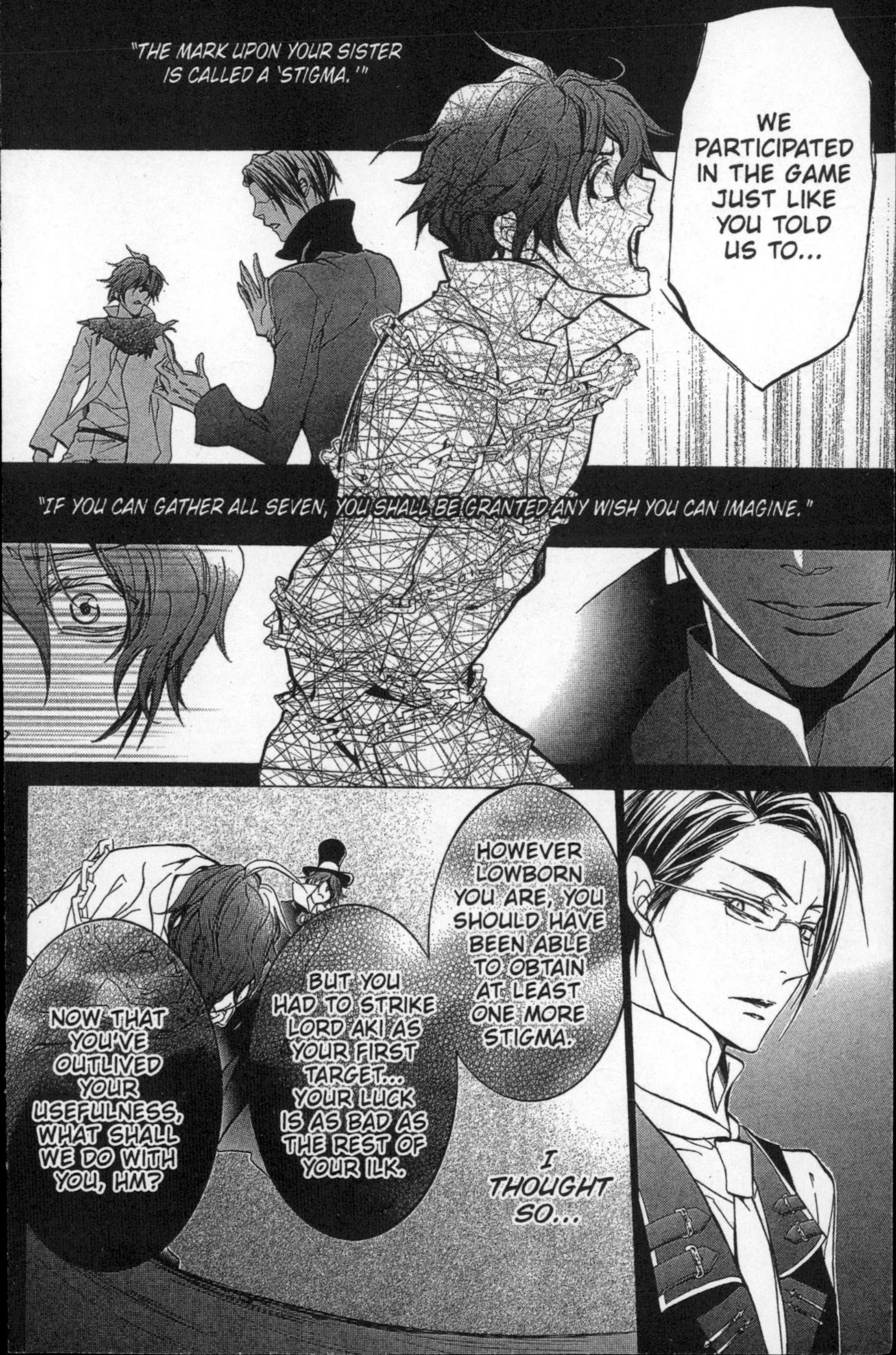
"THE MARK UPON YOUR SISTER IS CALLED A 'STIGMA.'"
WE PARTICIPATED IN THE GAME JUST LIKE YOU TOLD US TO...
"IF YOU CAN GATHER ALL SEVEN, YOU SHALL BE GRANTED ANY WISH YOU CAN IMAGINE."
HOWEVER LOWBORN YOU ARE, YOU SHOULD HAVE BEEN ABLE TO OBTAIN AT LEAST ONE MORE STIGMA.
BUT YOU HAD TO STRIKE LORD AKI AS YOUR FIRST TARGET... YOUR LUCK IS AS BAD AS THE REST OF YOUR ILK.
NOW THAT YOU'VE OUTLIVED YOUR USEFULNESS, WHAT SHALL WE DO WITH YOU, HM?
I THOUGHT SO...

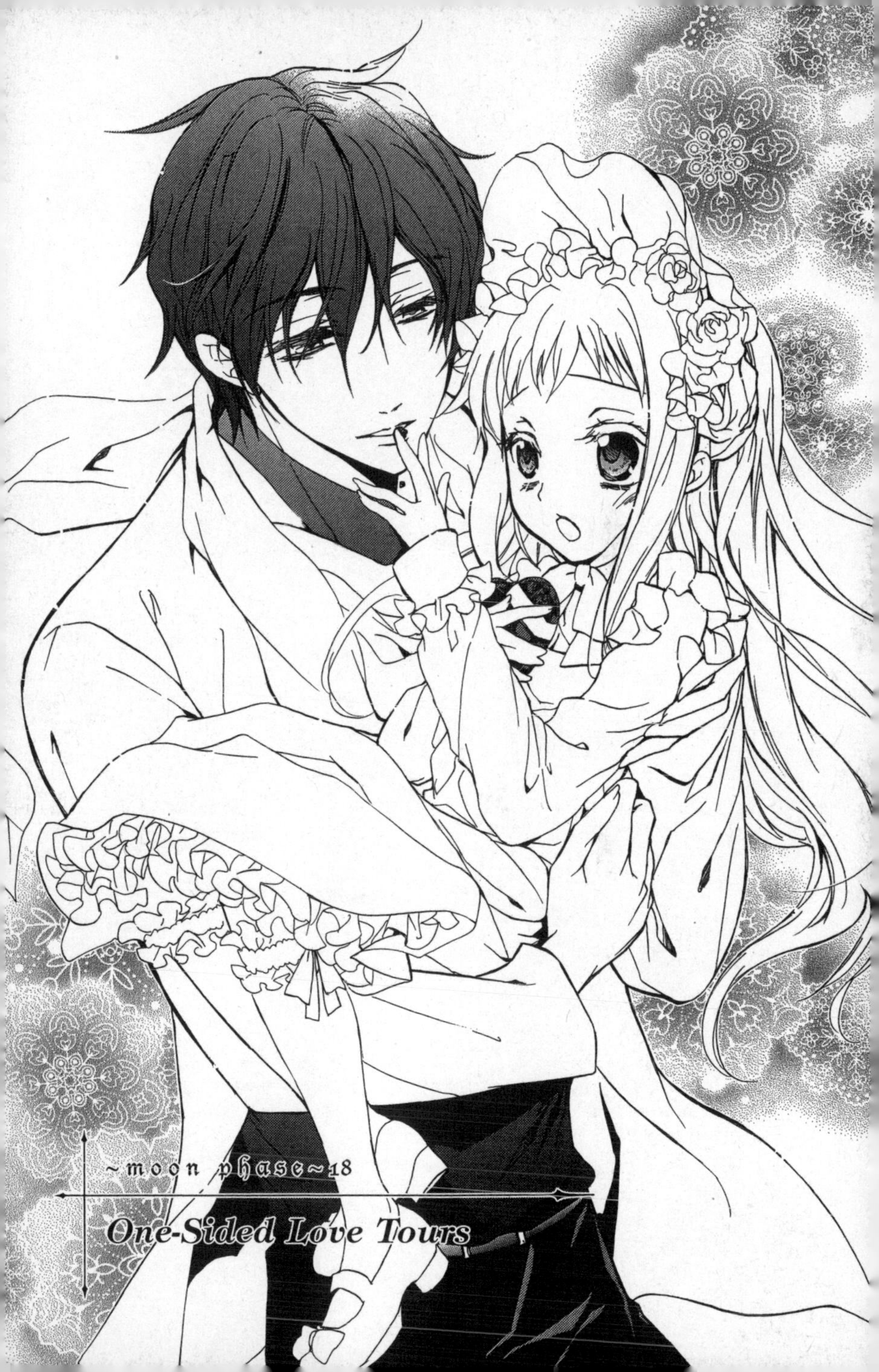
~moon phase~18
One-Sided Love Tours

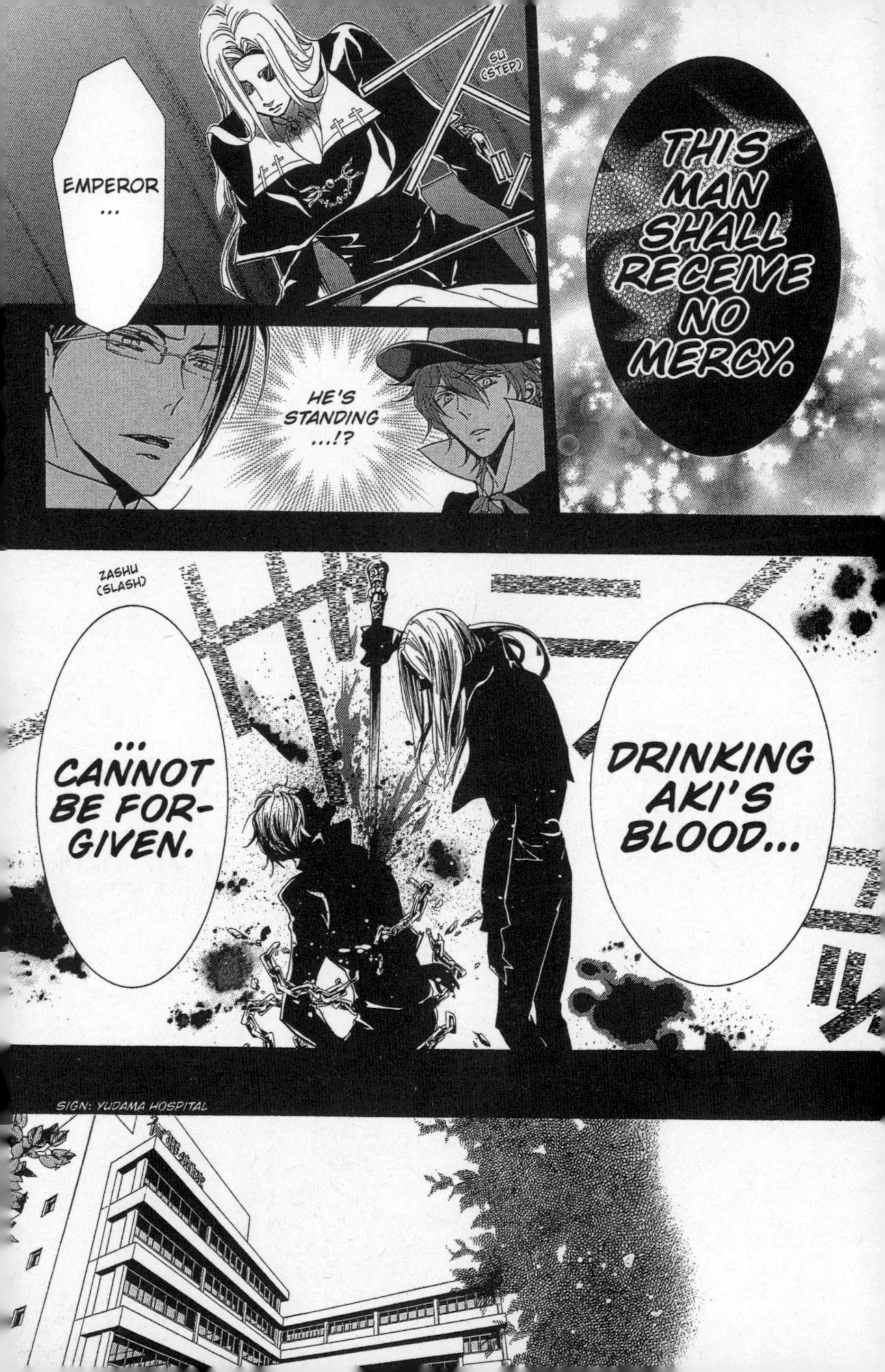
THIS MAN SHALL RECEIVE NO MERCY.
SU (STEP)
EMPEROR ...
HE'S STANDING ...!?
DRINKING AKI'S BLOOD...
ZASHU (SLASH)
... CANNOT BE FOR-GIVEN.
SIGN: YUDAMA HOSPITAL

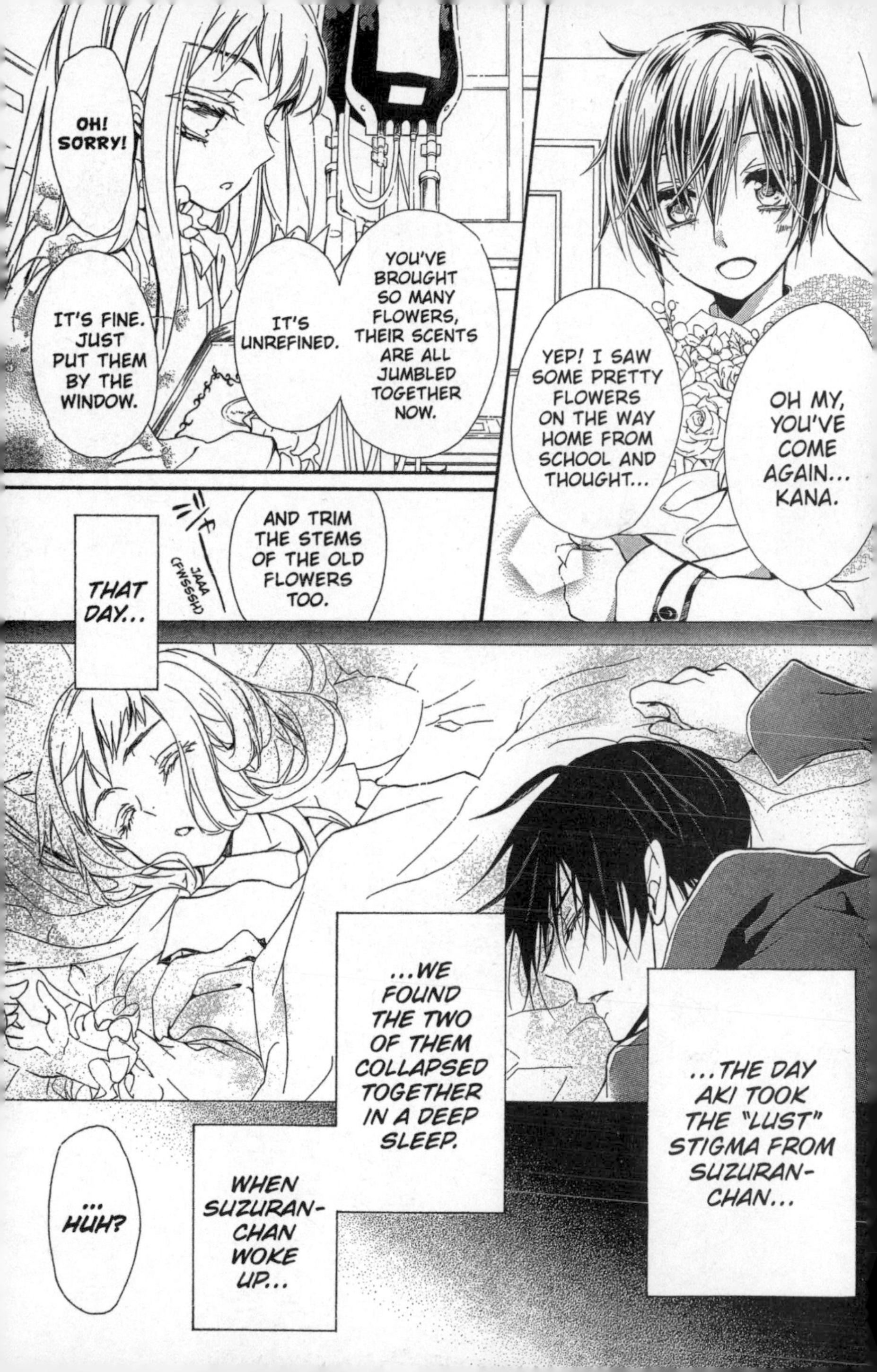
OH MY, YOU'VE COME AGAIN... KANA.
YEP! I SAW SOME PRETTY FLOWERS ON THE WAY HOME FROM SCHOOL AND THOUGHT...
YOU'VE BROUGHT SO MANY FLOWERS, THEIR SCENTS ARE ALL JUMBLED TOGETHER NOW.
IT'S UNREFINED.
OH! SORRY!
IT'S FINE. JUST PUT THEM BY THE WINDOW.
AND TRIM THE STEMS OF THE OLD FLOWERS TOO.
JAAA (FWSSSH)
THAT DAY...
...THE DAY AKI TOOK THE "LUST" STIGMA FROM SUZURAN-CHAN...
...WE FOUND THE TWO OF THEM COLLAPSED TOGETHER IN A DEEP SLEEP.
WHEN SUZURAN-CHAN WOKE UP...
... HUH?

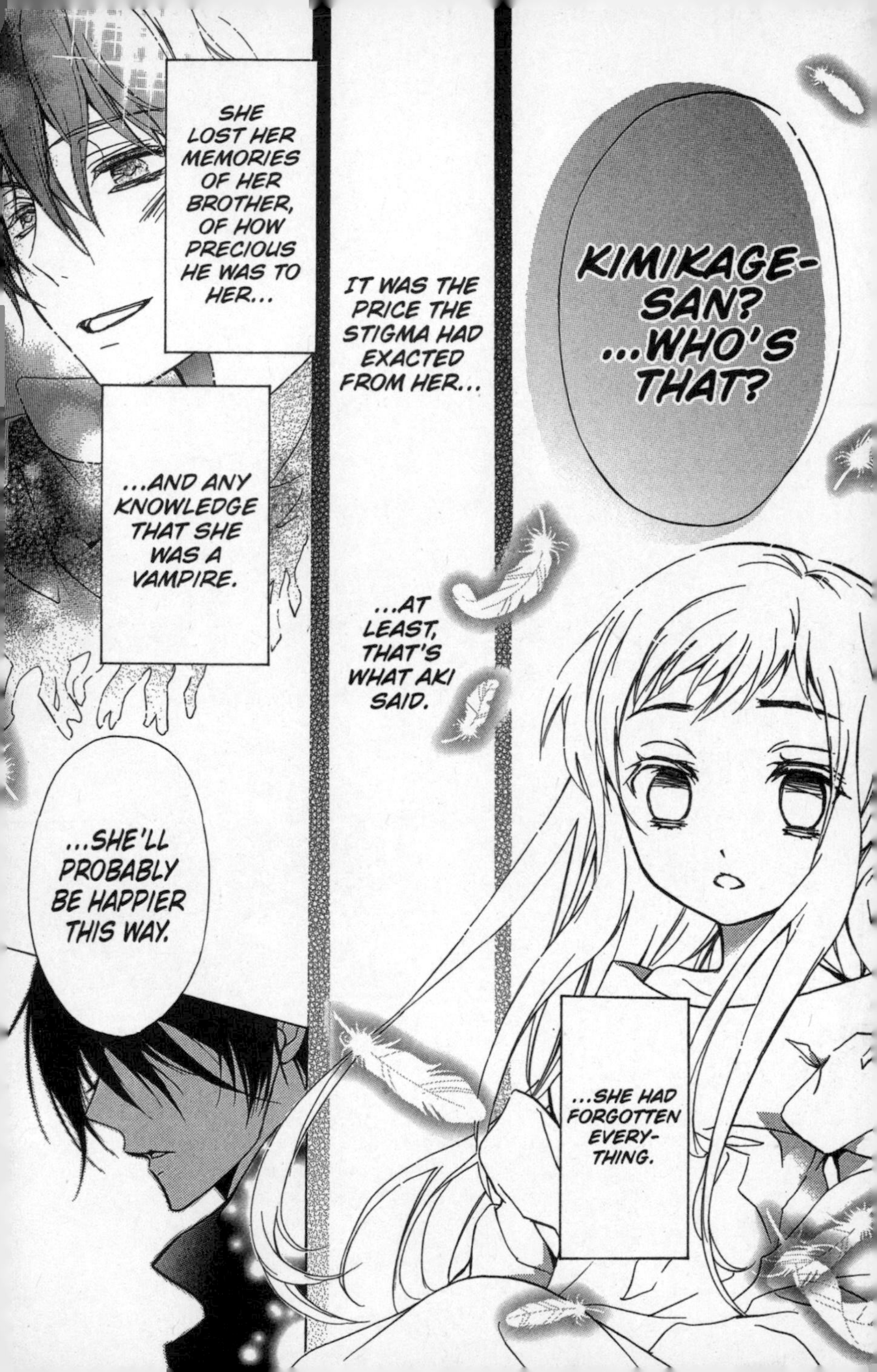
KIMIKAGE-SAN? ...WHO'S THAT?
...SHE HAD FORGOTTEN EVERYTHING.
IT WAS THE PRICE THE STIGMA HAD EXACTED FROM HER...
...AT LEAST, THAT'S WHAT AKI SAID.
SHE LOST HER MEMORIES OF HER BROTHER, OF HOW PRECIOUS HE WAS TO HER...
...AND ANY KNOWLEDGE THAT SHE WAS A VAMPIRE.
...SHE'LL PROBABLY BE HAPPIER THIS WAY.

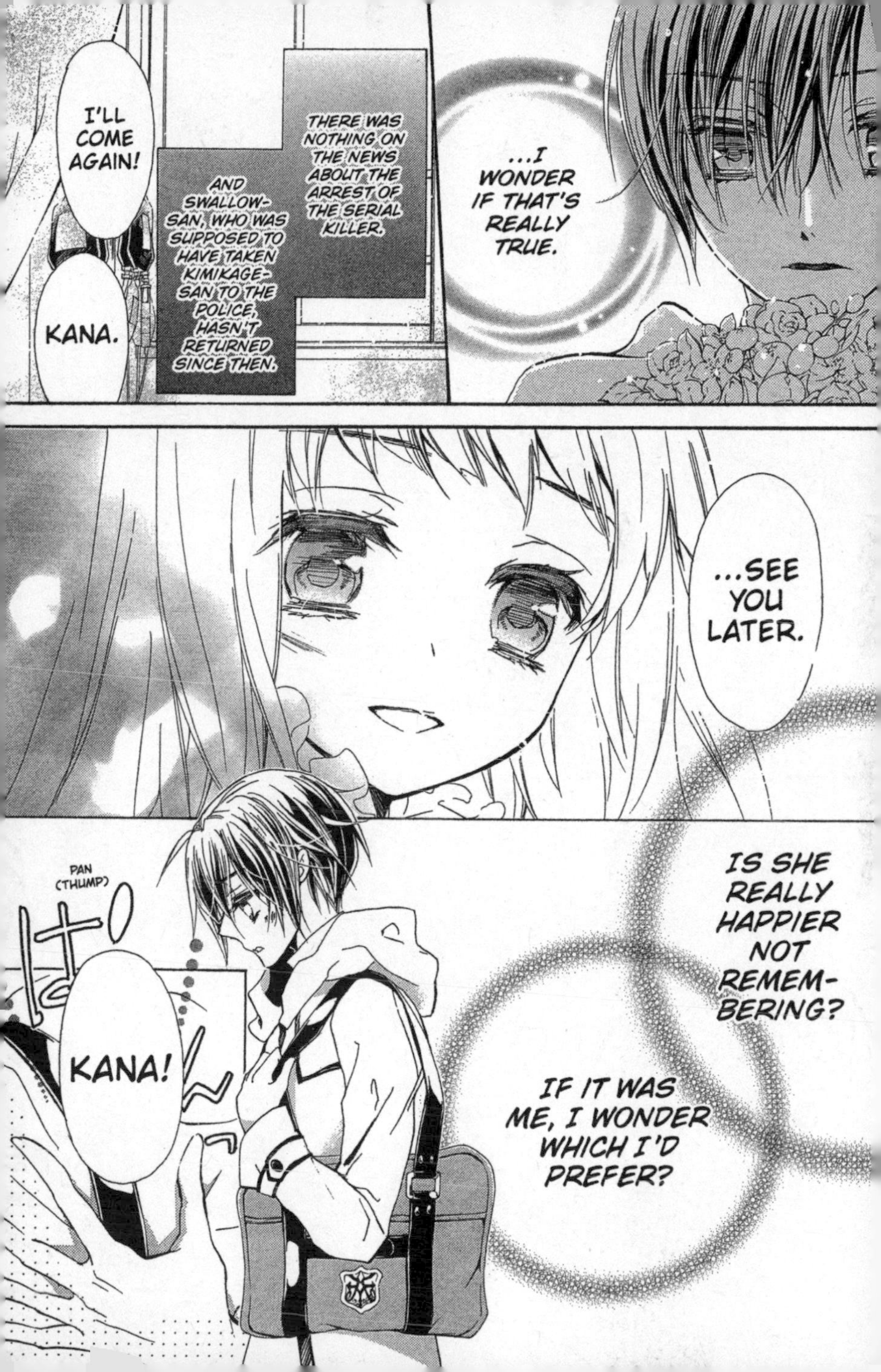
...I WONDER IF THAT'S REALLY TRUE.
THERE WAS NOTHING ON THE NEWS ABOUT THE ARREST OF THE SERIAL KILLER.
AND SWALLOW-SAN, WHO WAS SUPPOSED TO HAVE TAKEN KIMIKAGE-SAN TO THE POLICE, HASN'T RETURNED SINCE THEN.
I'LL COME AGAIN!
KANA.
...SEE YOU LATER.
IS SHE REALLY HAPPIER NOT REMEMBERING?
IF IT WAS ME, I WONDER WHICH I'D PREFER?
PAN (THUMP)
KANA!

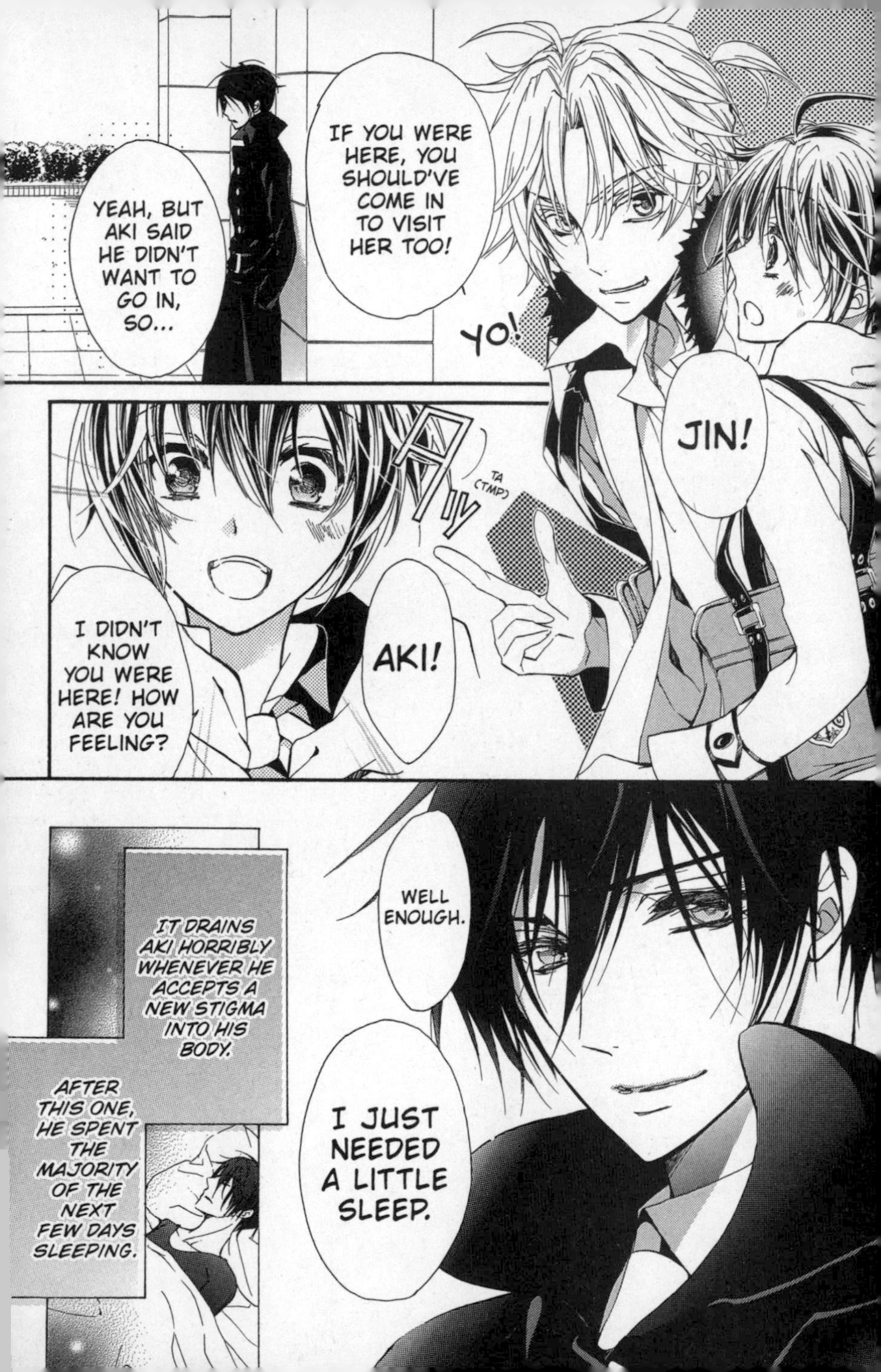
YO!
JIN!
IF YOU WERE HERE, YOU SHOULD'VE COME IN TO VISIT HER TOO!
YEAH, BUT AKI SAID HE DIDN'T WANT TO GO IN, SO...
TA (TMP)
AKI!
I DIDN'T KNOW YOU WERE HERE! HOW ARE YOU FEELING?
WELL ENOUGH.
I JUST NEEDED A LITTLE SLEEP.
IT DRAINS AKI HORRIBLY WHENEVER HE ACCEPTS A NEW STIGMA INTO HIS BODY.
AFTER THIS ONE, HE SPENT THE MAJORITY OF THE NEXT FEW DAYS SLEEPING.

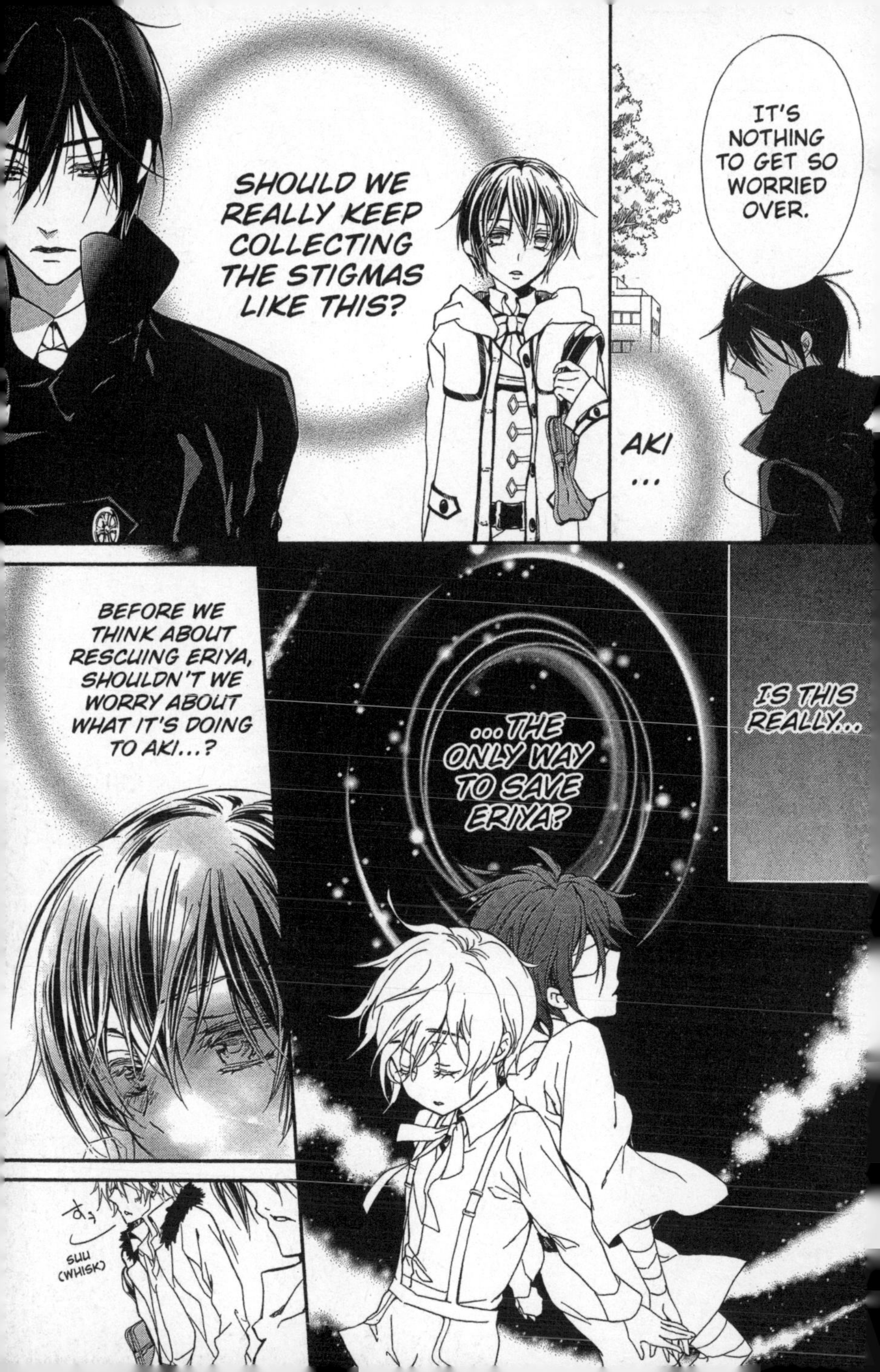

IT'S NOTHING TO GET SO WORRIED OVER.
AKI ...
SHOULD WE REALLY KEEP COLLECTING THE STIGMAS LIKE THIS?
IS THIS REALLY...
...THE ONLY WAY TO SAVE ERIYA?
BEFORE WE THINK ABOUT RESCUING ERIYA, SHOULDN'T WE WORRY ABOUT WHAT IT'S DOING TO AKI...?
すっ
SUU (WHISK)

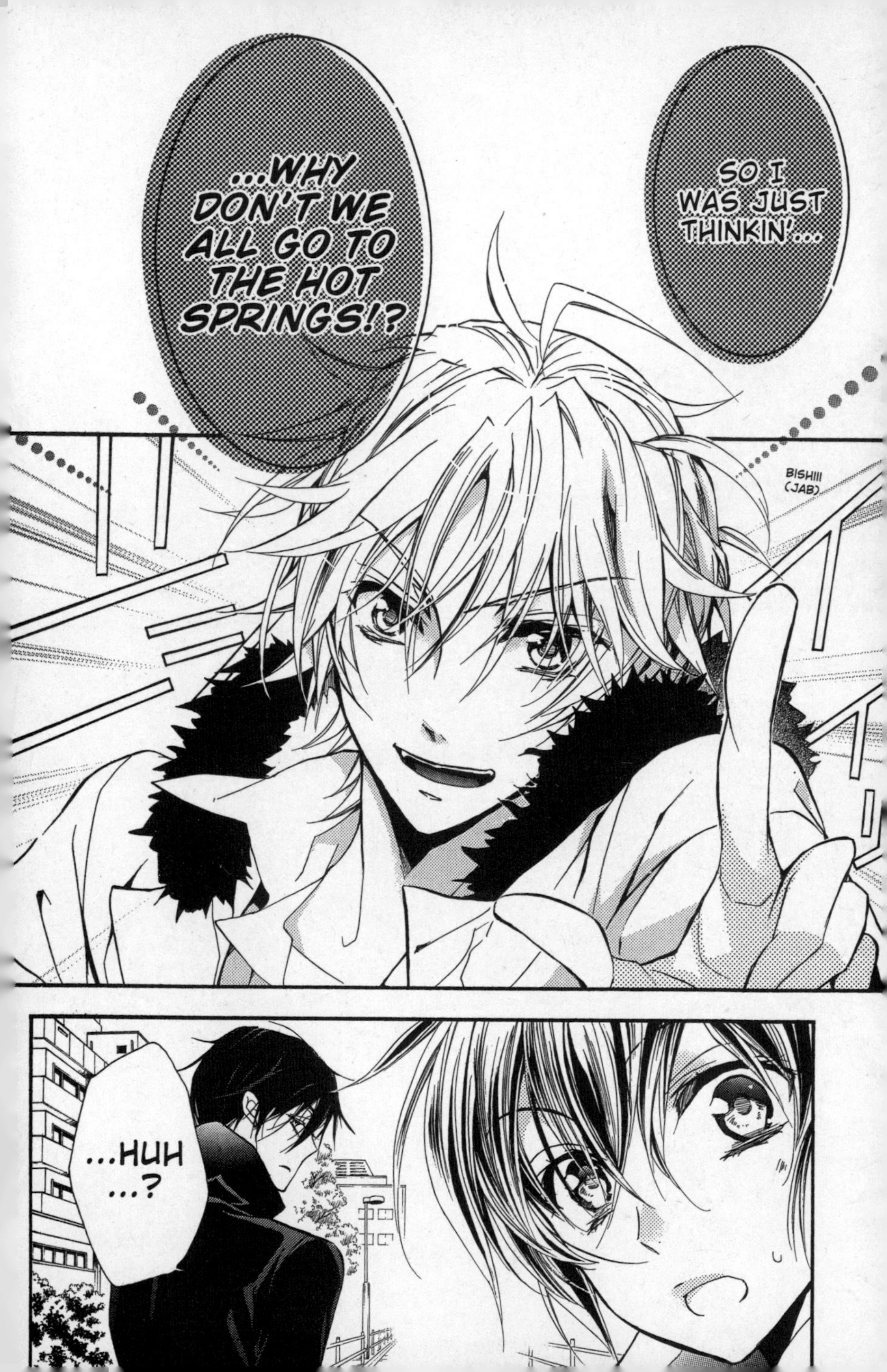
SO I WAS JUST THINKIN'...
...WHY DON'T WE ALL GO TO THE HOT SPRINGS!?
BISHIII (JAB)
...HUH ...?

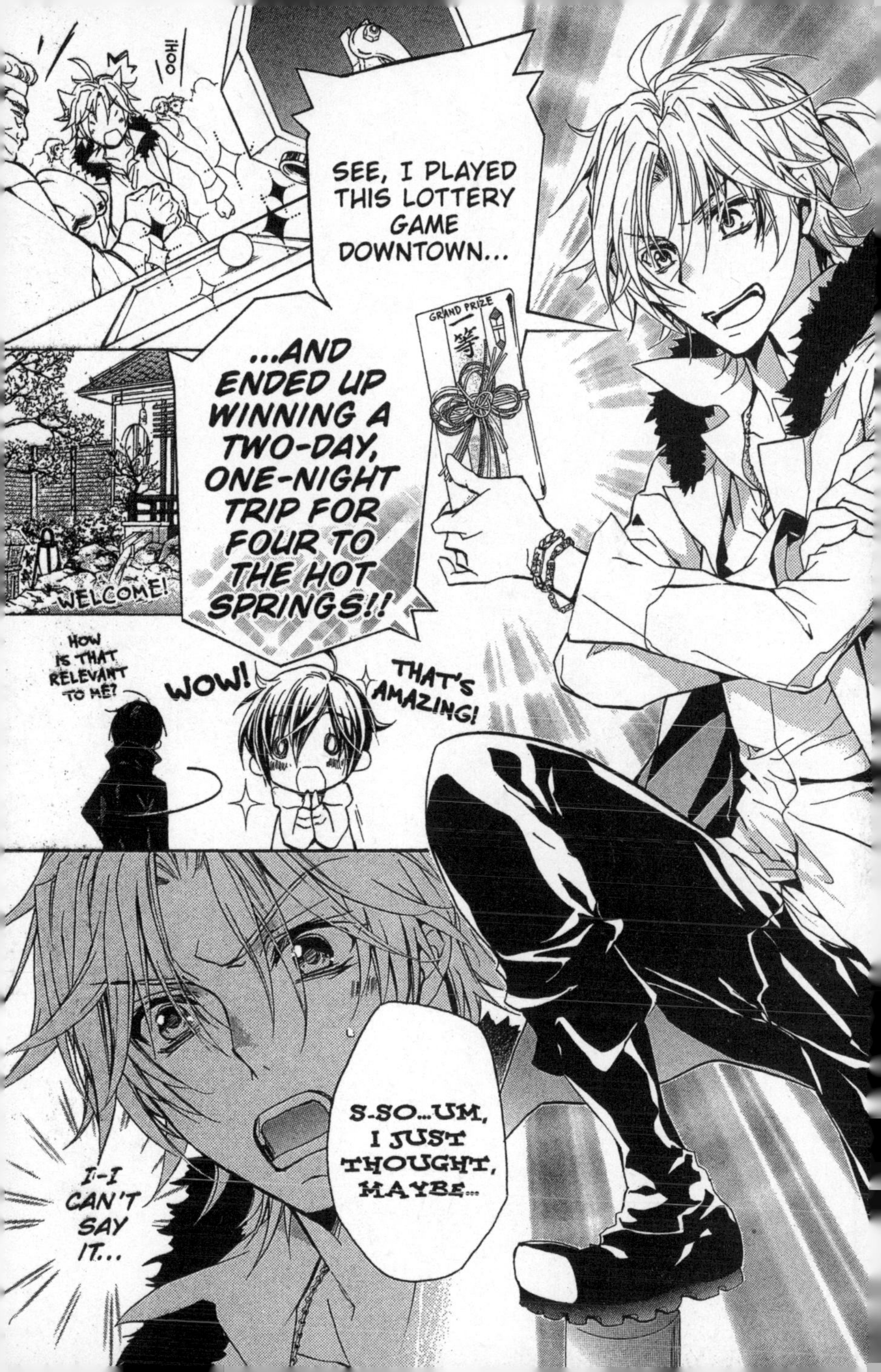
SEE, I PLAYED THIS LOTTERY GAME DOWNTOWN...
OOH!
GRAND PRIZE
...AND ENDED UP WINNING A TWO-DAY, ONE-NIGHT TRIP FOR FOUR TO THE HOT SPRINGS!!
WELCOME!
THAT'S AMAZING!
WOW!
HOW IS THAT RELEVANT TO ME?
S-SO...UM, I JUST THOUGHT, MAYBE...
I-I CAN'T SAY IT...

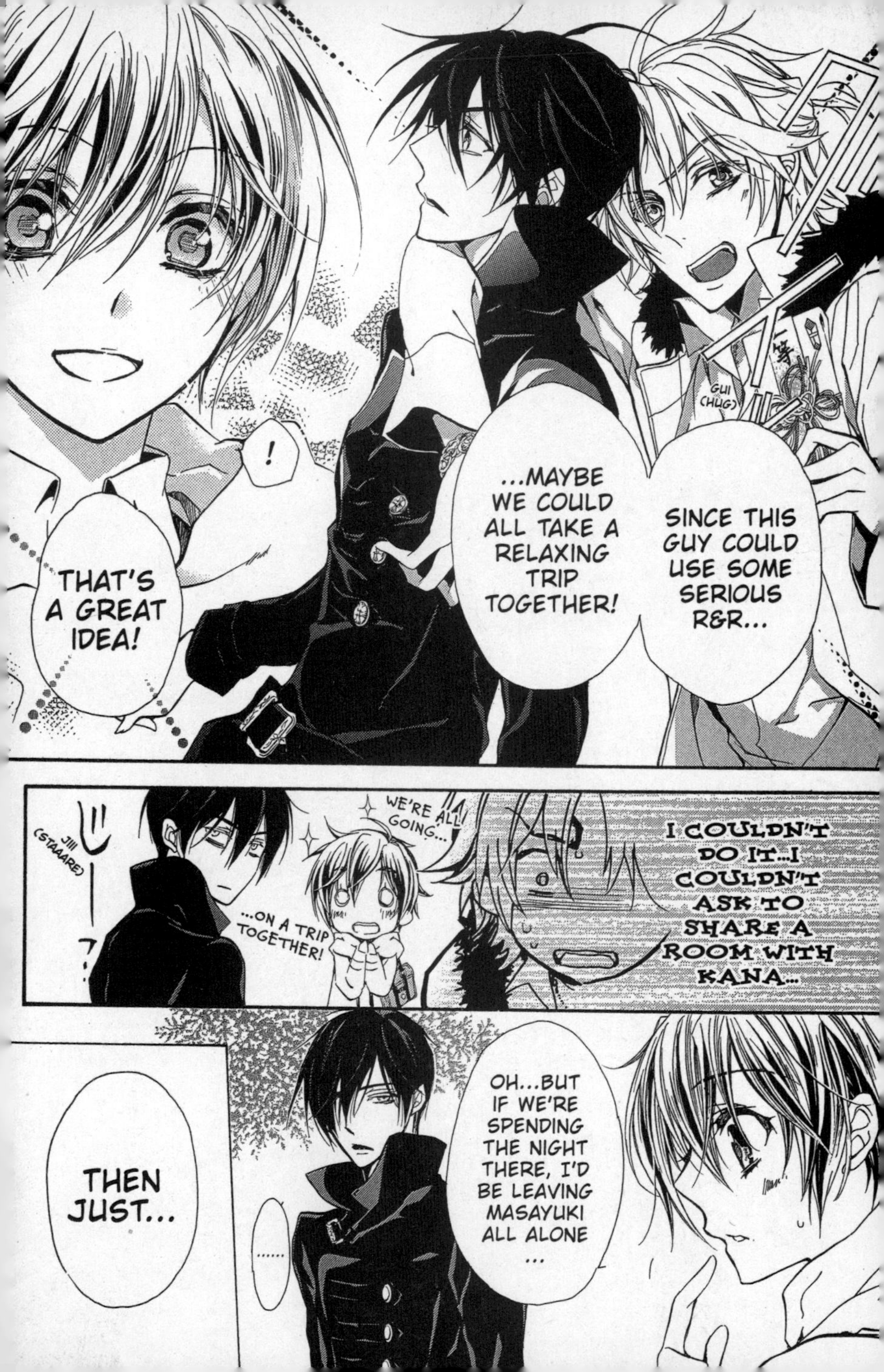
GUI (HUG)
SINCE THIS GUY COULD USE SOME SERIOUS R&R...
...MAYBE WE COULD ALL TAKE A RELAXING TRIP TOGETHER!
!
THAT'S A GREAT IDEA!
I COULDN'T DO IT...I COULDN'T ASK TO SHARE A ROOM WITH KANA...
WE'RE ALL GOING...
...ON A TRIP TOGETHER!
JIII (STAAARE)
OH...BUT IF WE'RE SPENDING THE NIGHT THERE, I'D BE LEAVING MASAYUKI ALL ALONE...
......
THEN JUST...

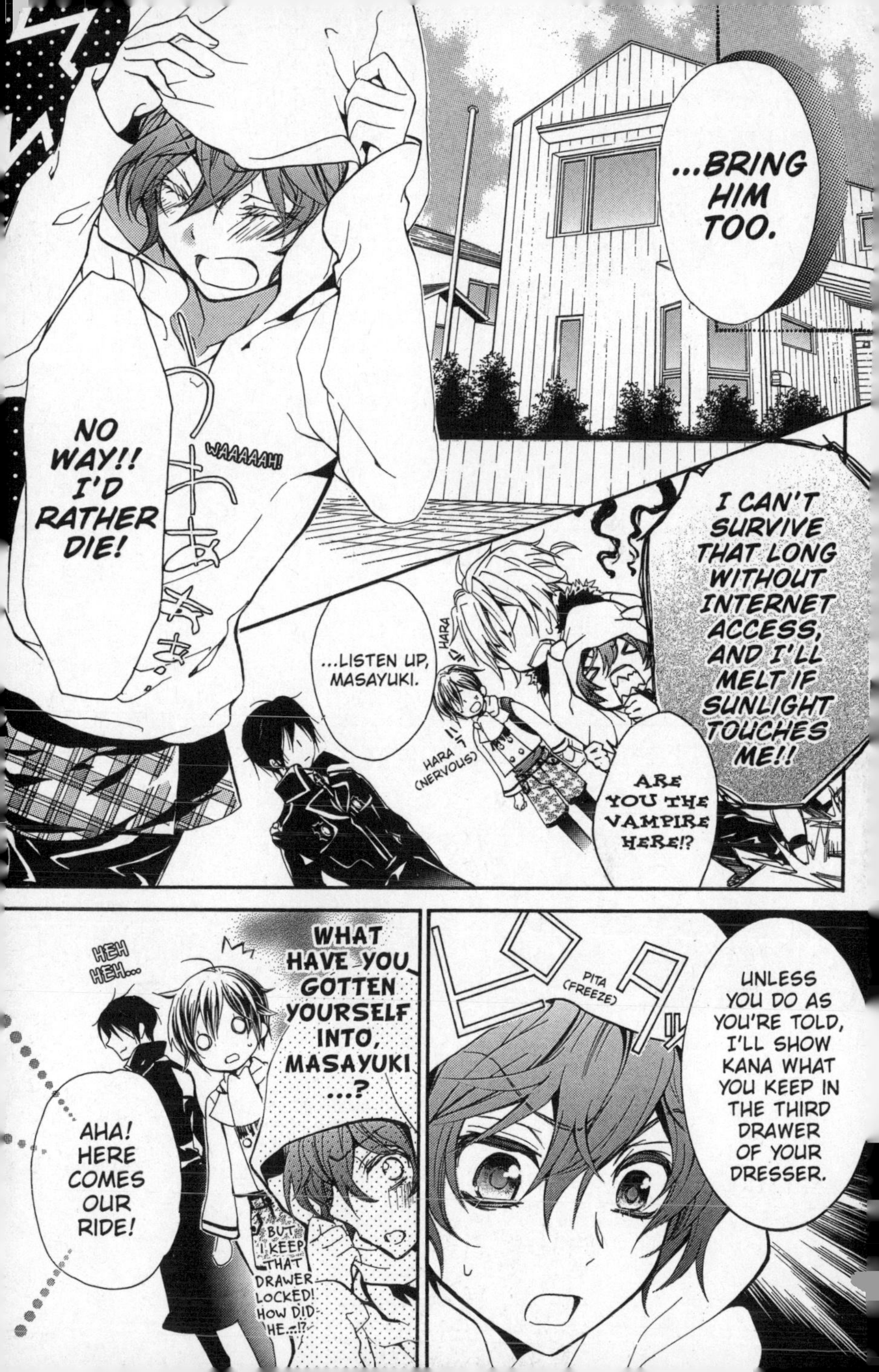
...BRING HIM TOO.
I CAN'T SURVIVE THAT LONG WITHOUT INTERNET ACCESS, AND I'LL MELT IF SUNLIGHT TOUCHES ME!!
ARE YOU THE VAMPIRE HERE!?
HARA
...LISTEN UP, MASAYUKI.
HARA (NERVOUS)
NO WAY!! I'D RATHER DIE!
WAAAAAH!
UNLESS YOU DO AS YOU'RE TOLD, I'LL SHOW KANA WHAT YOU KEEP IN THE THIRD DRAWER OF YOUR DRESSER.
PITA (FREEZE)
WHAT HAVE YOU GOTTEN YOURSELF INTO, MASAYUKI ...?
HEH HEH...
AHA! HERE COMES OUR RIDE!
BUT I KEEP THAT DRAWER LOCKED! HOW DID HE...!?

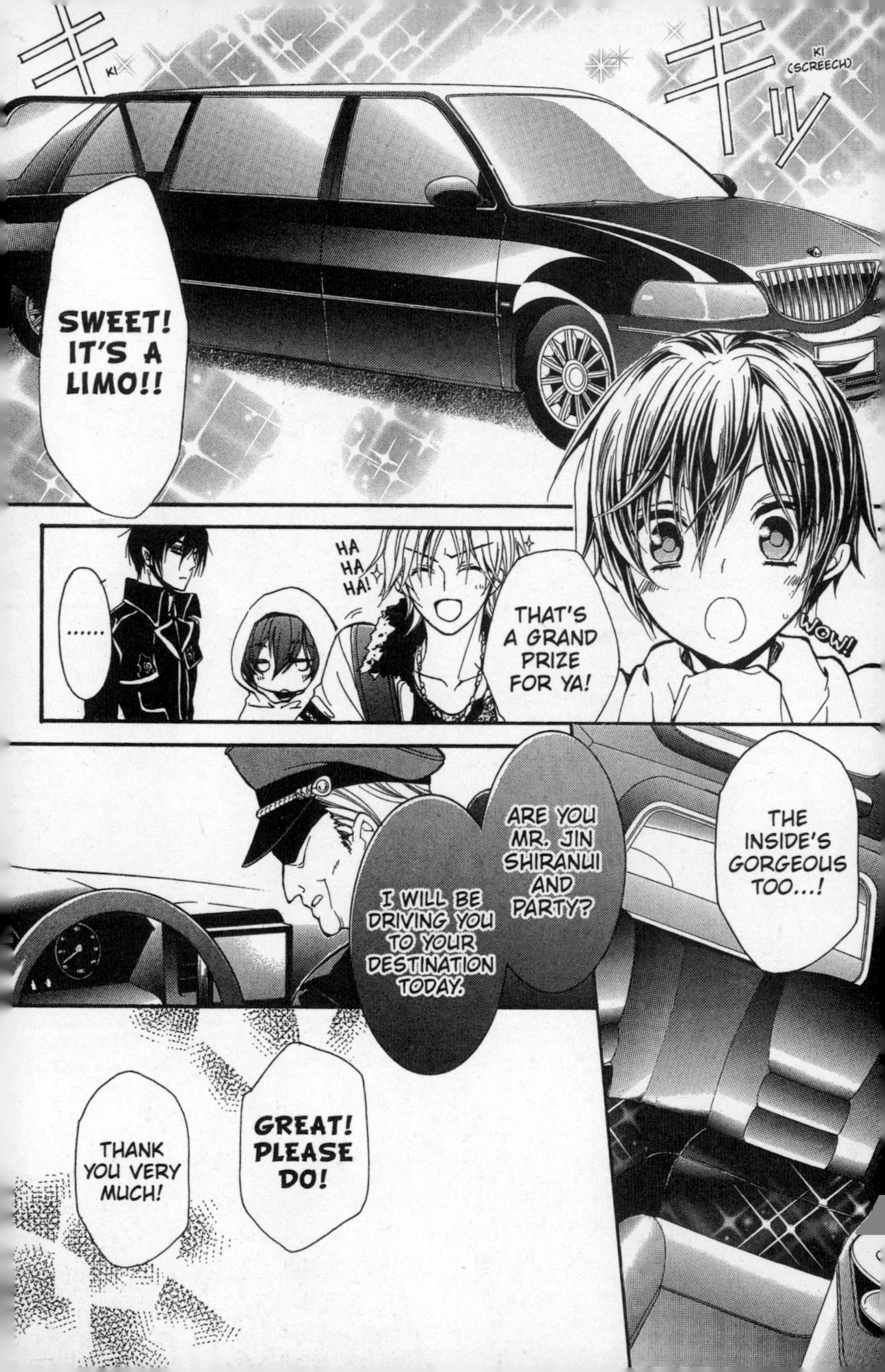
キッ
KI (SCREECH)
キ
KI
SWEET! IT'S A LIMO!!
WOW!
THAT'S A GRAND PRIZE FOR YA!
HA HA HA!
......
THE INSIDE'S GORGEOUS TOO...!
ARE YOU MR. JIN SHIRANUI AND PARTY?
I WILL BE DRIVING YOU TO YOUR DESTINATION TODAY.
GREAT! PLEASE DO!
THANK YOU VERY MUCH!

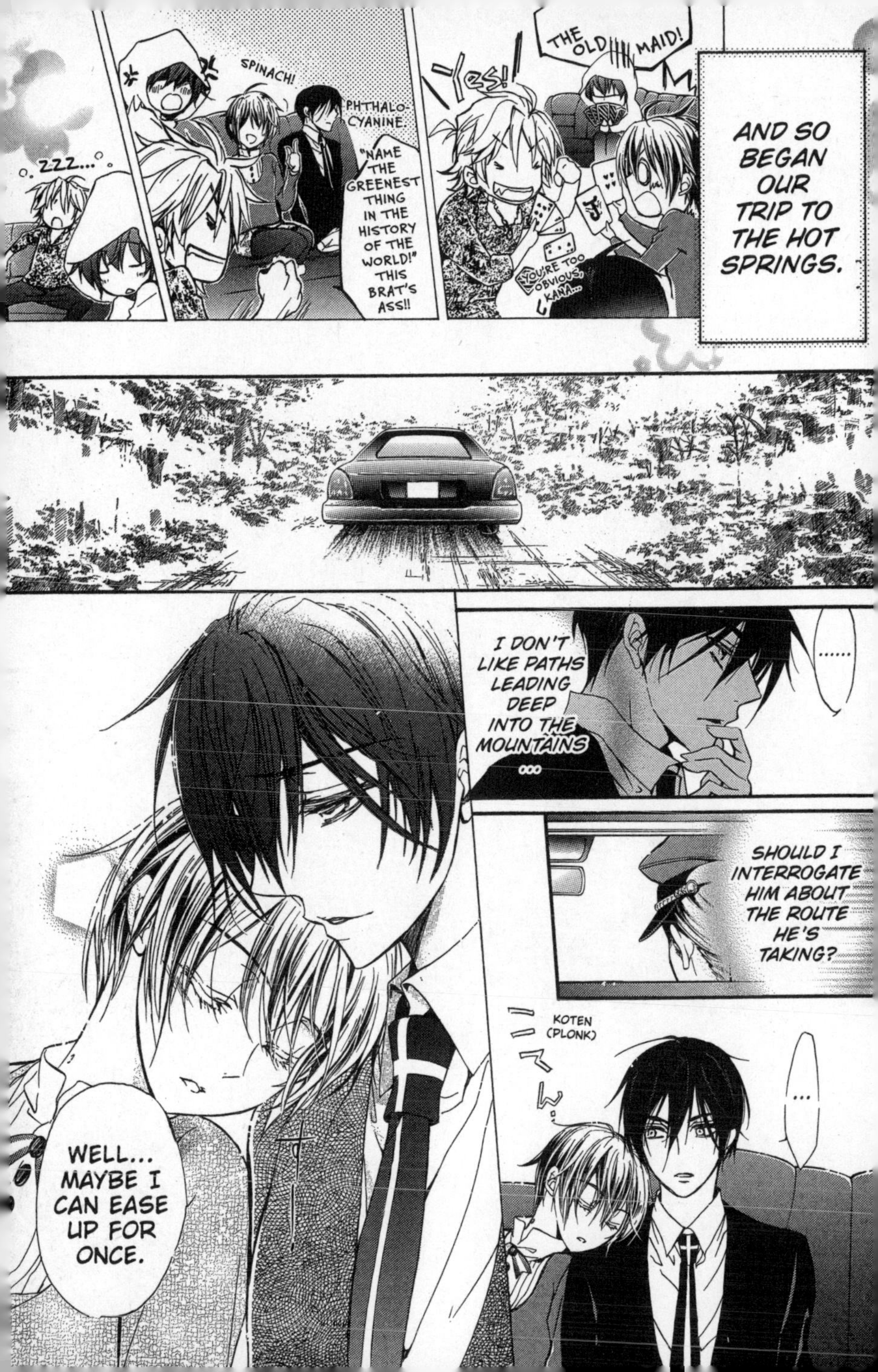
AND SO BEGAN OUR TRIP TO THE HOT SPRINGS.
THE OLD MAID!
YES!
YOU'RE TOO OBVIOUS, KANA...
SPINACH!
PHTHALO-CYANINE.
"NAME THE GREENEST THING IN THE HISTORY OF THE WORLD!" THIS BRAT'S ASS!!
ZZZ...
......
I DON'T LIKE PATHS LEADING DEEP INTO THE MOUNTAINS...
SHOULD I INTERROGATE HIM ABOUT THE ROUTE HE'S TAKING?
...
KOTEN (PLONK)
WELL... MAYBE I CAN EASE UP FOR ONCE.

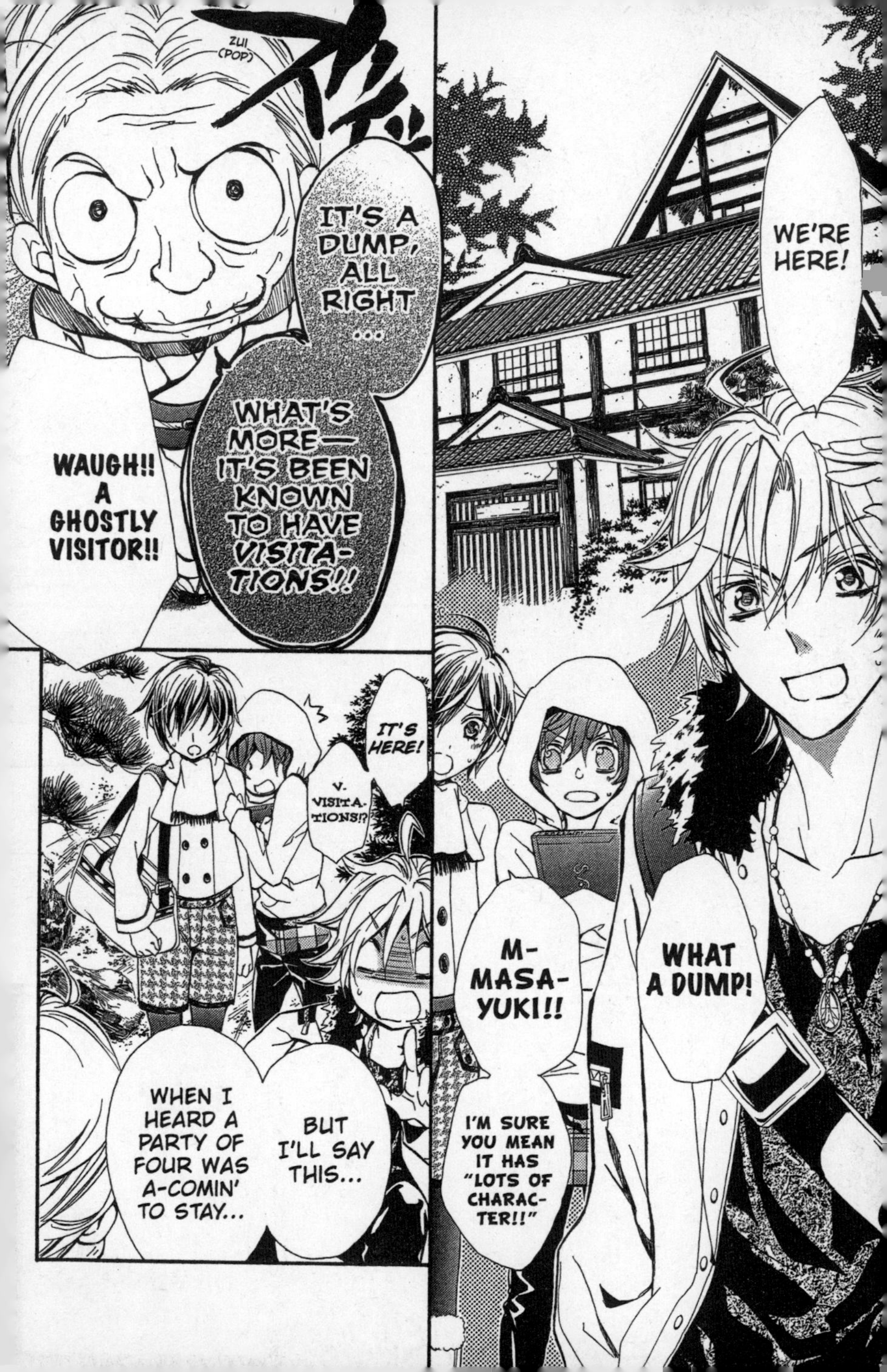
WE'RE HERE!
WHAT A DUMP!
M-MASAYUKI!!
I'M SURE YOU MEAN IT HAS "LOTS OF CHARACTER!!"
ZUI (POP)
IT'S A DUMP, ALL RIGHT...
WHAT'S MORE— IT'S BEEN KNOWN TO HAVE VISITATIONS!!
WAUGH!! A GHOSTLY VISITOR!!
IT'S HERE!
V. VISITATIONS!?
BUT I'LL SAY THIS...
WHEN I HEARD A PARTY OF FOUR WAS A-COMIN' TO STAY...

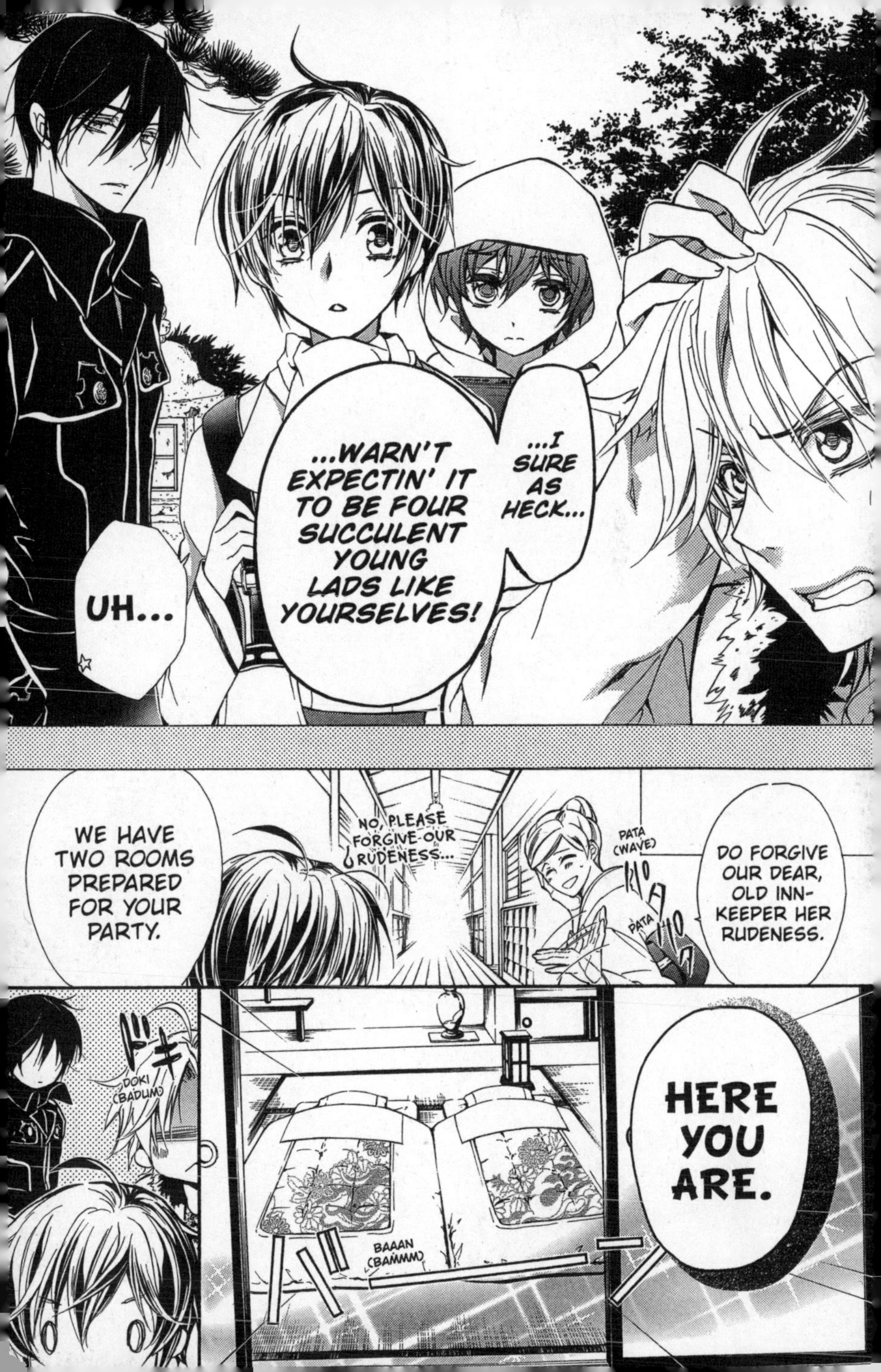
...I SURE AS HECK...
...WARN'T EXPECTIN' IT TO BE FOUR SUCCULENT YOUNG LADS LIKE YOURSELVES!
UH...
DO FORGIVE OUR DEAR, OLD INN-KEEPER HER RUDENESS.
PATA (WAVE)
PATA
NO, PLEASE FORGIVE OUR RUDENESS...
WE HAVE TWO ROOMS PREPARED FOR YOUR PARTY.
HERE YOU ARE.
BAAAN (BAMMM)
DOKI (BADUM)

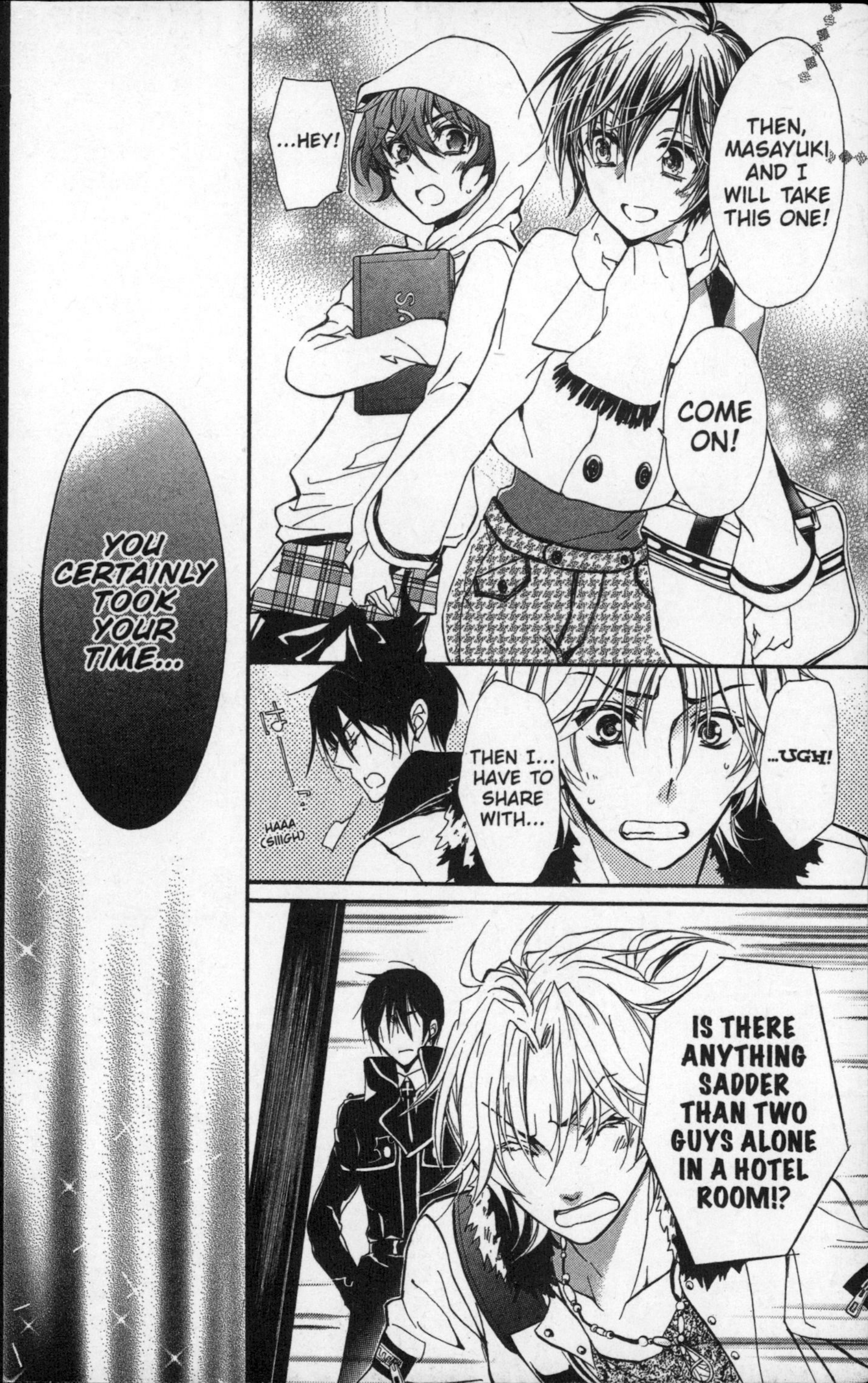
THEN, MASAYUKI AND I WILL TAKE THIS ONE!
COME ON!
...HEY!
...UGH!
THEN I... HAVE TO SHARE WITH...
HAAA (SIIIGH)
IS THERE ANYTHING SADDER THAN TWO GUYS ALONE IN A HOTEL ROOM!?
YOU CERTAINLY TOOK YOUR TIME...

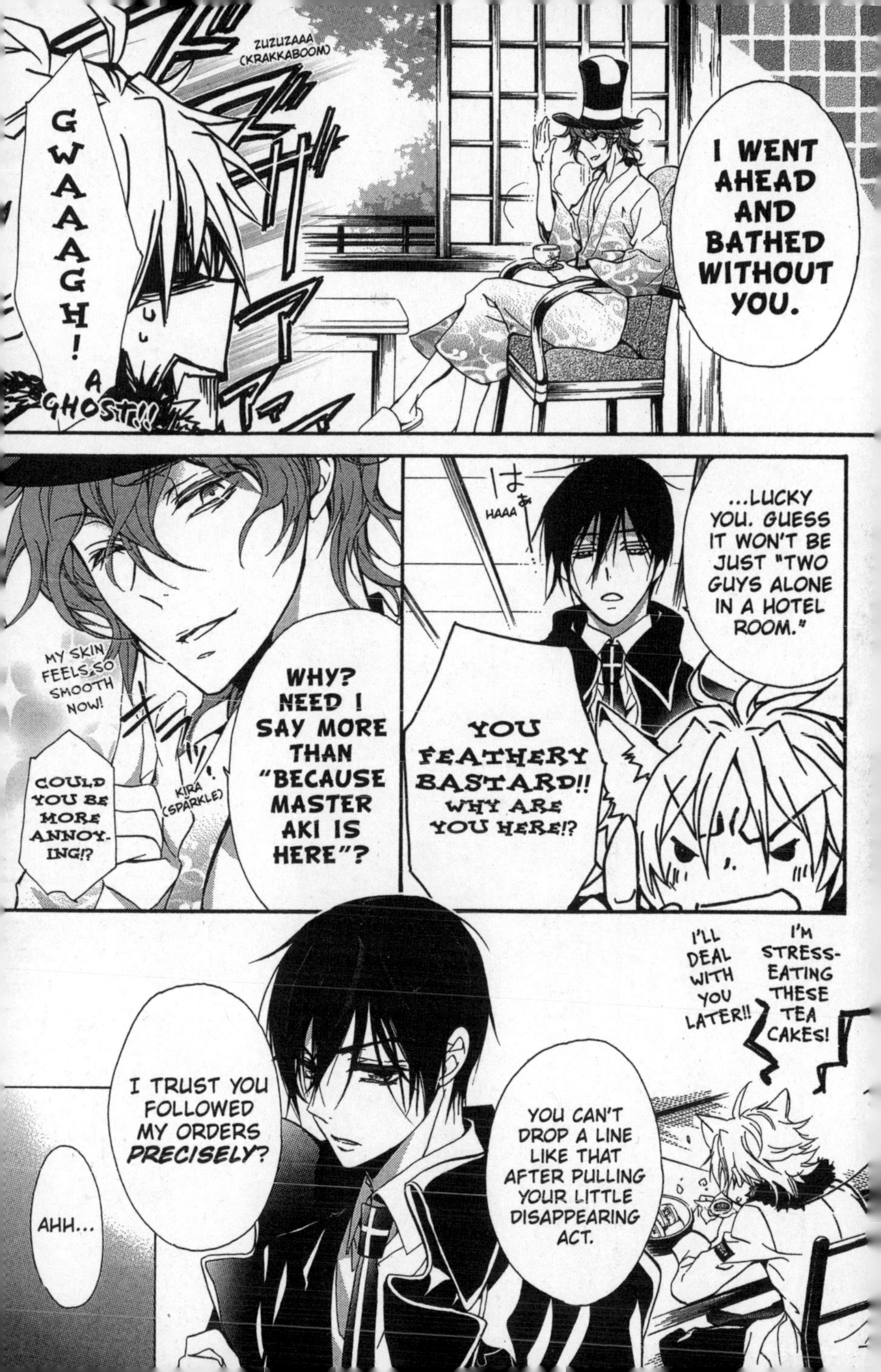

I WENT AHEAD AND BATHED WITHOUT YOU.
ZUZUZAAA (KRAKKABOOM)
GWAAAAGH!
A GHOST!!
はぁ
HAAA
...LUCKY YOU. GUESS IT WON'T BE JUST "TWO GUYS ALONE IN A HOTEL ROOM."
YOU FEATHERY BASTARD!! WHY ARE YOU HERE!?
WHY? NEED I SAY MORE THAN "BECAUSE MASTER AKI IS HERE"?
KIRA (SPARKLE)
MY SKIN FEELS SO SMOOTH NOW!
COULD YOU BE MORE ANNOY-ING!?
I'M STRESS-EATING THESE TEA CAKES!
I'LL DEAL WITH YOU LATER!!
YOU CAN'T DROP A LINE LIKE THAT AFTER PULLING YOUR LITTLE DISAPPEARING ACT.
I TRUST YOU FOLLOWED MY ORDERS *PRECISELY*?
AHH...

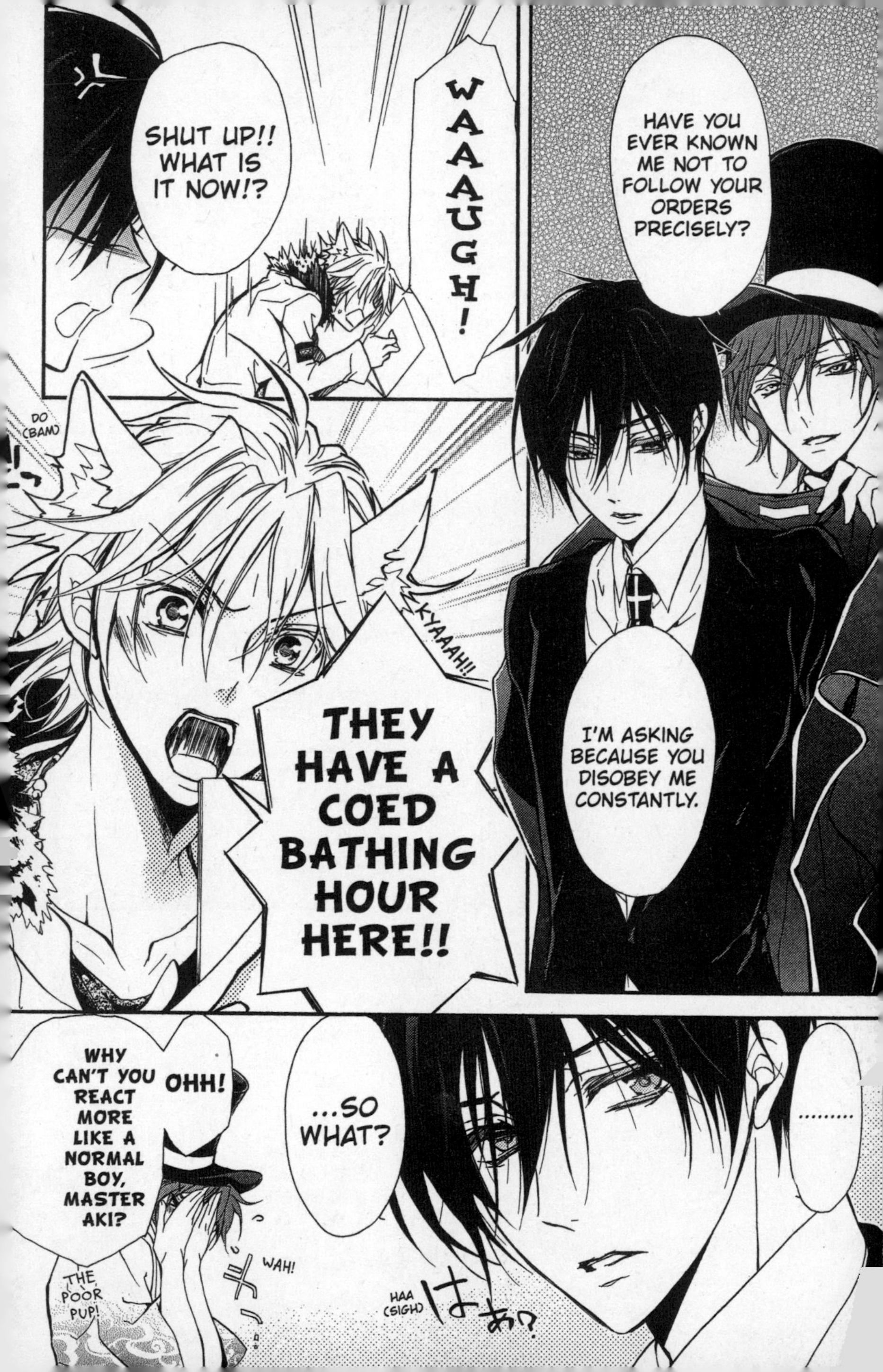
HAVE YOU EVER KNOWN ME NOT TO FOLLOW YOUR ORDERS PRECISELY?
I'M ASKING BECAUSE YOU DISOBEY ME CONSTANTLY.
WAAAUGH!
SHUT UP!! WHAT IS IT NOW!?
DO (BAM)
KYAAAH!!
THEY HAVE A COED BATHING HOUR HERE!!
....
...SO WHAT?
OHH!
WHY CAN'T YOU REACT MORE LIKE A NORMAL BOY, MASTER AKI?
HAA (SIGH)
WAH!
THE POOR PUP!

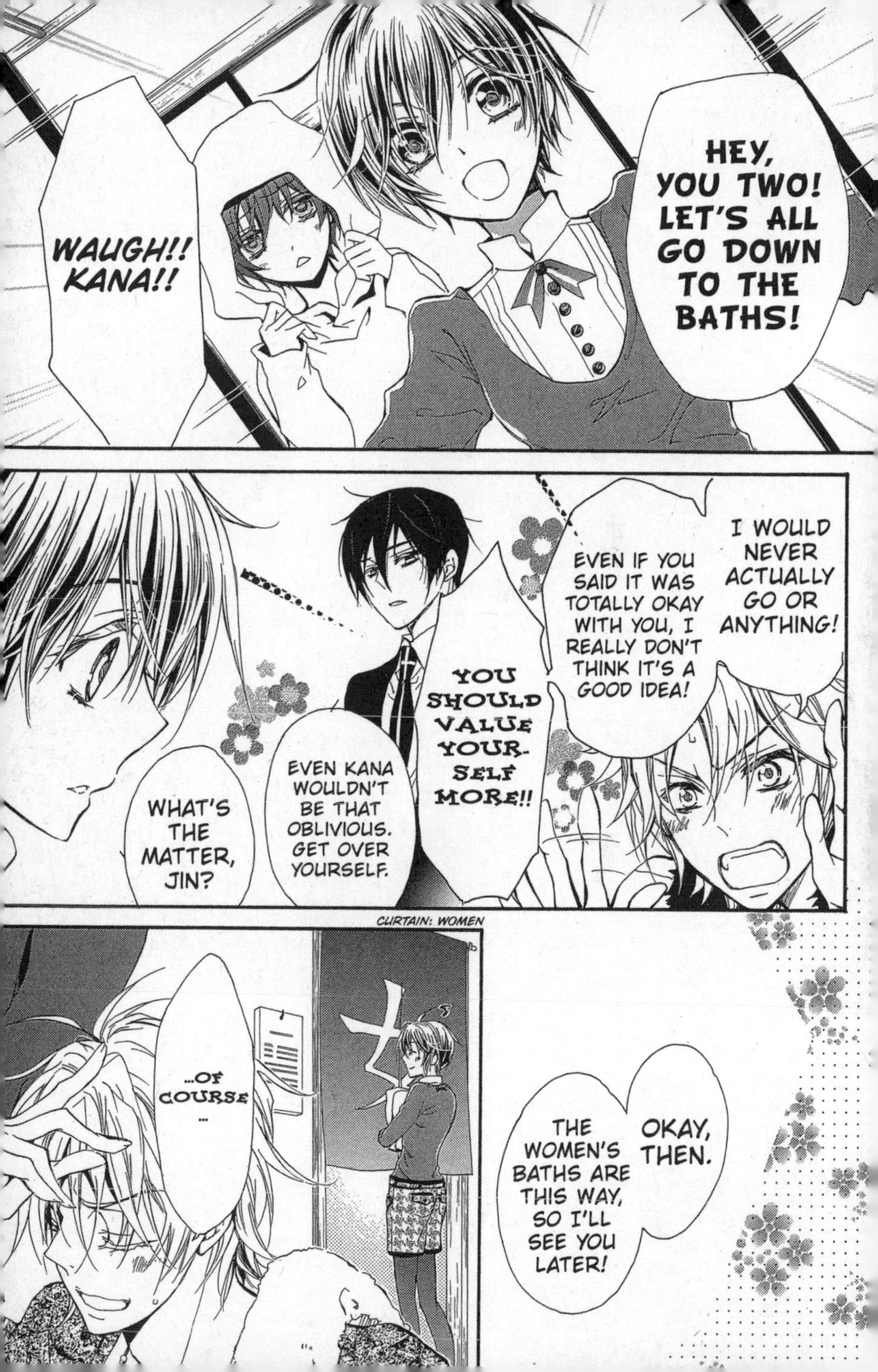
HEY, YOU TWO! LET'S ALL GO DOWN TO THE BATHS!
WAUGH!! KANA!!
I WOULD NEVER ACTUALLY GO OR ANYTHING!
EVEN IF YOU SAID IT WAS TOTALLY OKAY WITH YOU, I REALLY DON'T THINK IT'S A GOOD IDEA!
YOU SHOULD VALUE YOURSELF MORE!!
EVEN KANA WOULDN'T BE THAT OBLIVIOUS. GET OVER YOURSELF.
WHAT'S THE MATTER, JIN?
CURTAIN: WOMEN
OKAY, THEN.
THE WOMEN'S BATHS ARE THIS WAY, SO I'LL SEE YOU LATER!
...OF COURSE...

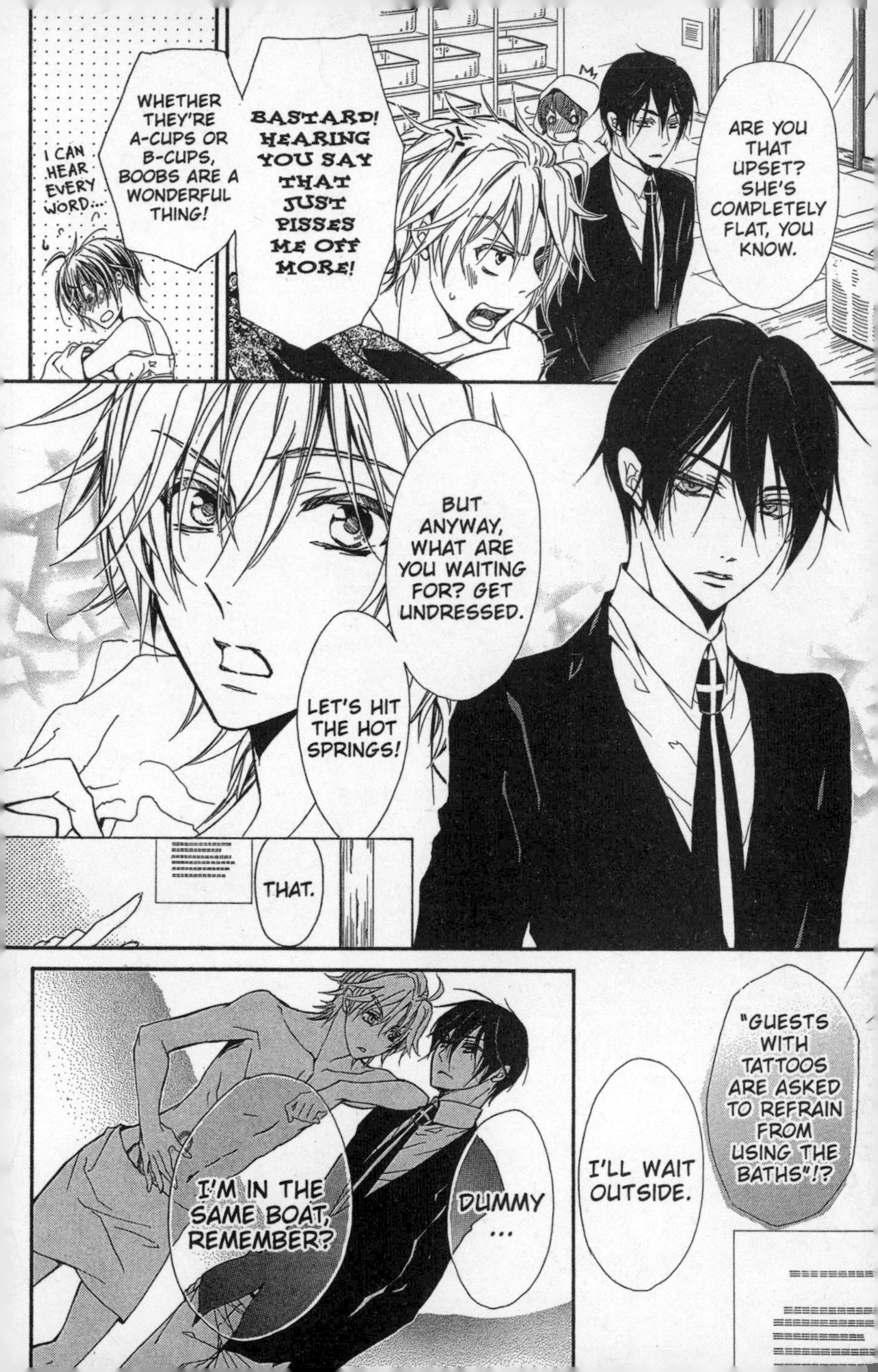
ARE YOU THAT UPSET? SHE'S COMPLETELY FLAT, YOU KNOW.
BASTARD! HEARING YOU SAY THAT JUST PISSES ME OFF MORE!
WHETHER THEY'RE A-CUPS OR B-CUPS, BOOBS ARE A WONDERFUL THING!
I CAN HEAR EVERY WORD...
BUT ANYWAY, WHAT ARE YOU WAITING FOR? GET UNDRESSED.
LET'S HIT THE HOT SPRINGS!
THAT.
"GUESTS WITH TATTOOS ARE ASKED TO REFRAIN FROM USING THE BATHS"!?
I'LL WAIT OUTSIDE.
DUMMY...
I'M IN THE SAME BOAT, REMEMBER?

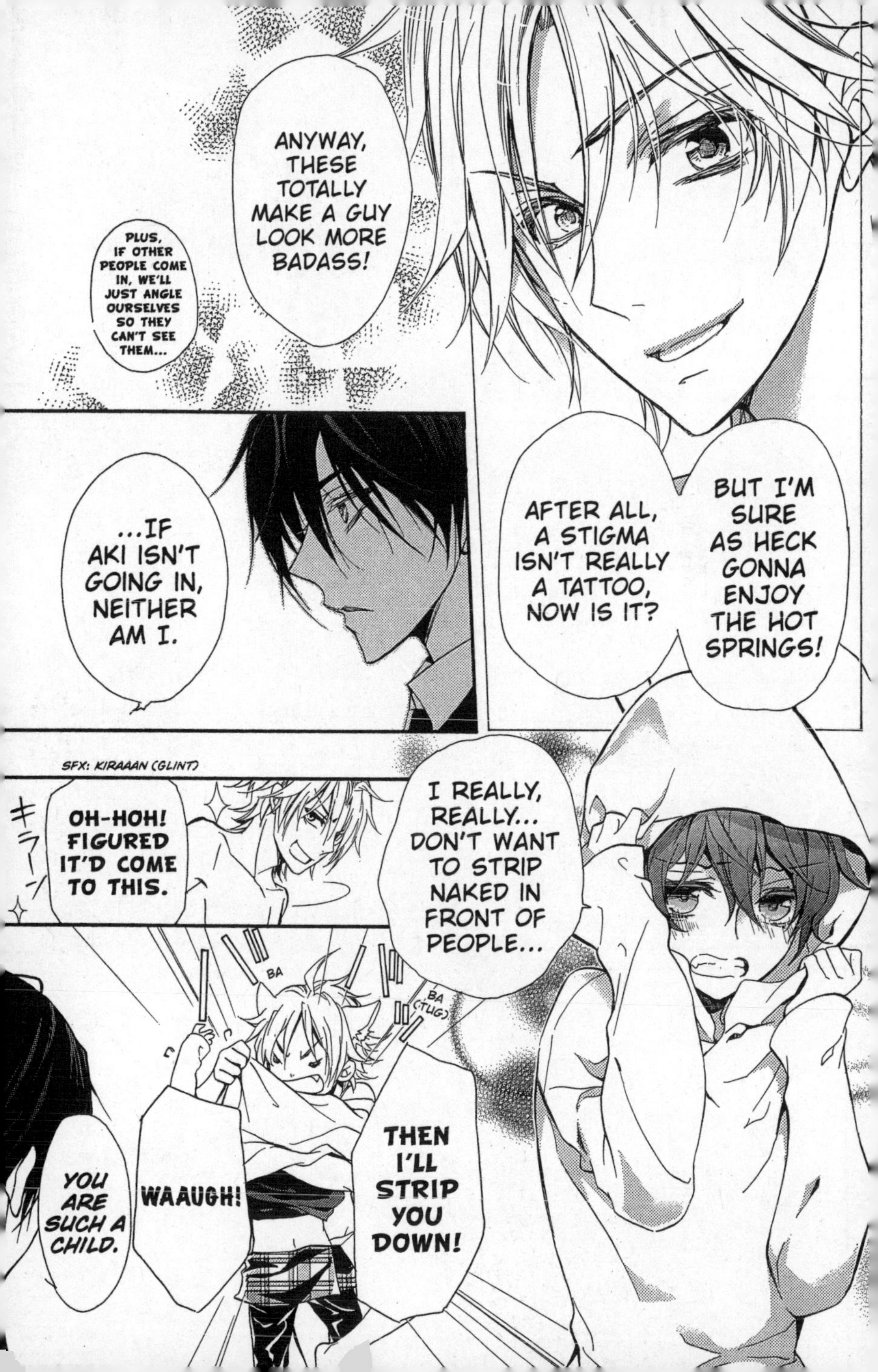
ANYWAY, THESE TOTALLY MAKE A GUY LOOK MORE BADASS!
PLUS, IF OTHER PEOPLE COME IN, WE'LL JUST ANGLE OURSELVES SO THEY CAN'T SEE THEM...
BUT I'M SURE AS HECK GONNA ENJOY THE HOT SPRINGS!
AFTER ALL, A STIGMA ISN'T REALLY A TATTOO, NOW IS IT?
...IF AKI ISN'T GOING IN, NEITHER AM I.
I REALLY, REALLY... DON'T WANT TO STRIP NAKED IN FRONT OF PEOPLE...
SFX: KIRAAAN (GLINT)
キラーン
OH-HOH! FIGURED IT'D COME TO THIS.
THEN I'LL STRIP YOU DOWN!
BA
BA (TUG)
WAAUGH!
YOU ARE SUCH A CHILD.

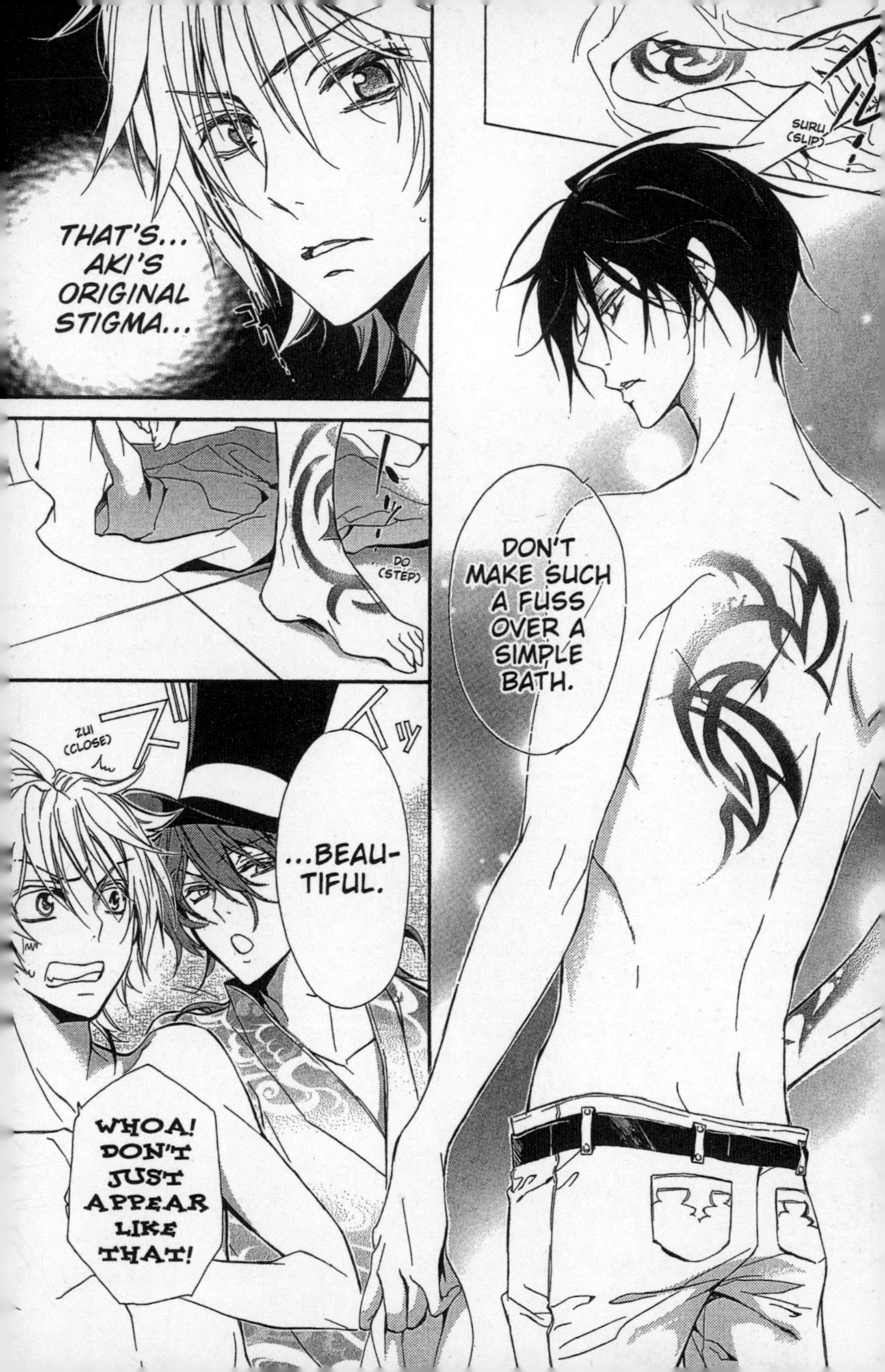
SURU (SLIP)
DON'T MAKE SUCH A FUSS OVER A SIMPLE BATH.
THAT'S... AKI'S ORIGINAL STIGMA...
DO (STEP)
...BEAU-TIFUL.
ZUI (CLOSE)
WHOA! DON'T JUST APPEAR LIKE THAT!

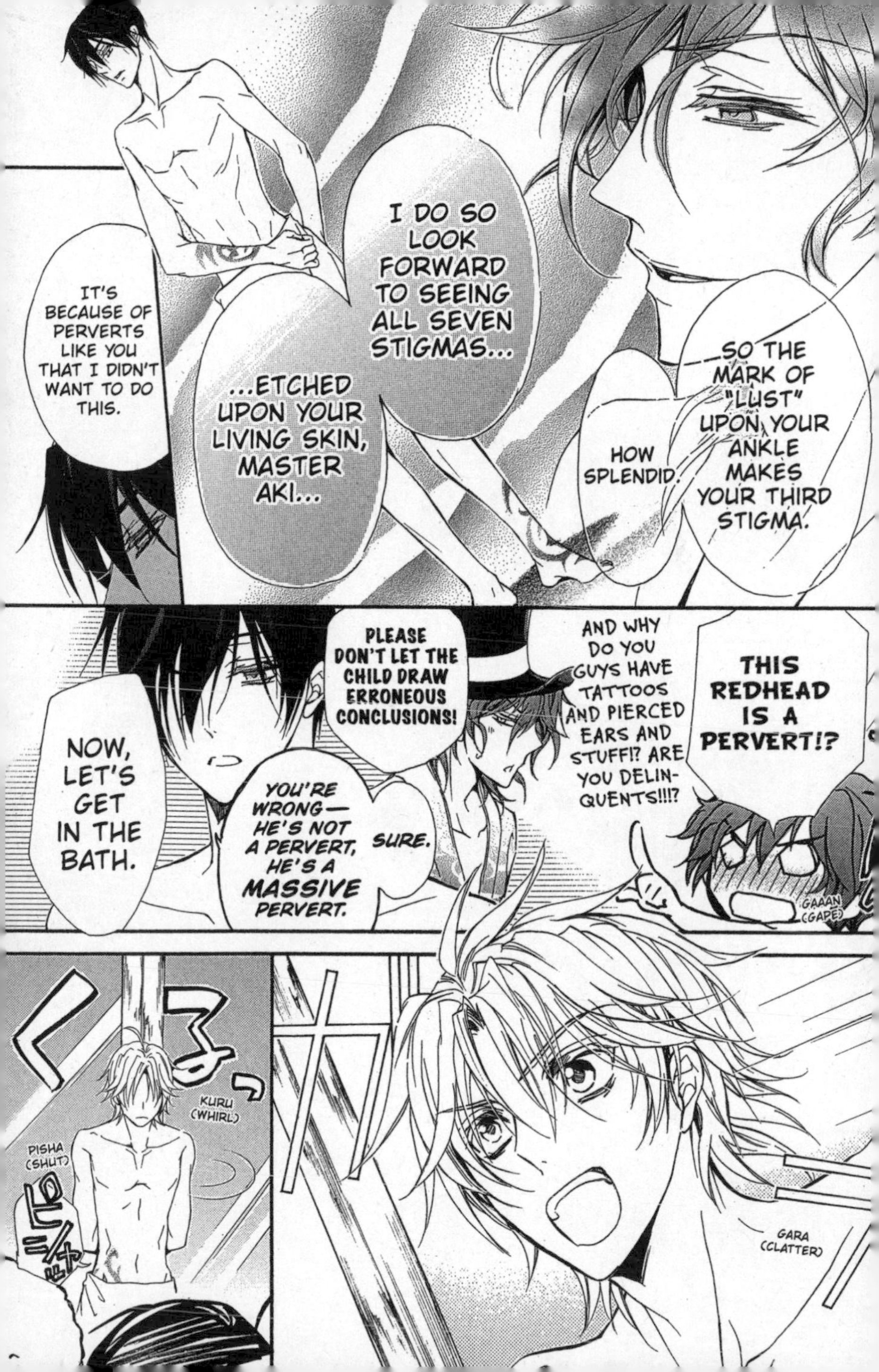
...SO THE MARK OF "LUST" UPON YOUR ANKLE MAKES YOUR THIRD STIGMA.
HOW SPLENDID.
I DO SO LOOK FORWARD TO SEEING ALL SEVEN STIGMAS...
...ETCHED UPON YOUR LIVING SKIN, MASTER AKI...
IT'S BECAUSE OF PERVERTS LIKE YOU THAT I DIDN'T WANT TO DO THIS.
THIS REDHEAD IS A PERVERT!?
AND WHY DO YOU GUYS HAVE TATTOOS AND PIERCED EARS AND STUFF!? ARE YOU DELIN-QUENTS!!!?
GAAAN (GAPE)
PLEASE DON'T LET THE CHILD DRAW ERRONEOUS CONCLUSIONS!
YOU'RE WRONG—HE'S NOT A PERVERT, HE'S A MASSIVE PERVERT.
SURE.
NOW, LET'S GET IN THE BATH.
GARA (CLATTER)
KURU (WHIRL)
PISHA (SHUT)

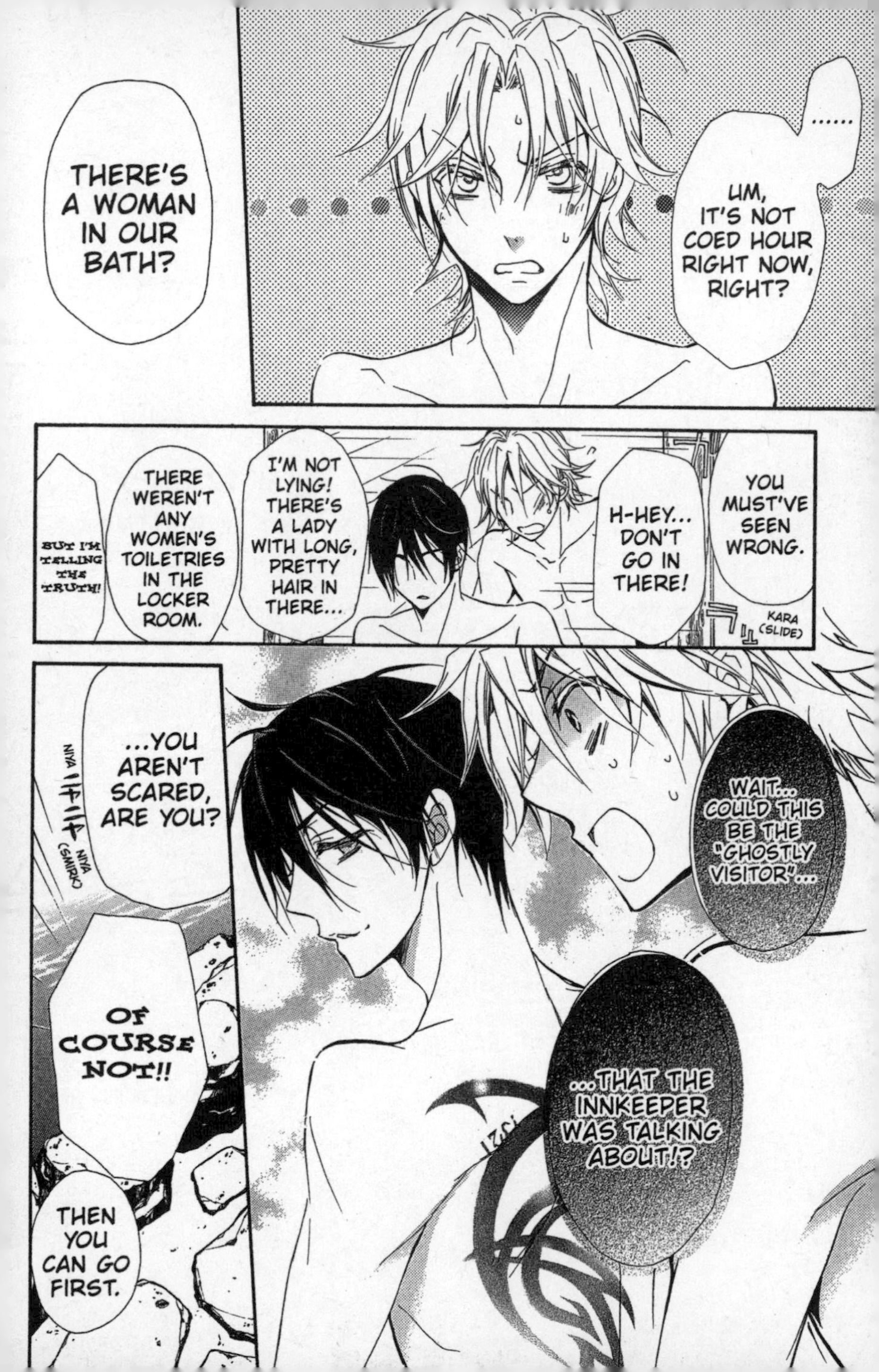
......
UM, IT'S NOT COED HOUR RIGHT NOW, RIGHT?
THERE'S A WOMAN IN OUR BATH?
YOU MUST'VE SEEN WRONG.
KARA (SLIDE)
H-HEY... DON'T GO IN THERE!
I'M NOT LYING! THERE'S A LADY WITH LONG, PRETTY HAIR IN THERE...
THERE WEREN'T ANY WOMEN'S TOILETRIES IN THE LOCKER ROOM.
BUT I'M TELLING THE TRUTH!
WAIT... COULD THIS BE THE "GHOSTLY VISITOR"...
...YOU AREN'T SCARED, ARE YOU?
NIYA (SMIRK)
...THAT THE INNKEEPER WAS TALKING ABOUT!?
OF COURSE NOT!!
THEN YOU CAN GO FIRST.

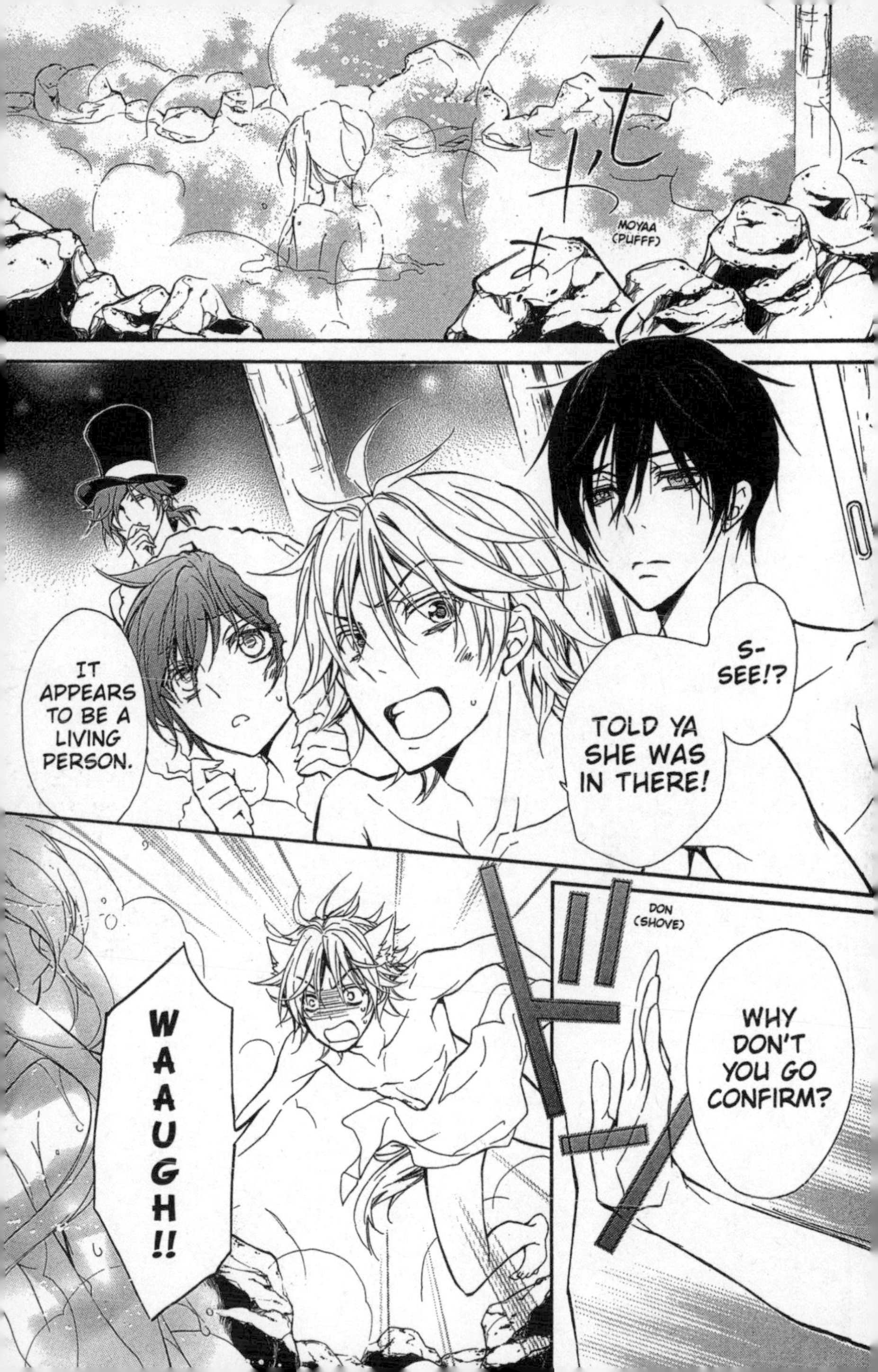
MOYAA (PUFFF)
S- SEE!?
TOLD YA SHE WAS IN THERE!
IT APPEARS TO BE A LIVING PERSON.
DON (SHOVE)
WHY DON'T YOU GO CONFIRM?
WAAAUGH!!

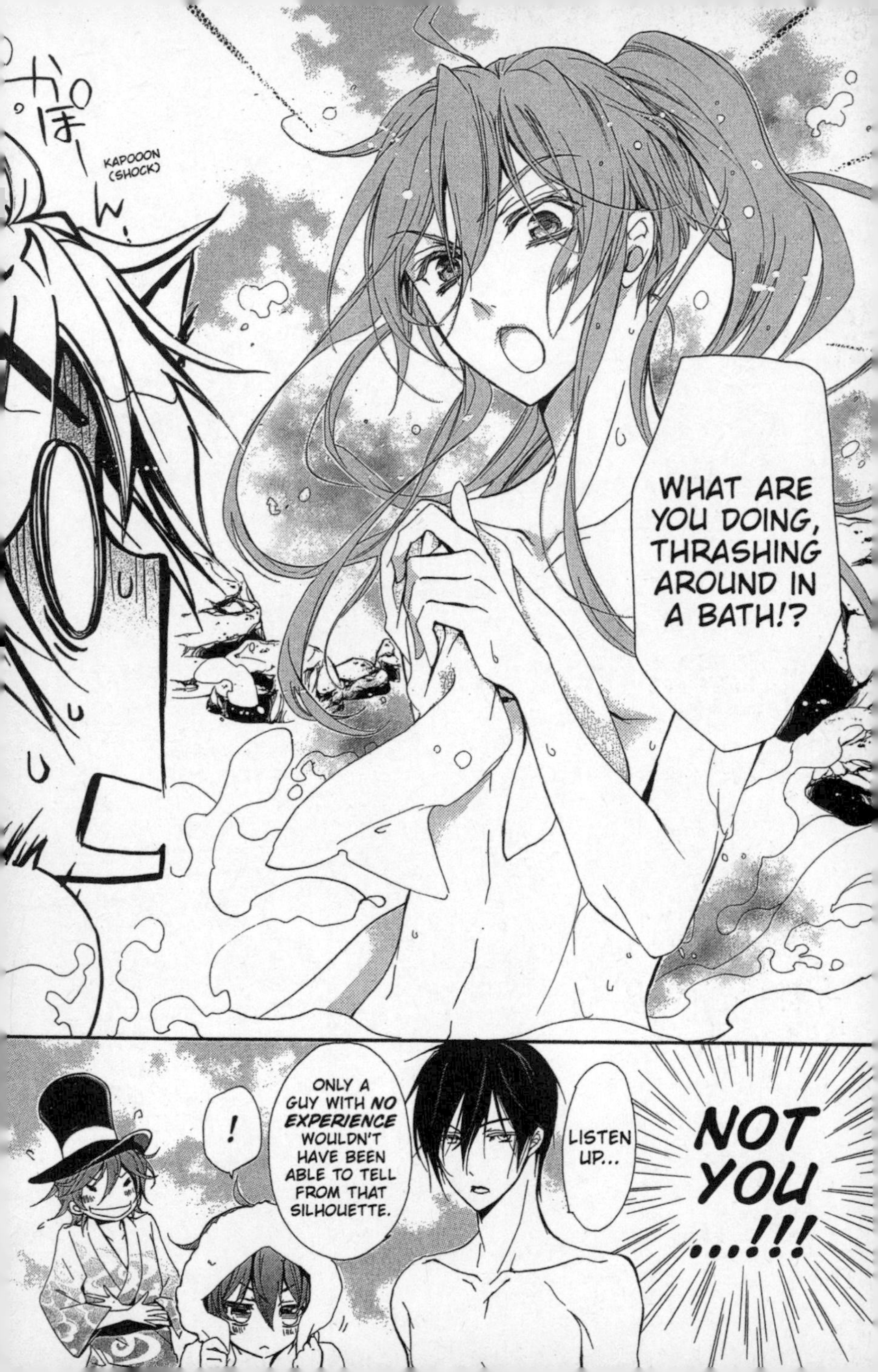

WHAT ARE YOU DOING, THRASHING AROUND IN A BATH!?
かぽーん!
KAPOOON (SHOCK)
NOT YOU ...!!!
LISTEN UP...
ONLY A GUY WITH *NO EXPERIENCE* WOULDN'T HAVE BEEN ABLE TO TELL FROM THAT SILHOUETTE.
!

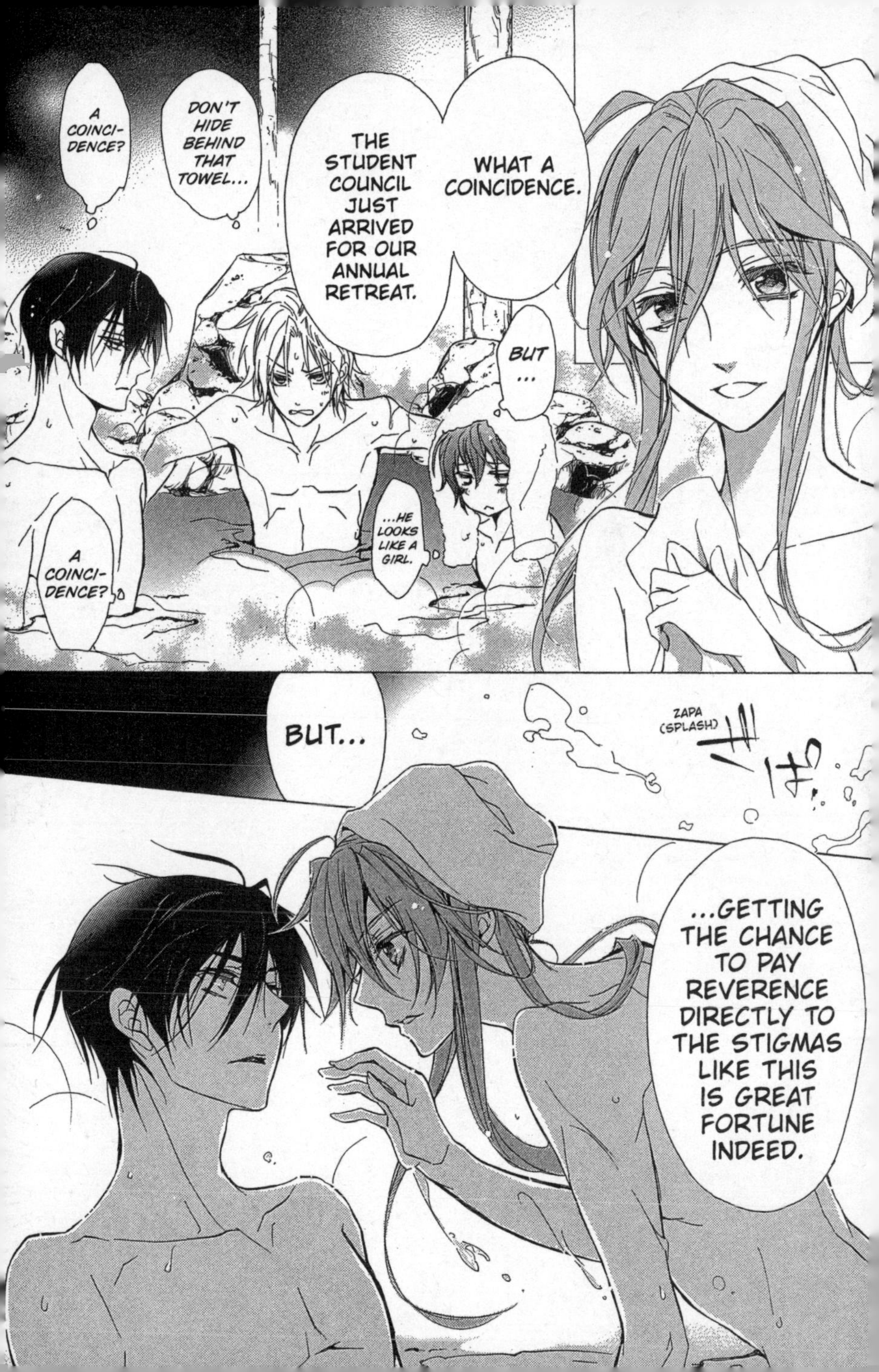
WHAT A COINCIDENCE.
THE STUDENT COUNCIL JUST ARRIVED FOR OUR ANNUAL RETREAT.
DON'T HIDE BEHIND THAT TOWEL...
A COINCIDENCE?
BUT...
...HE LOOKS LIKE A GIRL.
A COINCIDENCE?
ZAPA (SPLASH)
BUT...
...GETTING THE CHANCE TO PAY REVERENCE DIRECTLY TO THE STIGMAS LIKE THIS IS GREAT FORTUNE INDEED.

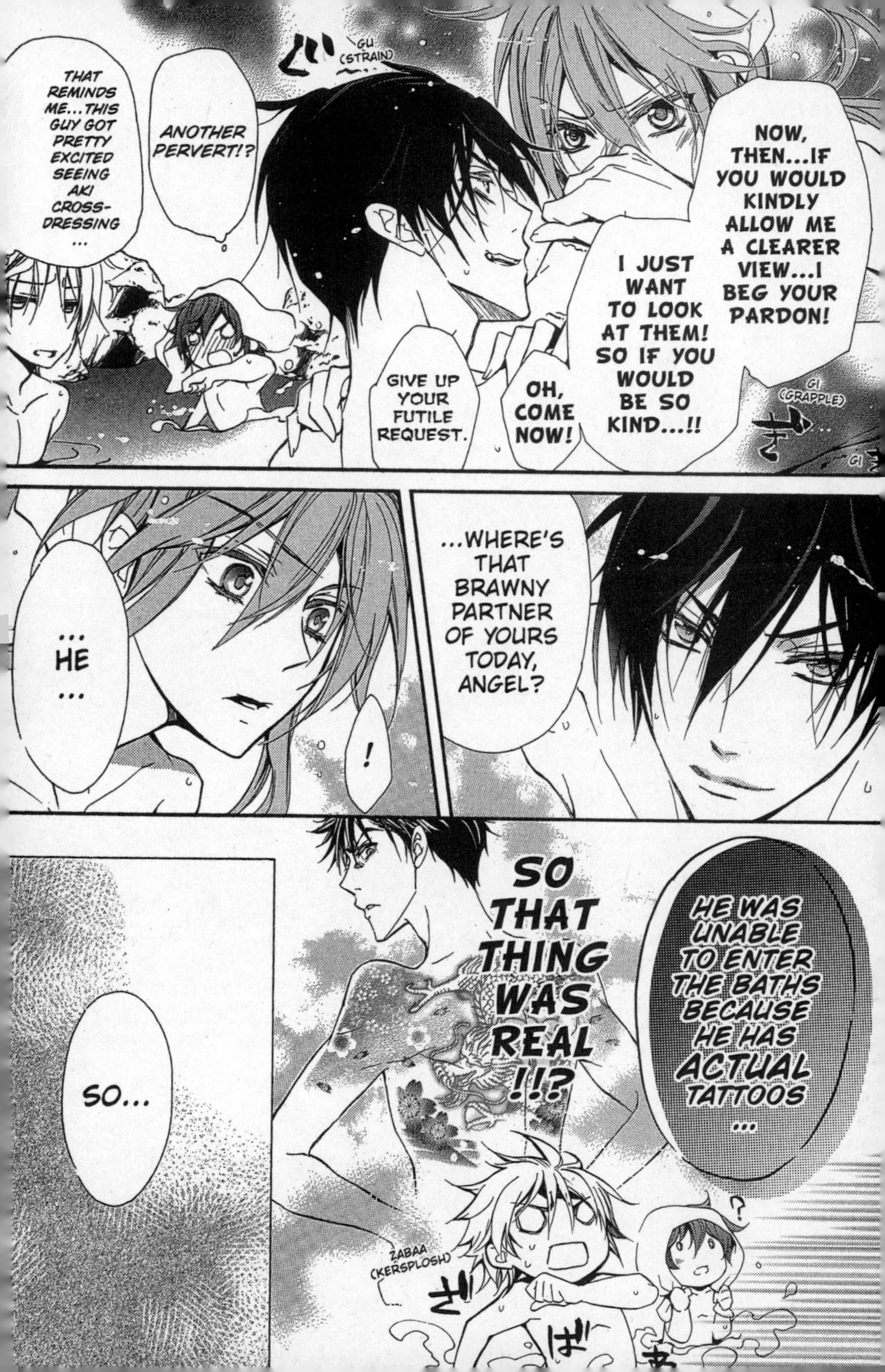
NOW, THEN...IF YOU WOULD KINDLY ALLOW ME A CLEARER VIEW...I BEG YOUR PARDON!
GI (GRAPPLE)
GI
I JUST WANT TO LOOK AT THEM! SO IF YOU WOULD BE SO KIND...!!
OH, COME NOW!
GIVE UP YOUR FUTILE REQUEST.
GU (STRAIN)
ANOTHER PERVERT!?
THAT REMINDS ME...THIS GUY GOT PRETTY EXCITED SEEING AKI CROSS-DRESSING...
...WHERE'S THAT BRAWNY PARTNER OF YOURS TODAY, ANGEL?
!
... HE ...
HE WAS UNABLE TO ENTER THE BATHS BECAUSE HE HAS ACTUAL TATTOOS ...
SO THAT THING WAS REAL!!?
?
ZABAA (KERSPLOSH)
SO...

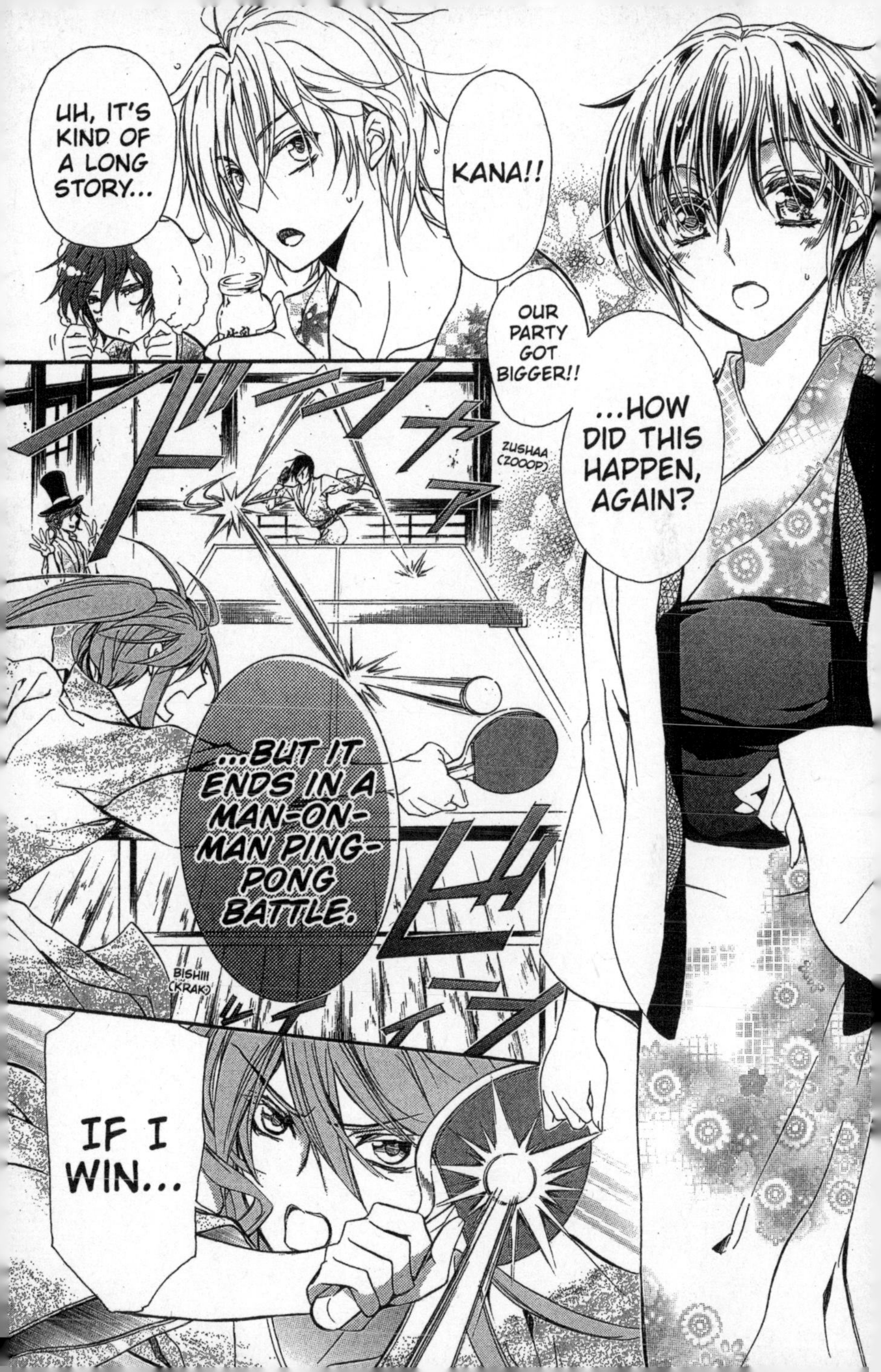
KANA!!
OUR PARTY GOT BIGGER!!
UH, IT'S KIND OF A LONG STORY...
...HOW DID THIS HAPPEN, AGAIN?
ZUSHAA (ZOOOP)
...BUT IT ENDS IN A MAN-ON-MAN PING-PONG BATTLE.
BISHIII (KRAK)
IF I WIN...

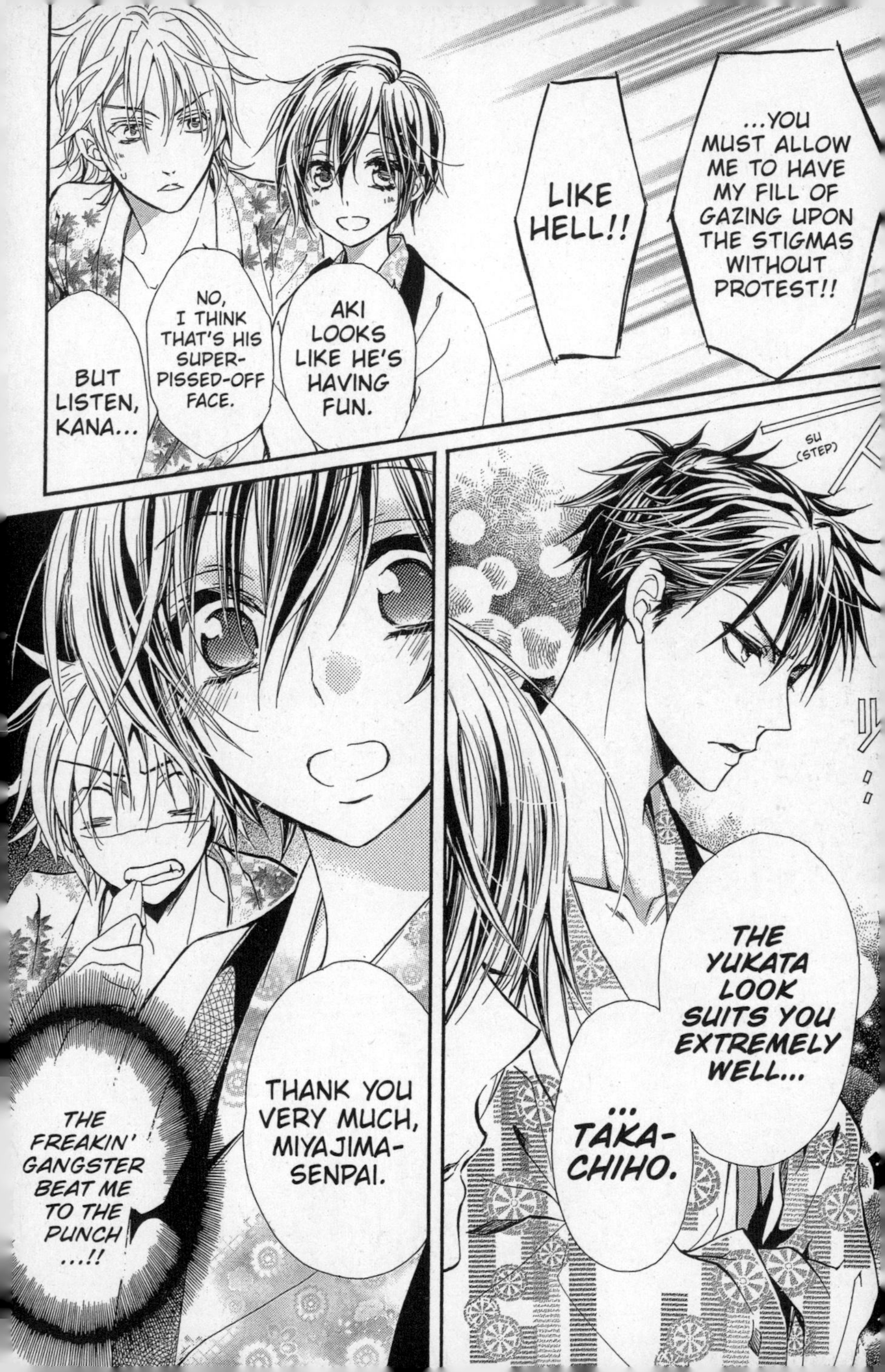

...YOU MUST ALLOW ME TO HAVE MY FILL OF GAZING UPON THE STIGMAS WITHOUT PROTEST!!
LIKE HELL!!
AKI LOOKS LIKE HE'S HAVING FUN.
NO, I THINK THAT'S HIS SUPER-PISSED-OFF FACE.
BUT LISTEN, KANA...
SU (STEP)
THE YUKATA LOOK SUITS YOU EXTREMELY WELL...
...TAKA-CHIHO.
THANK YOU VERY MUCH, MIYAJIMA-SENPAI.
THE FREAKIN' GANGSTER BEAT ME TO THE PUNCH...!!

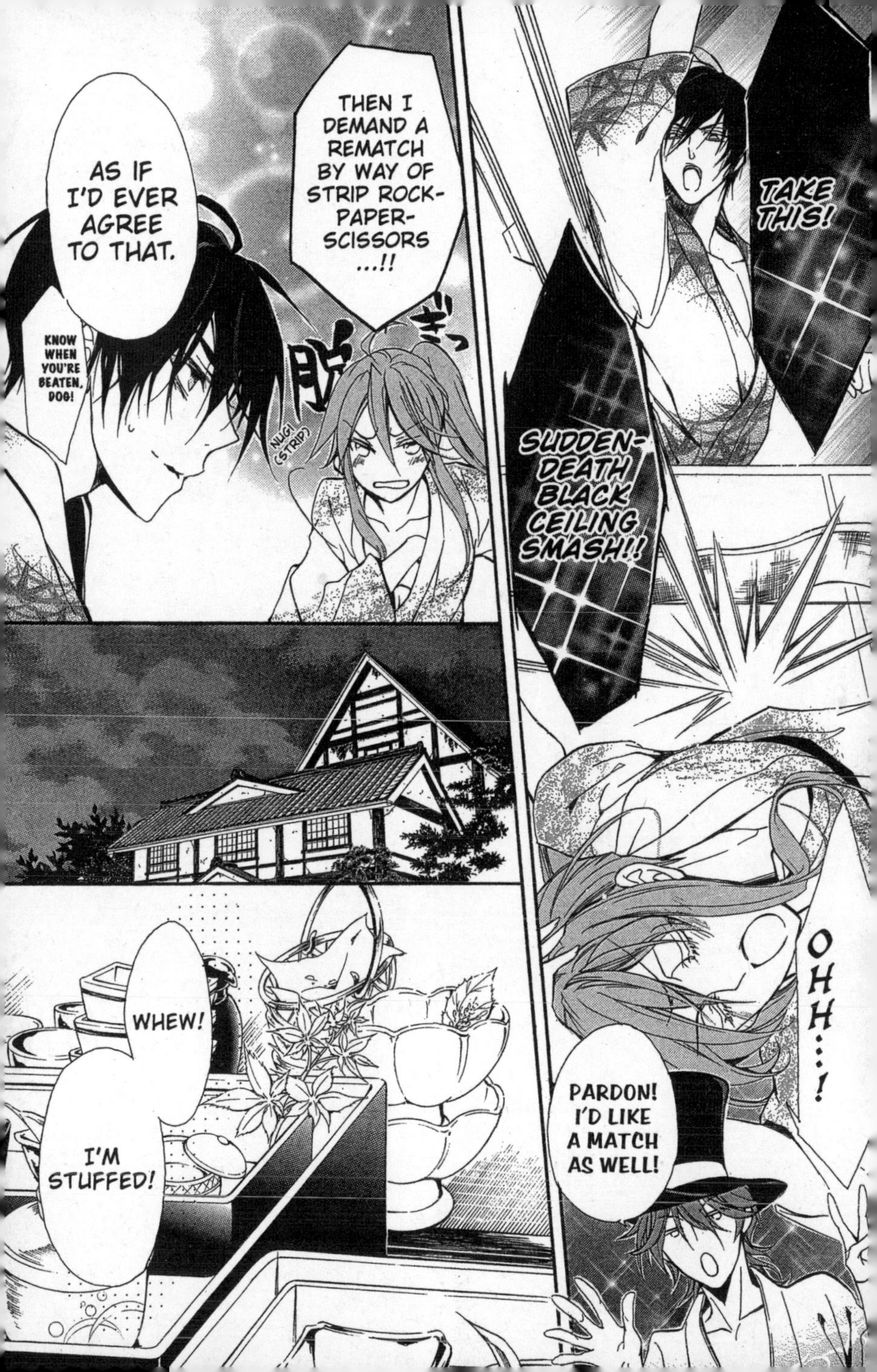
TAKE THIS!
SUDDEN-DEATH BLACK CEILING SMASH!!
THEN I DEMAND A REMATCH BY WAY OF STRIP ROCK-PAPER-SCISSORS ...!!
AS IF I'D EVER AGREE TO THAT.
KNOW WHEN YOU'RE BEATEN, DOG!
NUGI (STRIP)
OHH...!
PARDON! I'D LIKE A MATCH AS WELL!
WHEW!
I'M STUFFED!

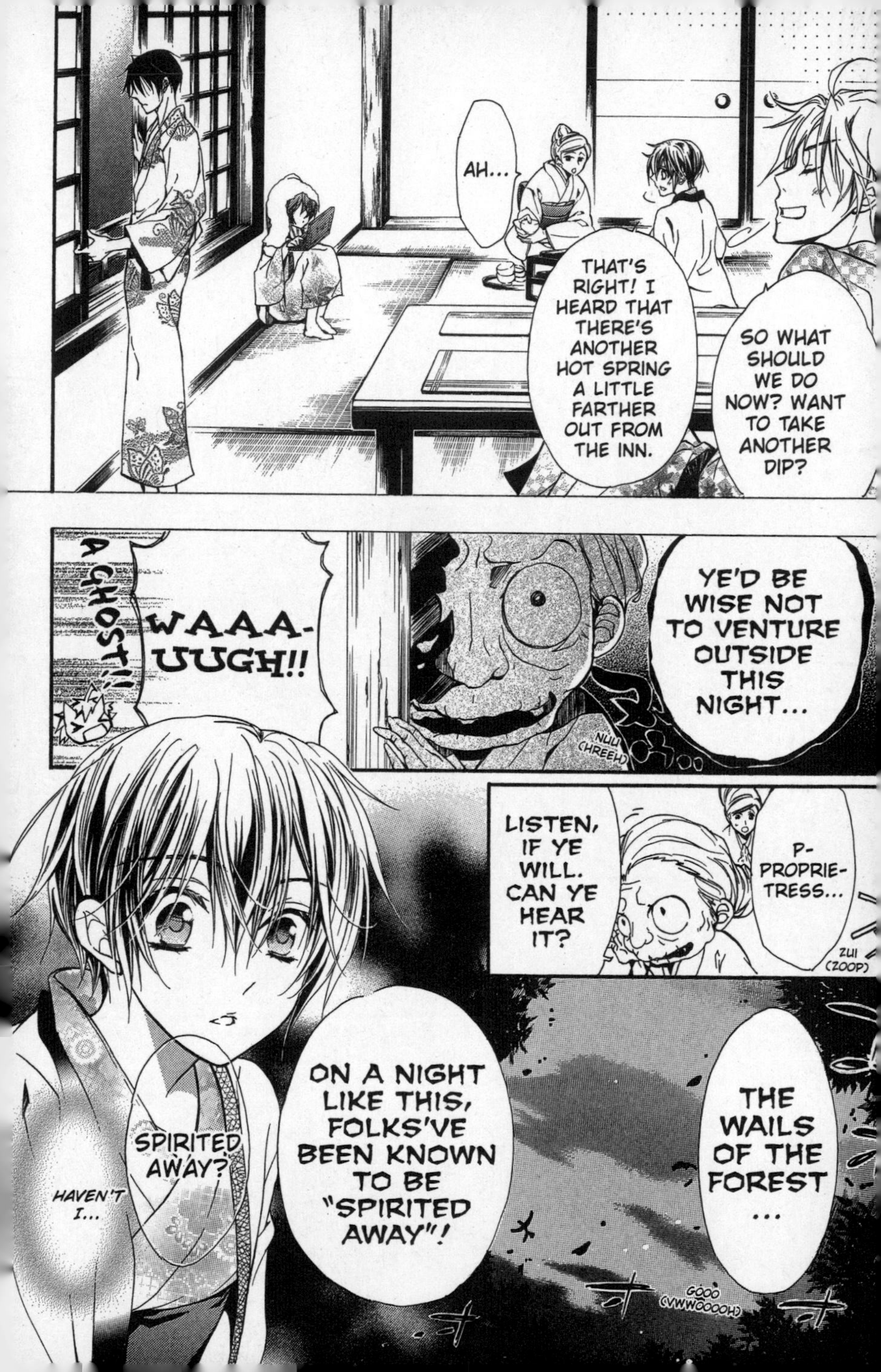
SO WHAT SHOULD WE DO NOW? WANT TO TAKE ANOTHER DIP?
THAT'S RIGHT! I HEARD THAT THERE'S ANOTHER HOT SPRING A LITTLE FARTHER OUT FROM THE INN.
AH...
YE'D BE WISE NOT TO VENTURE OUTSIDE THIS NIGHT...
NUU (HREEH)
WAAA-UUGH!!
A GHOST!!
P-PROPRIETRESS...
LISTEN, IF YE WILL. CAN YE HEAR IT?
ZUI (ZOOP)
THE WAILS OF THE FOREST...
GOOO (VWWOOOOH)
ON A NIGHT LIKE THIS, FOLKS'VE BEEN KNOWN TO BE "SPIRITED AWAY"!
SPIRITED AWAY?
HAVEN'T I...

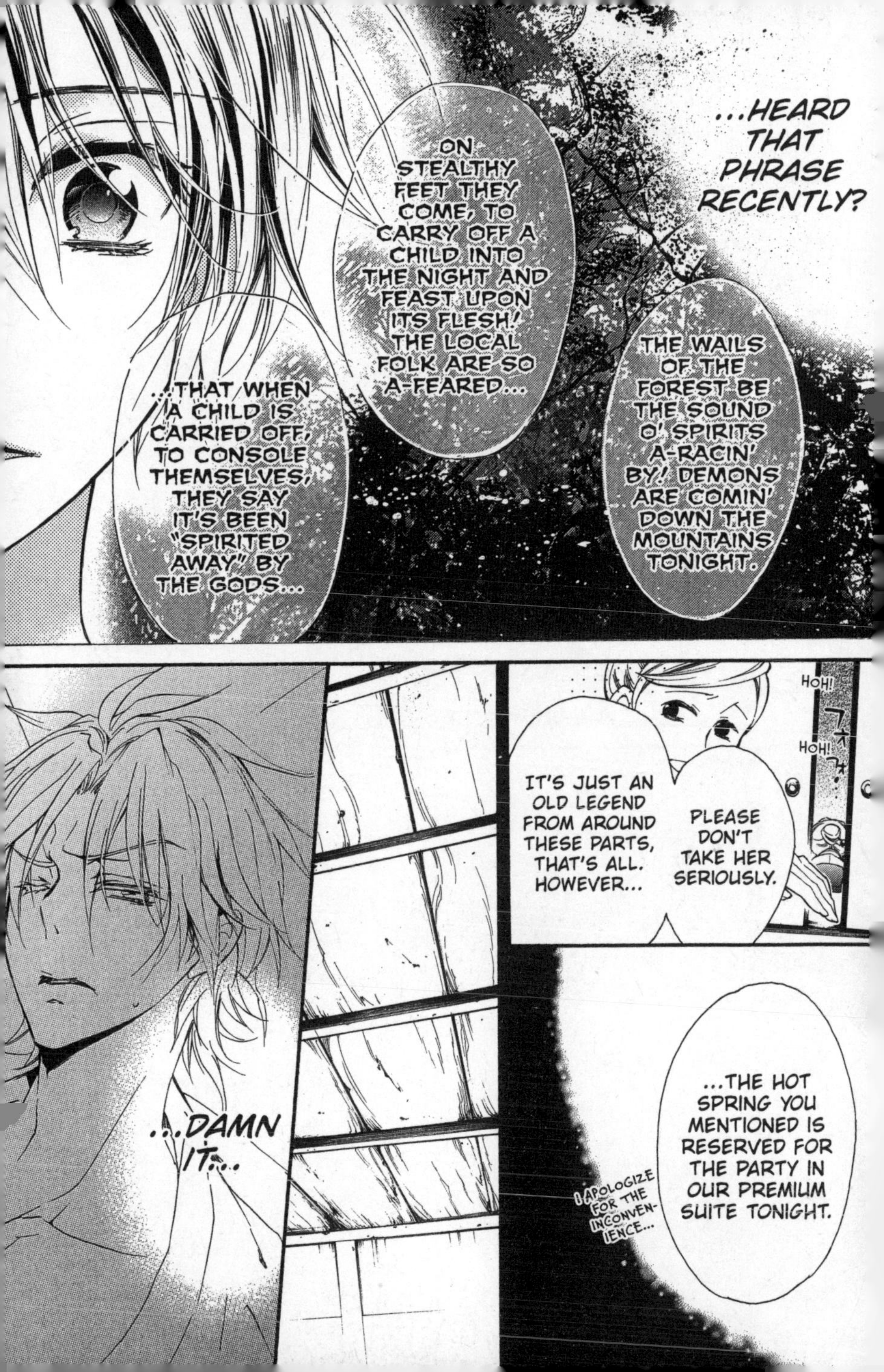

...HEARD THAT PHRASE RECENTLY?
THE WAILS OF THE FOREST BE THE SOUND O' SPIRITS A-RACIN' BY! DEMONS ARE COMIN' DOWN THE MOUNTAINS TONIGHT.
ON STEALTHY FEET THEY COME, TO CARRY OFF A CHILD INTO THE NIGHT AND FEAST UPON ITS FLESH! THE LOCAL FOLK ARE SO A-FEARED...
...THAT WHEN A CHILD IS CARRIED OFF, TO CONSOLE THEMSELVES, THEY SAY IT'S BEEN "SPIRITED AWAY" BY THE GODS...
HOH!
HOH!
PLEASE DON'T TAKE HER SERIOUSLY.
IT'S JUST AN OLD LEGEND FROM AROUND THESE PARTS, THAT'S ALL. HOWEVER...
...THE HOT SPRING YOU MENTIONED IS RESERVED FOR THE PARTY IN OUR PREMIUM SUITE TONIGHT.
I APOLOGIZE FOR THE INCONVEN-IENCE...
...DAMN IT...

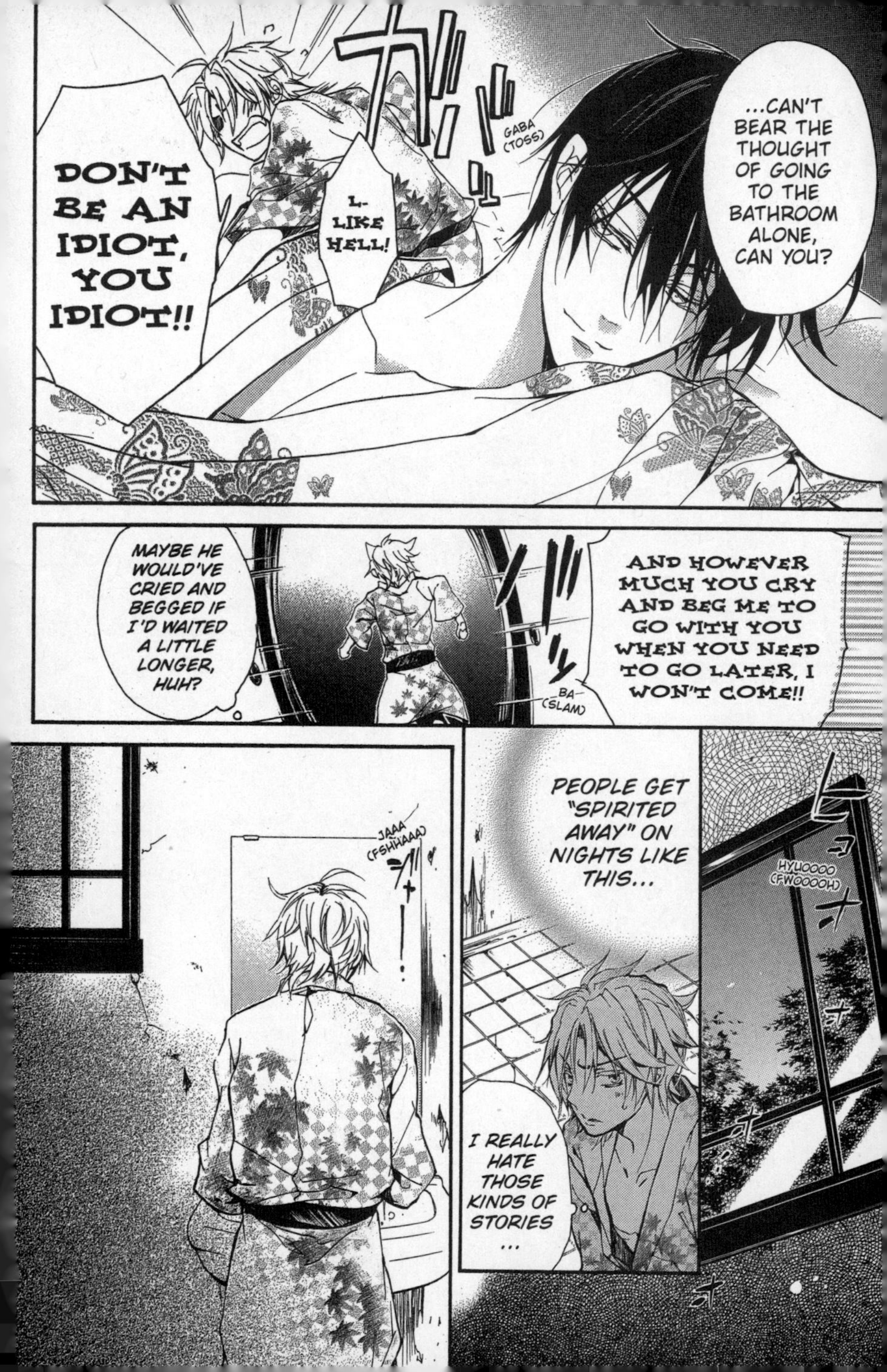
...CAN'T BEAR THE THOUGHT OF GOING TO THE BATHROOM ALONE, CAN YOU?
GABA (TOSS)
L-LIKE HELL!
DON'T BE AN IDIOT, YOU IDIOT!!
AND HOWEVER MUCH YOU CRY AND BEG ME TO GO WITH YOU WHEN YOU NEED TO GO LATER, I WON'T COME!!
BA (SLAM)
MAYBE HE WOULD'VE CRIED AND BEGGED IF I'D WAITED A LITTLE LONGER, HUH?
HYUOOOO (FWOOOOH)
PEOPLE GET "SPIRITED AWAY" ON NIGHTS LIKE THIS...
I REALLY HATE THOSE KINDS OF STORIES ...
JAAA (FSHHAAA)

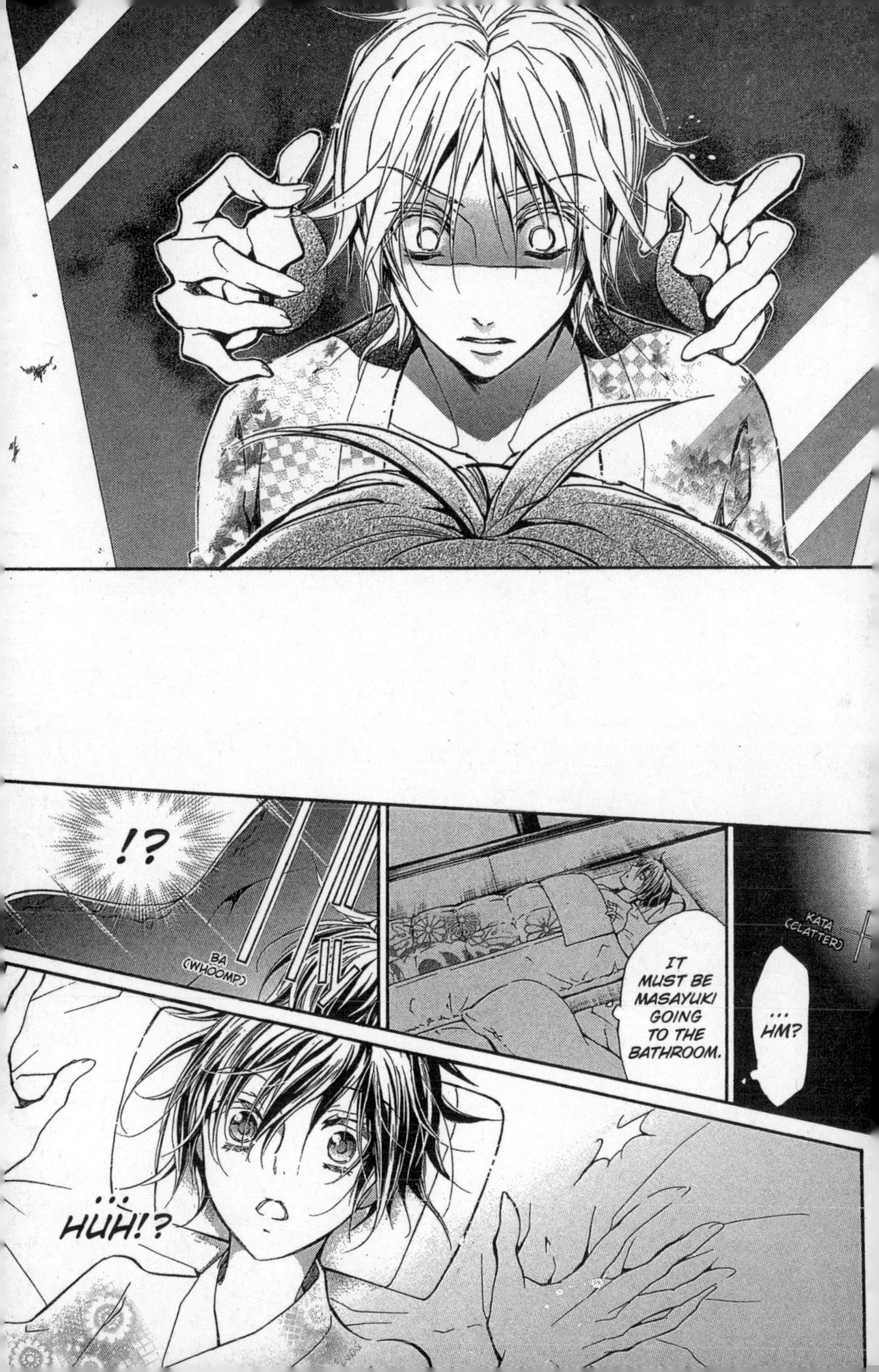
KATA (CLATTER)
...HM?
IT MUST BE MASAYUKI GOING TO THE BATHROOM.
!?
BA (WHOOMP)
...HUH!?

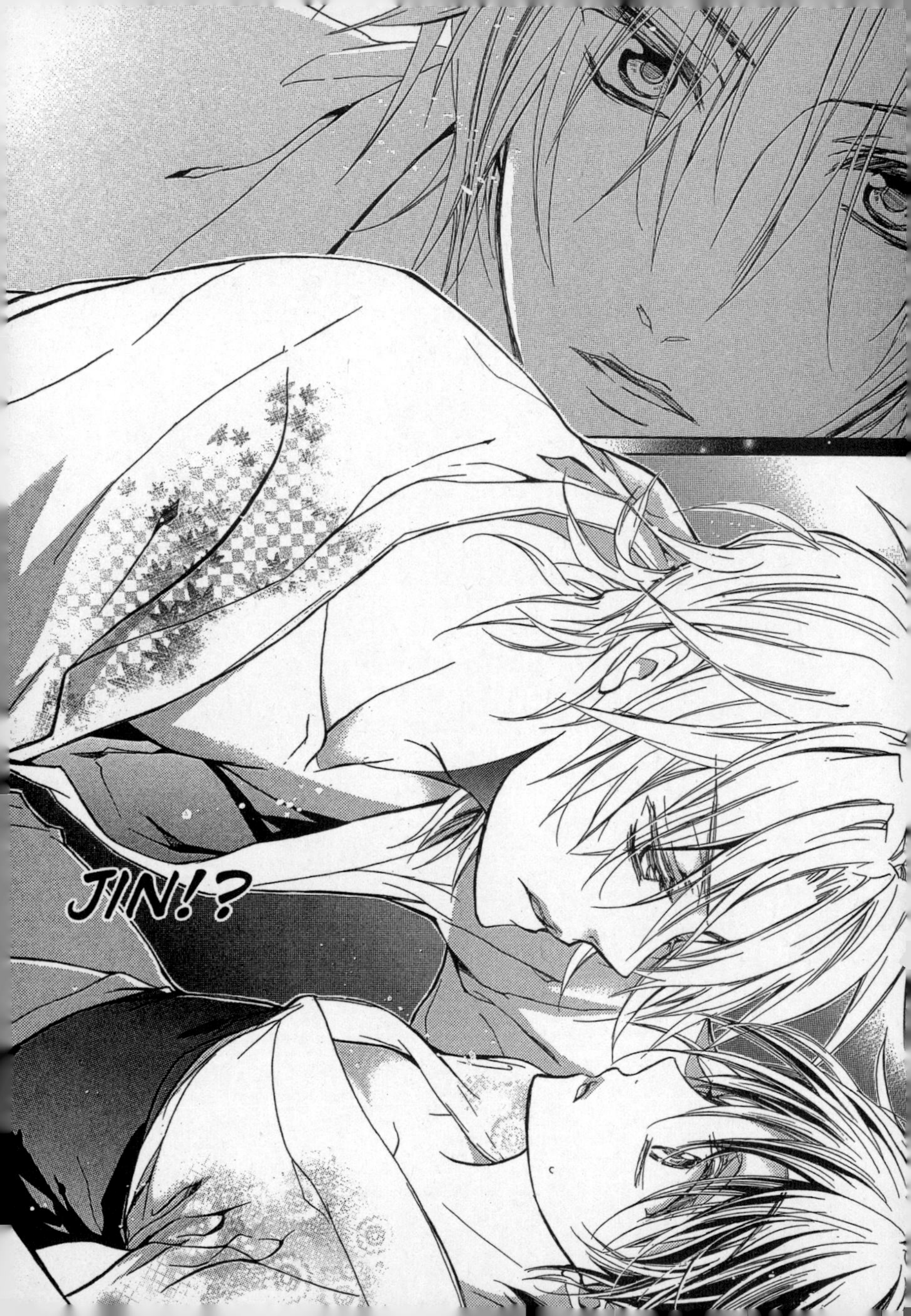
JIN!?

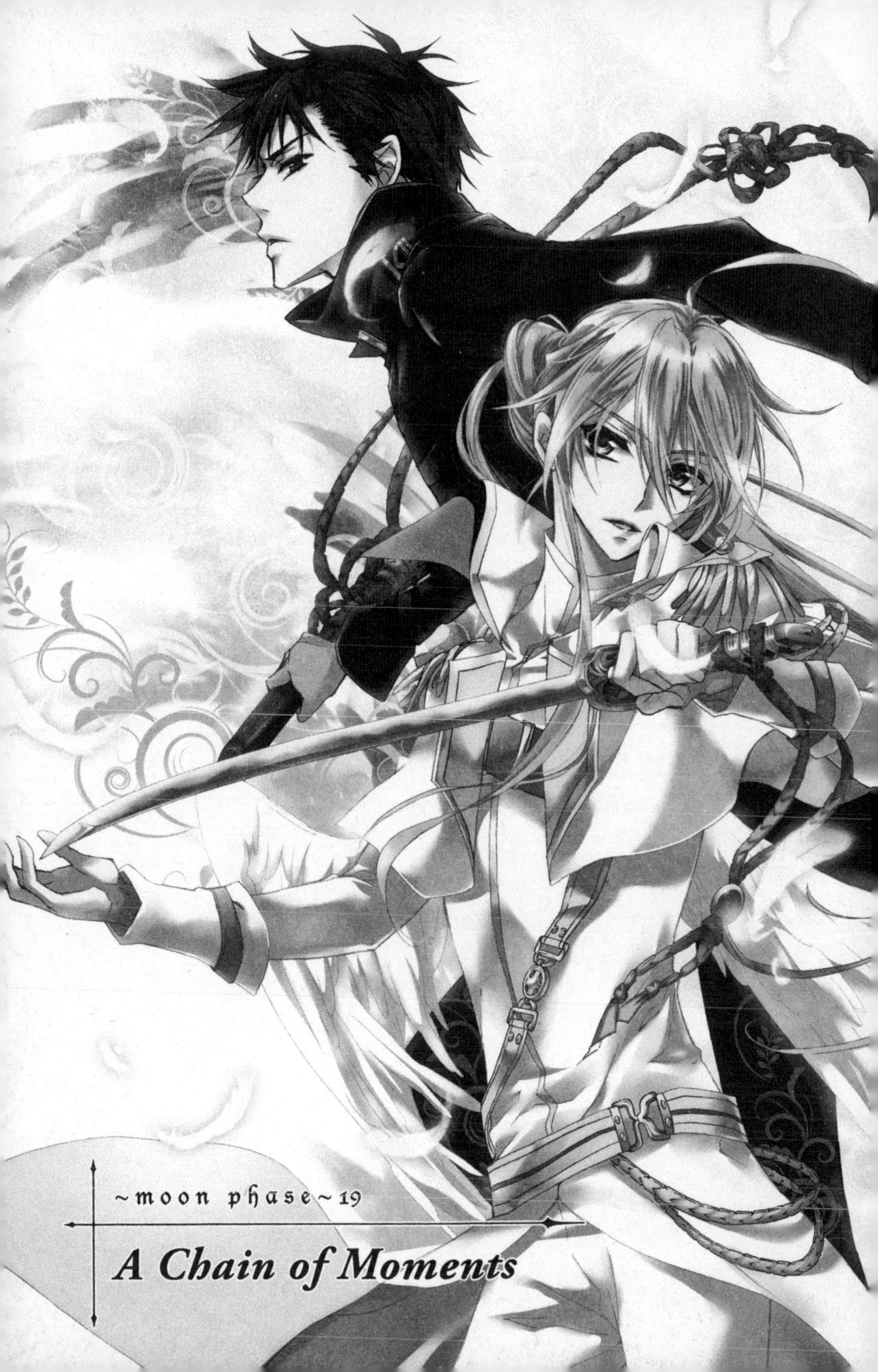
~moon phase~19
A Chain of Moments

He's my only vampire
Aya Shouoto

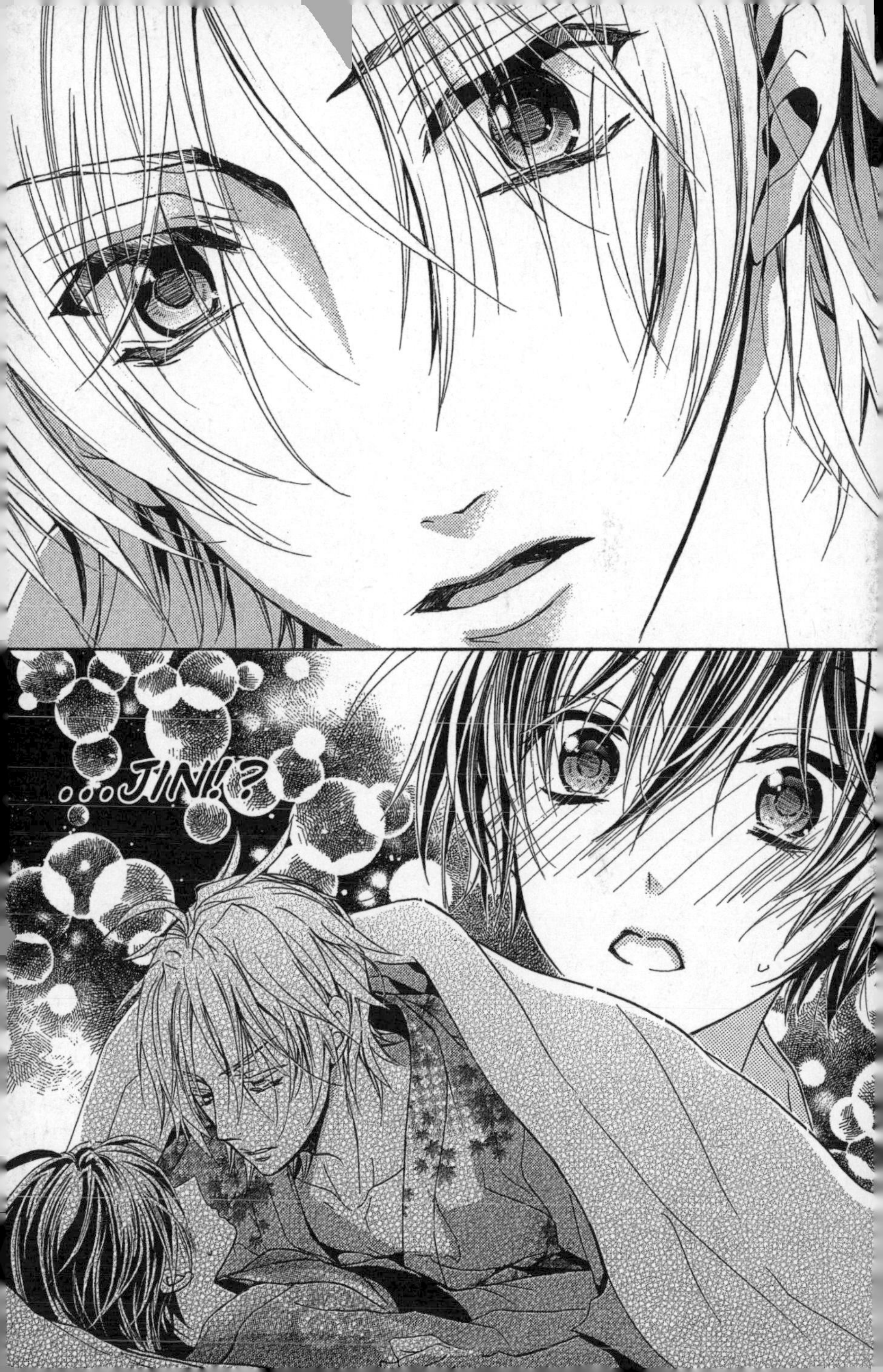
...JIN!?

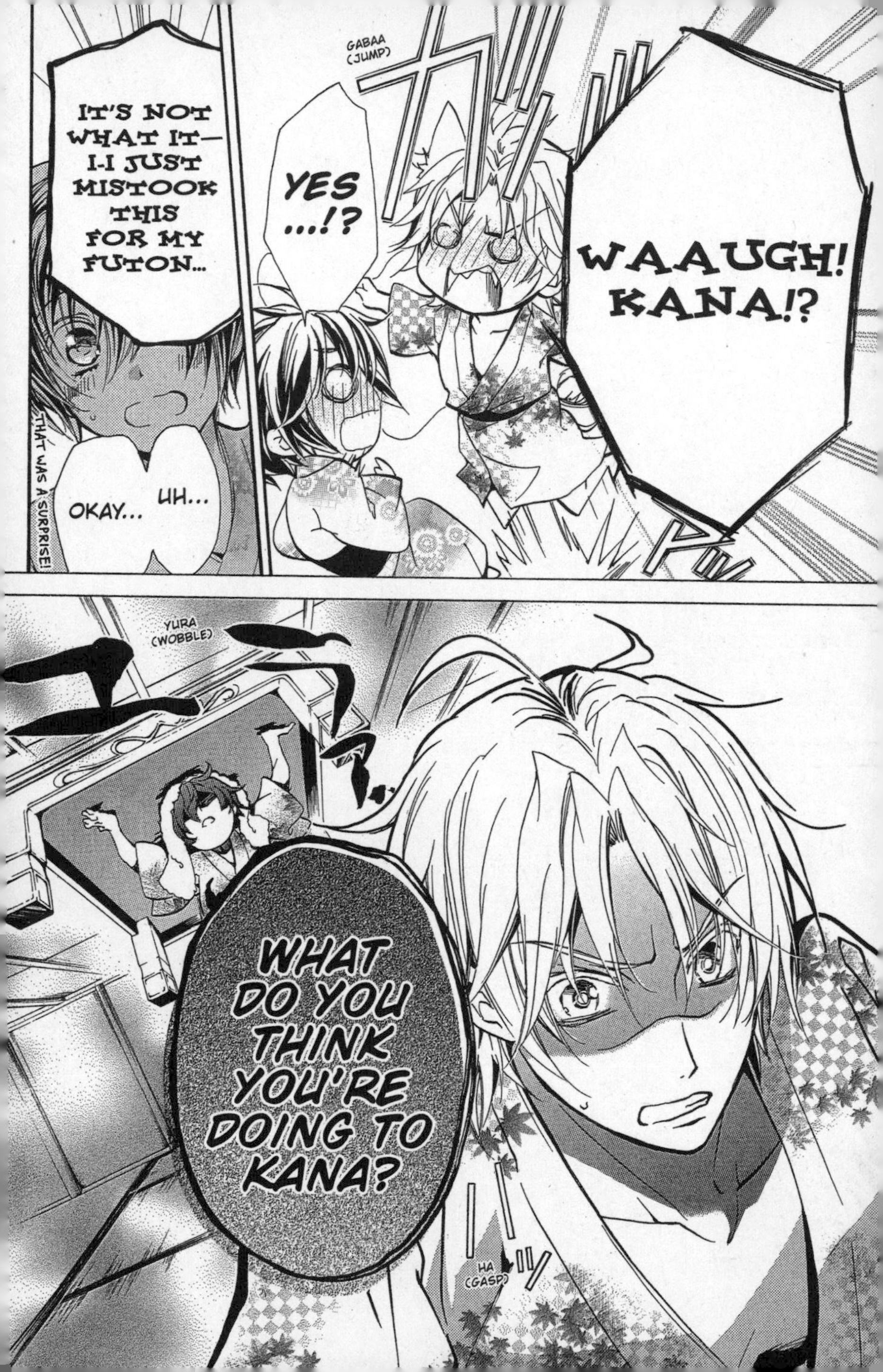
GABAA (JUMP)
WAAUGH! KANA!?
YES ...!?
IT'S NOT WHAT IT— I-I JUST MISTOOK THIS FOR MY FUTON...
UH... OKAY...
THAT WAS A SURPRISE!
YURA (WOBBLE)
WHAT DO YOU THINK YOU'RE DOING TO KANA?
HA (GASP)

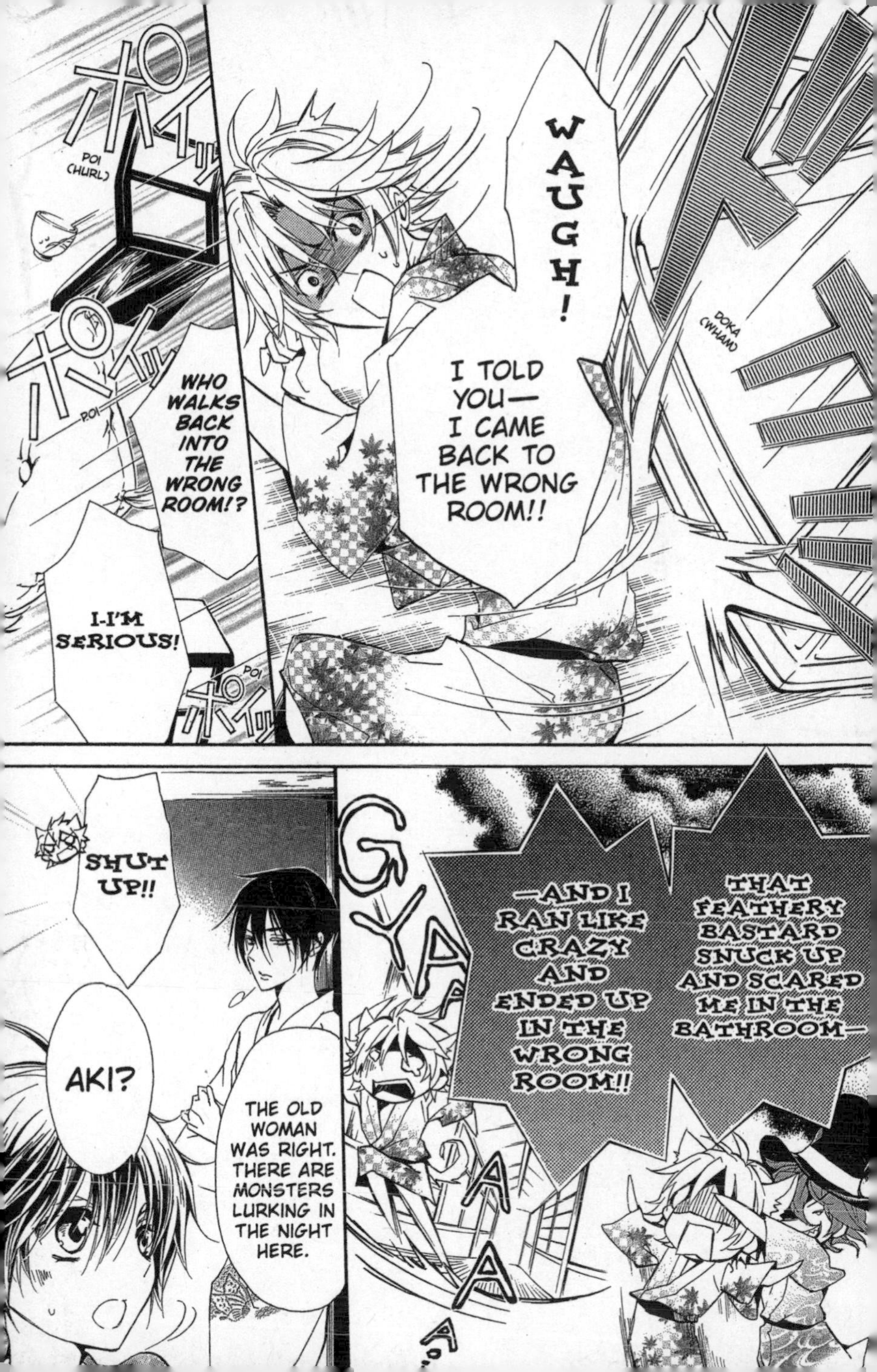
WAUGH!
DOKA (WHAM)
I TOLD YOU— I CAME BACK TO THE WRONG ROOM!!
POI (HURL)
WHO WALKS BACK INTO THE WRONG ROOM!?
POI
I-I'M SERIOUS!
POI
THAT FEATHERY BASTARD SNUCK UP AND SCARED ME IN THE BATHROOM—
—AND I RAN LIKE CRAZY AND ENDED UP IN THE WRONG ROOM!!
GYAAAAA
SHUT UP!!
THE OLD WOMAN WAS RIGHT. THERE ARE MONSTERS LURKING IN THE NIGHT HERE.
AKI?

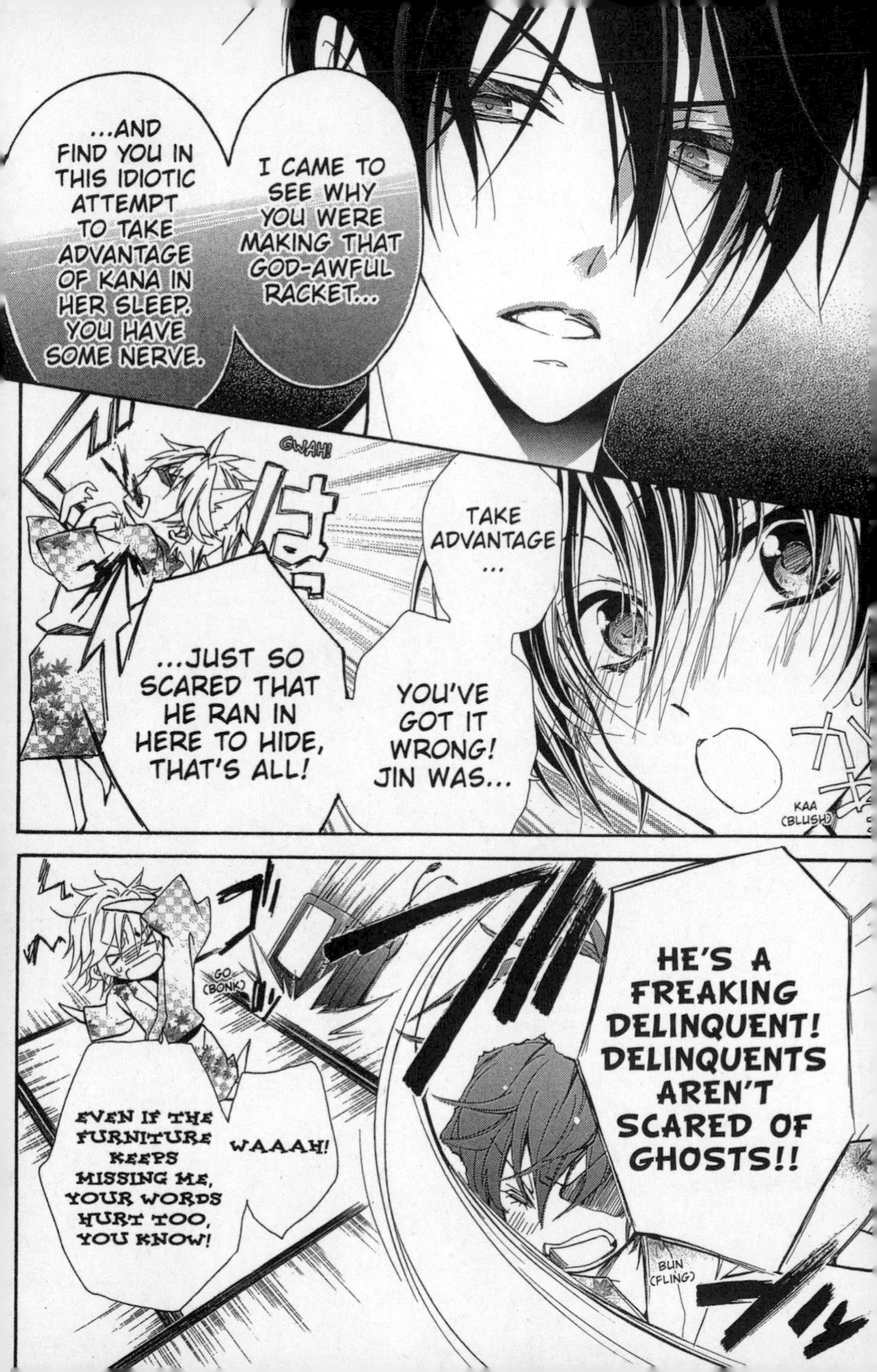
I CAME TO SEE WHY YOU WERE MAKING THAT GOD-AWFUL RACKET...
...AND FIND YOU IN THIS IDIOTIC ATTEMPT TO TAKE ADVANTAGE OF KANA IN HER SLEEP. YOU HAVE SOME NERVE.
TAKE ADVANTAGE ...
KAA (BLUSH)
YOU'VE GOT IT WRONG! JIN WAS...
...JUST SO SCARED THAT HE RAN IN HERE TO HIDE, THAT'S ALL!
GWAH!
HE'S A FREAKING DELINQUENT! DELINQUENTS AREN'T SCARED OF GHOSTS!!
BUN (FLING)
GO (BONK)
WAAAH!
EVEN IF THE FURNITURE KEEPS MISSING ME, YOUR WORDS HURT TOO, YOU KNOW!

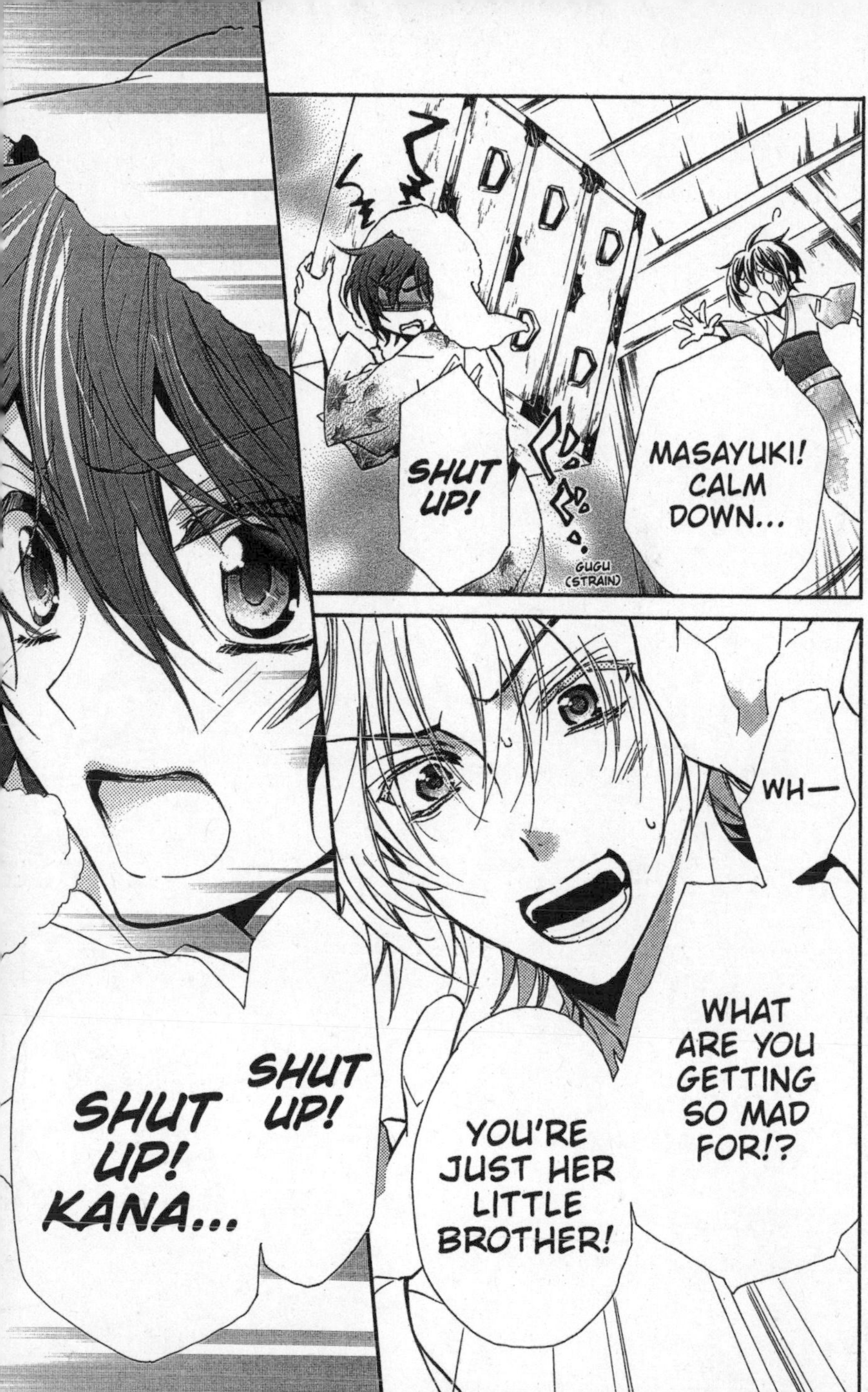
MASAYUKI! CALM DOWN...
GUGU (STRAIN)
SHUT UP!
WH—
WHAT ARE YOU GETTING SO MAD FOR!?
YOU'RE JUST HER LITTLE BROTHER!
SHUT UP!
SHUT UP! KANA...

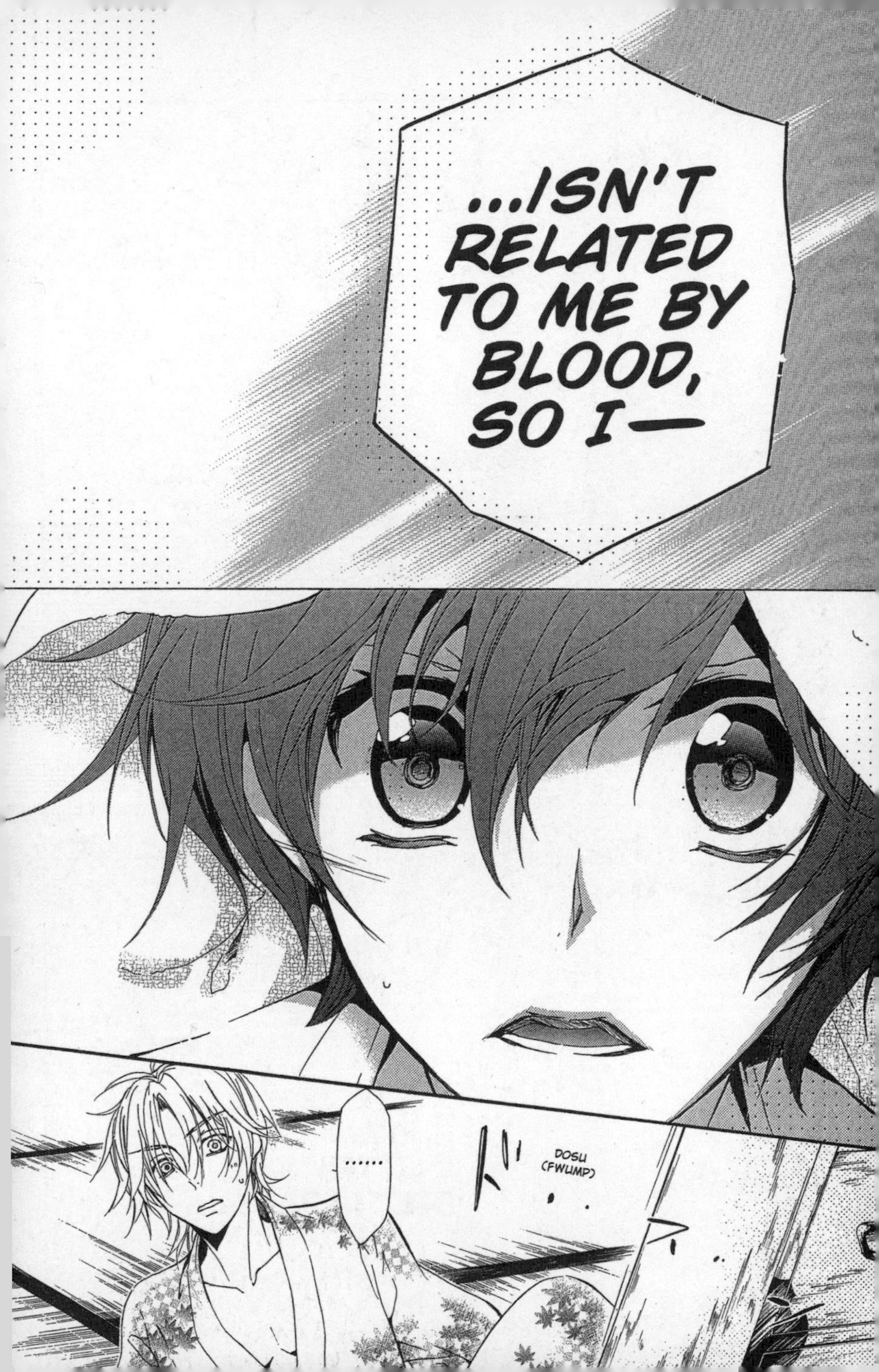
...ISN'T RELATED TO ME BY BLOOD, SO I—
ド
DOSU (FWUMP)
......

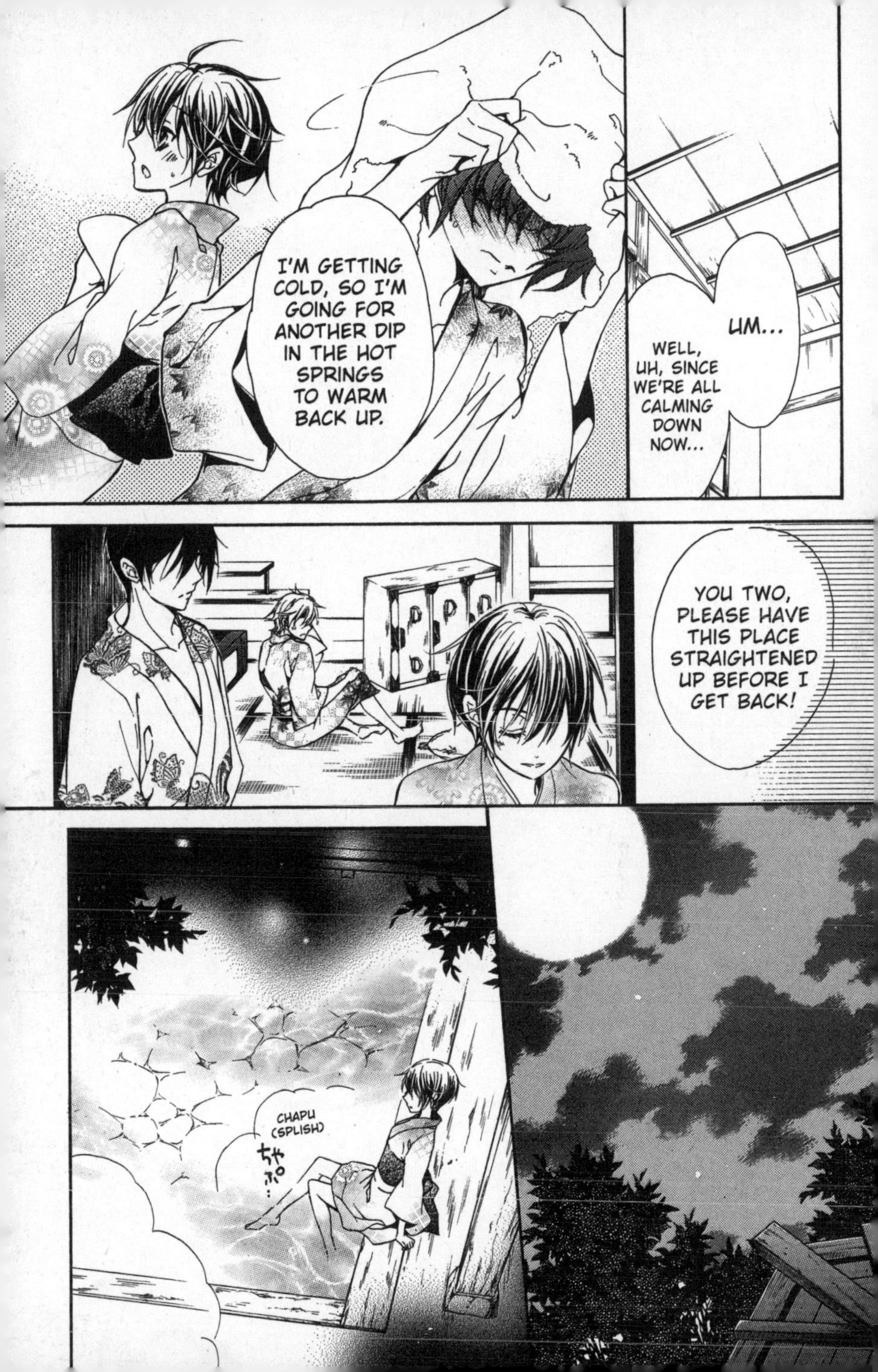
UM...
WELL, UH, SINCE WE'RE ALL CALMING DOWN NOW...
I'M GETTING COLD, SO I'M GOING FOR ANOTHER DIP IN THE HOT SPRINGS TO WARM BACK UP.
YOU TWO, PLEASE HAVE THIS PLACE STRAIGHTENED UP BEFORE I GET BACK!
CHAPU (SPLISH)
ちゃぷ…

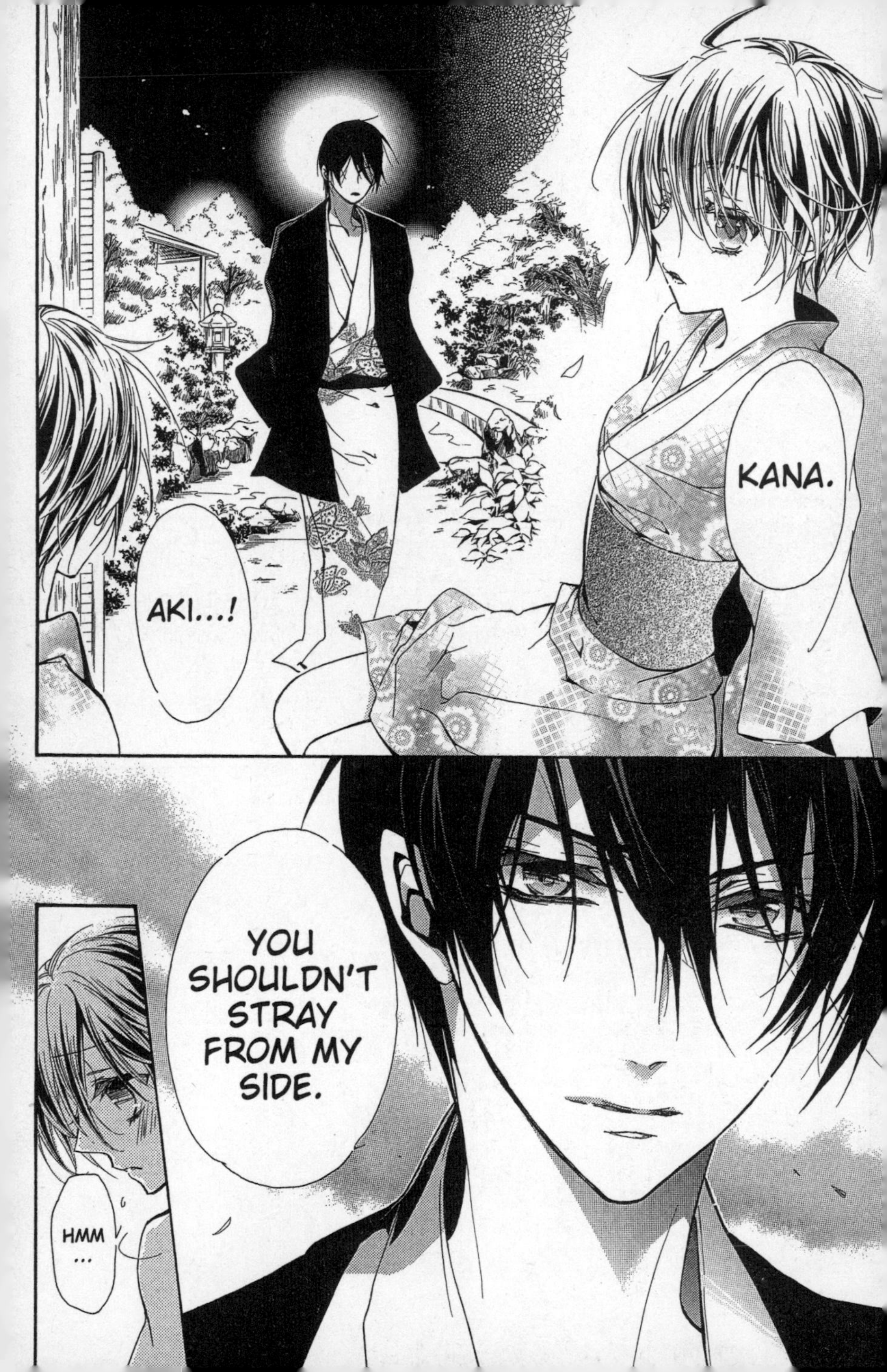
KANA.
AKI...!
YOU SHOULDN'T STRAY FROM MY SIDE.
HMM ...

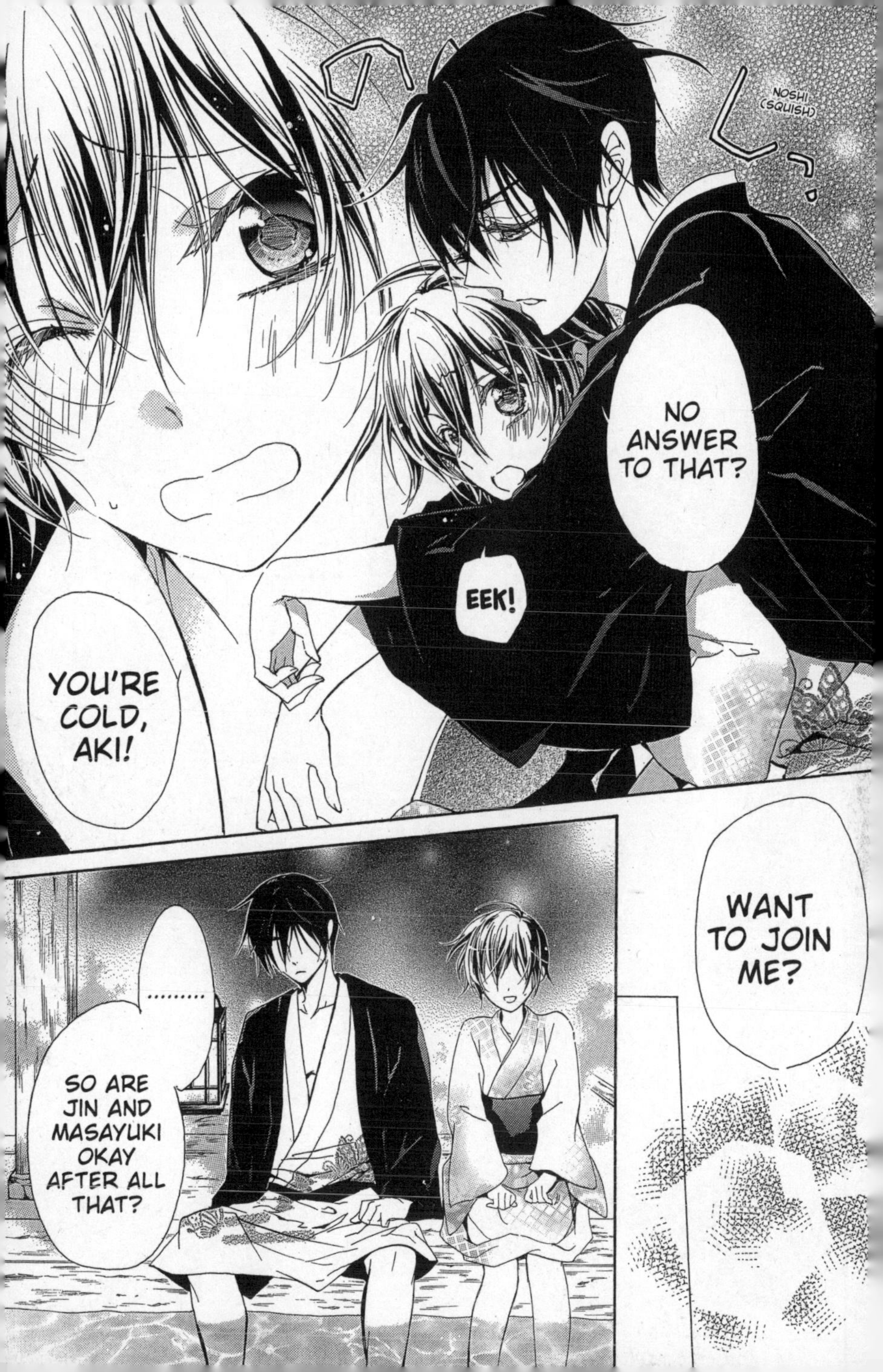
NOSHI (SQUISH)
NO ANSWER TO THAT?
EEK!
YOU'RE COLD, AKI!
WANT TO JOIN ME?
....
SO ARE JIN AND MASAYUKI OKAY AFTER ALL THAT?

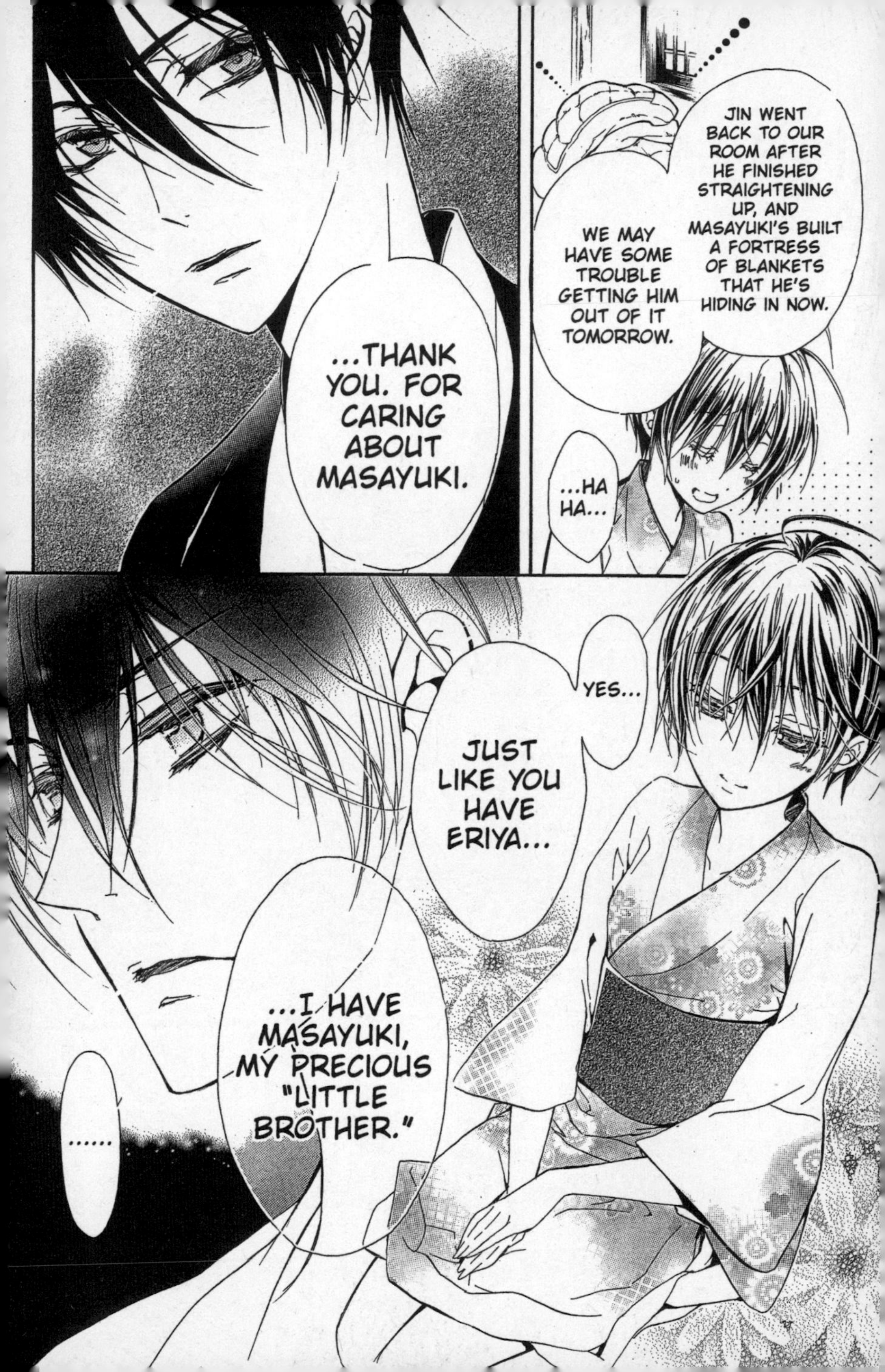
JIN WENT BACK TO OUR ROOM AFTER HE FINISHED STRAIGHTENING UP, AND MASAYUKI'S BUILT A FORTRESS OF BLANKETS THAT HE'S HIDING IN NOW.
WE MAY HAVE SOME TROUBLE GETTING HIM OUT OF IT TOMORROW.
...HA HA...
...THANK YOU. FOR CARING ABOUT MASAYUKI.
YES...
JUST LIKE YOU HAVE ERIYA...
...I HAVE MASAYUKI, MY PRECIOUS "LITTLE BROTHER."
......

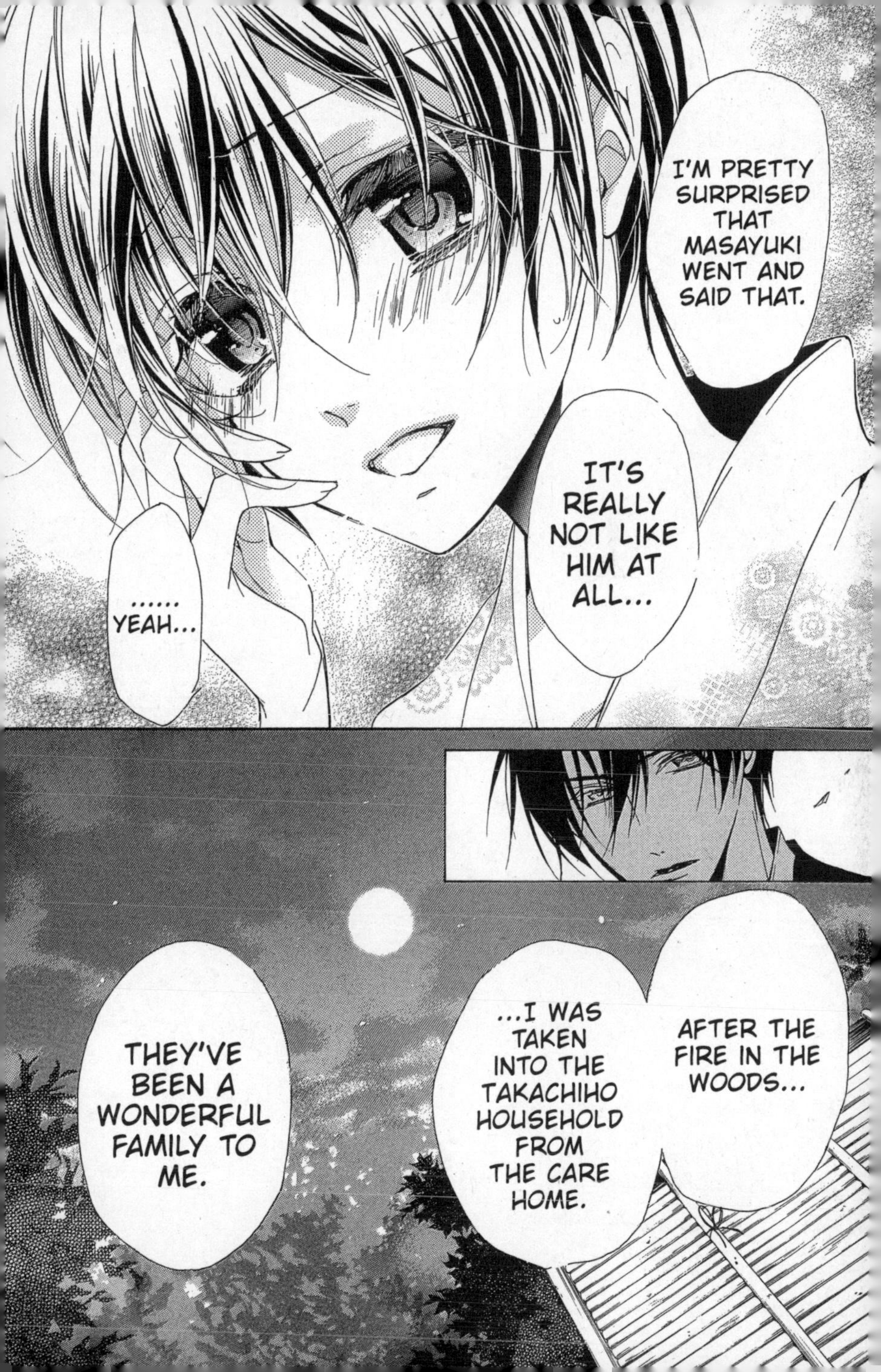
I'M PRETTY SURPRISED THAT MASAYUKI WENT AND SAID THAT.
IT'S REALLY NOT LIKE HIM AT ALL...
...... YEAH...
AFTER THE FIRE IN THE WOODS...
...I WAS TAKEN INTO THE TAKACHIHO HOUSEHOLD FROM THE CARE HOME.
THEY'VE BEEN A WONDERFUL FAMILY TO ME.

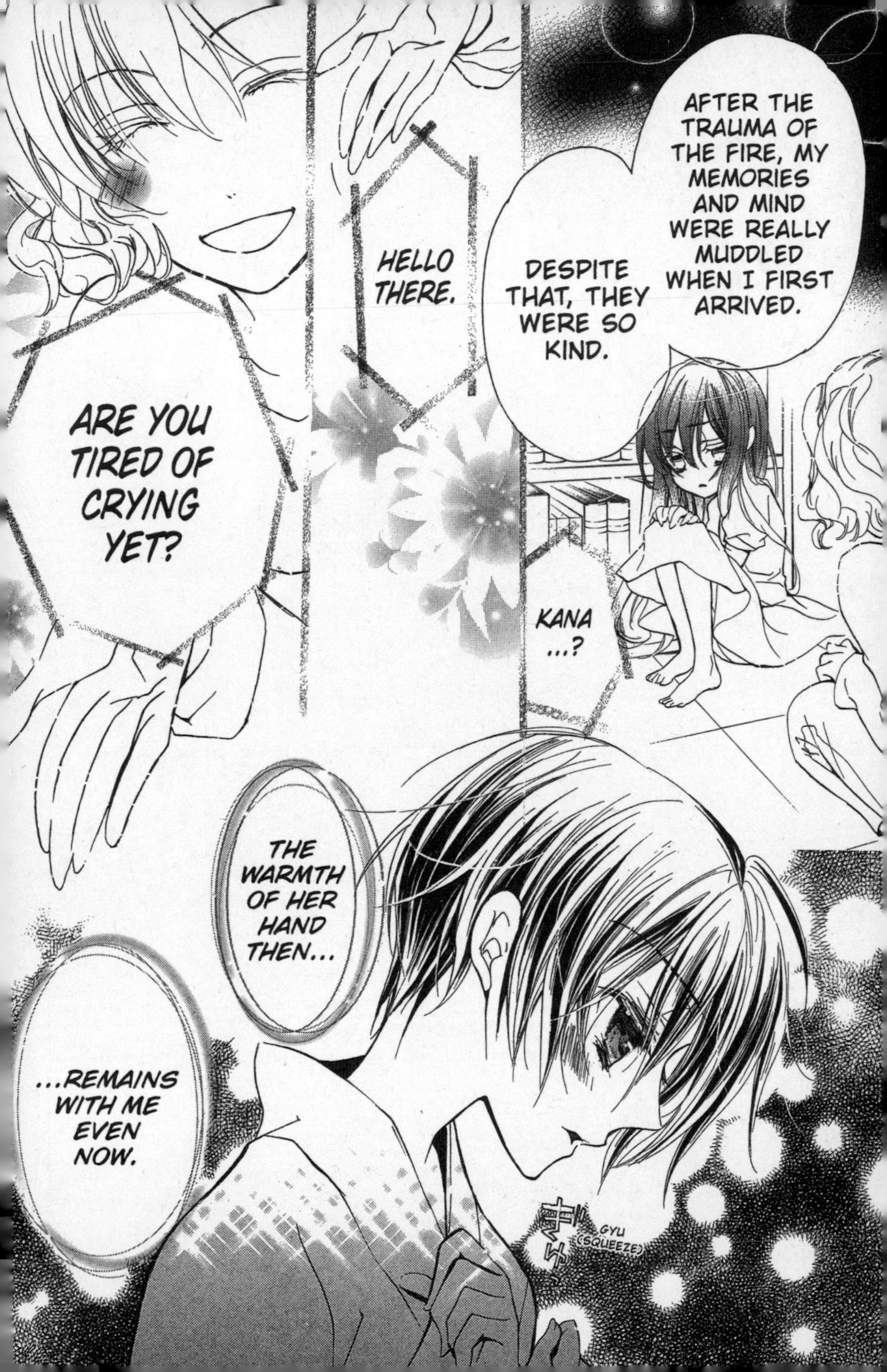

AFTER THE TRAUMA OF THE FIRE, MY MEMORIES AND MIND WERE REALLY MUDDLED WHEN I FIRST ARRIVED.
DESPITE THAT, THEY WERE SO KIND.
KANA ...?
HELLO THERE.
ARE YOU TIRED OF CRYING YET?
THE WARMTH OF HER HAND THEN...
...REMAINS WITH ME EVEN NOW.
GYU (SQUEEZE)

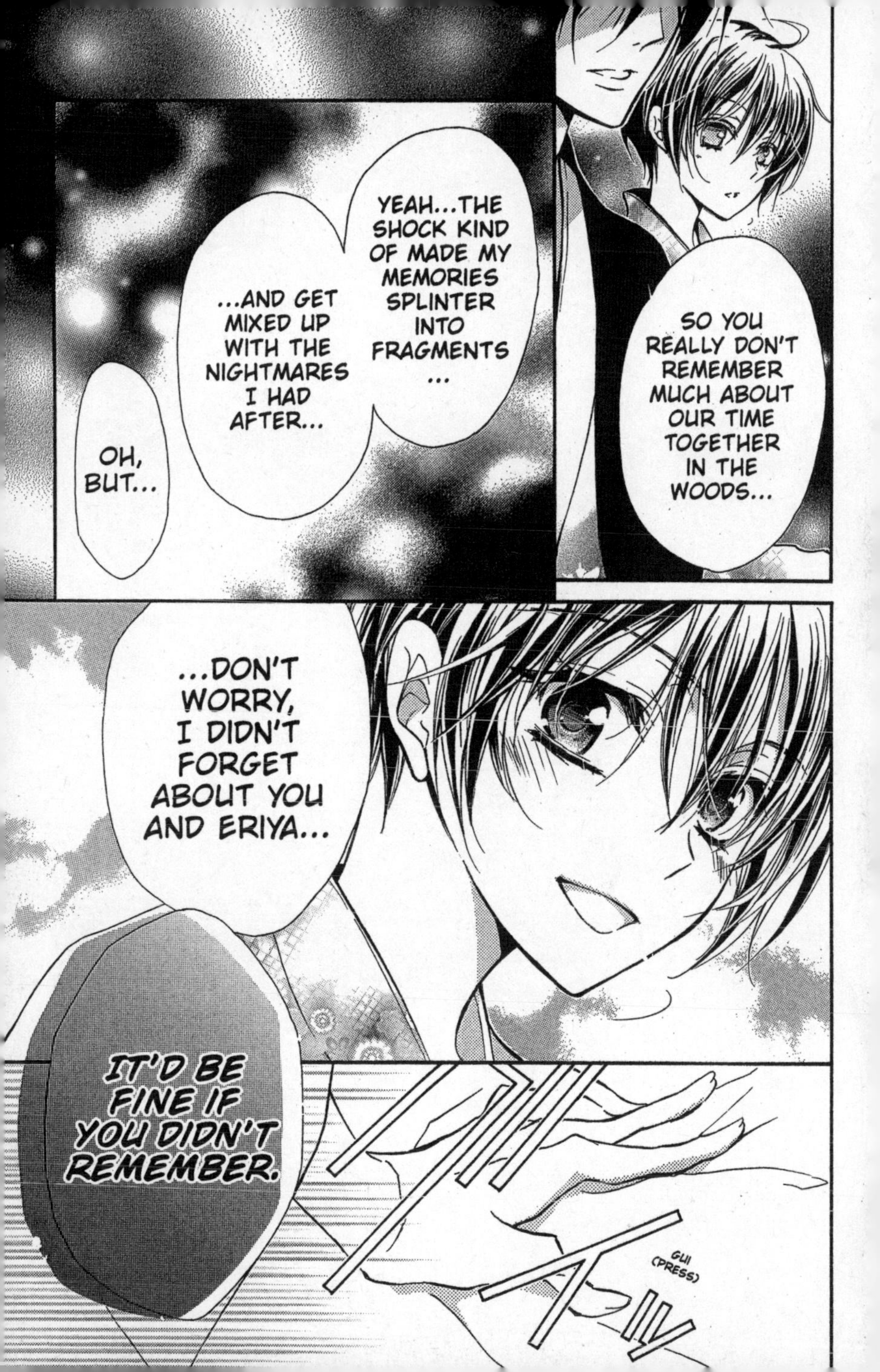
SO YOU REALLY DON'T REMEMBER MUCH ABOUT OUR TIME TOGETHER IN THE WOODS...
YEAH...THE SHOCK KIND OF MADE MY MEMORIES SPLINTER INTO FRAGMENTS...
...AND GET MIXED UP WITH THE NIGHTMARES I HAD AFTER...
OH, BUT...
...DON'T WORRY, I DIDN'T FORGET ABOUT YOU AND ERIYA...
IT'D BE FINE IF YOU DIDN'T REMEMBER.
GUI (PRESS)

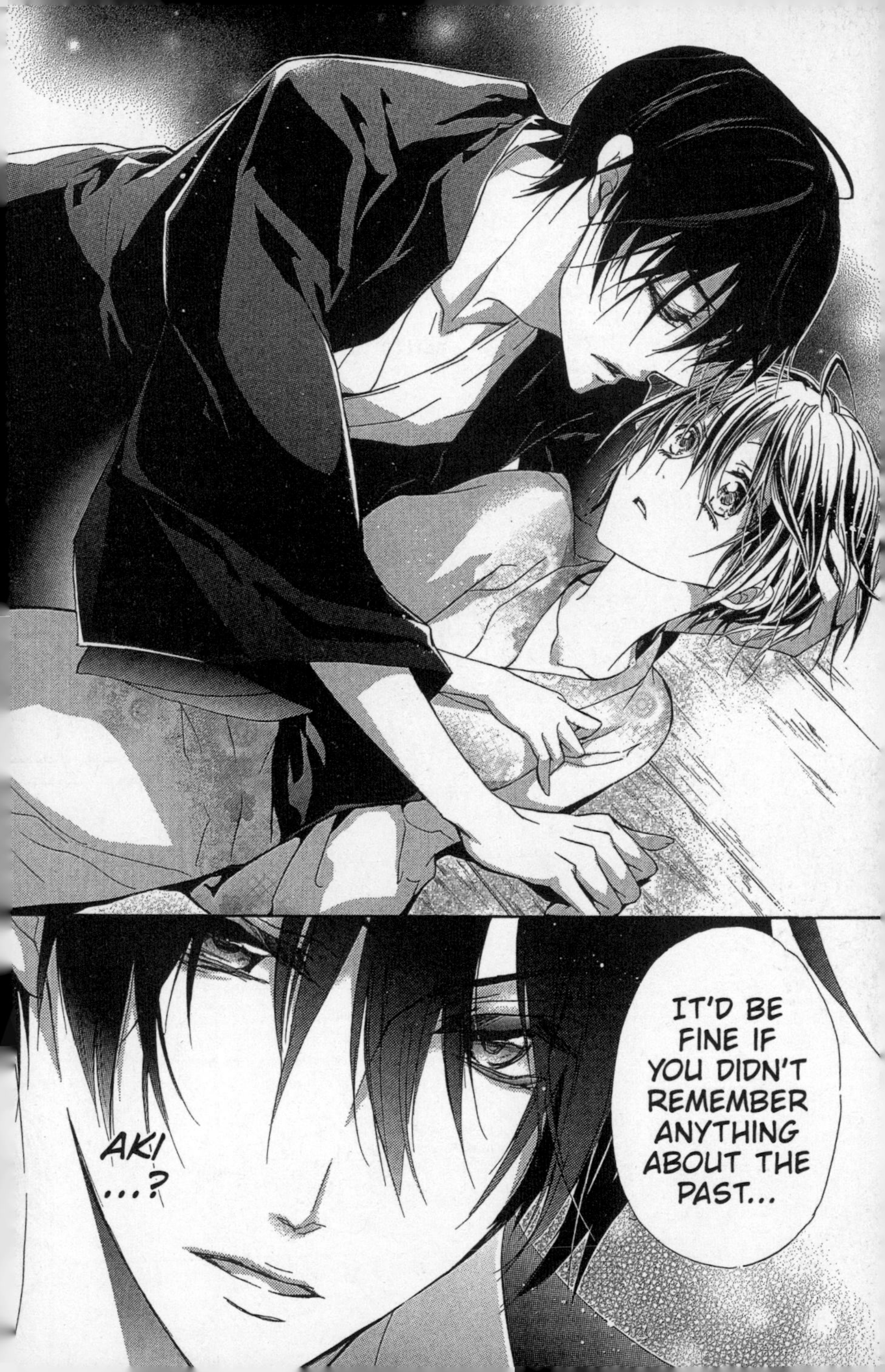
IT'D BE FINE IF YOU DIDN'T REMEMBER ANYTHING ABOUT THE PAST...
AKI ...?

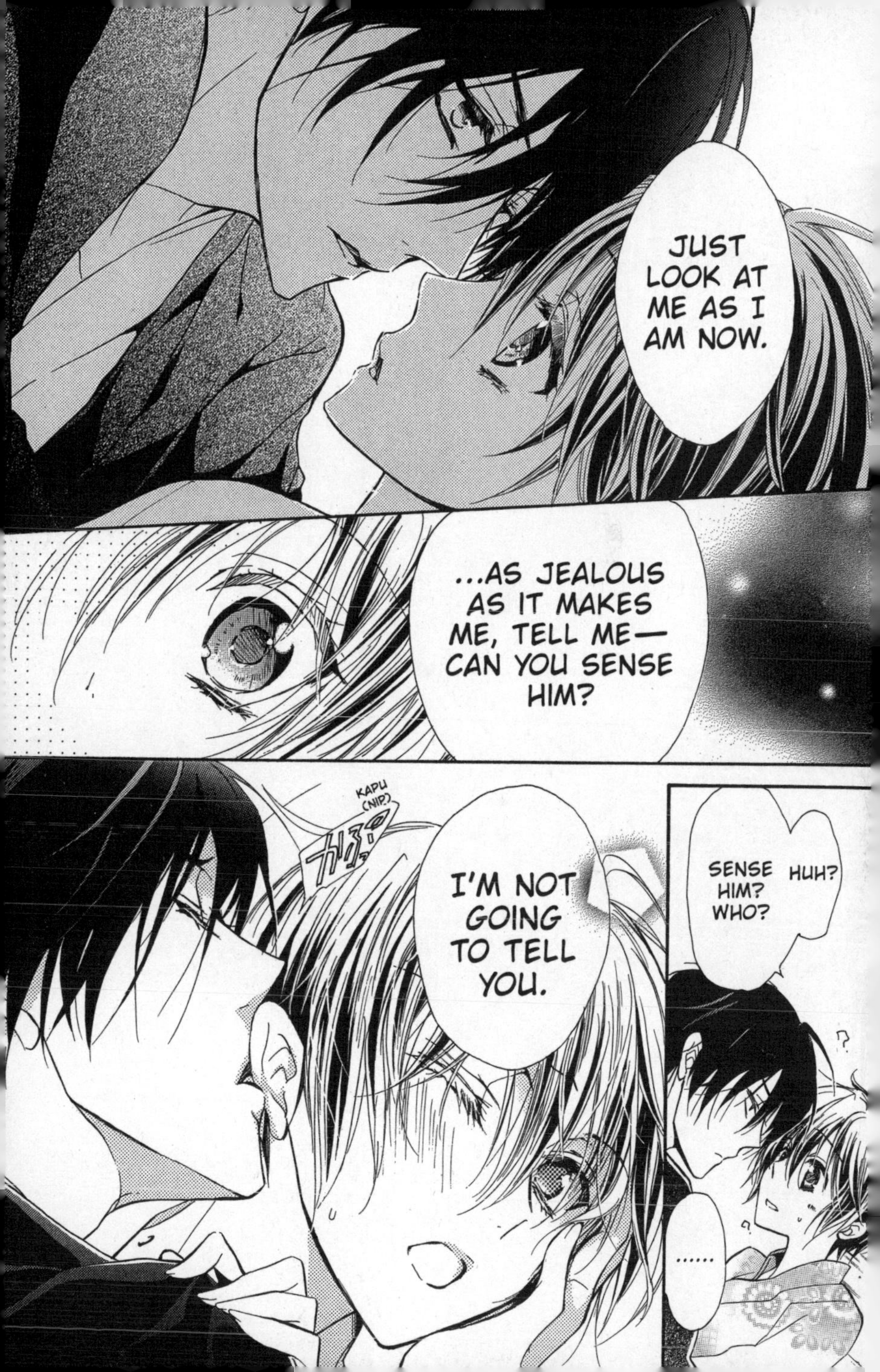
JUST LOOK AT ME AS I AM NOW.
...AS JEALOUS AS IT MAKES ME, TELL ME— CAN YOU SENSE HIM?
HUH?
SENSE HIM? WHO?
......
I'M NOT GOING TO TELL YOU.
KAPU (NIP)

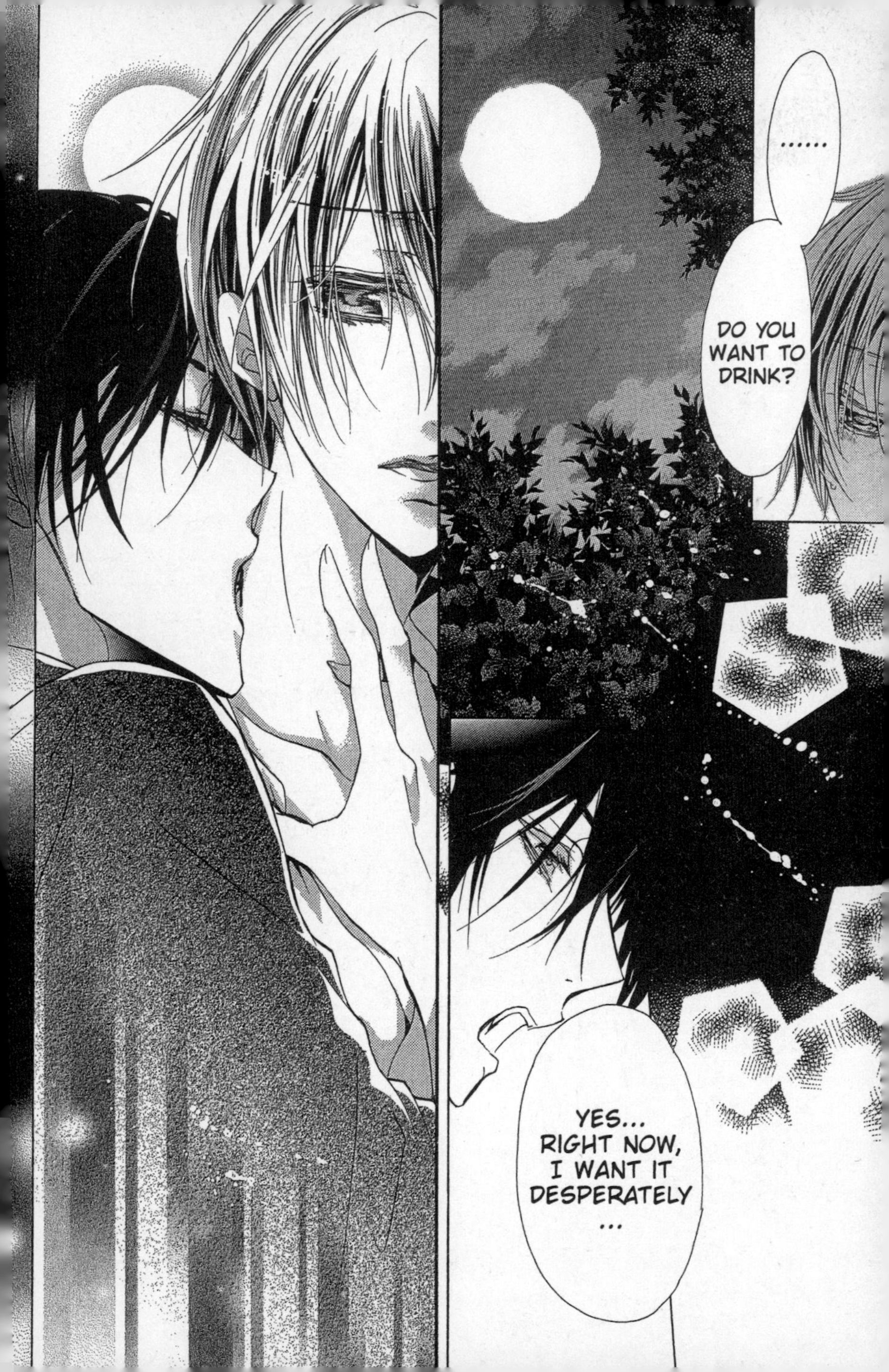
......
DO YOU WANT TO DRINK?
YES... RIGHT NOW, I WANT IT DESPERATELY ...

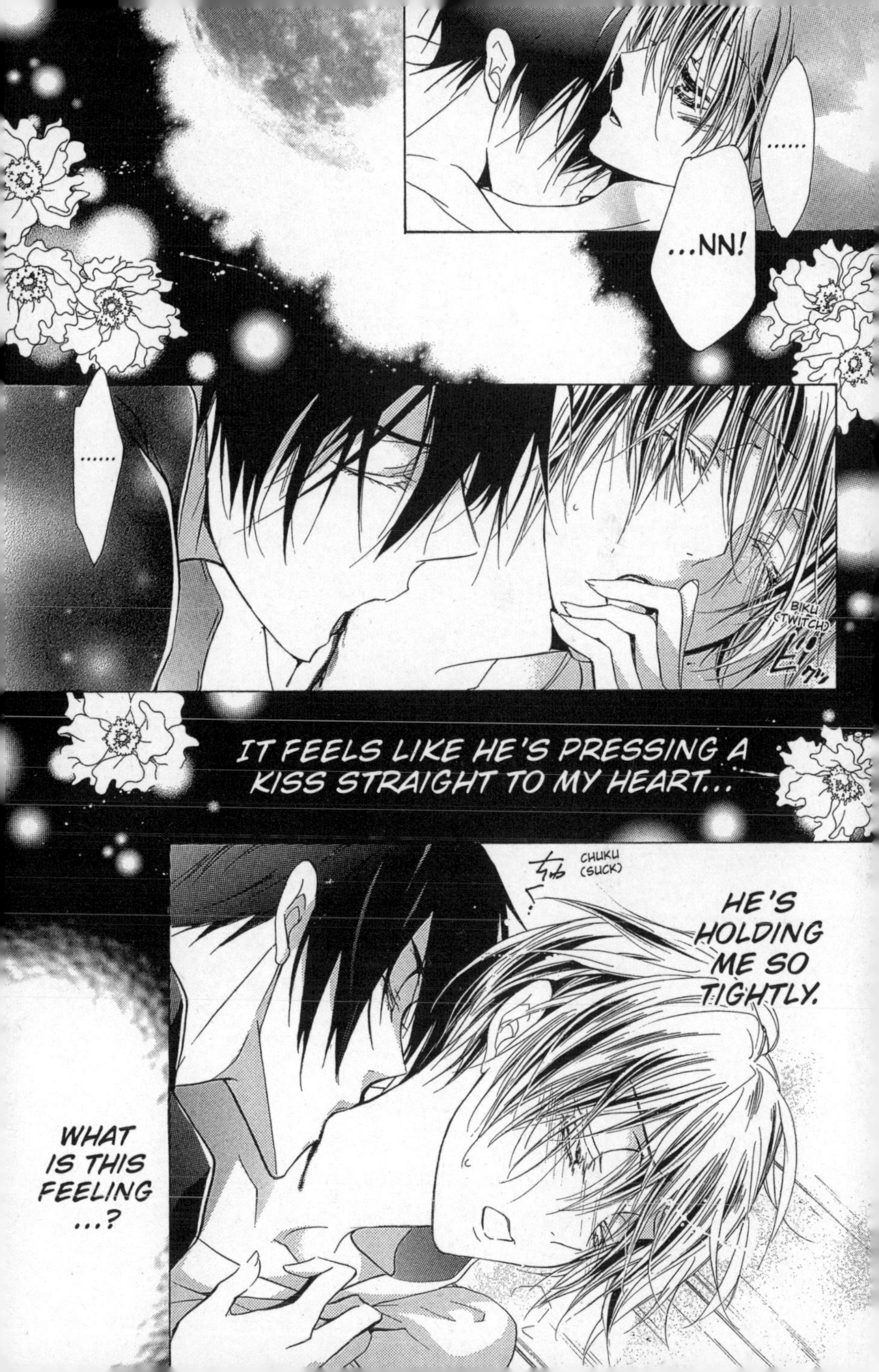
......
...NN!
BIKU (TWITCH)
......
IT FEELS LIKE HE'S PRESSING A KISS STRAIGHT TO MY HEART...
CHUKU (SUCK)
HE'S HOLDING ME SO TIGHTLY.
WHAT IS THIS FEELING ...?

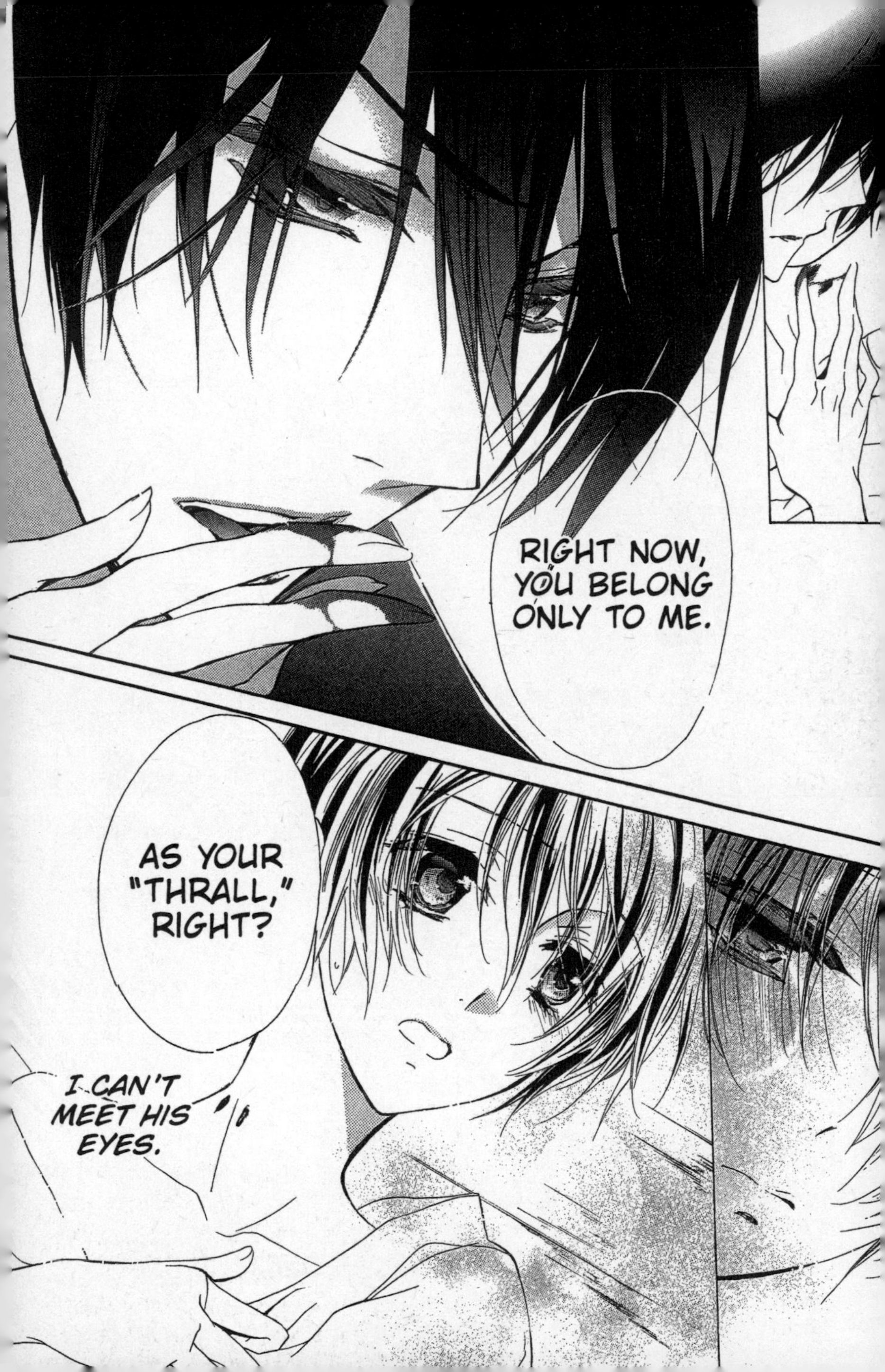
RIGHT NOW, YOU BELONG ONLY TO ME.
AS YOUR "THRALL," RIGHT?
I CAN'T MEET HIS EYES.

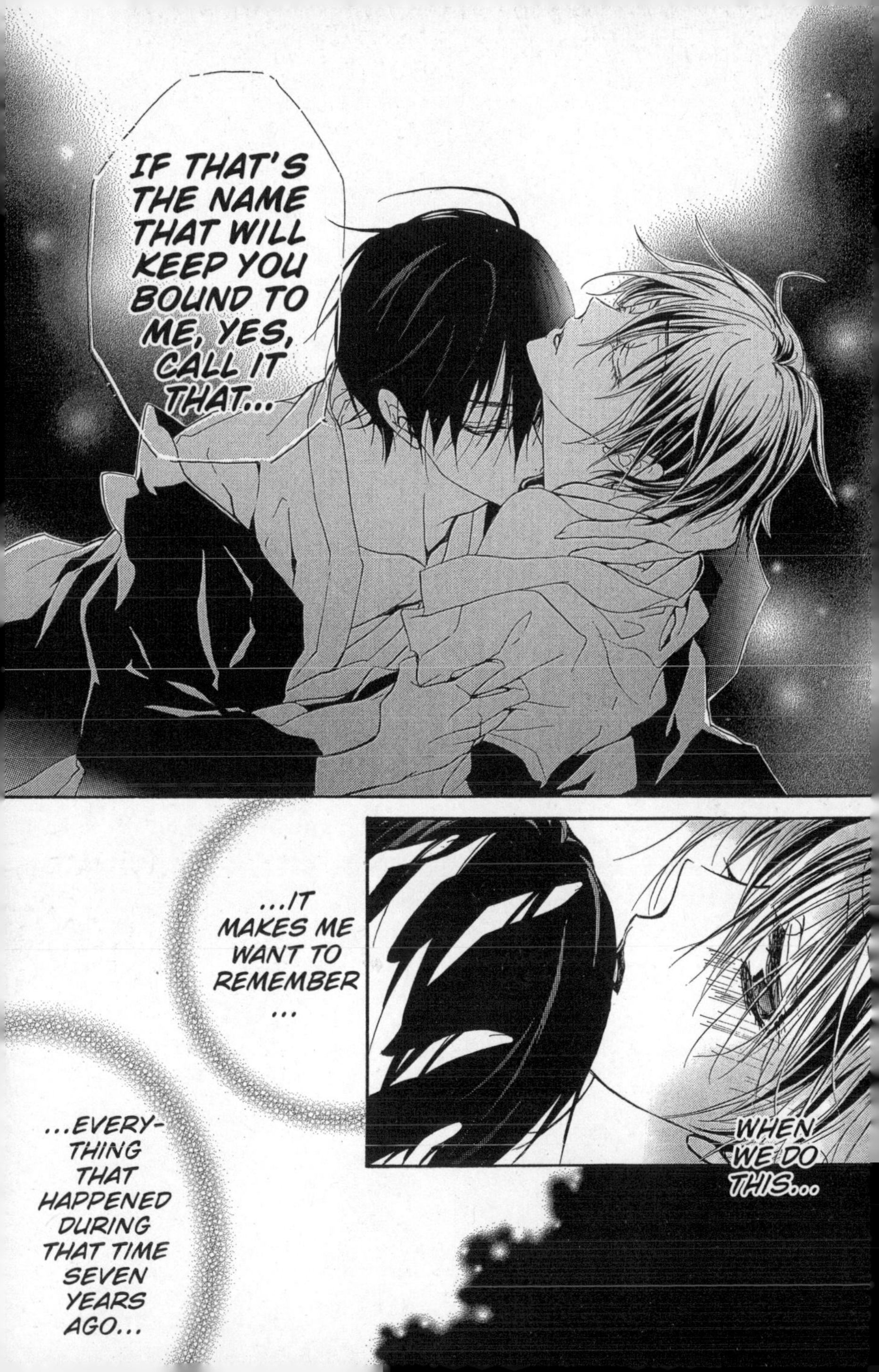
IF THAT'S THE NAME THAT WILL KEEP YOU BOUND TO ME, YES, CALL IT THAT...
WHEN WE DO THIS...
...IT MAKES ME WANT TO REMEMBER...
...EVERYTHING THAT HAPPENED DURING THAT TIME SEVEN YEARS AGO...

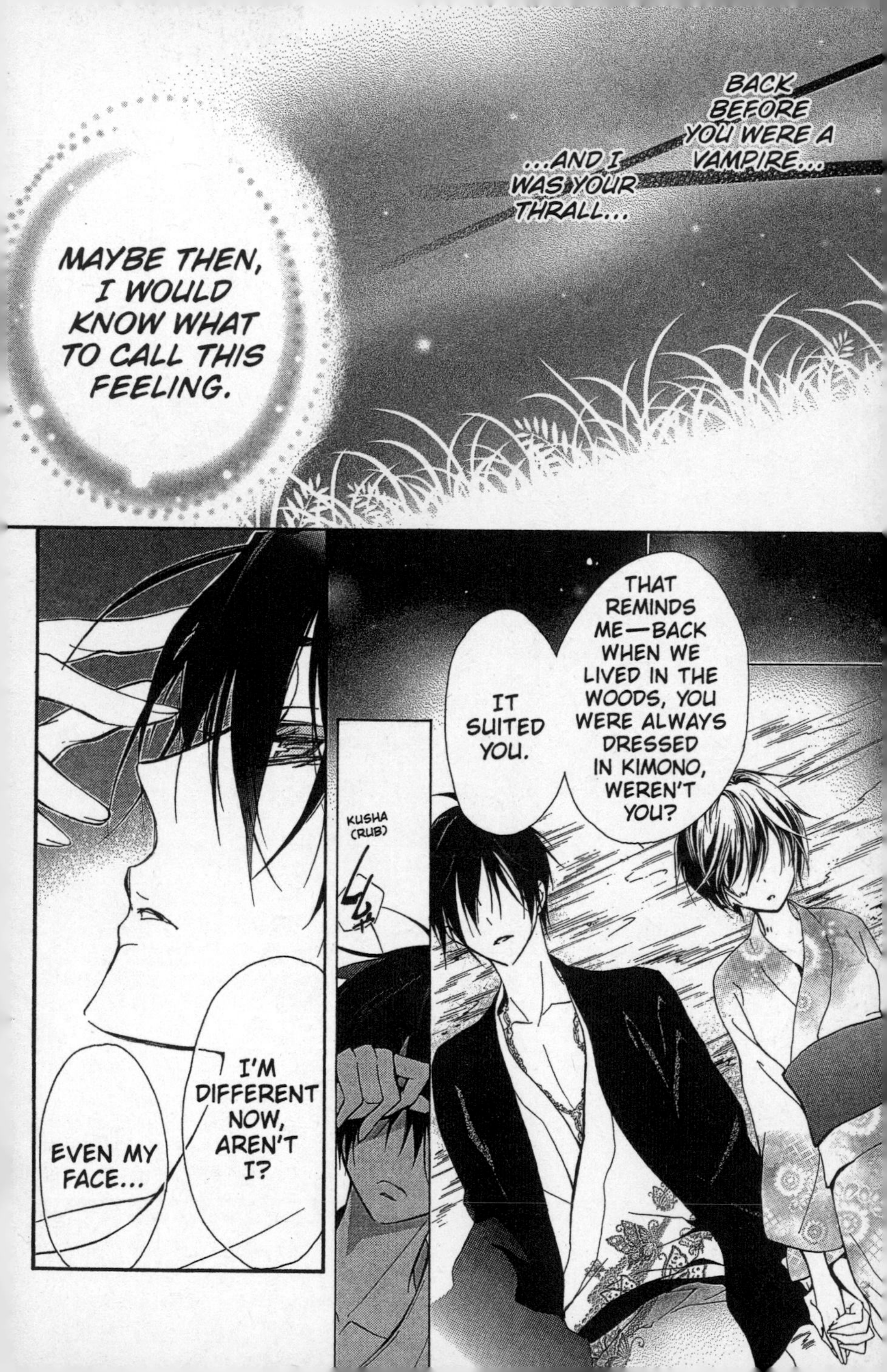
BACK BEFORE YOU WERE A VAMPIRE...
...AND I WAS YOUR THRALL...
MAYBE THEN, I WOULD KNOW WHAT TO CALL THIS FEELING.
THAT REMINDS ME—BACK WHEN WE LIVED IN THE WOODS, YOU WERE ALWAYS DRESSED IN KIMONO, WEREN'T YOU?
IT SUITED YOU.
KUSHA (RUB)
I'M DIFFERENT NOW, AREN'T I?
EVEN MY FACE...

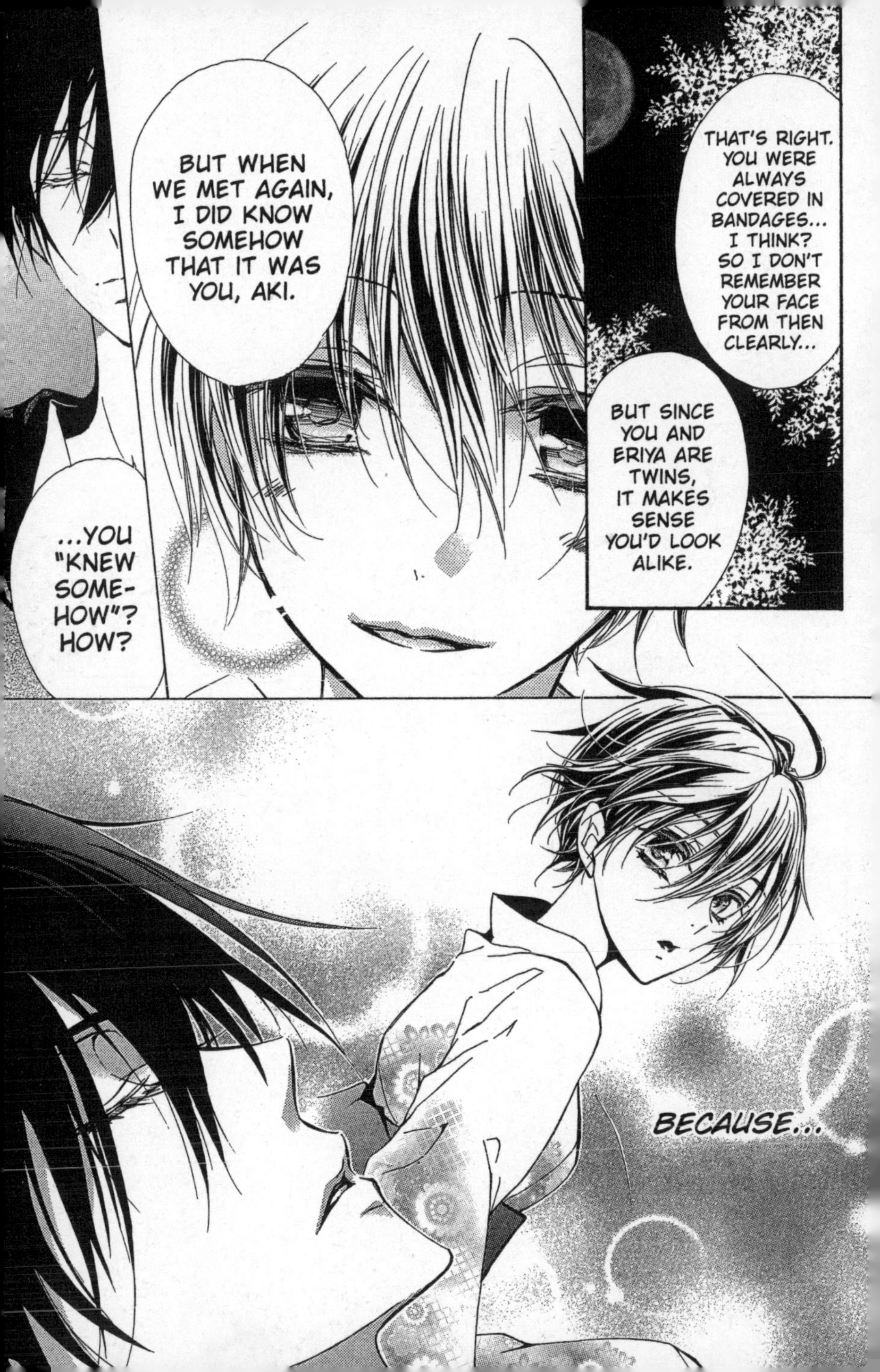

THAT'S RIGHT. YOU WERE ALWAYS COVERED IN BANDAGES... I THINK? SO I DON'T REMEMBER YOUR FACE FROM THEN CLEARLY...
BUT SINCE YOU AND ERIYA ARE TWINS, IT MAKES SENSE YOU'D LOOK ALIKE.
BUT WHEN WE MET AGAIN, I DID KNOW SOMEHOW THAT IT WAS YOU, AKI.
...YOU "KNEW SOME-HOW"? HOW?
BECAUSE...

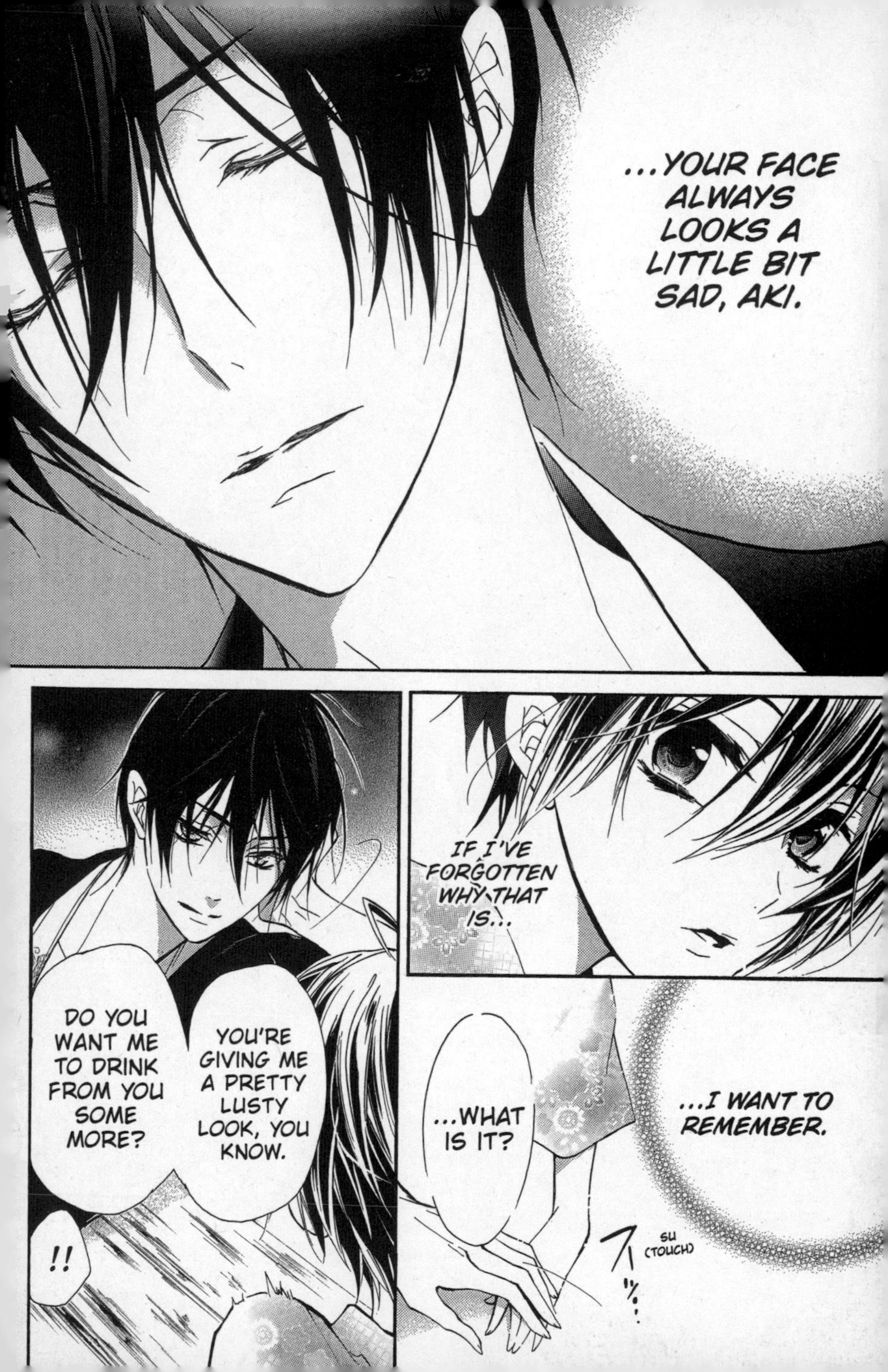
...YOUR FACE ALWAYS LOOKS A LITTLE BIT SAD, AKI.
IF I'VE FORGOTTEN WHY THAT IS...
...I WANT TO REMEMBER.
...WHAT IS IT?
SU (TOUCH)
YOU'RE GIVING ME A PRETTY LUSTY LOOK, YOU KNOW.
DO YOU WANT ME TO DRINK FROM YOU SOME MORE?
!!

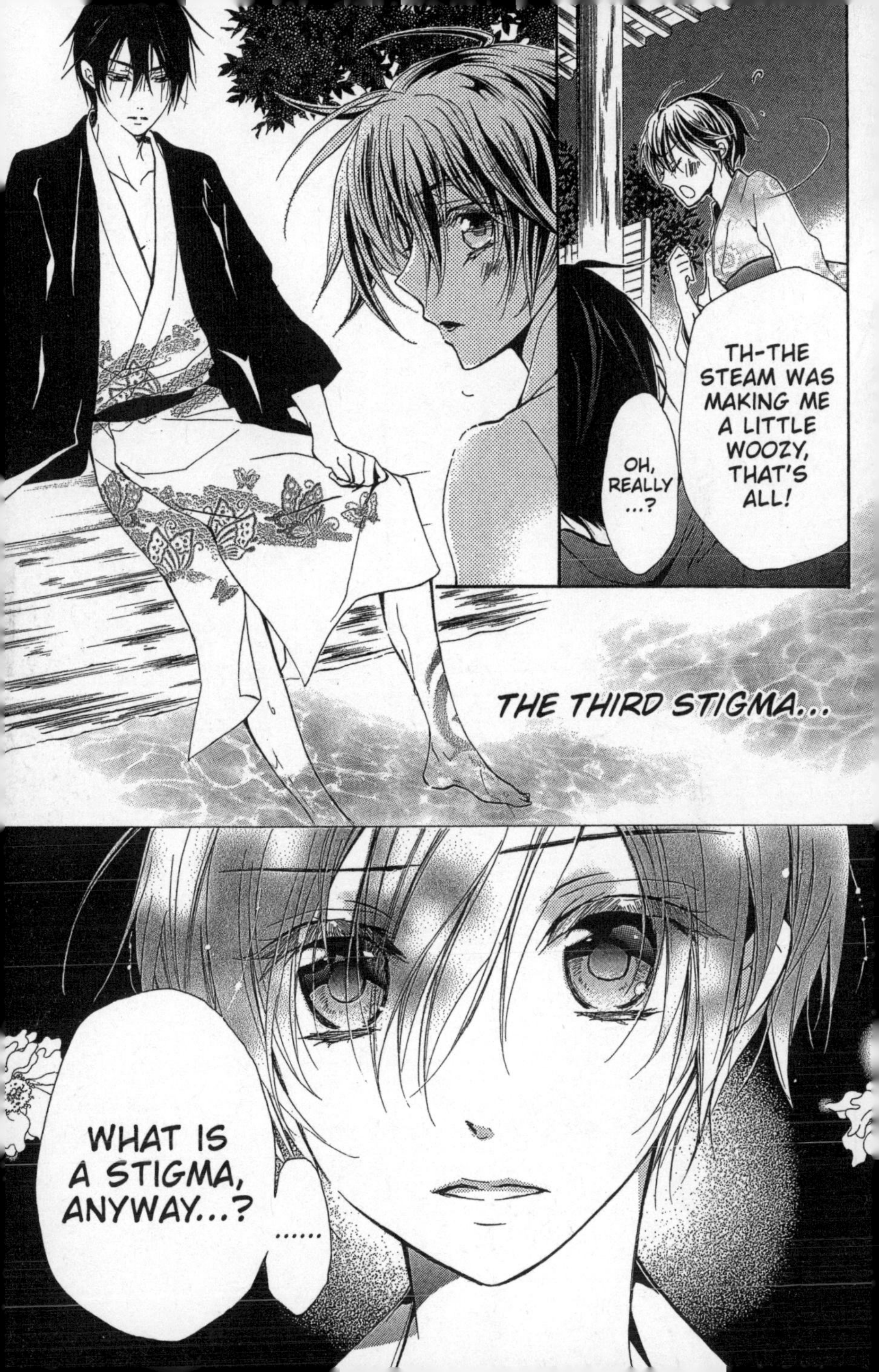
TH-THE STEAM WAS MAKING ME A LITTLE WOOZY, THAT'S ALL!
OH, REALLY ...?
THE THIRD STIGMA...
WHAT IS A STIGMA, ANYWAY...?
......

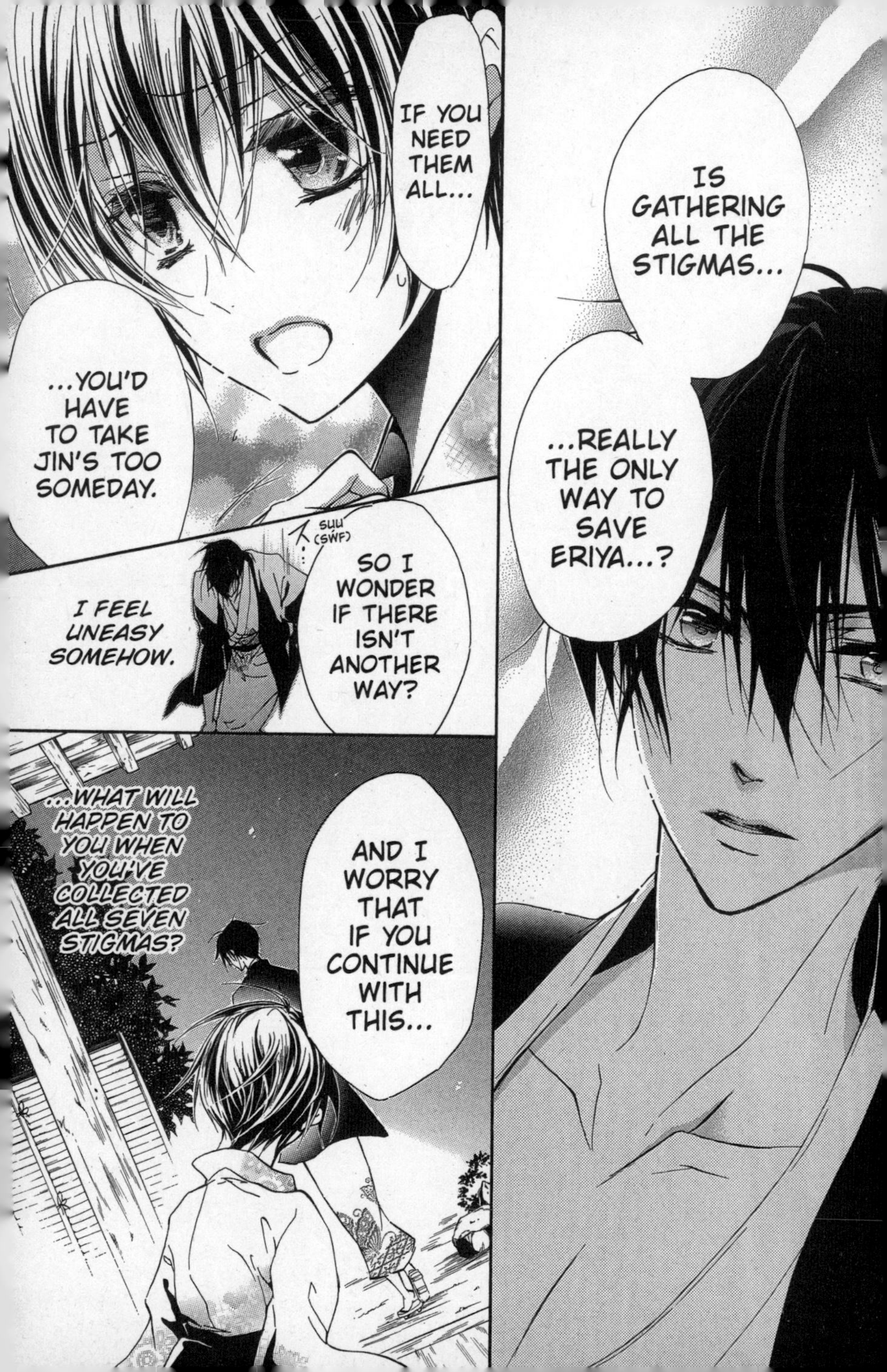

IS GATHERING ALL THE STIGMAS...
...REALLY THE ONLY WAY TO SAVE ERIYA...?
IF YOU NEED THEM ALL...
...YOU'D HAVE TO TAKE JIN'S TOO SOMEDAY.
SUU (SWF)
SO I WONDER IF THERE ISN'T ANOTHER WAY?
I FEEL UNEASY SOMEHOW.
AND I WORRY THAT IF YOU CONTINUE WITH THIS...
...WHAT WILL HAPPEN TO YOU WHEN YOU'VE COLLECTED ALL SEVEN STIGMAS?

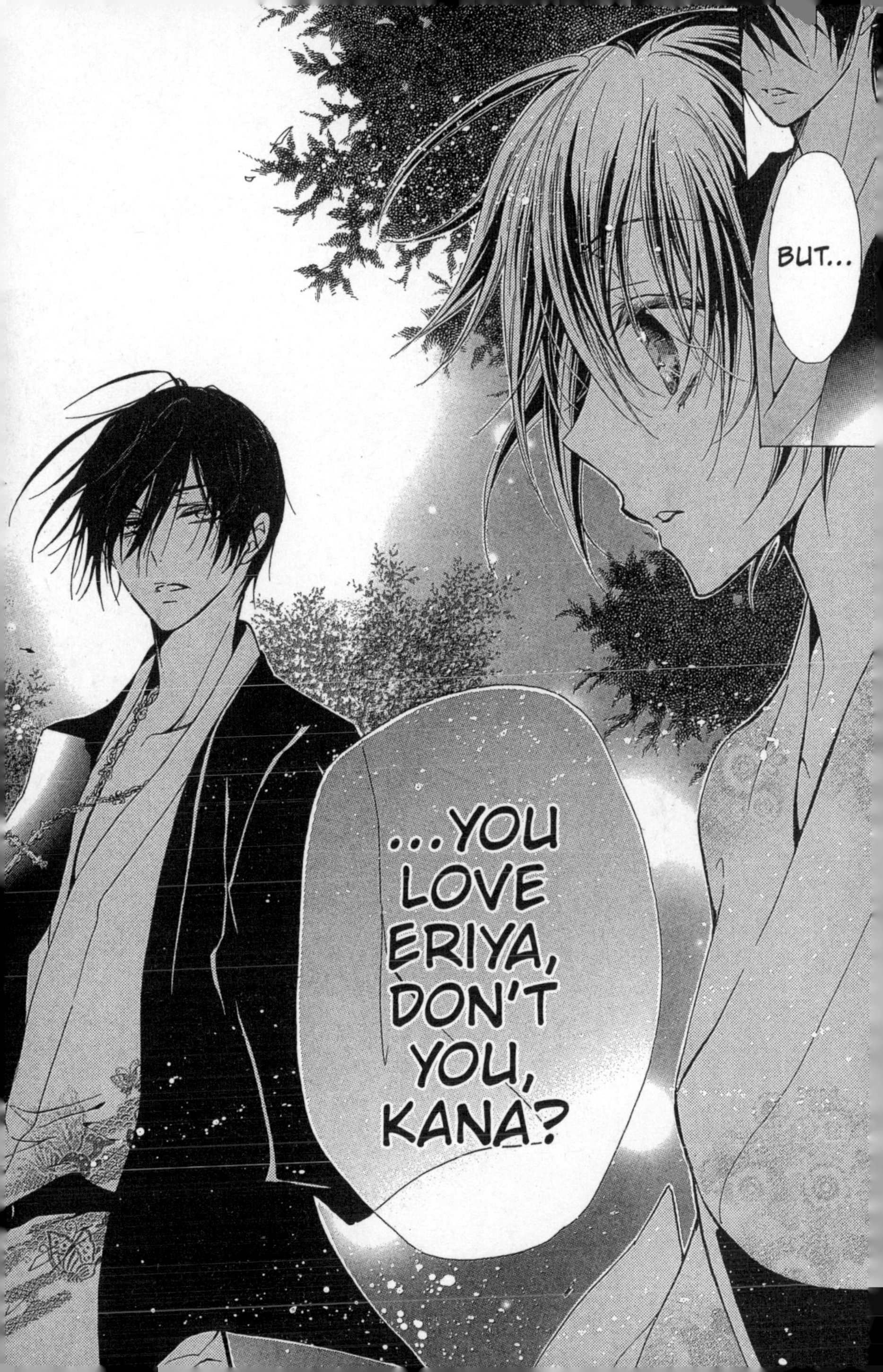
BUT...
...YOU LOVE ERIYA, DON'T YOU, KANA?

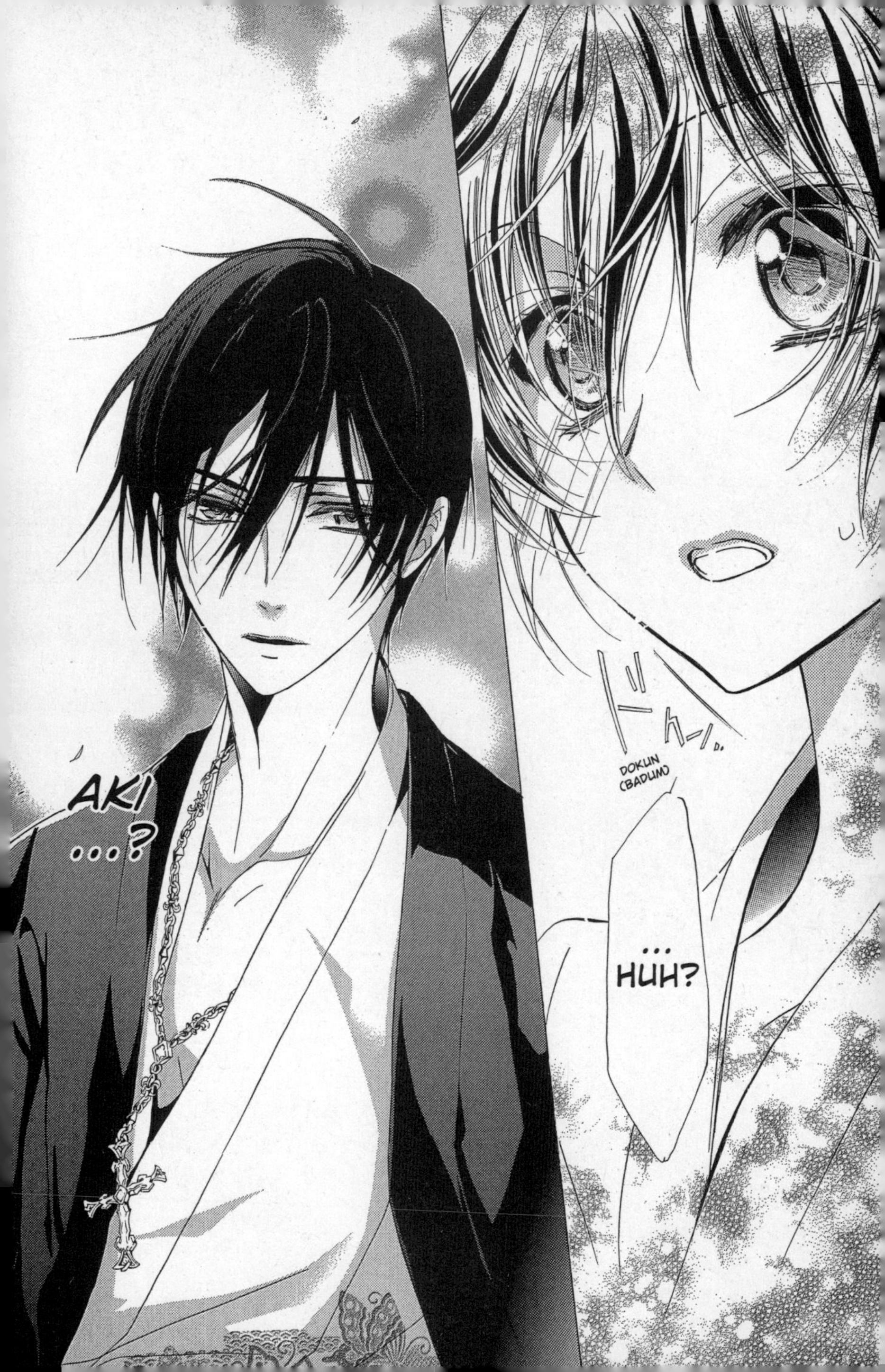
ドクン。
DOKUN (BADUM)
...HUH?
AKI ...?

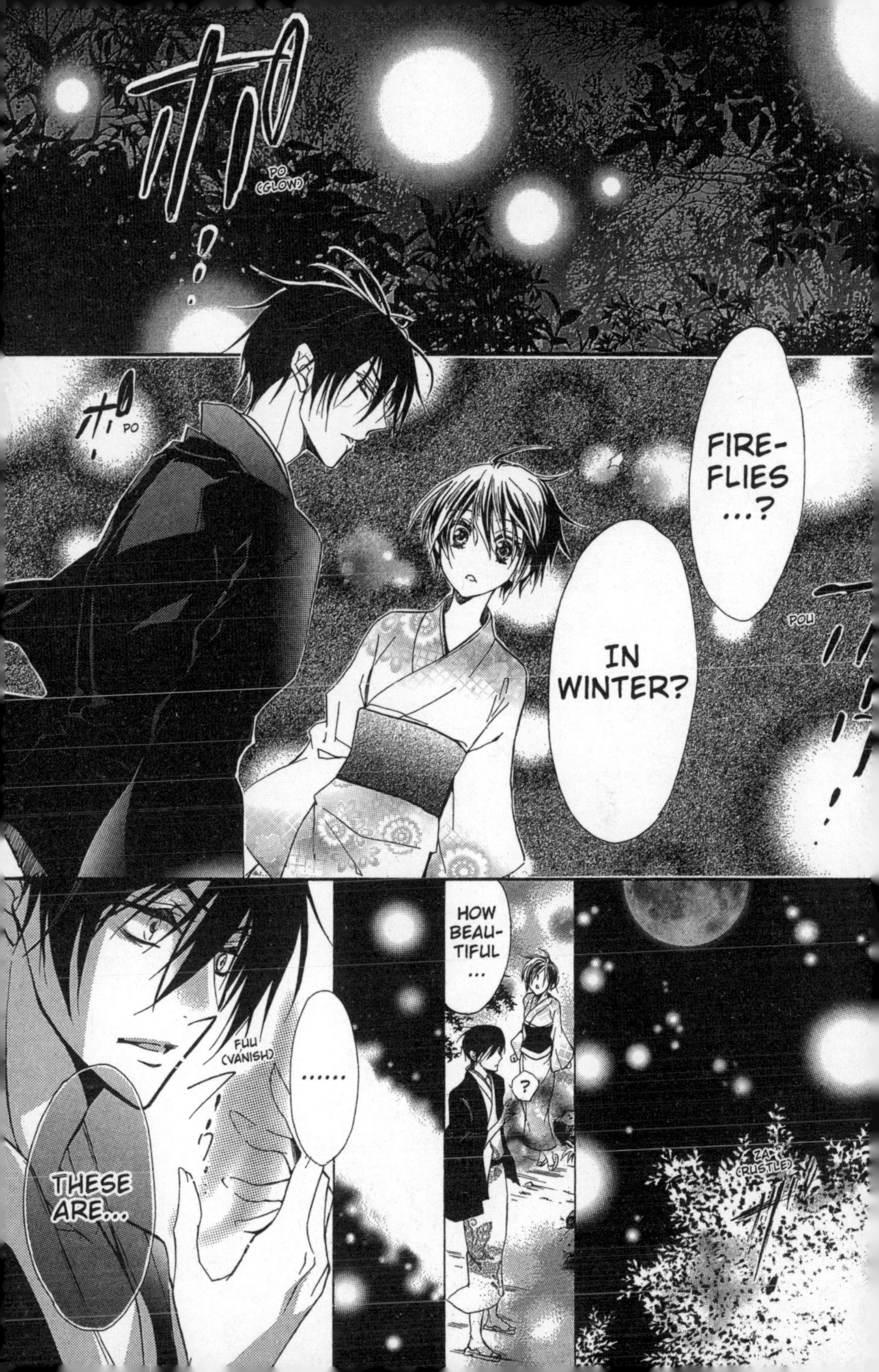
PO (GLOW)
FIRE-FLIES...?
POU
IN WINTER?
PO
ZA (RUSTLE)
HOW BEAU-TIFUL...
?
......
FUU (VANISH)
THESE ARE...

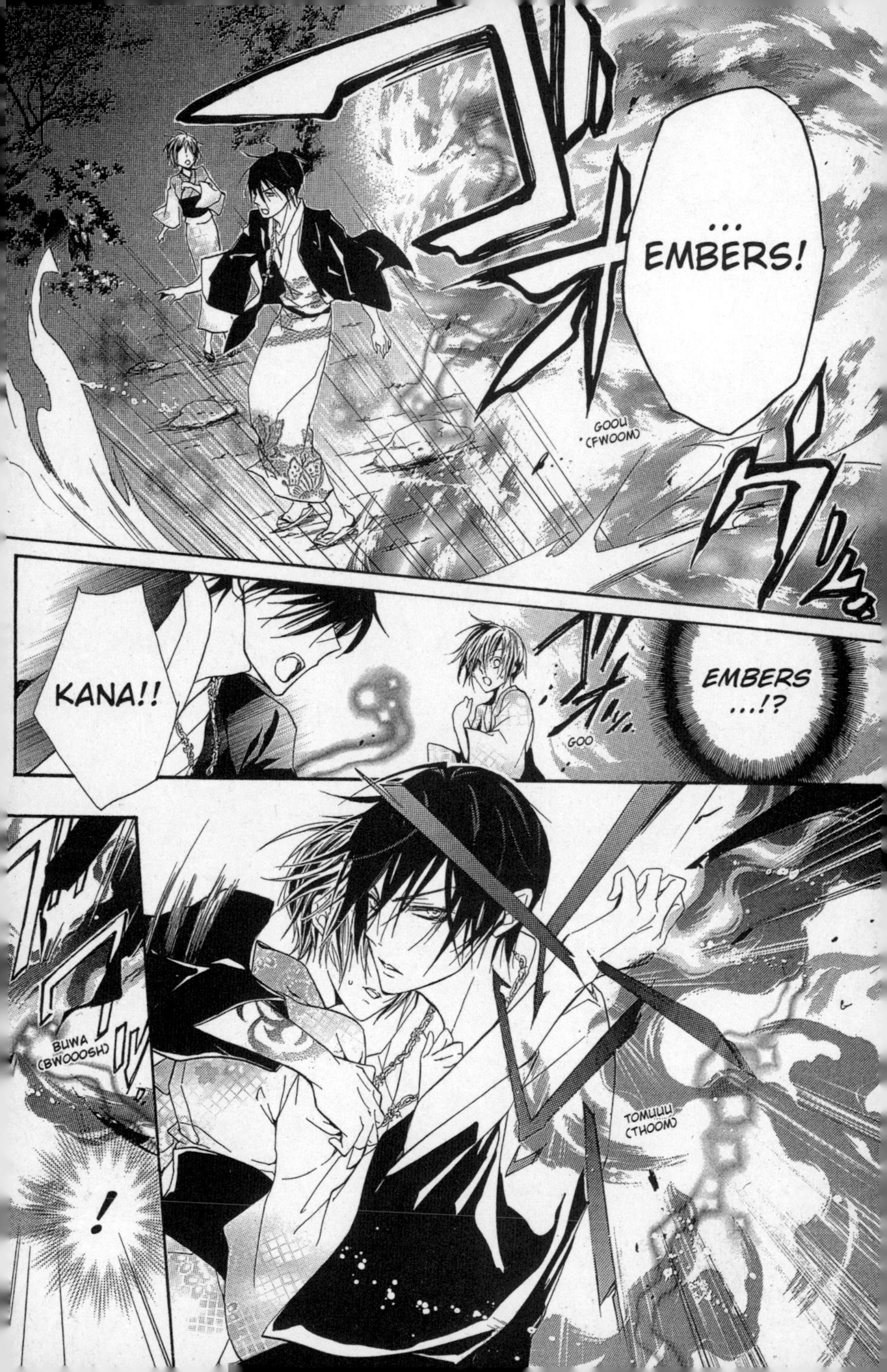
...
EMBERS!
GOOU
(FWOOM)
EMBERS
...!?
GOO
KANA!!
TOMUUU
(THOOM)
BUWA
(BWOOOSH)
!

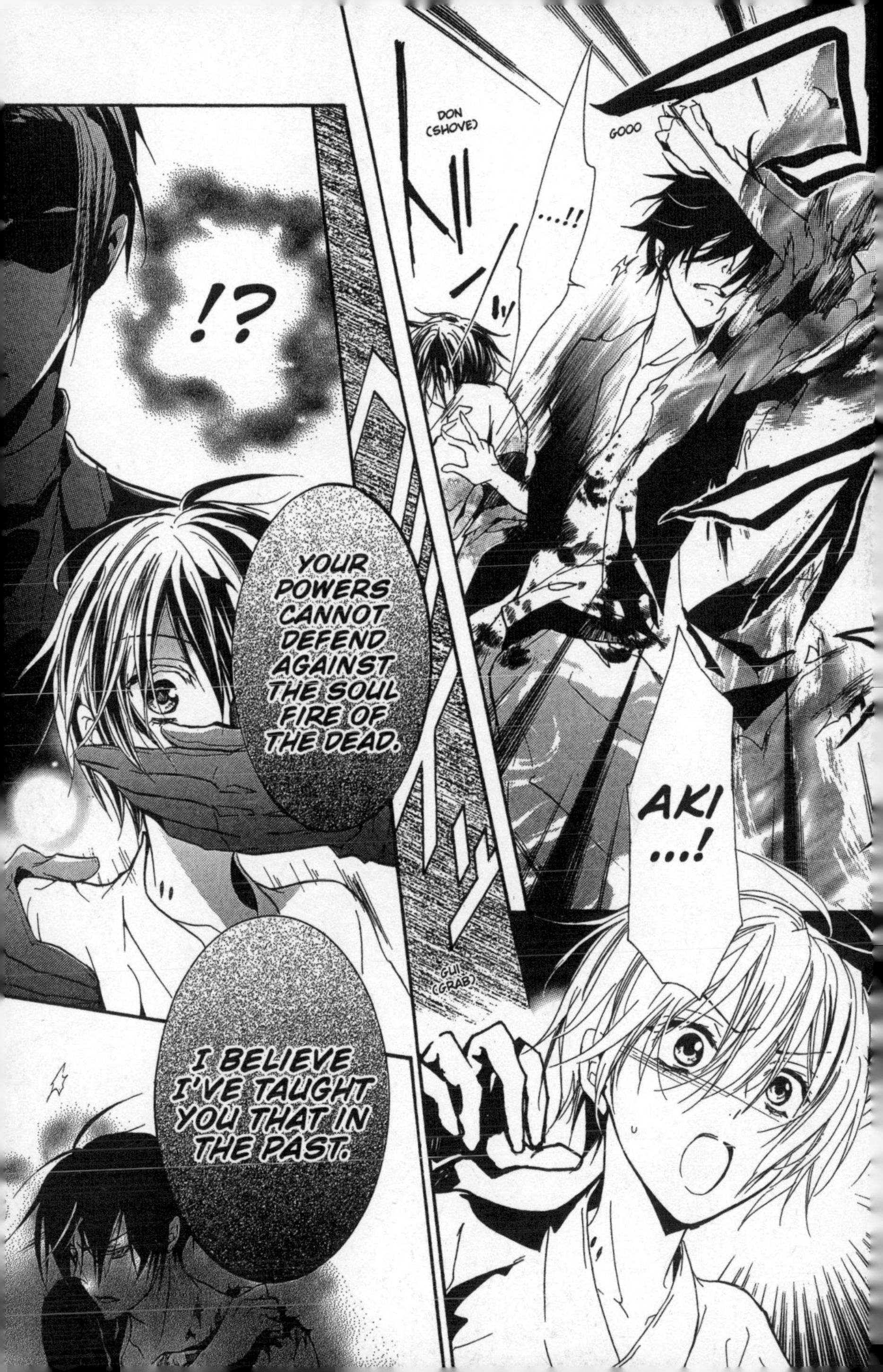
GOOO
DON (SHOVE)
...!!
!?
GUI (GRAB)
AKI ...!
YOUR POWERS CANNOT DEFEND AGAINST THE SOUL FIRE OF THE DEAD.
I BELIEVE I'VE TAUGHT YOU THAT IN THE PAST.

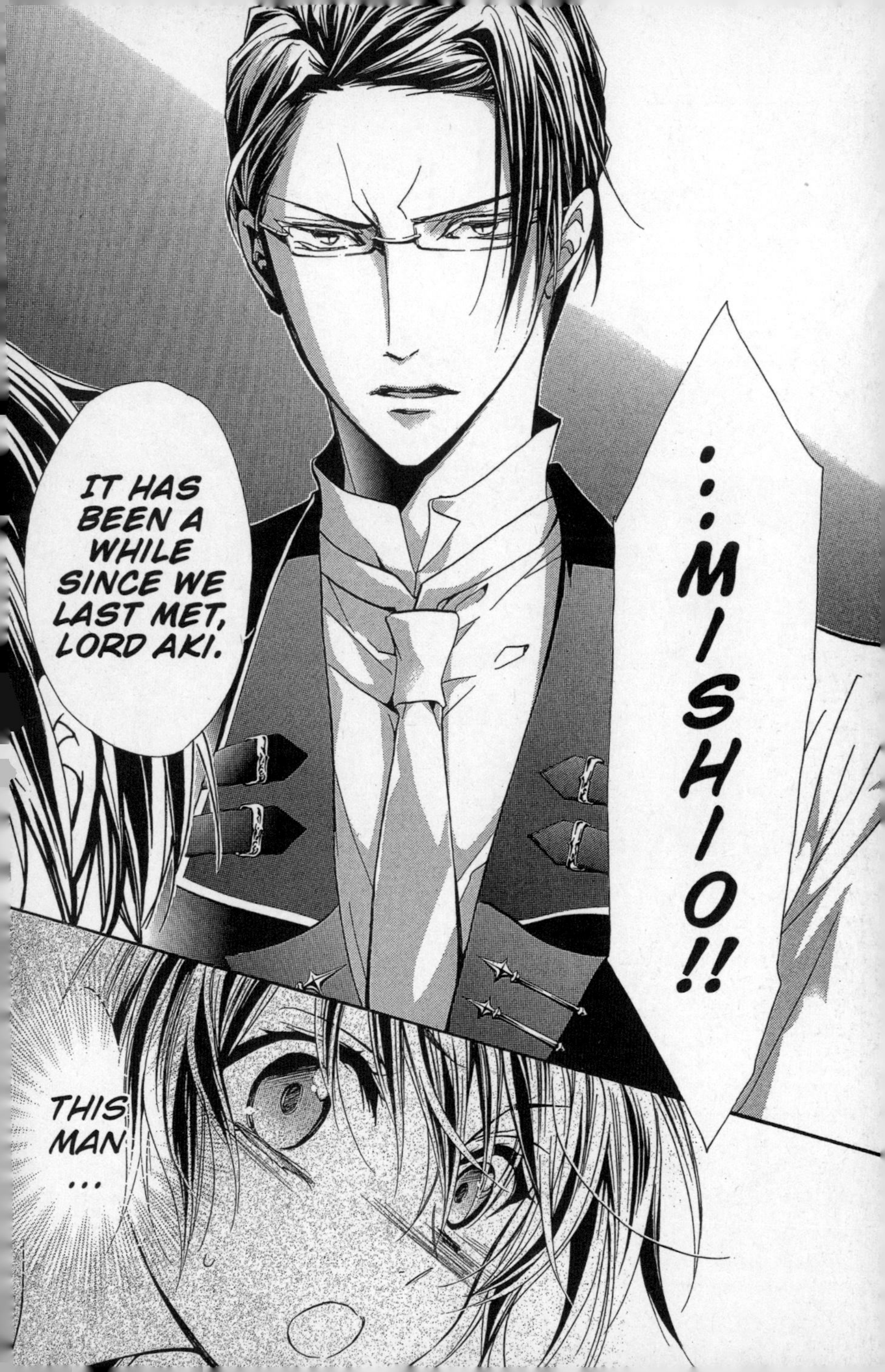
IT HAS BEEN A WHILE SINCE WE LAST MET, LORD AKI.
...MISHIO!!
THIS MAN
...

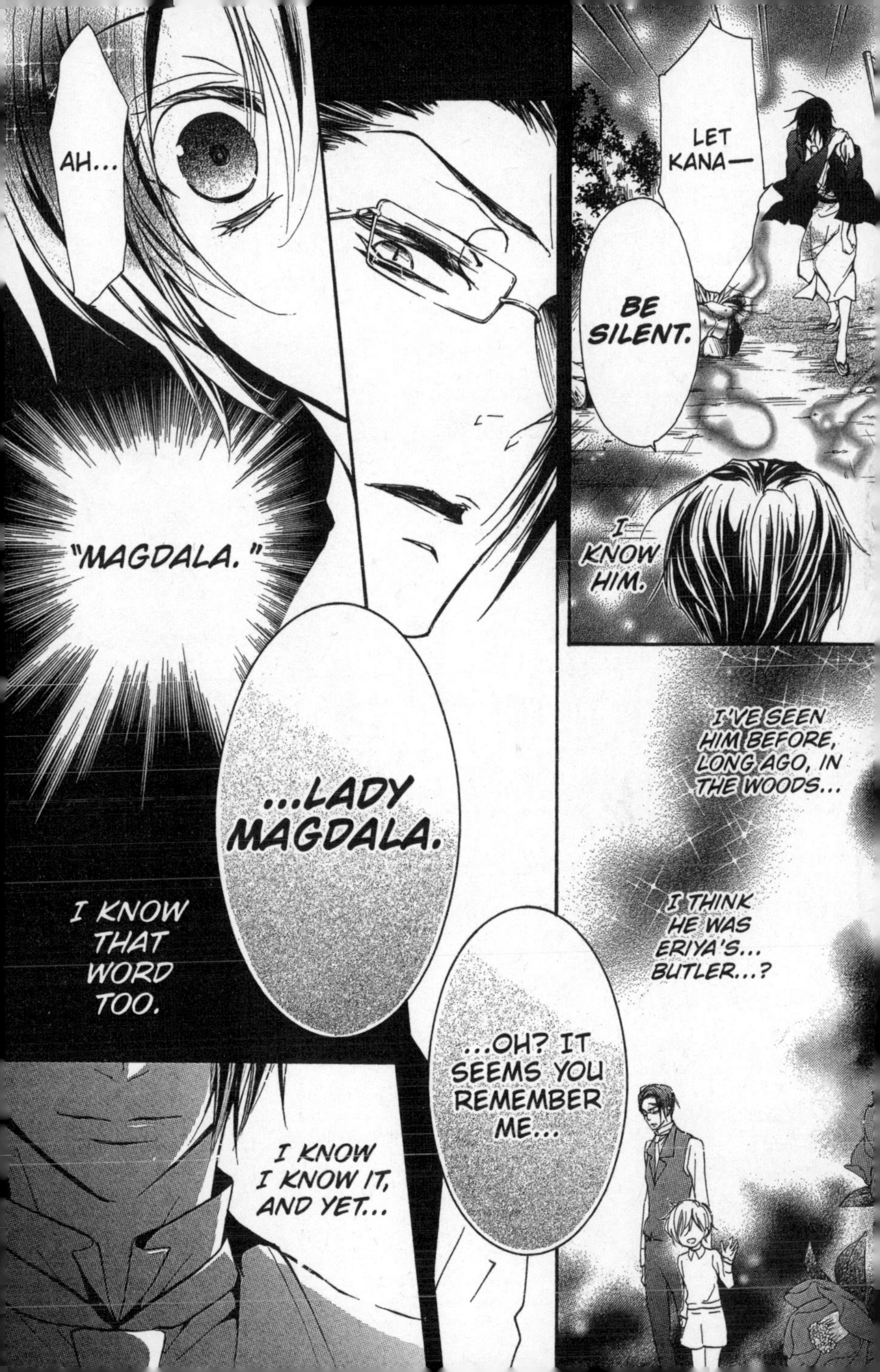
LET KANA—
BE SILENT.
I KNOW HIM.
I'VE SEEN HIM BEFORE, LONG AGO, IN THE WOODS...
I THINK HE WAS ERIYA'S... BUTLER...?
...OH? IT SEEMS YOU REMEMBER ME...
AH...
"MAGDALA."
...LADY MAGDALA.
I KNOW THAT WORD TOO.
I KNOW I KNOW IT, AND YET...

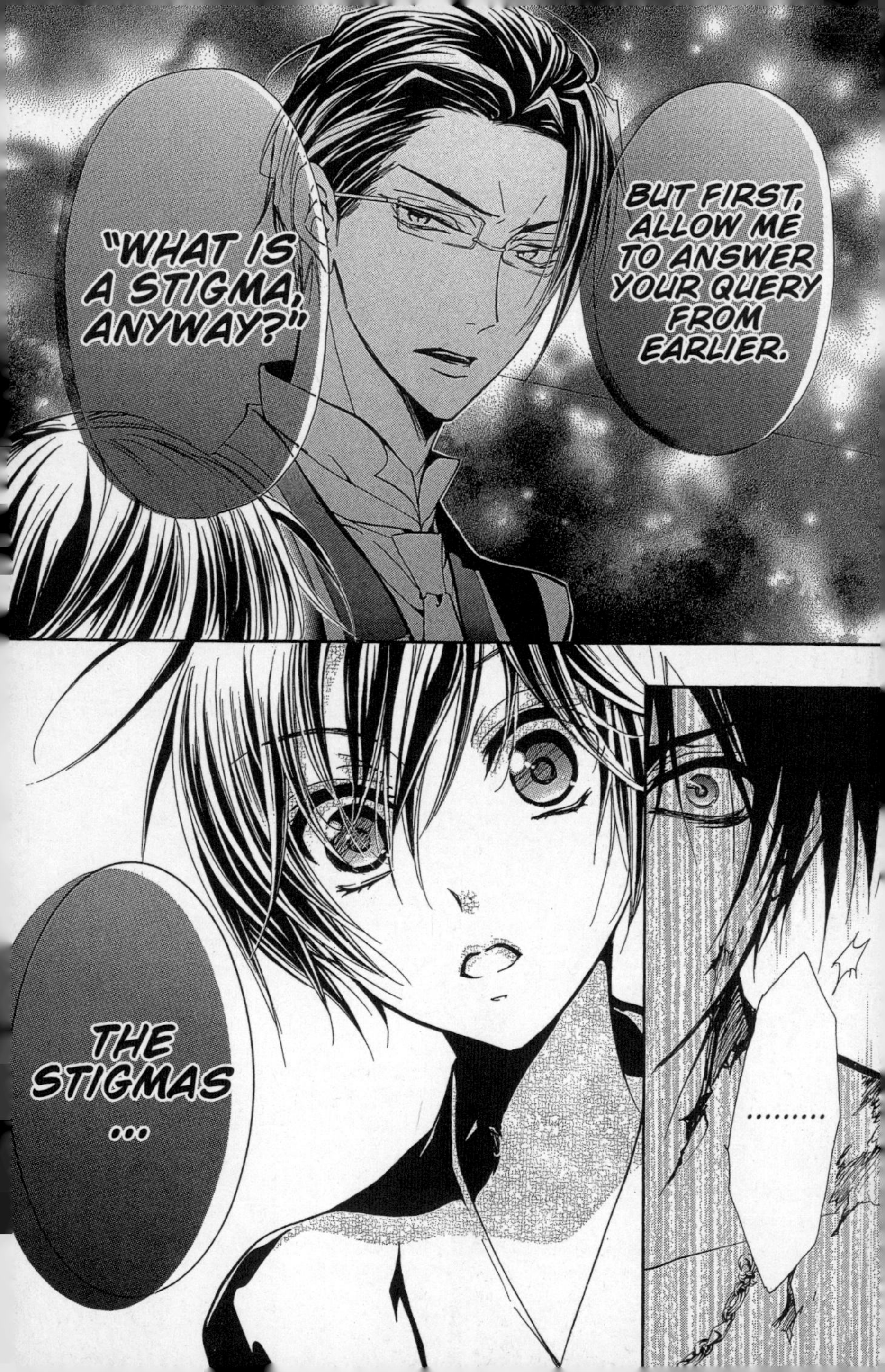
BUT FIRST, ALLOW ME TO ANSWER YOUR QUERY FROM EARLIER.
"WHAT IS A STIGMA, ANYWAY?"
....
THE STIGMAS ...

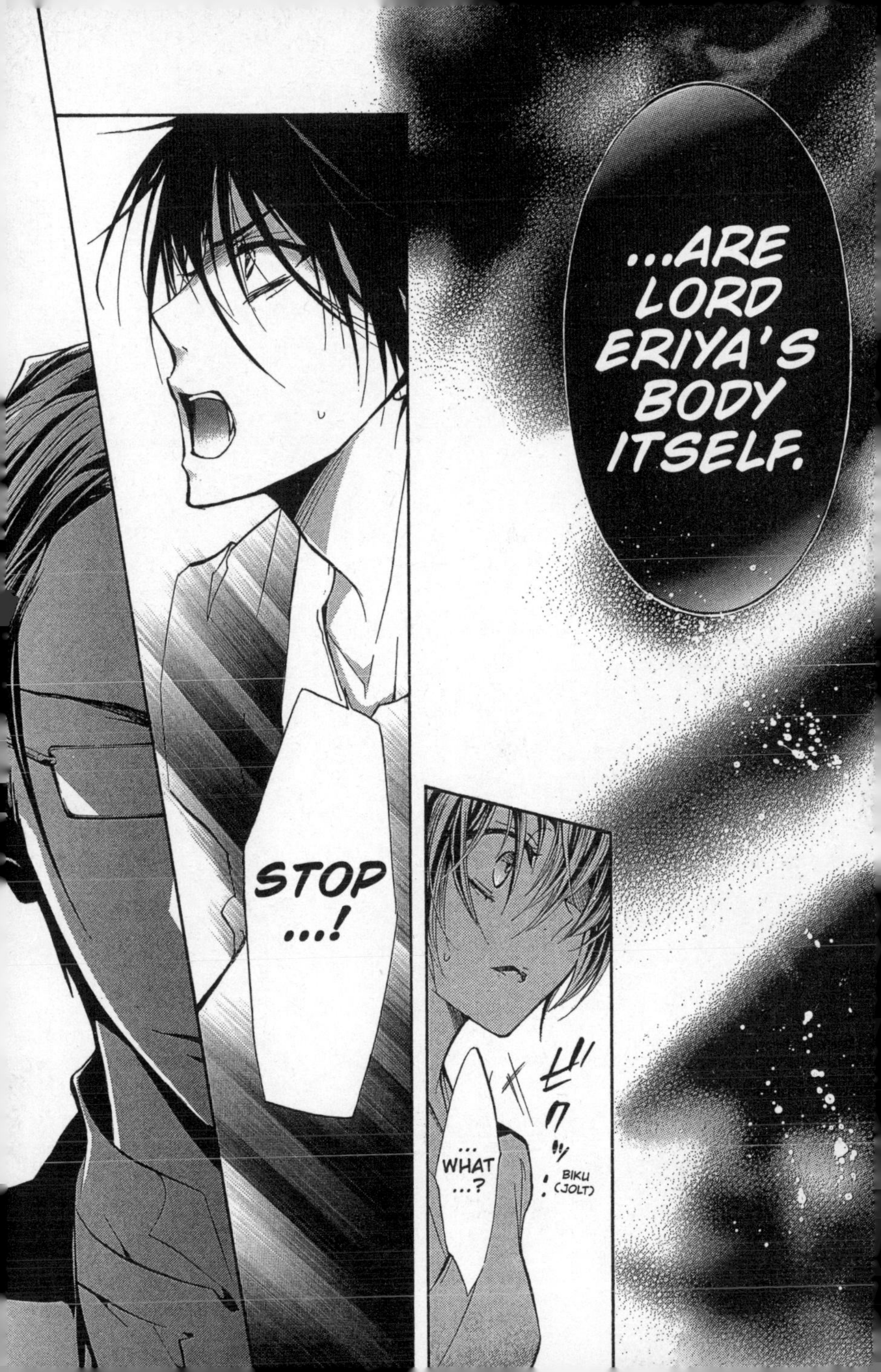
...ARE LORD ERIYA'S BODY ITSELF.
STOP ...!
... WHAT ...?
BIKU (JOLT)

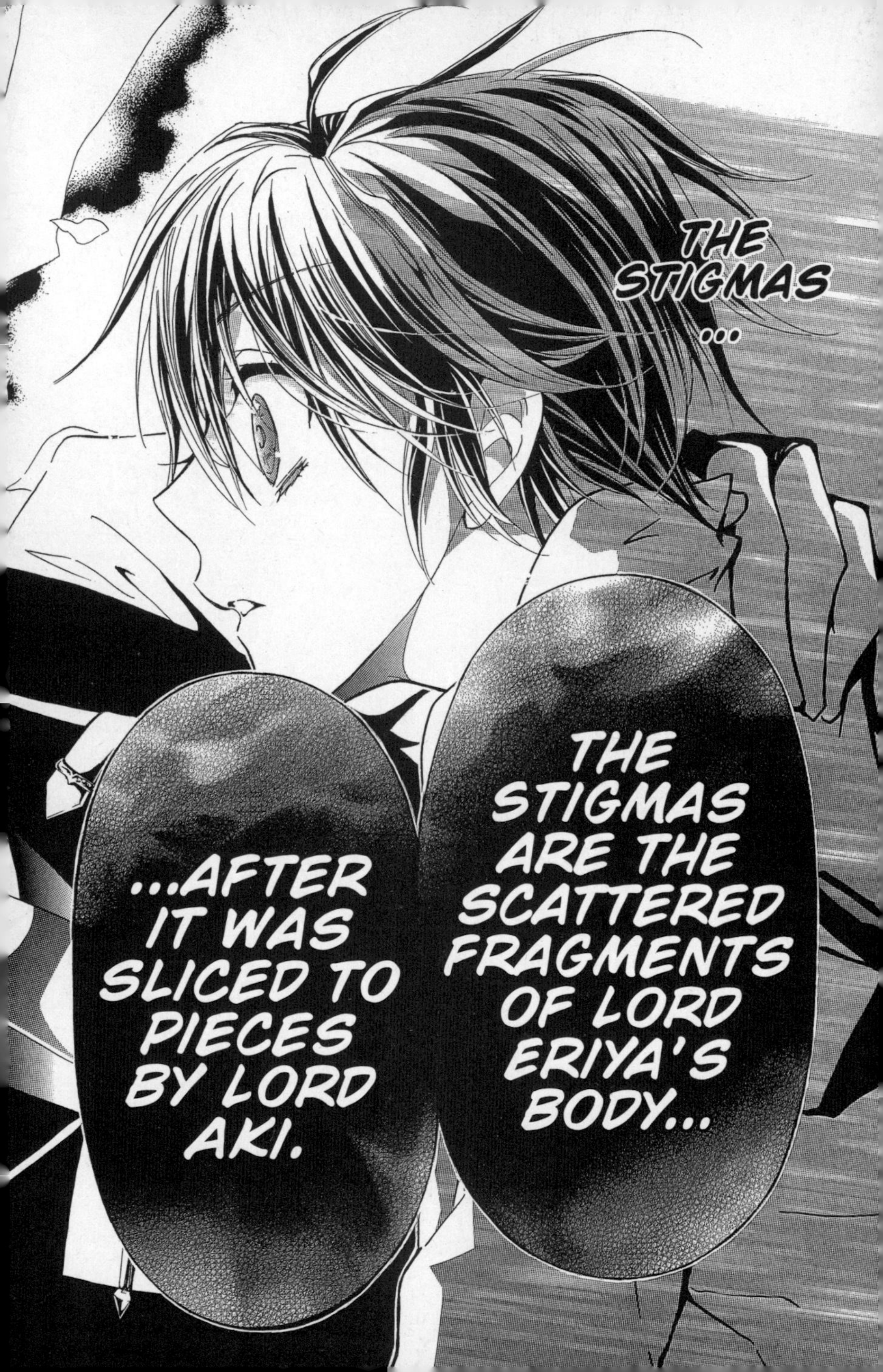
THE STIGMAS...
THE STIGMAS ARE THE SCATTERED FRAGMENTS OF LORD ERIYA'S BODY...
...AFTER IT WAS SLICED TO PIECES BY LORD AKI.

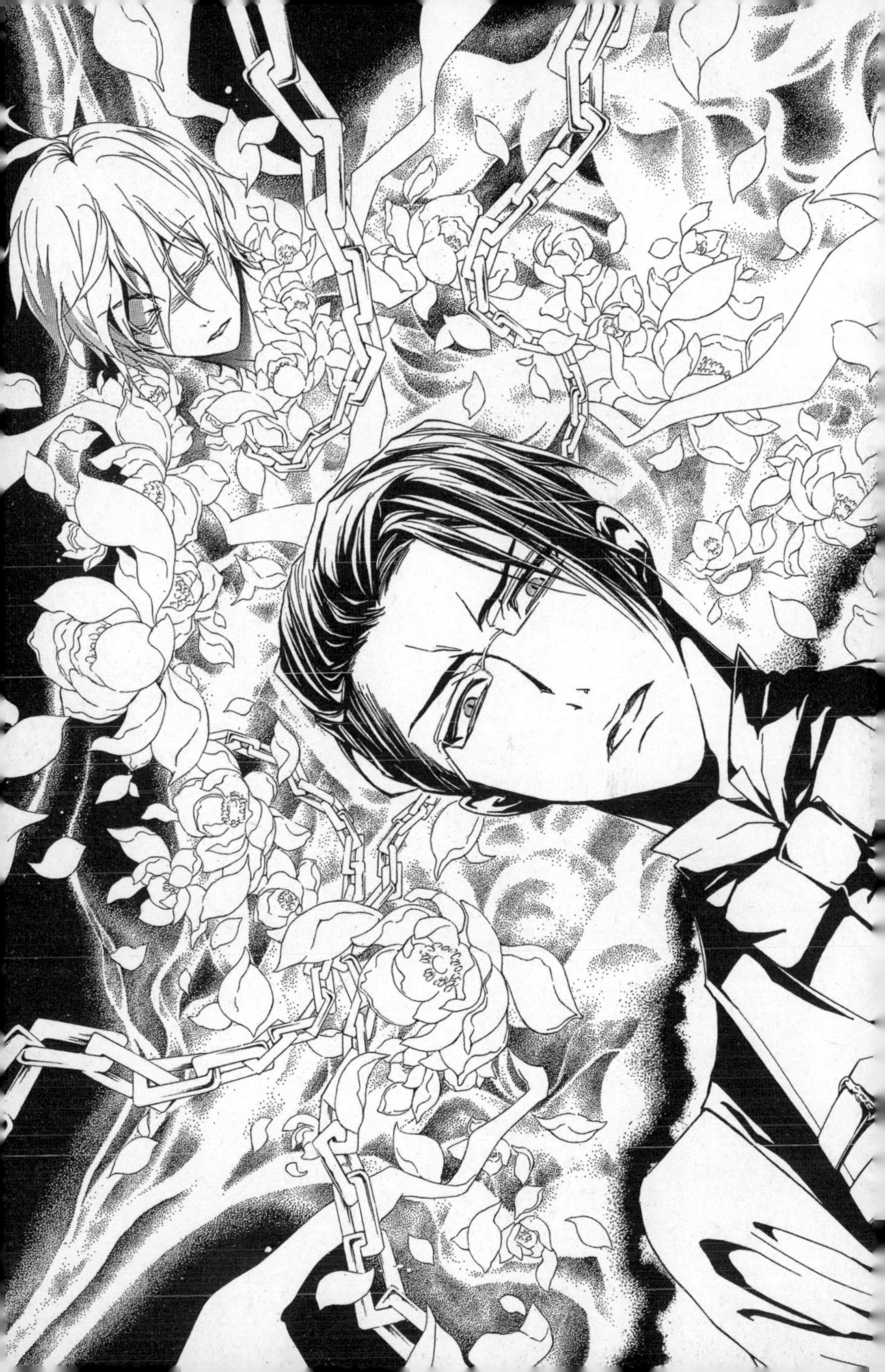

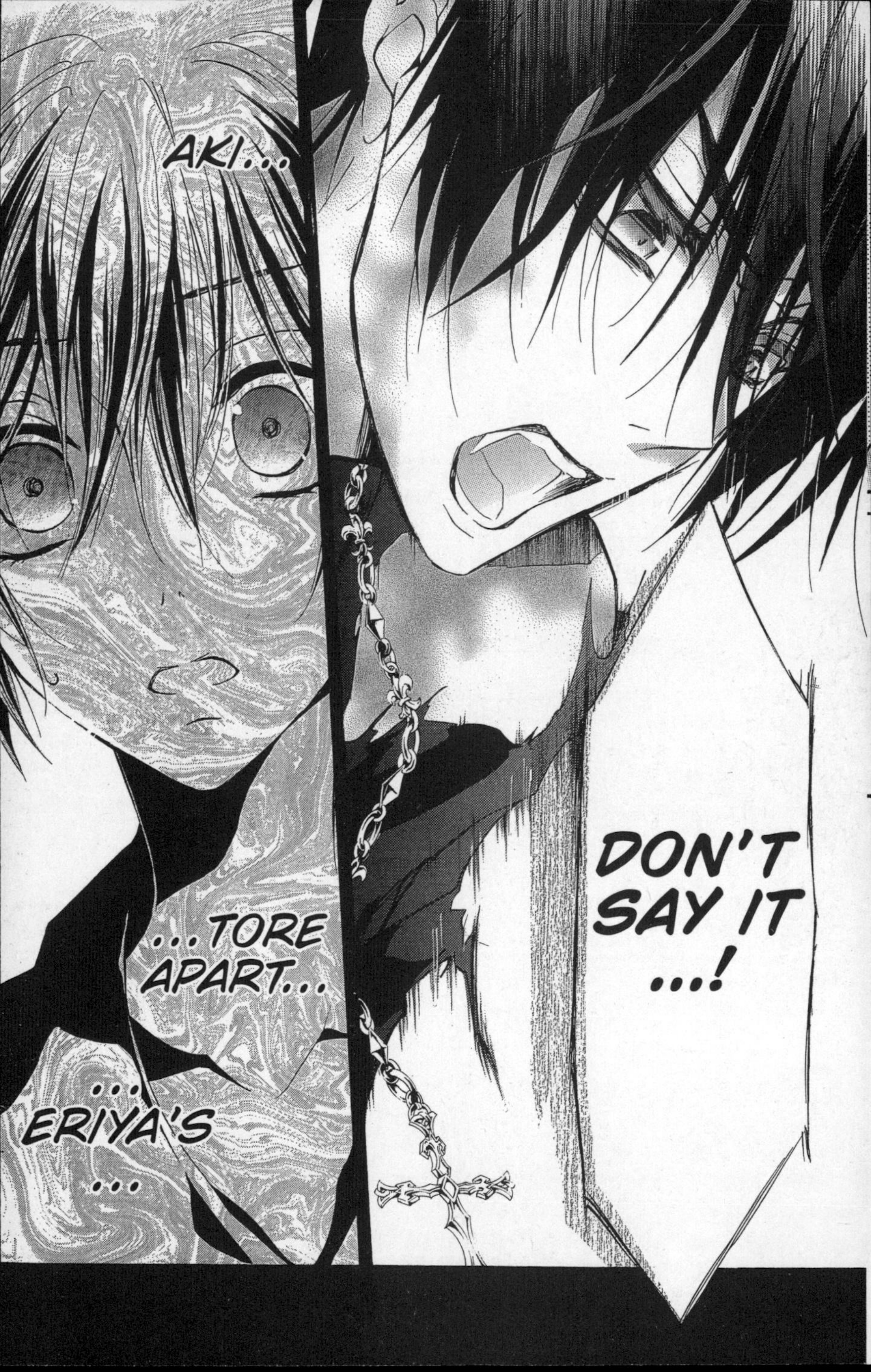
AKI...
DON'T SAY IT ...!
... TORE APART...
... ERIYA'S ...

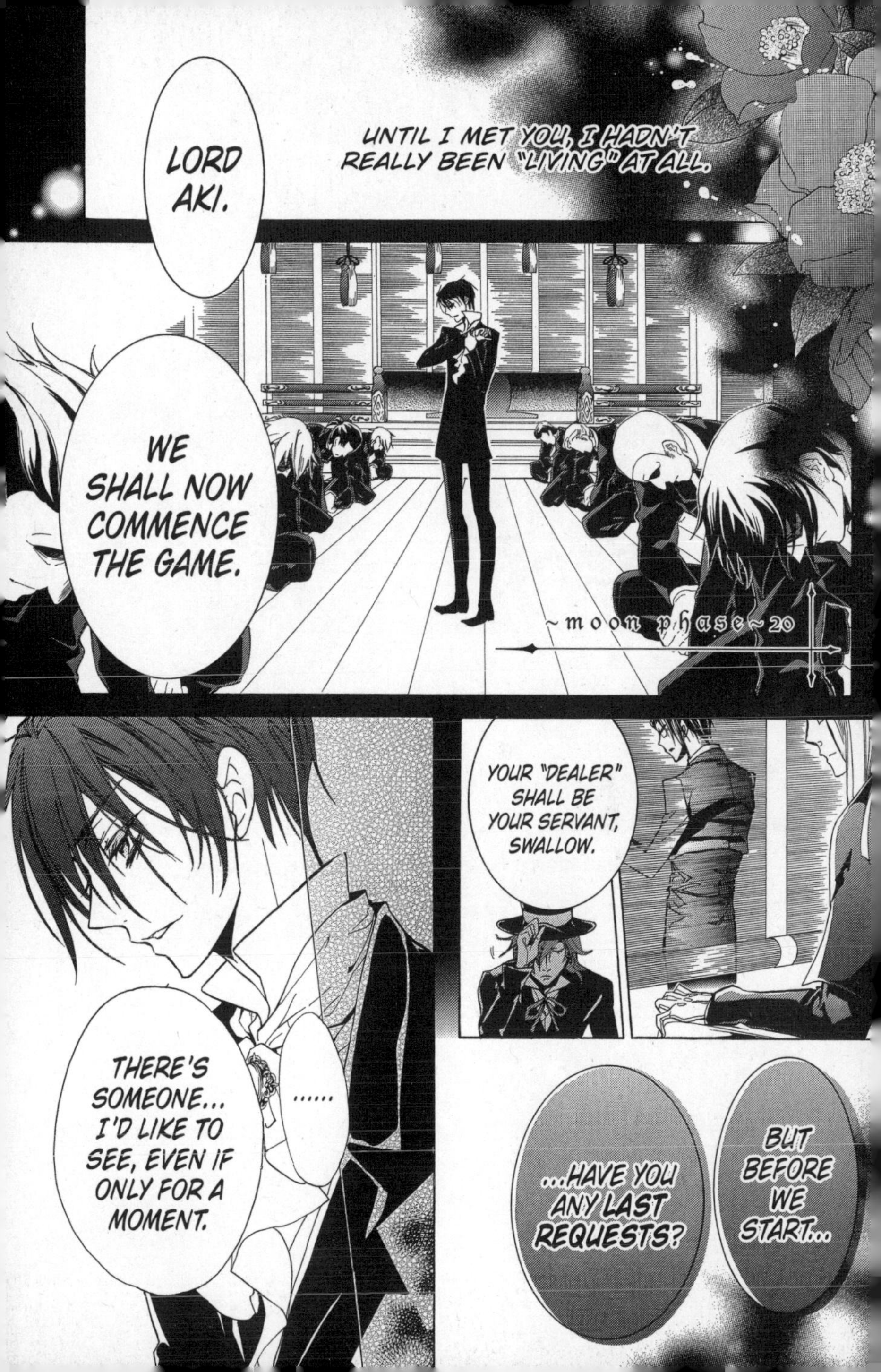
UNTIL I MET YOU, I HADN'T REALLY BEEN "LIVING" AT ALL.
LORD AKI.
WE SHALL NOW COMMENCE THE GAME.
~moon phase~20
YOUR "DEALER" SHALL BE YOUR SERVANT, SWALLOW.
BUT BEFORE WE START...
...HAVE YOU ANY LAST REQUESTS?
......
THERE'S SOMEONE... I'D LIKE TO SEE, EVEN IF ONLY FOR A MOMENT.

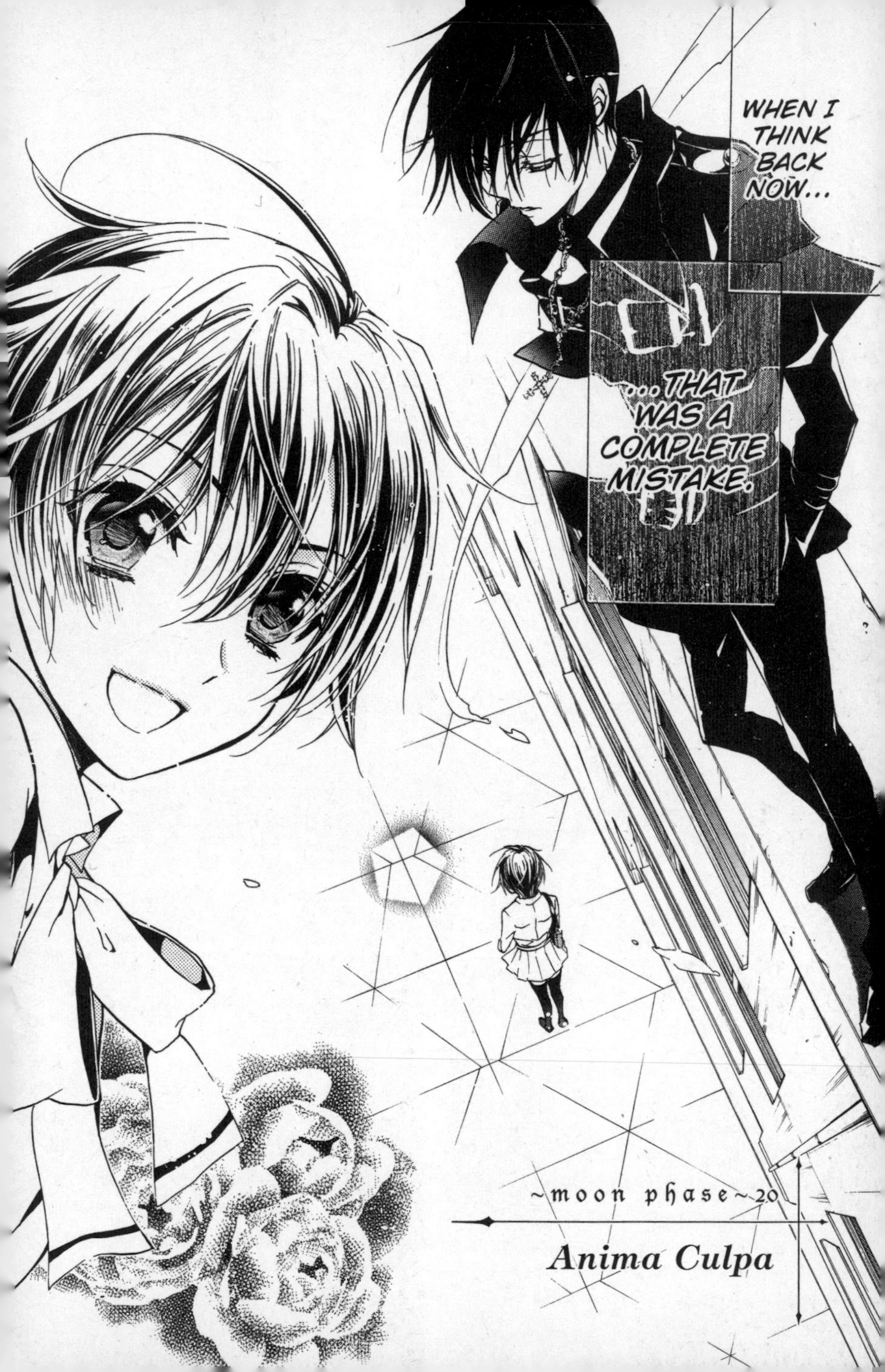
WHEN I THINK BACK NOW...
...THAT WAS A COMPLETE MISTAKE.
~moon phase~20
Anima Culpa

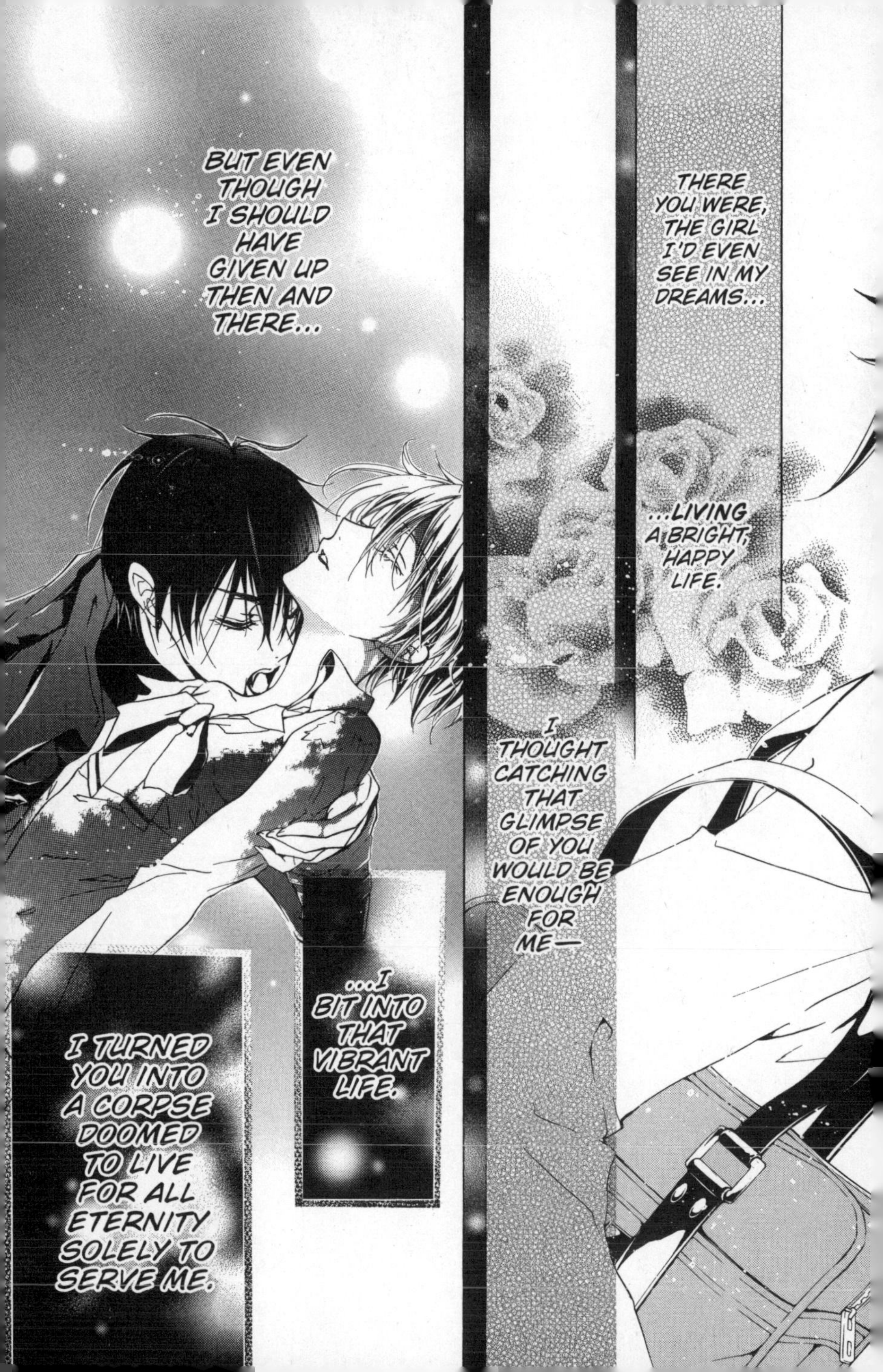
THERE YOU WERE, THE GIRL I'D EVEN SEE IN MY DREAMS...
...LIVING A BRIGHT, HAPPY LIFE.
I THOUGHT CATCHING THAT GLIMPSE OF YOU WOULD BE ENOUGH FOR ME—
BUT EVEN THOUGH I SHOULD HAVE GIVEN UP THEN AND THERE...
...I BIT INTO THAT VIBRANT LIFE.
I TURNED YOU INTO A CORPSE DOOMED TO LIVE FOR ALL ETERNITY SOLELY TO SERVE ME.

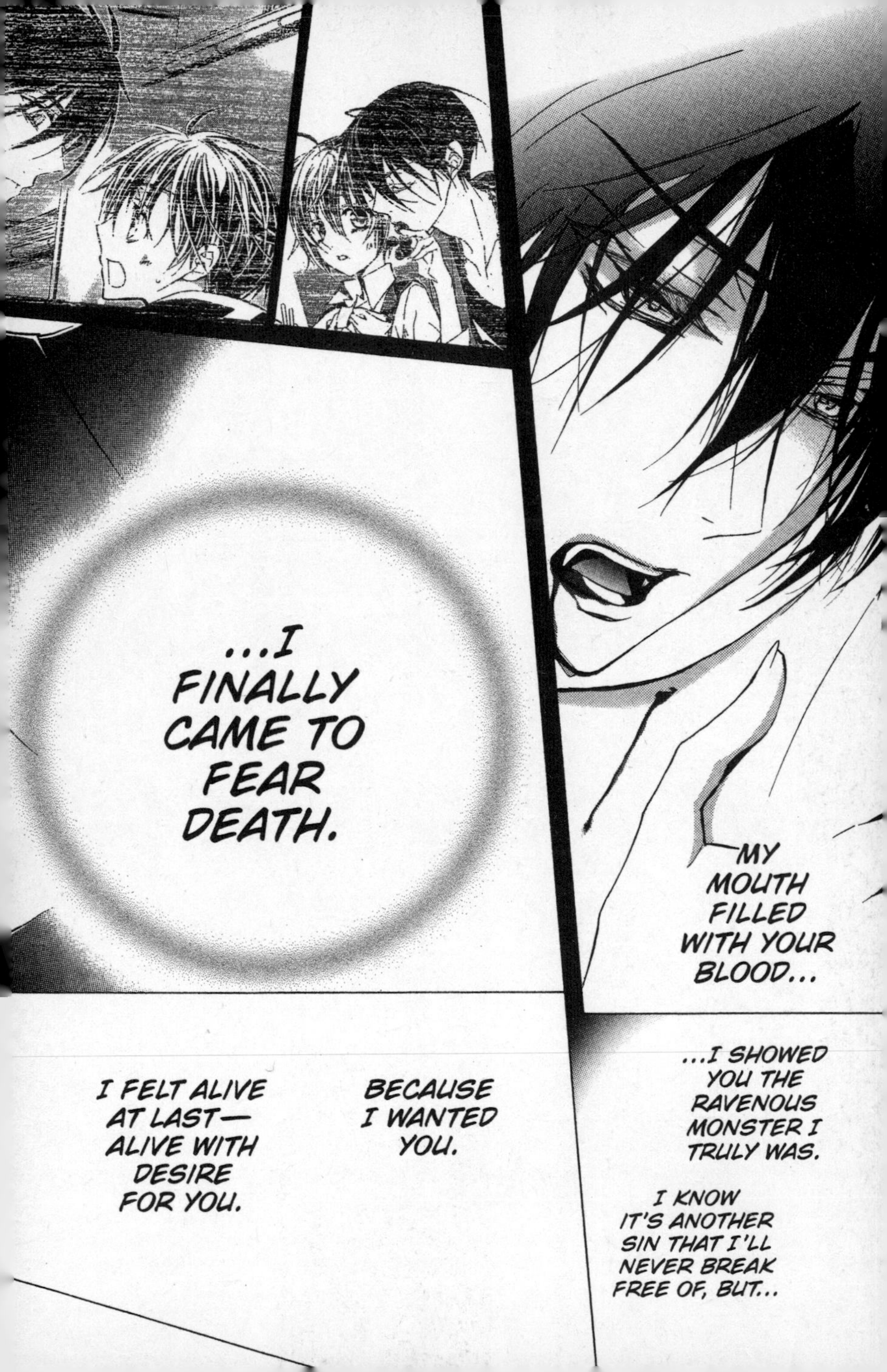
MY MOUTH FILLED WITH YOUR BLOOD...
...I FINALLY CAME TO FEAR DEATH.
...I SHOWED YOU THE RAVENOUS MONSTER I TRULY WAS.
I KNOW IT'S ANOTHER SIN THAT I'LL NEVER BREAK FREE OF, BUT...
BECAUSE I WANTED YOU.
I FELT ALIVE AT LAST—ALIVE WITH DESIRE FOR YOU.

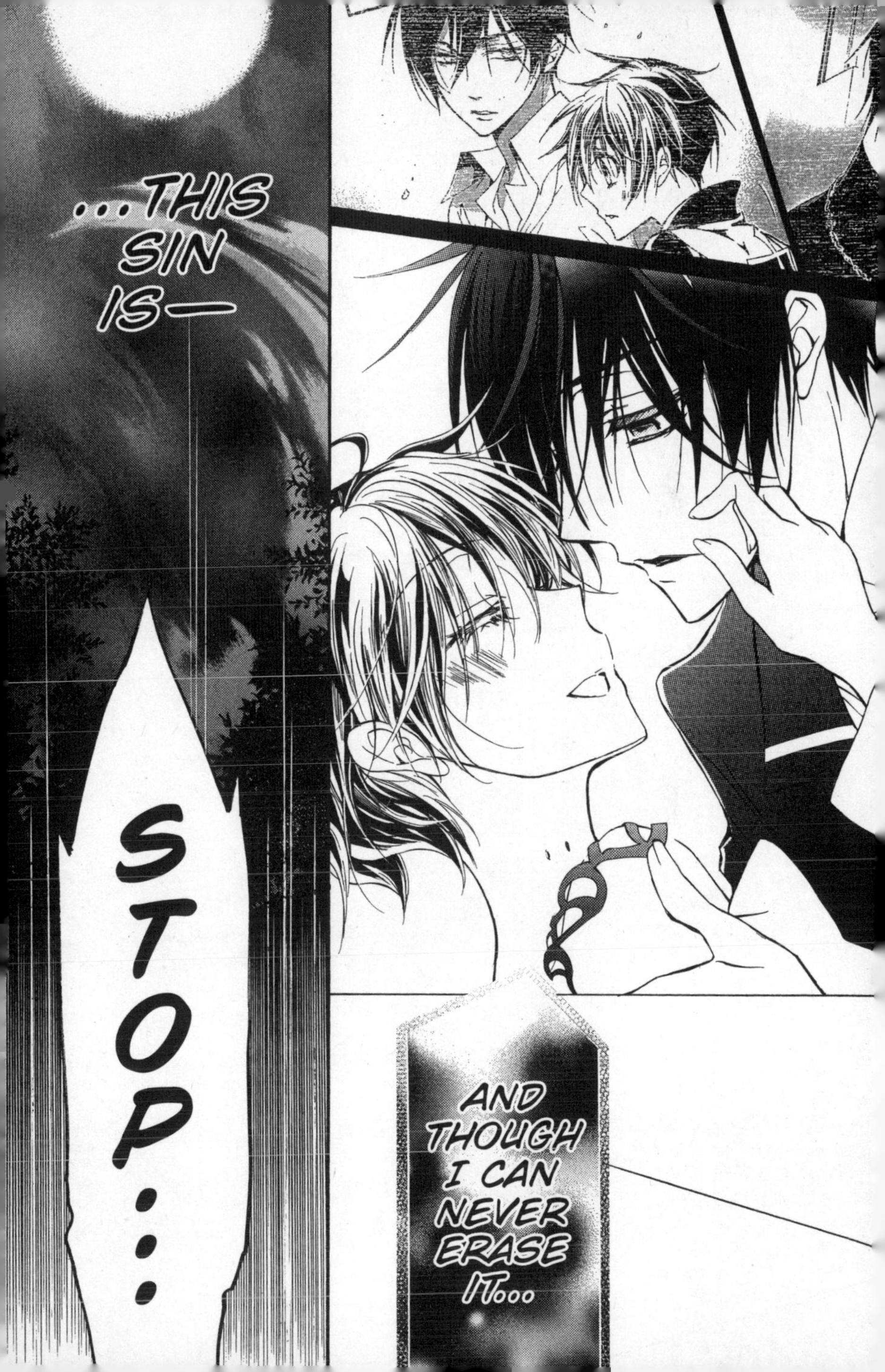
AND THOUGH I CAN NEVER ERASE IT...
...THIS SIN IS—
STOP...

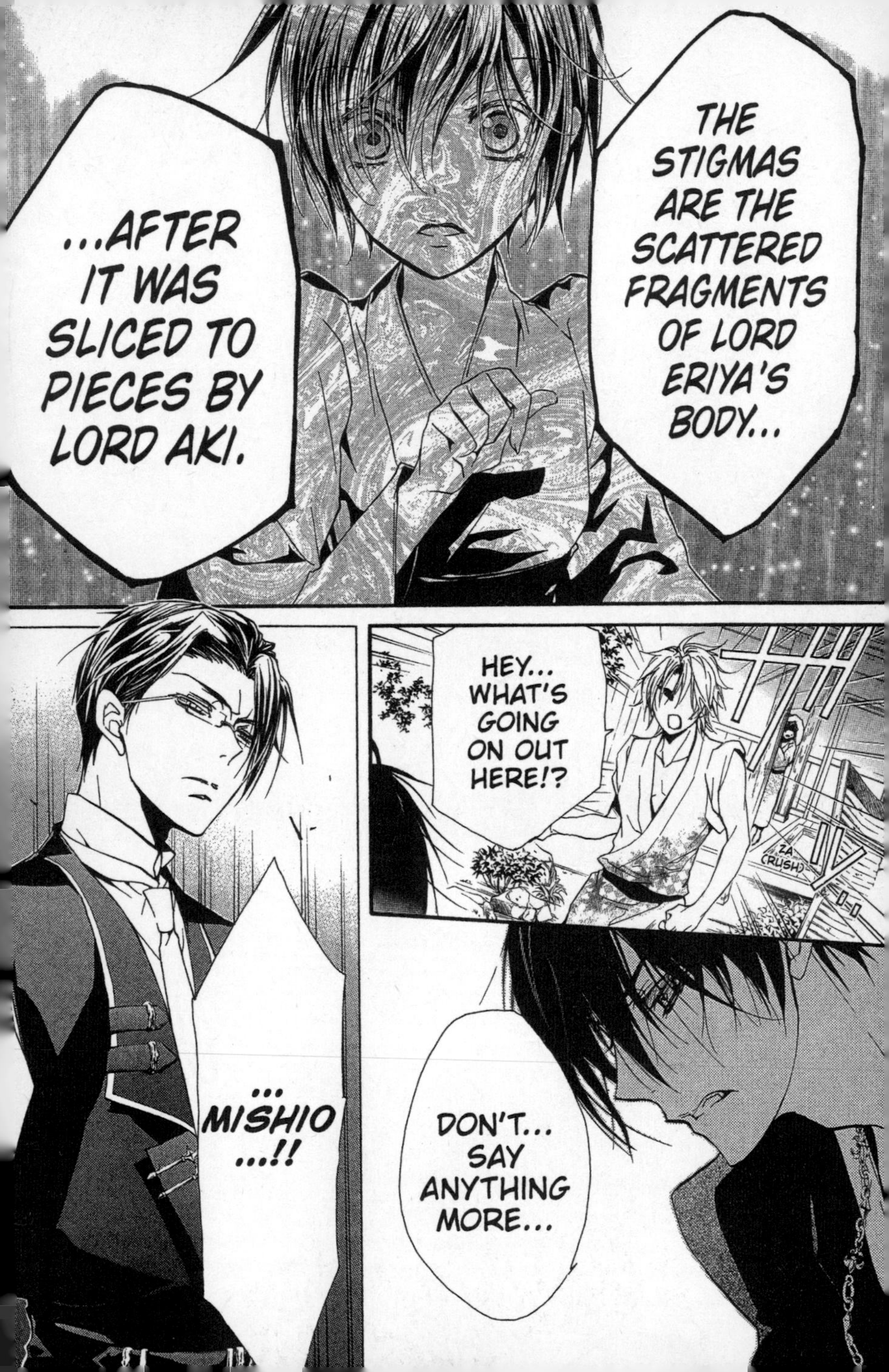
THE STIGMAS ARE THE SCATTERED FRAGMENTS OF LORD ERIYA'S BODY...
...AFTER IT WAS SLICED TO PIECES BY LORD AKI.
HEY... WHAT'S GOING ON OUT HERE!?
ZA (RUSH)
DON'T... SAY ANYTHING MORE...
... MISHIO ...!!

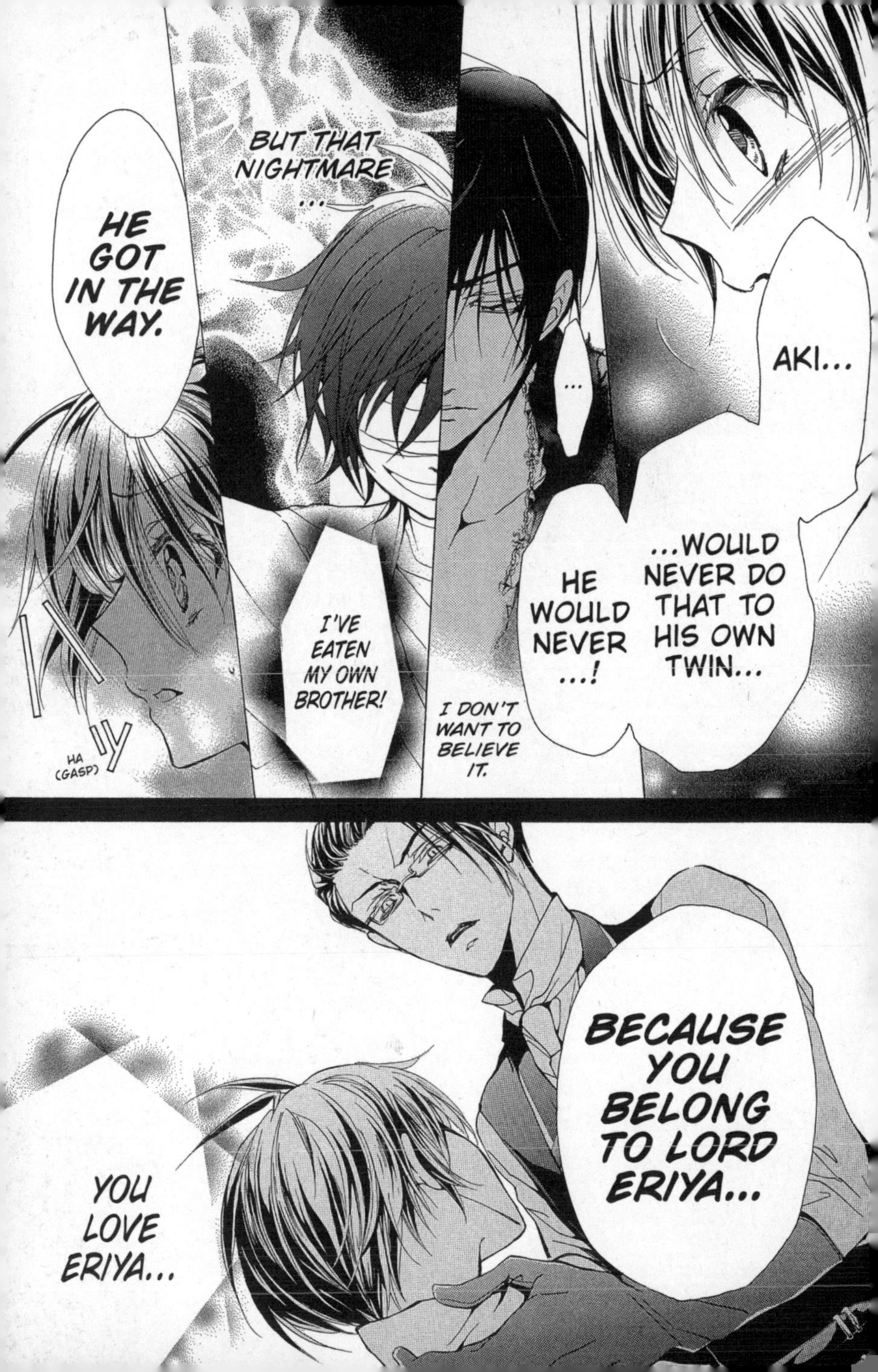
AKI...
...WOULD NEVER DO THAT TO HIS OWN TWIN...
HE WOULD NEVER ...!
...
I DON'T WANT TO BELIEVE IT.
BUT THAT NIGHTMARE ...
I'VE EATEN MY OWN BROTHER!
HE GOT IN THE WAY.
HA (GASP)
BECAUSE YOU BELONG TO LORD ERIYA...
YOU LOVE ERIYA...

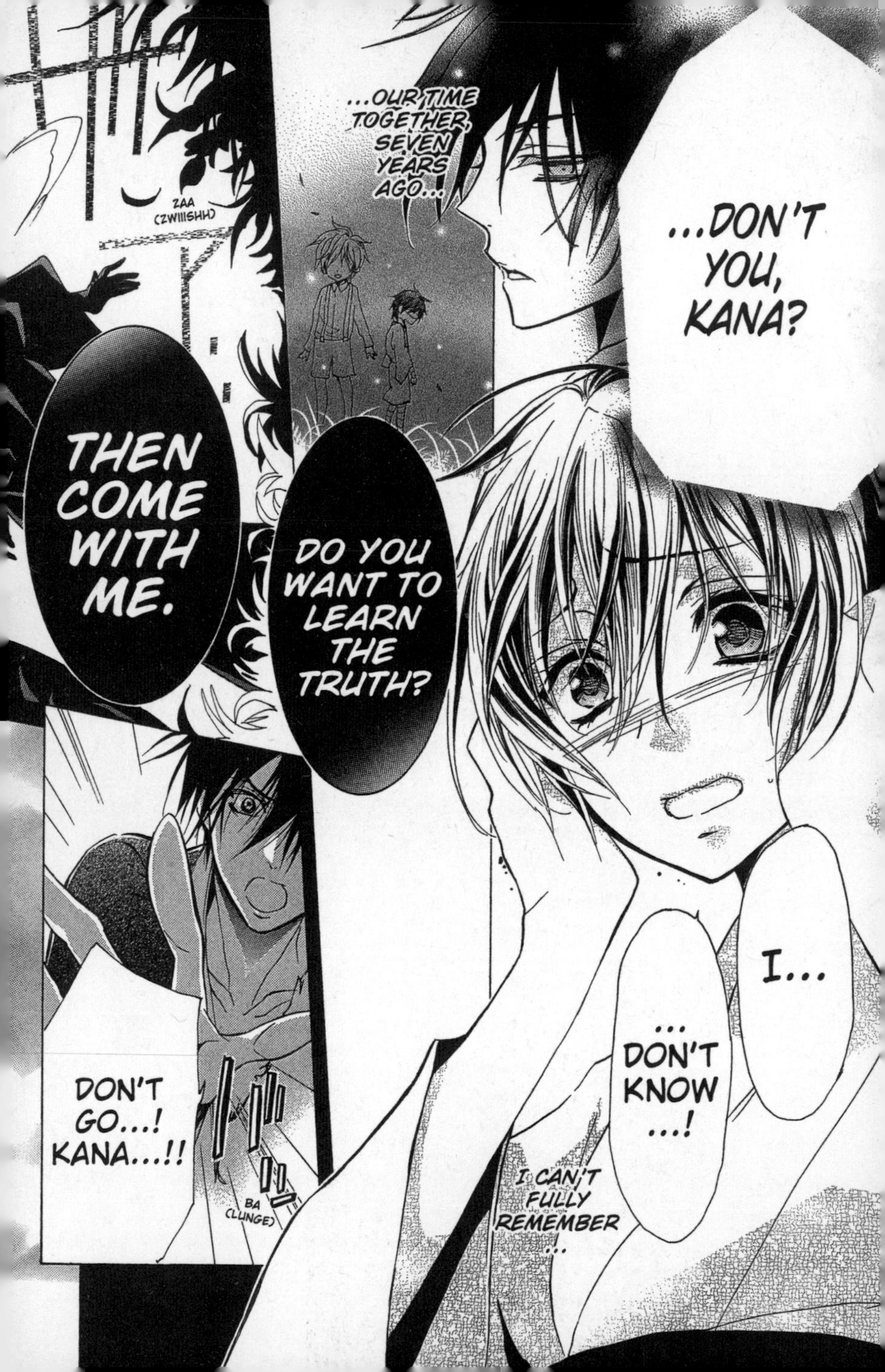
...OUR TIME TOGETHER, SEVEN YEARS AGO...
...DON'T YOU, KANA?
I...
...DON'T KNOW...!
I CAN'T FULLY REMEMBER...
ZAA (ZWIIISHH)
DO YOU WANT TO LEARN THE TRUTH?
THEN COME WITH ME.
DON'T GO...! KANA...!!
BA (LUNGE)

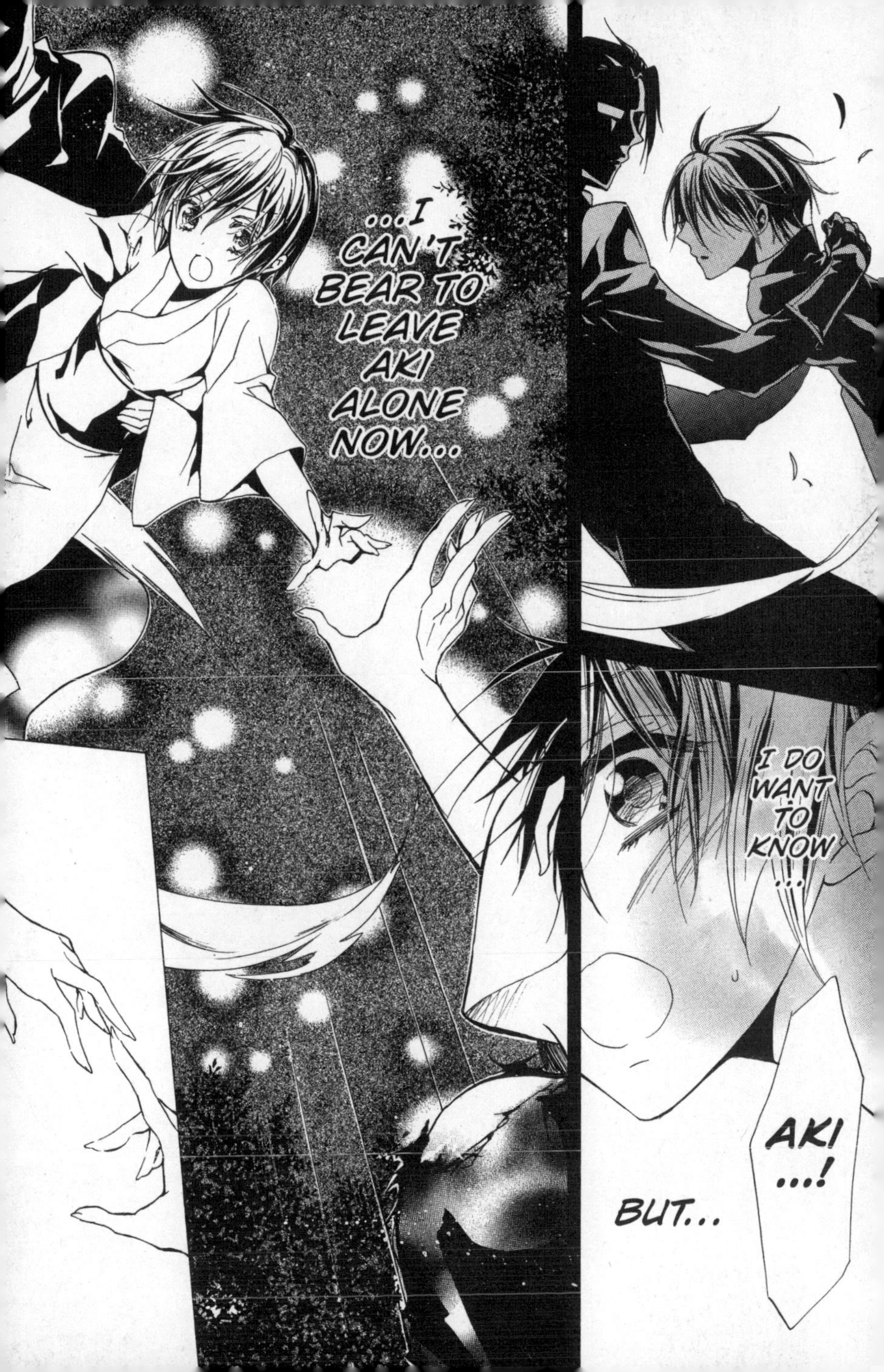
I DO WANT TO KNOW...
AKI...!
BUT...
...I CAN'T BEAR TO LEAVE AKI ALONE NOW...

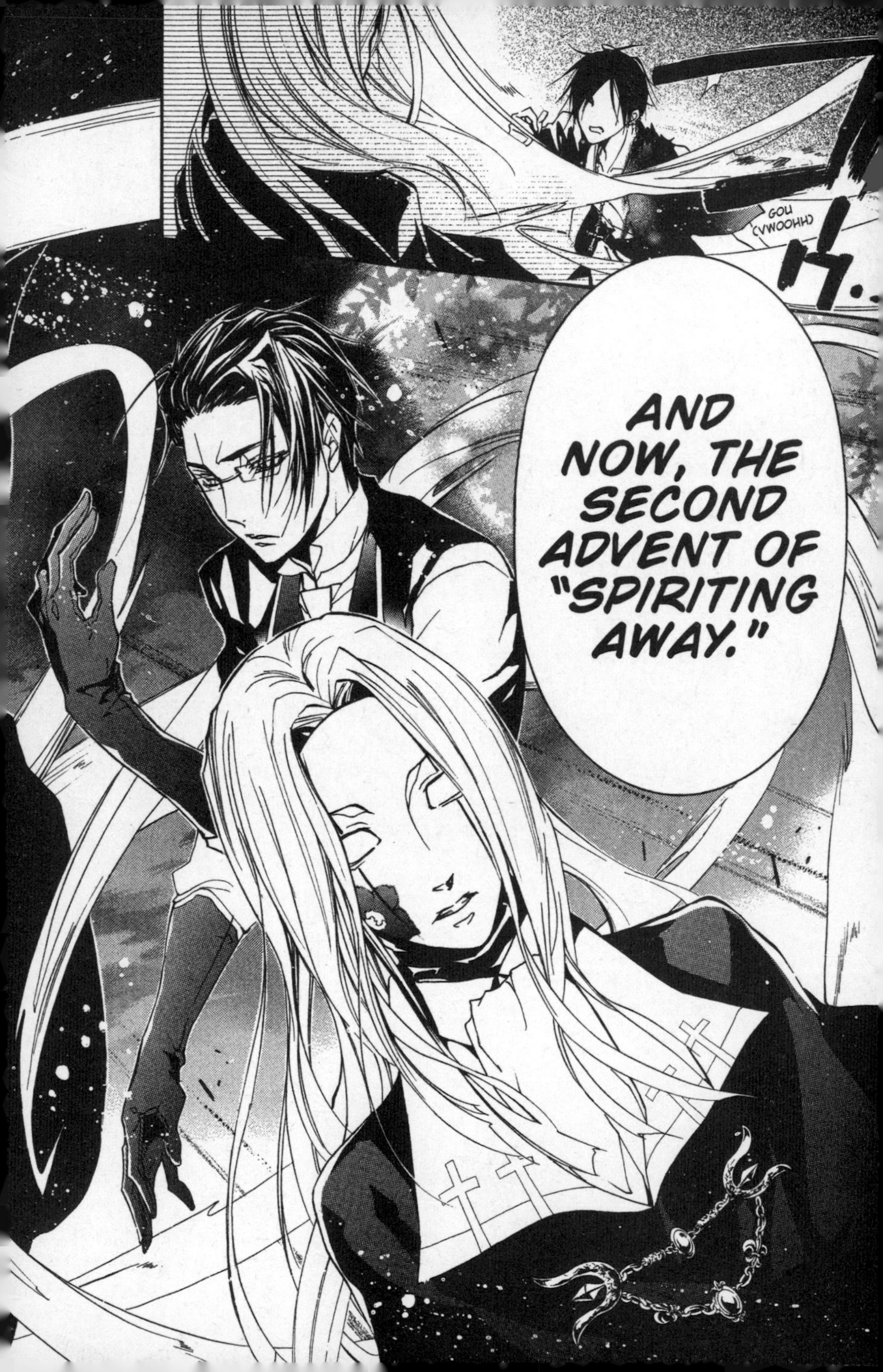
GOU
(VWOOHH)
AND NOW, THE SECOND ADVENT OF "SPIRITING AWAY."

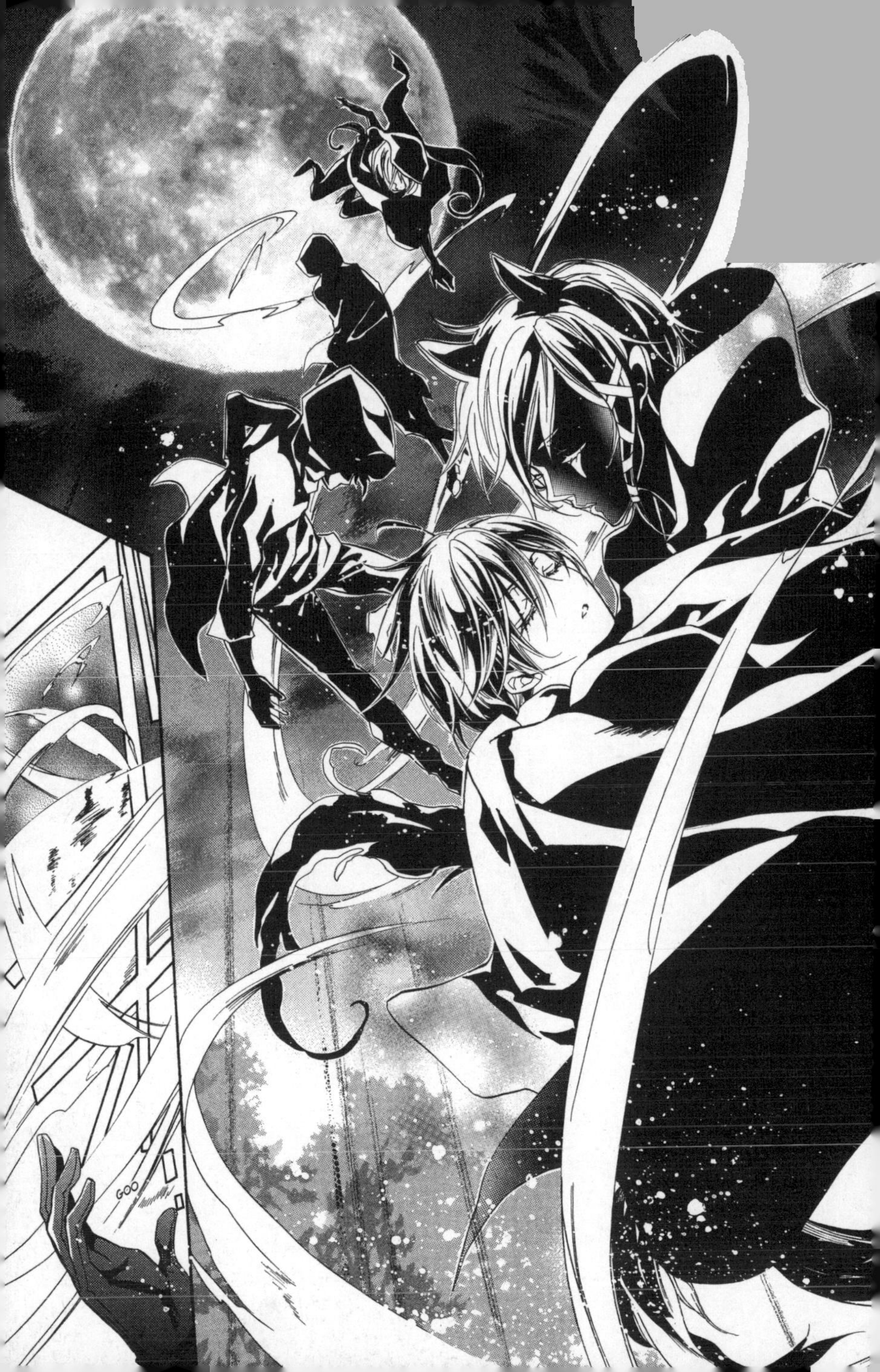
GOO

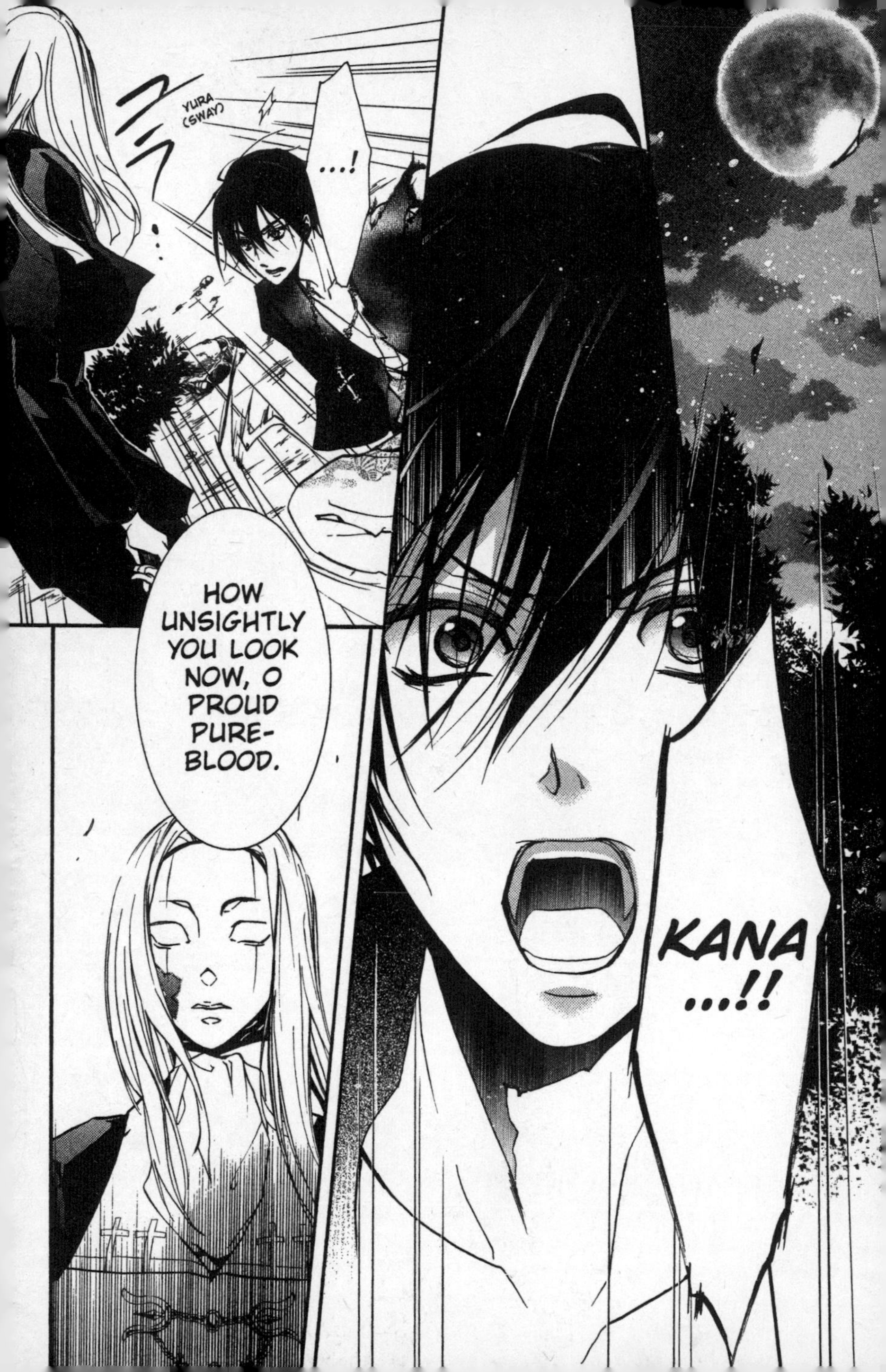
KANA...!!
...!
YURA (SWAY)
...
HOW UNSIGHTLY YOU LOOK NOW, O PROUD PURE-BLOOD.

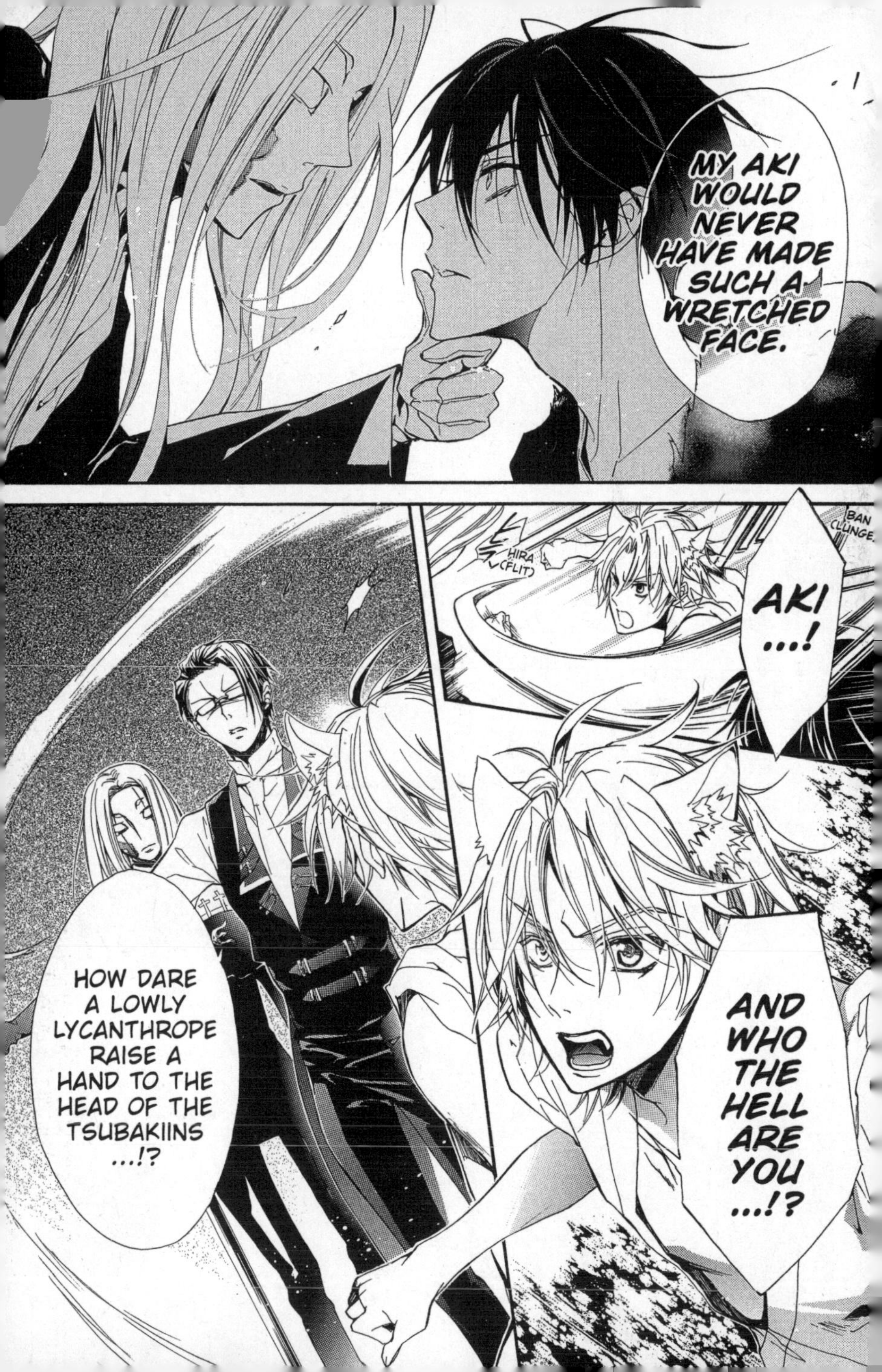
MY AKI WOULD NEVER HAVE MADE SUCH A WRETCHED FACE.
BAN
CLUNGE
HIRA
(FLIT)
AKI ...!
AND WHO THE HELL ARE YOU ...!?
HOW DARE A LOWLY LYCANTHROPE RAISE A HAND TO THE HEAD OF THE TSUBAKIINS ...!?

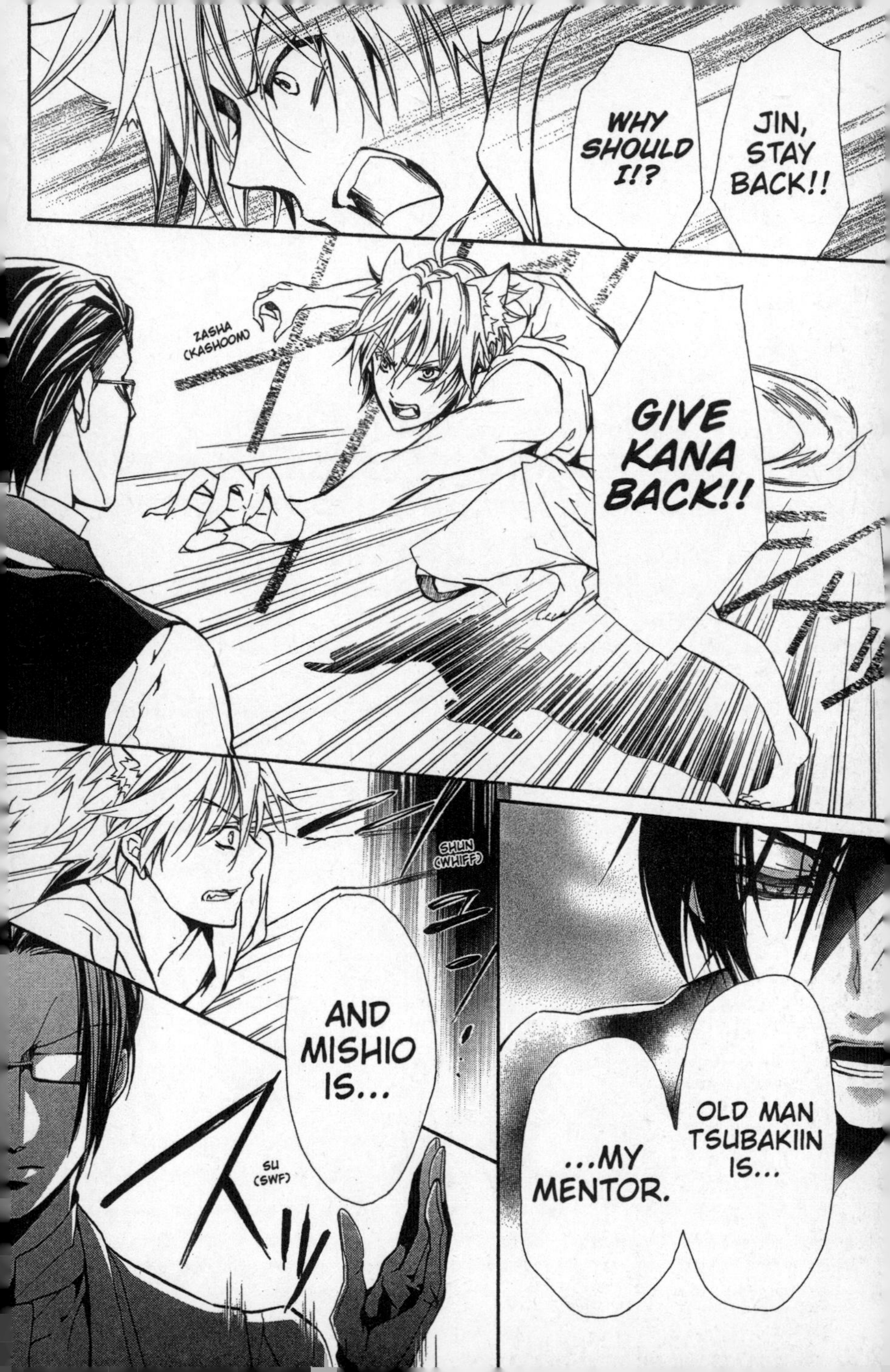
JIN, STAY BACK!!
WHY SHOULD I!?
GIVE KANA BACK!!
ZASHA (KASHOOM)
OLD MAN TSUBAKIIN IS...
...MY MENTOR.
SHUN (WHIFF)
AND MISHIO IS...
SU (SWF)

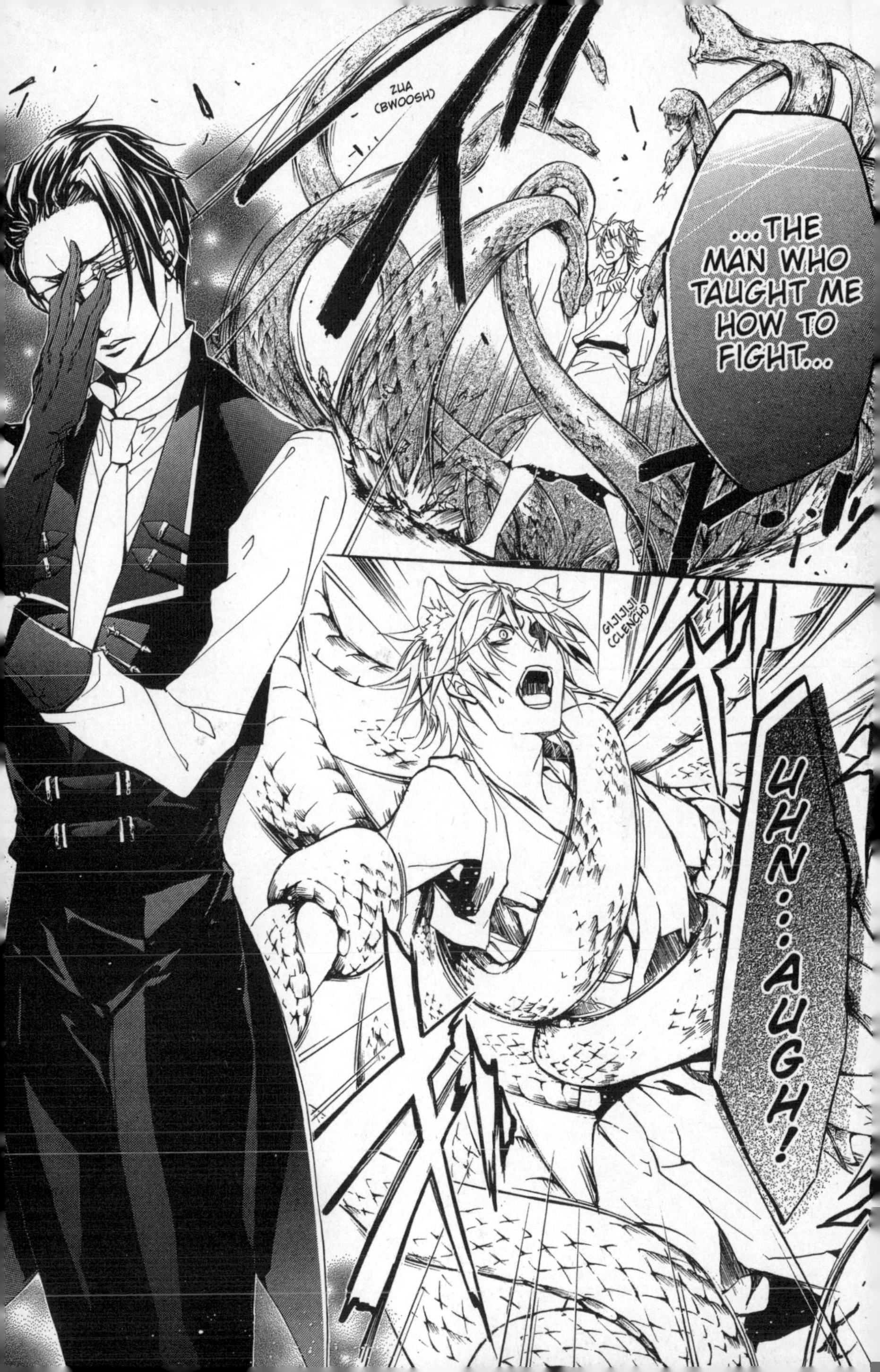
...THE MAN WHO TAUGHT ME HOW TO FIGHT...
ZUA (BWOOSH)
GIJIJIJI (CLENCH)
UHN...AUGH!

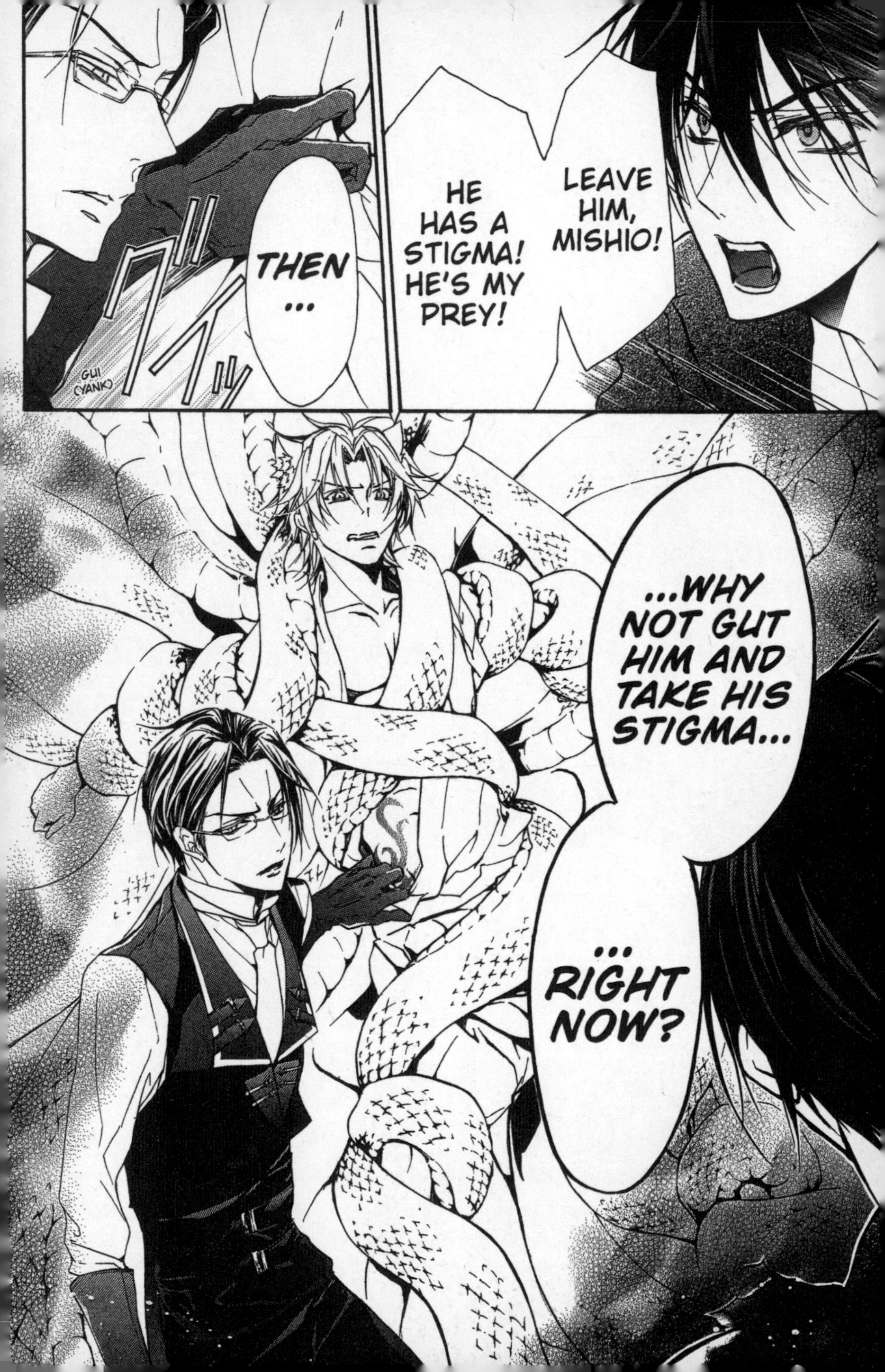
LEAVE HIM, MISHIO!
HE HAS A STIGMA! HE'S MY PREY!
THEN ...
GUI (YANK)
...WHY NOT GUT HIM AND TAKE HIS STIGMA...
... RIGHT NOW?

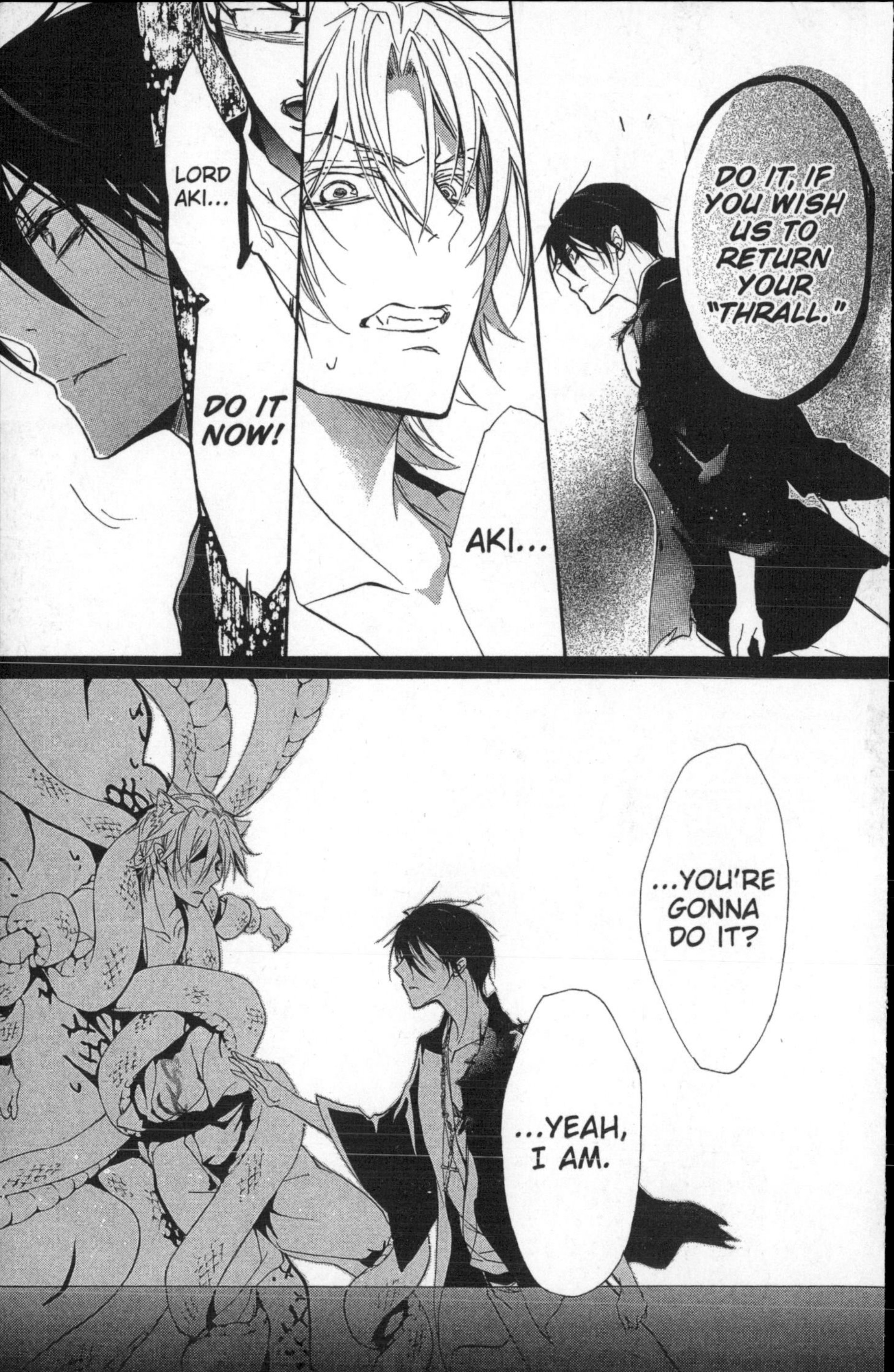
DO IT, IF YOU WISH US TO RETURN YOUR "THRALL."
AKI...
LORD AKI...
DO IT NOW!
...YOU'RE GONNA DO IT?
...YEAH, I AM.

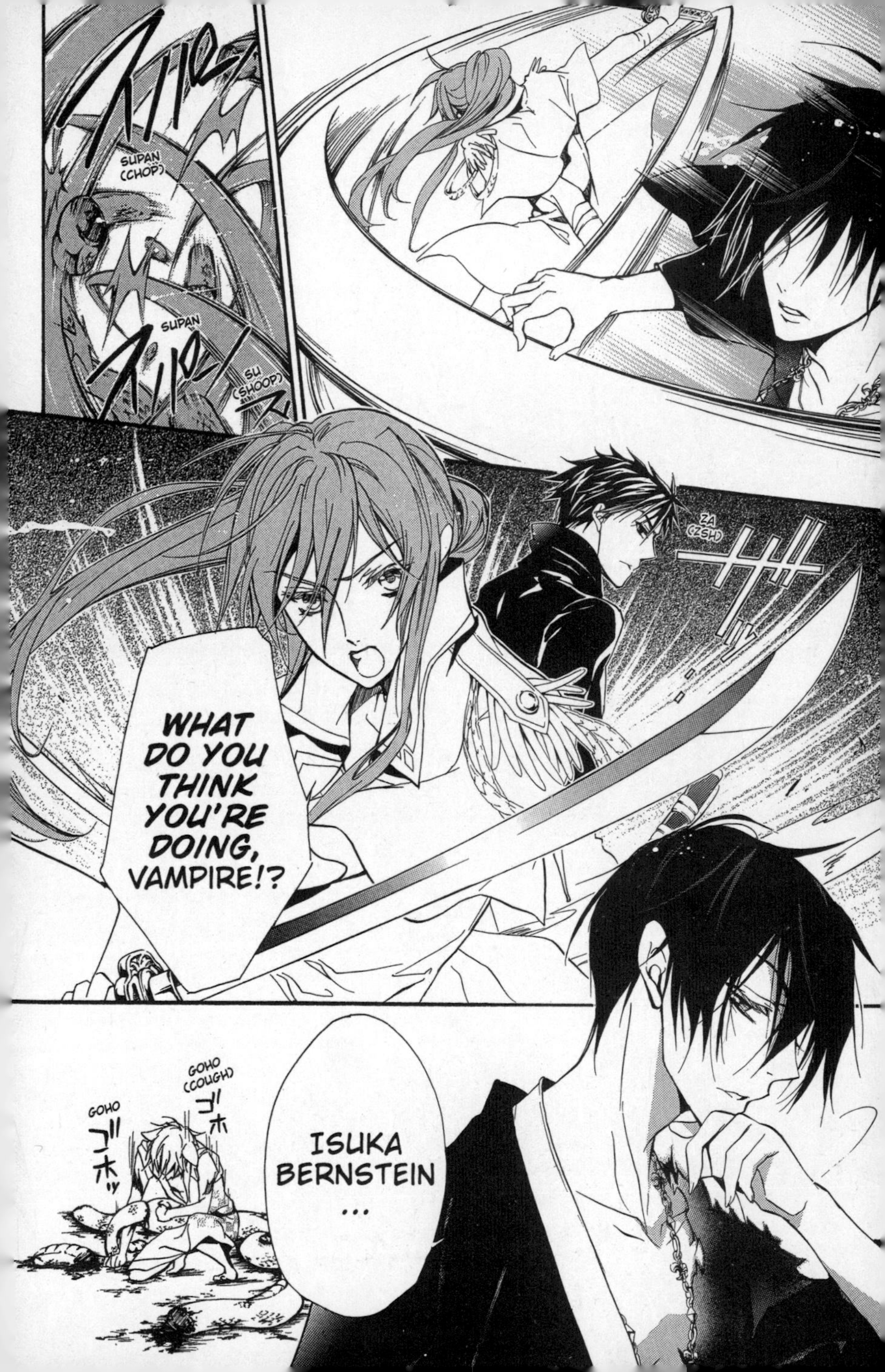
SUPAN (CHOP)
SUPAN
SU (SHOOP)
ZA (ZSH)
WHAT DO YOU THINK YOU'RE DOING, VAMPIRE!?
ISUKA BERNSTEIN ...
GOHO (COUGH)
GOHO

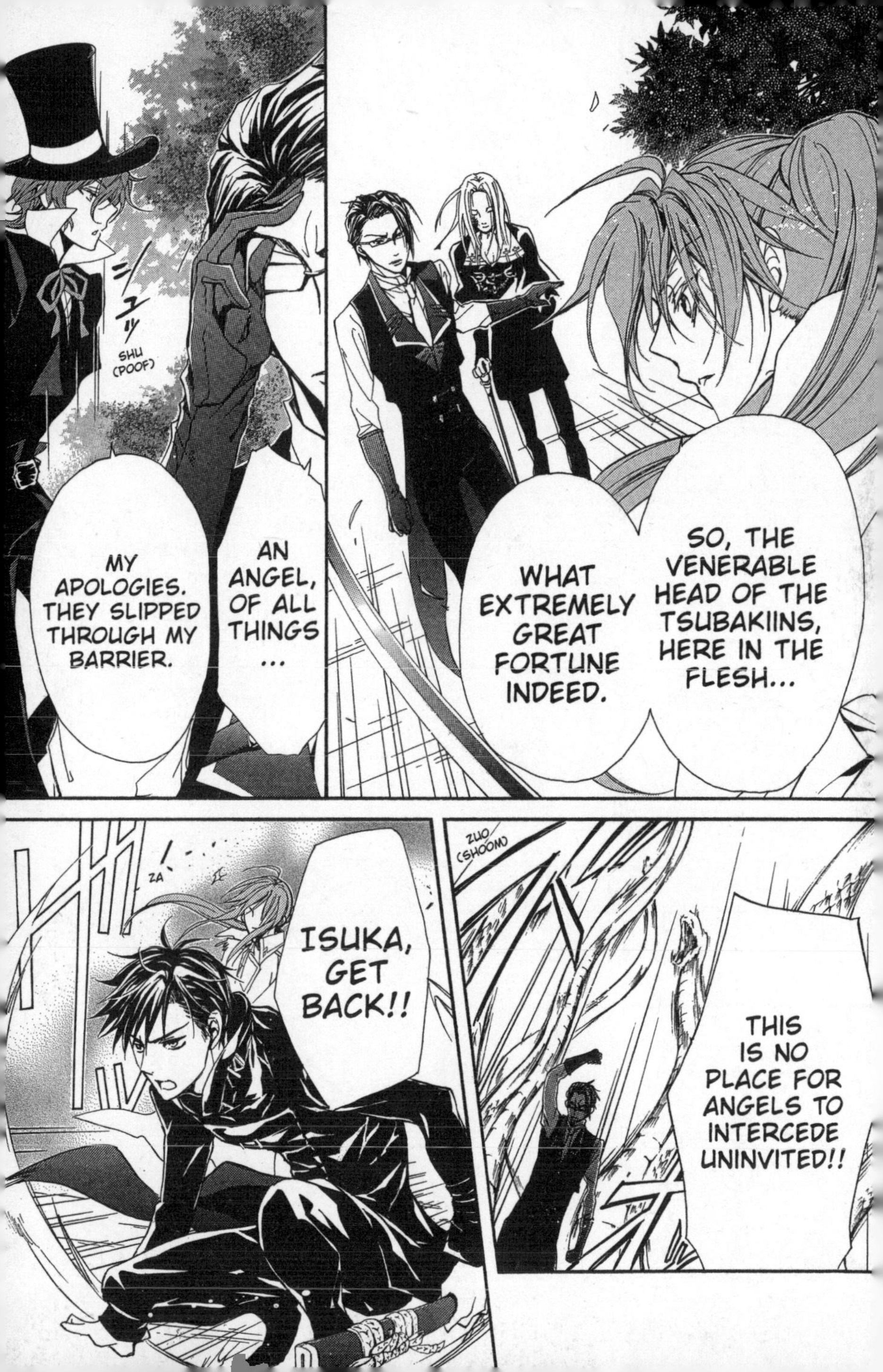
SO, THE VENERABLE HEAD OF THE TSUBAKIINS, HERE IN THE FLESH...
WHAT EXTREMELY GREAT FORTUNE INDEED.
SHU (POOF)
AN ANGEL, OF ALL THINGS...
MY APOLOGIES. THEY SLIPPED THROUGH MY BARRIER.
ZUO (SHOOM)
THIS IS NO PLACE FOR ANGELS TO INTERCEDE UNINVITED!!
ZA
ISUKA, GET BACK!!

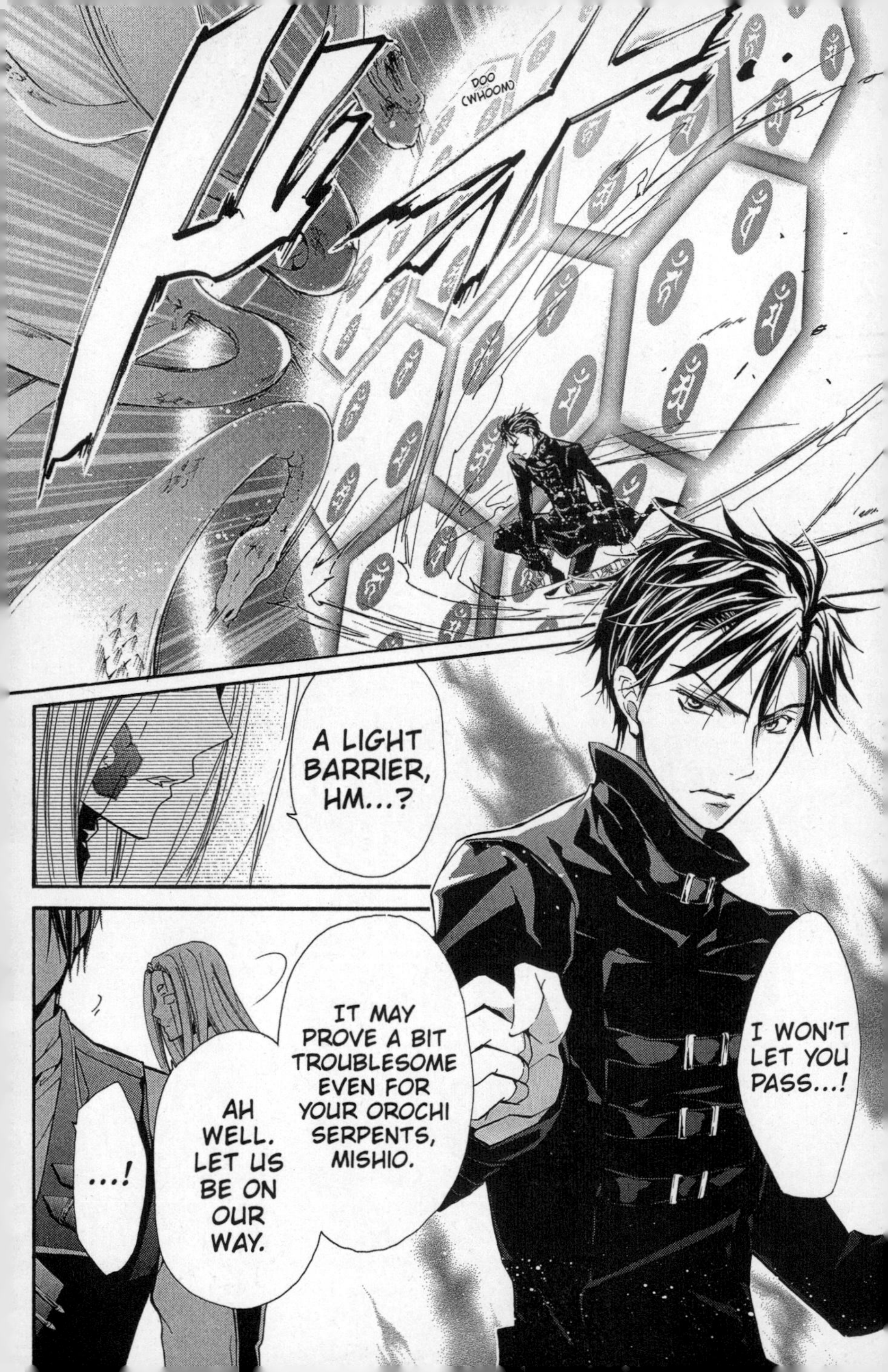
DOO (WHOOM)
A LIGHT BARRIER, HM...?
I WON'T LET YOU PASS...!
IT MAY PROVE A BIT TROUBLESOME EVEN FOR YOUR OROCHI SERPENTS, MISHIO.
AH WELL. LET US BE ON OUR WAY.
...!

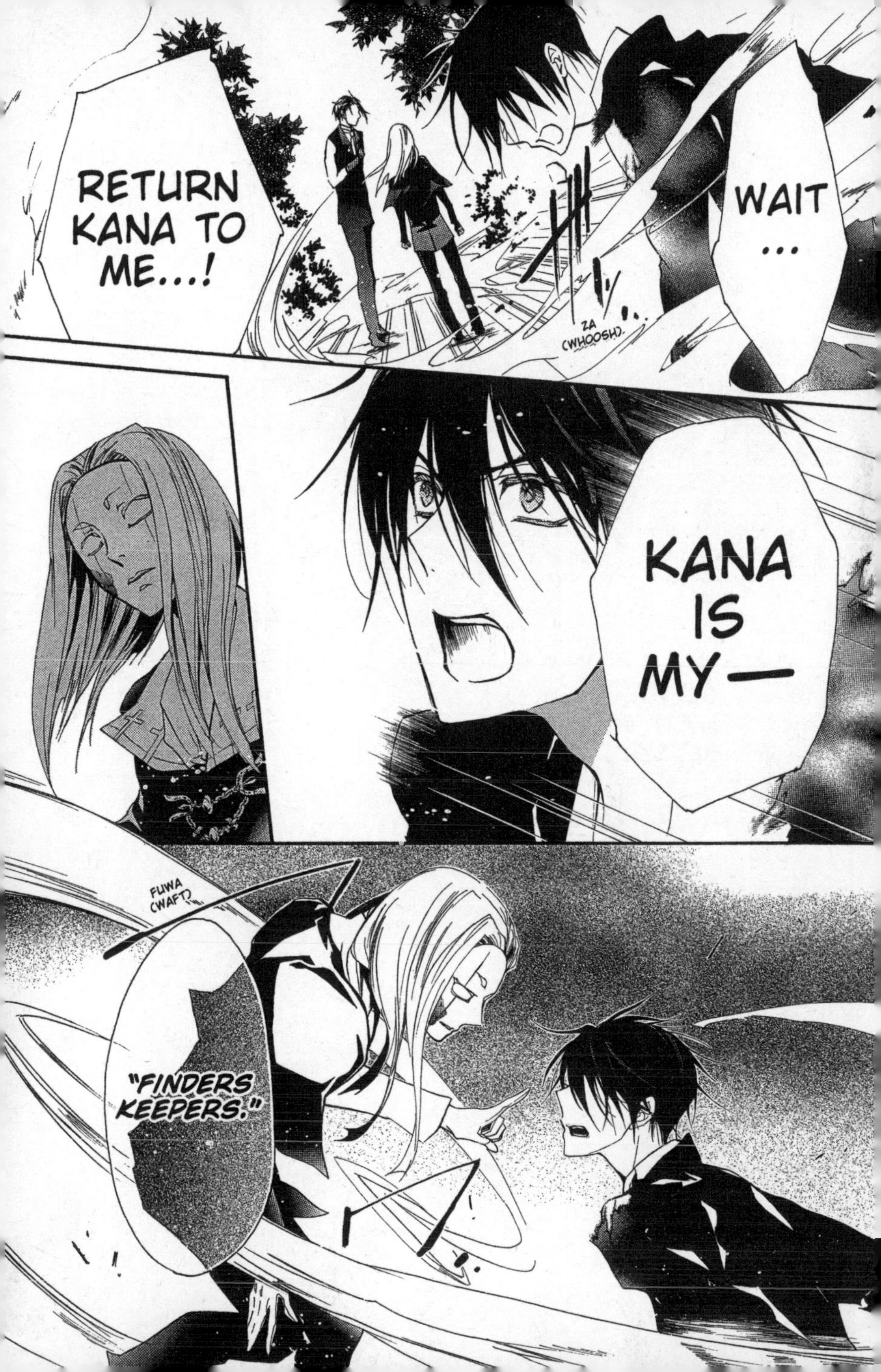
WAIT...
ZA (WHOOSH)
RETURN KANA TO ME...!
KANA IS MY—
FUWA (WAFT)
"FINDERS KEEPERS."

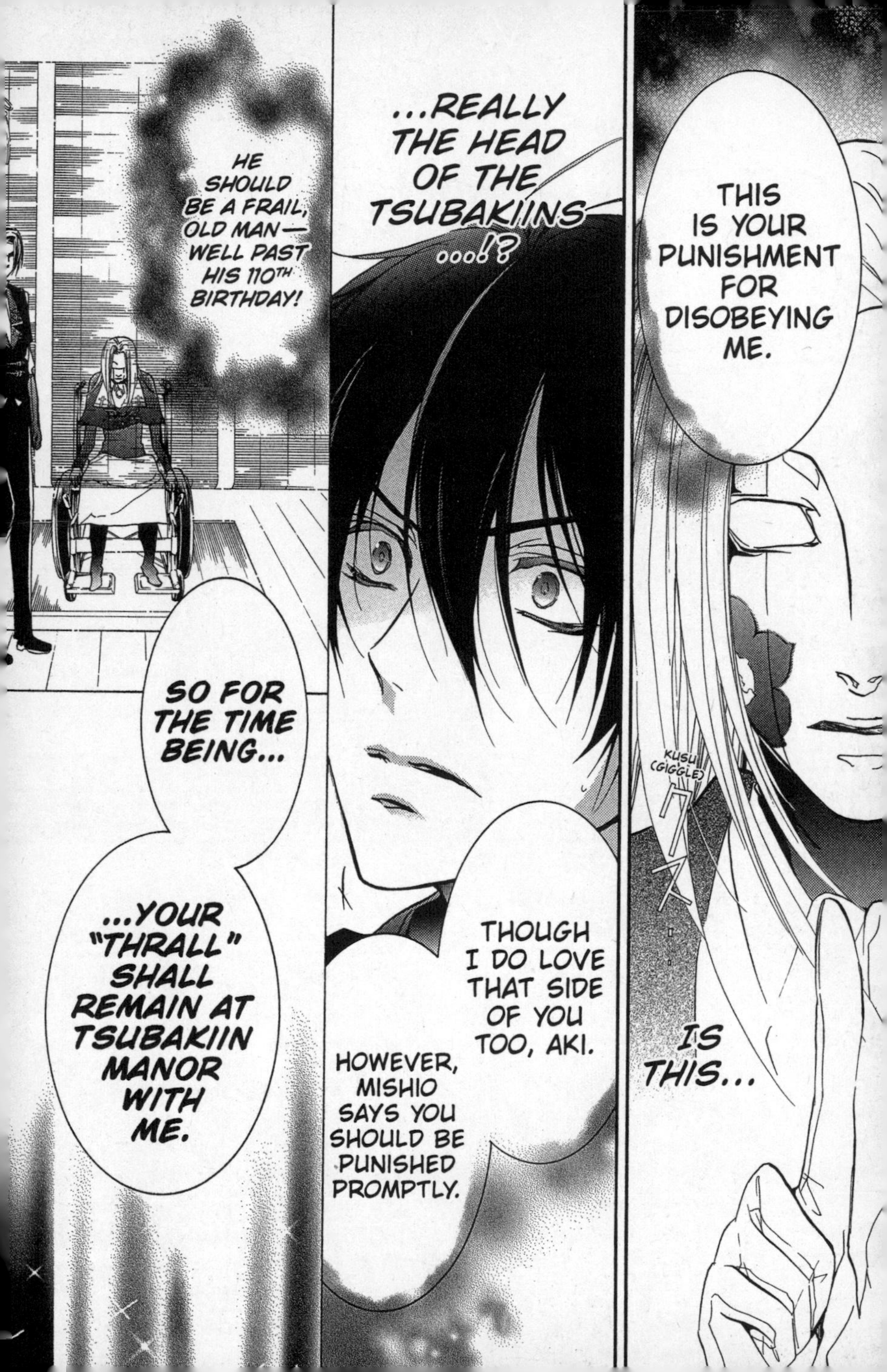
THIS IS YOUR PUNISHMENT FOR DISOBEYING ME.
KUSU (GIGGLE)
IS THIS...
...REALLY THE HEAD OF THE TSUBAKIINS ...!?
THOUGH I DO LOVE THAT SIDE OF YOU TOO, AKI.
HOWEVER, MISHIO SAYS YOU SHOULD BE PUNISHED PROMPTLY.
HE SHOULD BE A FRAIL, OLD MAN— WELL PAST HIS 110TH BIRTHDAY!
SO FOR THE TIME BEING...
...YOUR "THRALL" SHALL REMAIN AT TSUBAKIIN MANOR WITH ME.

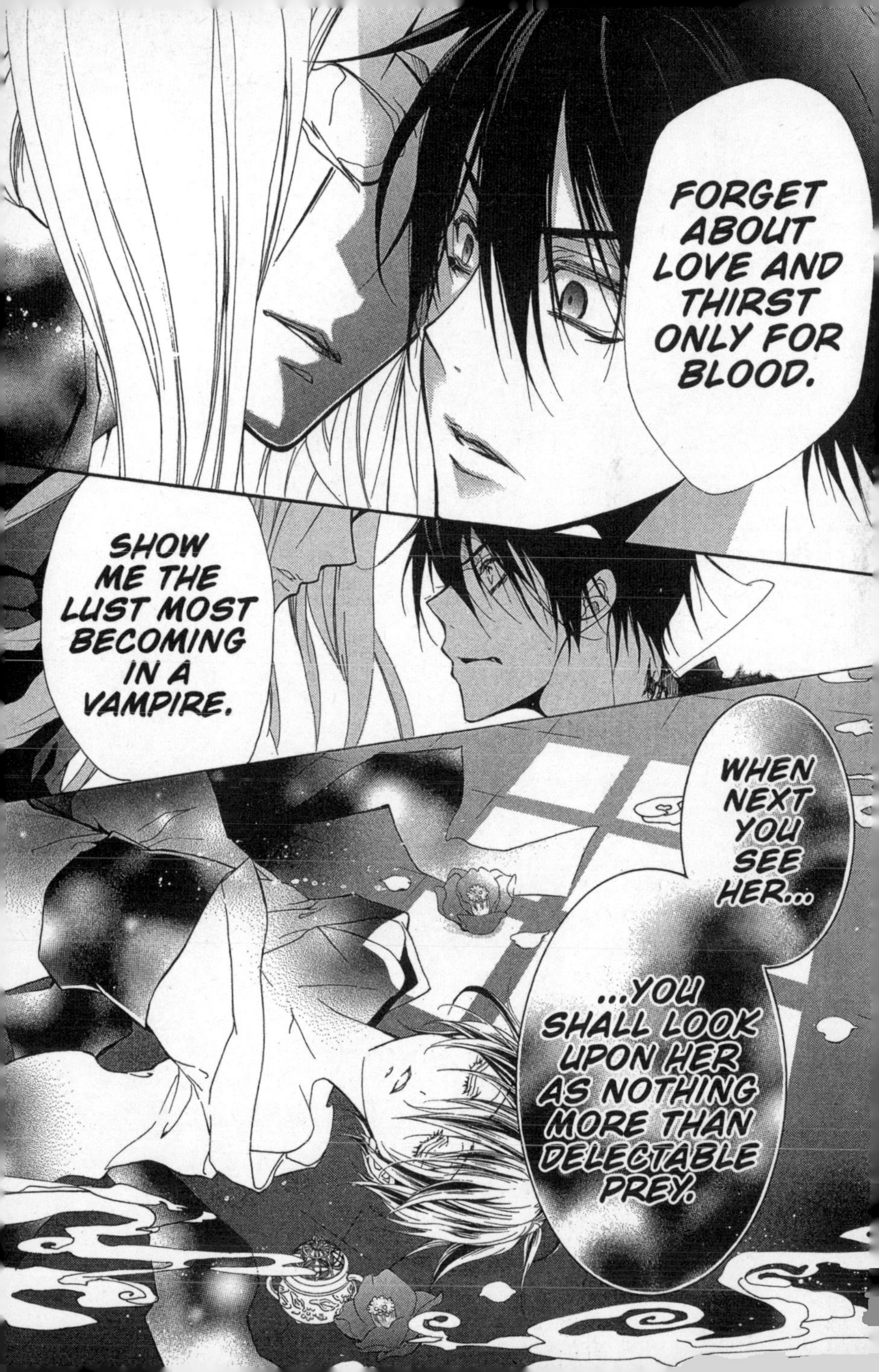
FORGET ABOUT LOVE AND THIRST ONLY FOR BLOOD.
SHOW ME THE LUST MOST BECOMING IN A VAMPIRE.
WHEN NEXT YOU SEE HER...
...YOU SHALL LOOK UPON HER AS NOTHING MORE THAN DELECTABLE PREY.

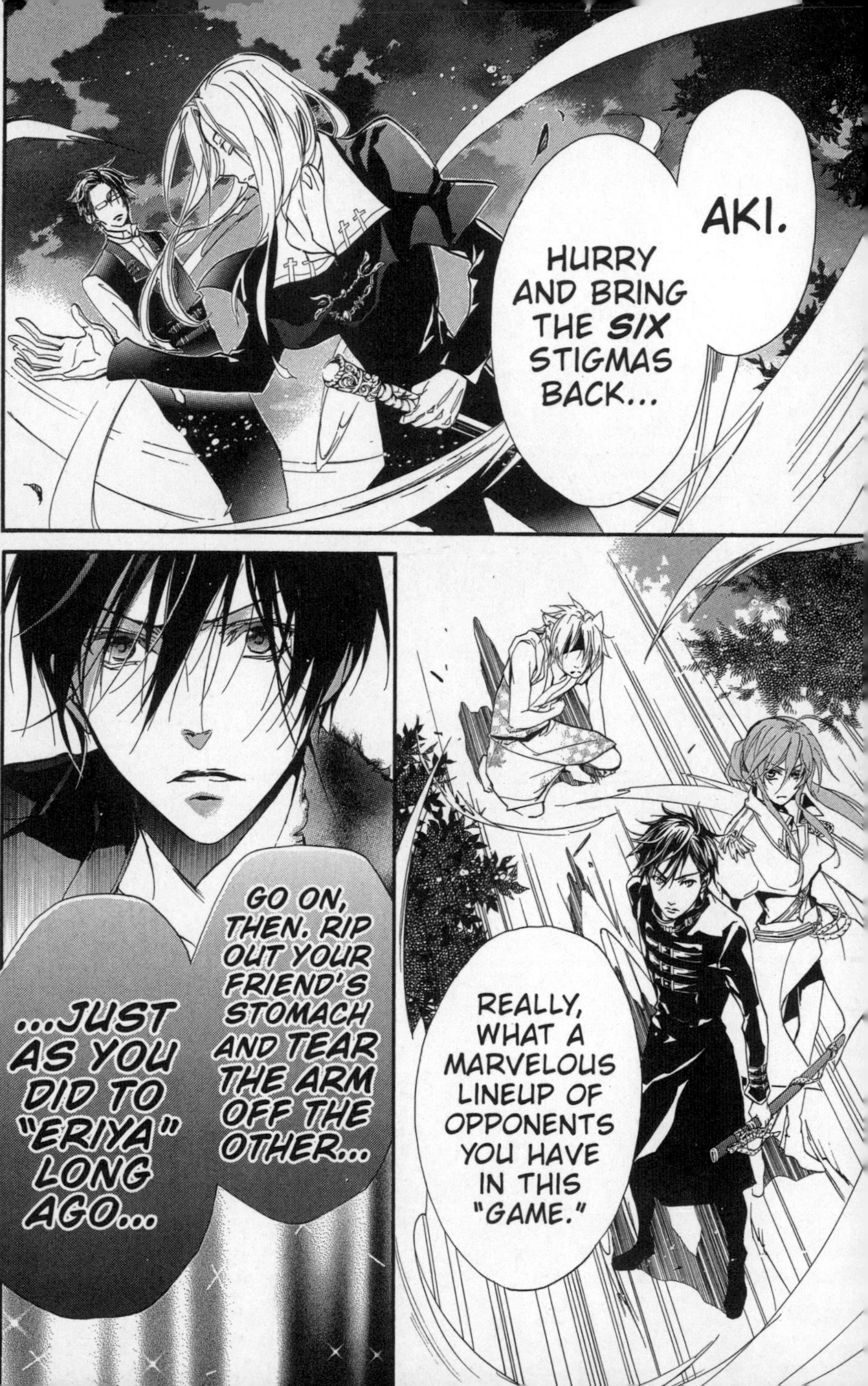
AKI.
HURRY AND BRING THE SIX STIGMAS BACK...
REALLY, WHAT A MARVELOUS LINEUP OF OPPONENTS YOU HAVE IN THIS "GAME."
GO ON, THEN. RIP OUT YOUR FRIEND'S STOMACH AND TEAR THE ARM OFF THE OTHER...
...JUST AS YOU DID TO "ERIYA" LONG AGO...

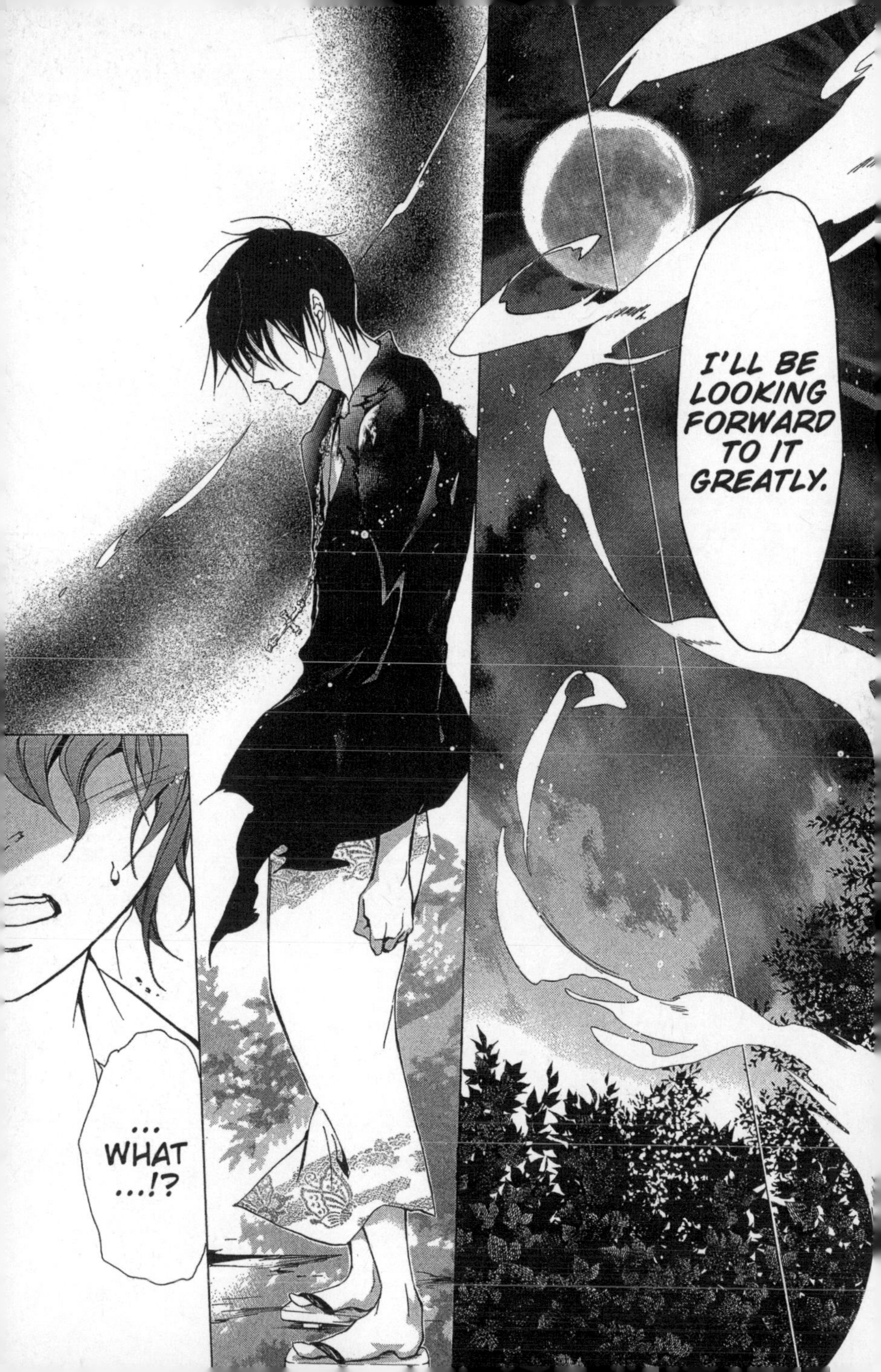
I'LL BE LOOKING FORWARD TO IT GREATLY.
... WHAT ...!?

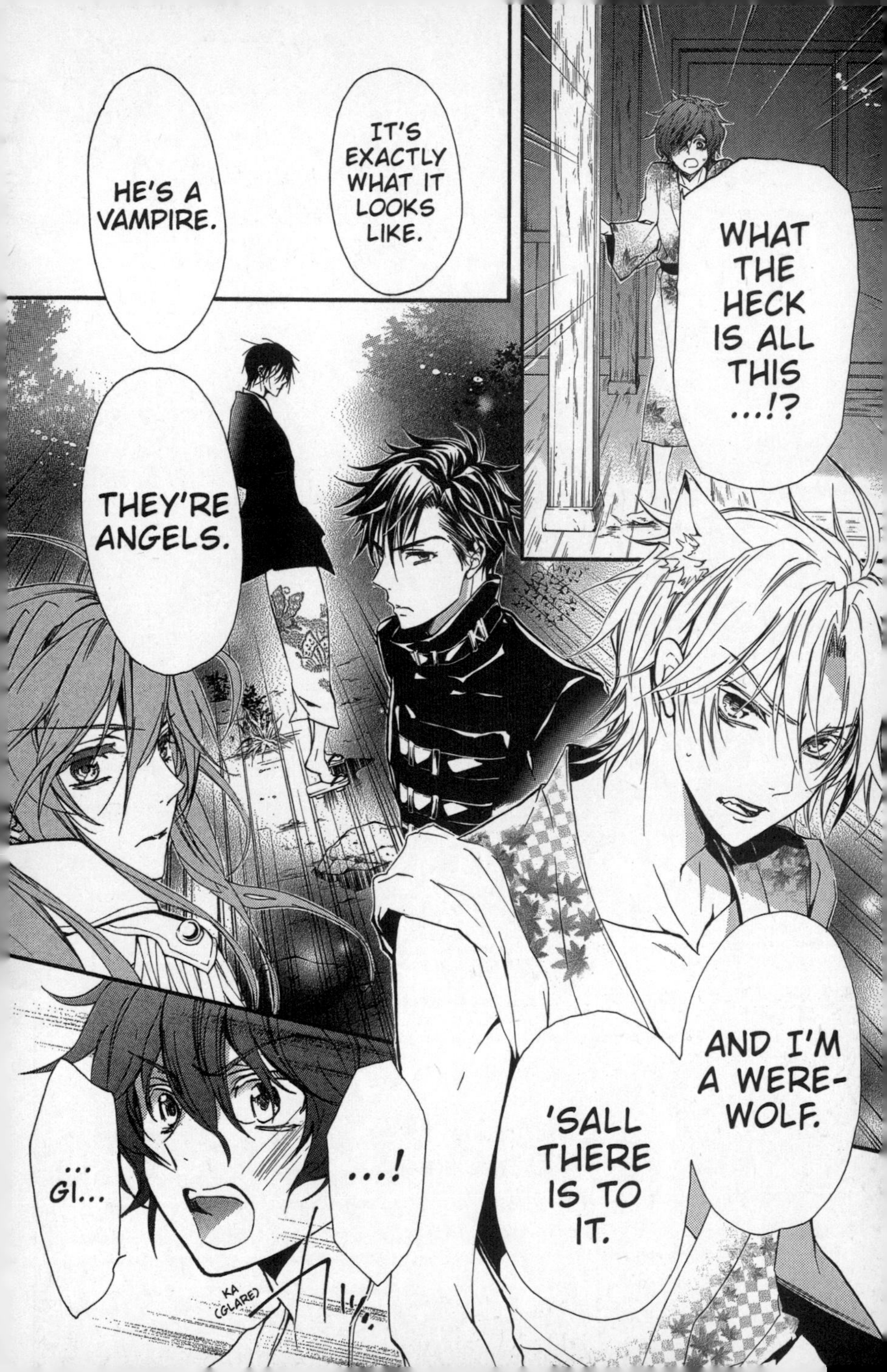
WHAT THE HECK IS ALL THIS ...!?
IT'S EXACTLY WHAT IT LOOKS LIKE.
HE'S A VAMPIRE.
THEY'RE ANGELS.
AND I'M A WERE-WOLF.
'SALL THERE IS TO IT.
...!
... GI...
KA (GLARE)

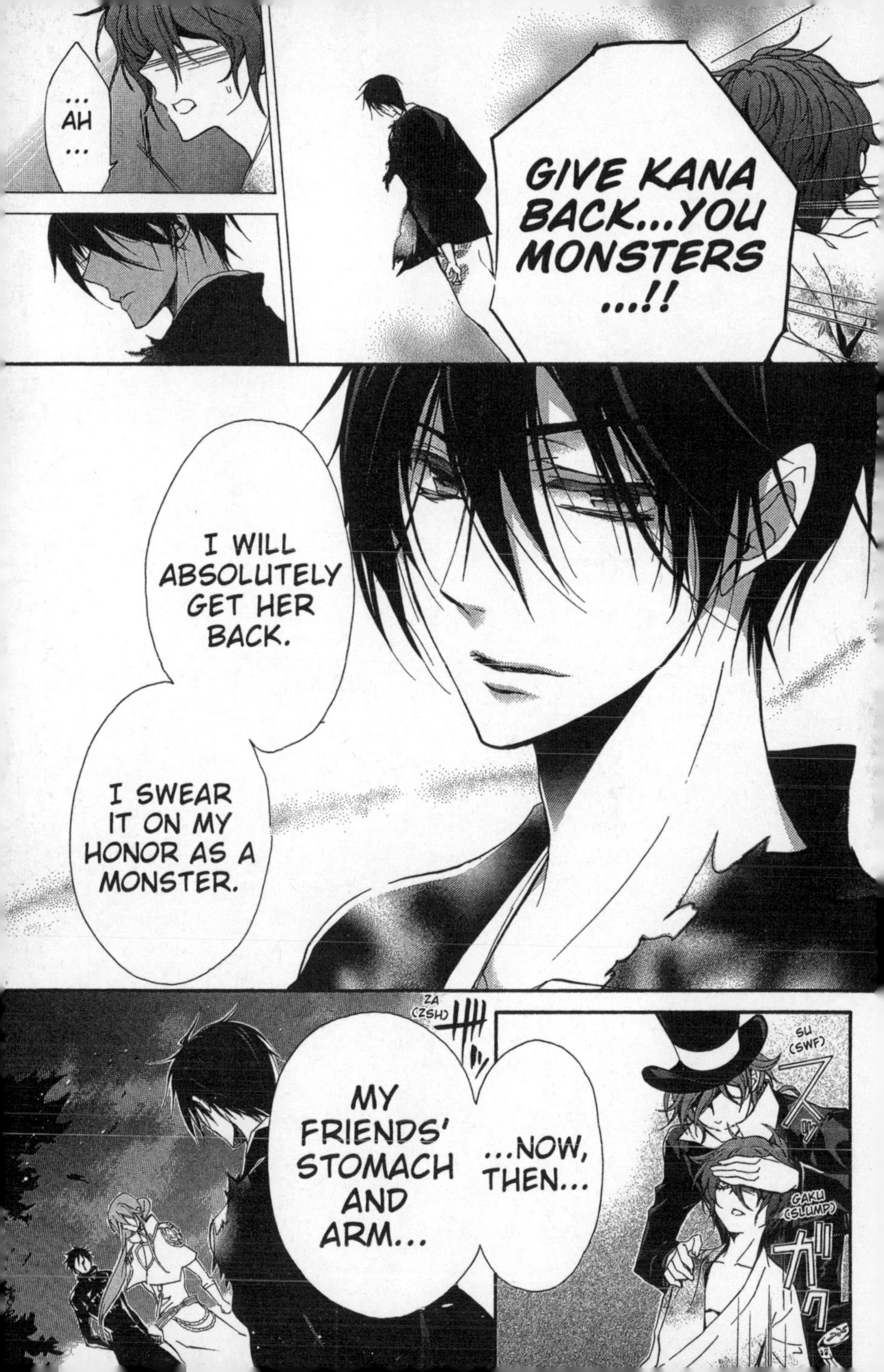
GIVE KANA BACK...YOU MONSTERS ...!!
...AH...
I WILL ABSOLUTELY GET HER BACK.
I SWEAR IT ON MY HONOR AS A MONSTER.
SU (SWF)
GAKU (SLUMP)
...NOW, THEN...
MY FRIENDS' STOMACH AND ARM...
ZA (ZSH)

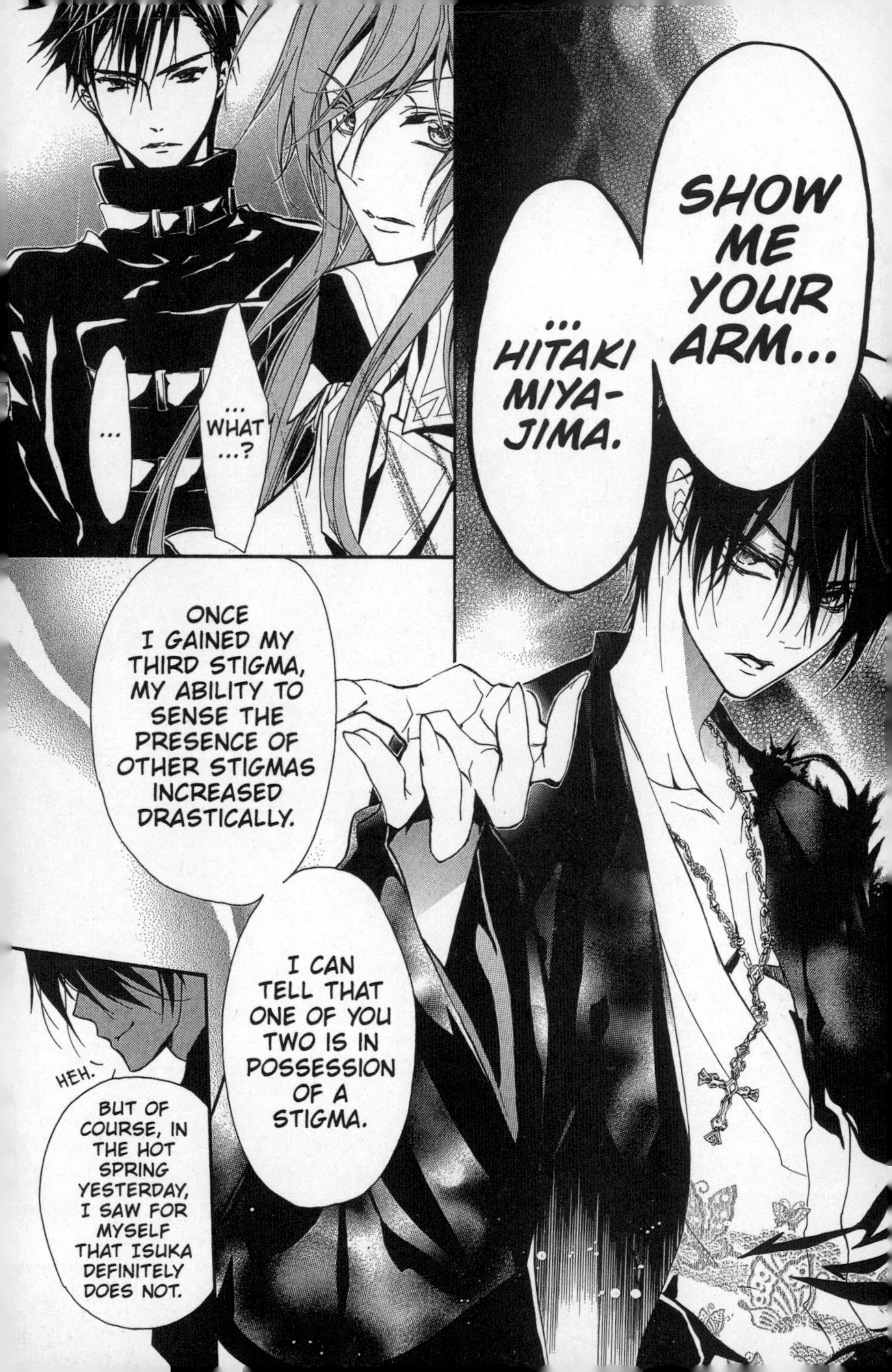
SHOW ME YOUR ARM...
...HITAKI MIYAJIMA.
...WHAT...?
...
ONCE I GAINED MY THIRD STIGMA, MY ABILITY TO SENSE THE PRESENCE OF OTHER STIGMAS INCREASED DRASTICALLY.
I CAN TELL THAT ONE OF YOU TWO IS IN POSSESSION OF A STIGMA.
HEH.
BUT OF COURSE, IN THE HOT SPRING YESTERDAY, I SAW FOR MYSELF THAT ISUKA DEFINITELY DOES NOT.

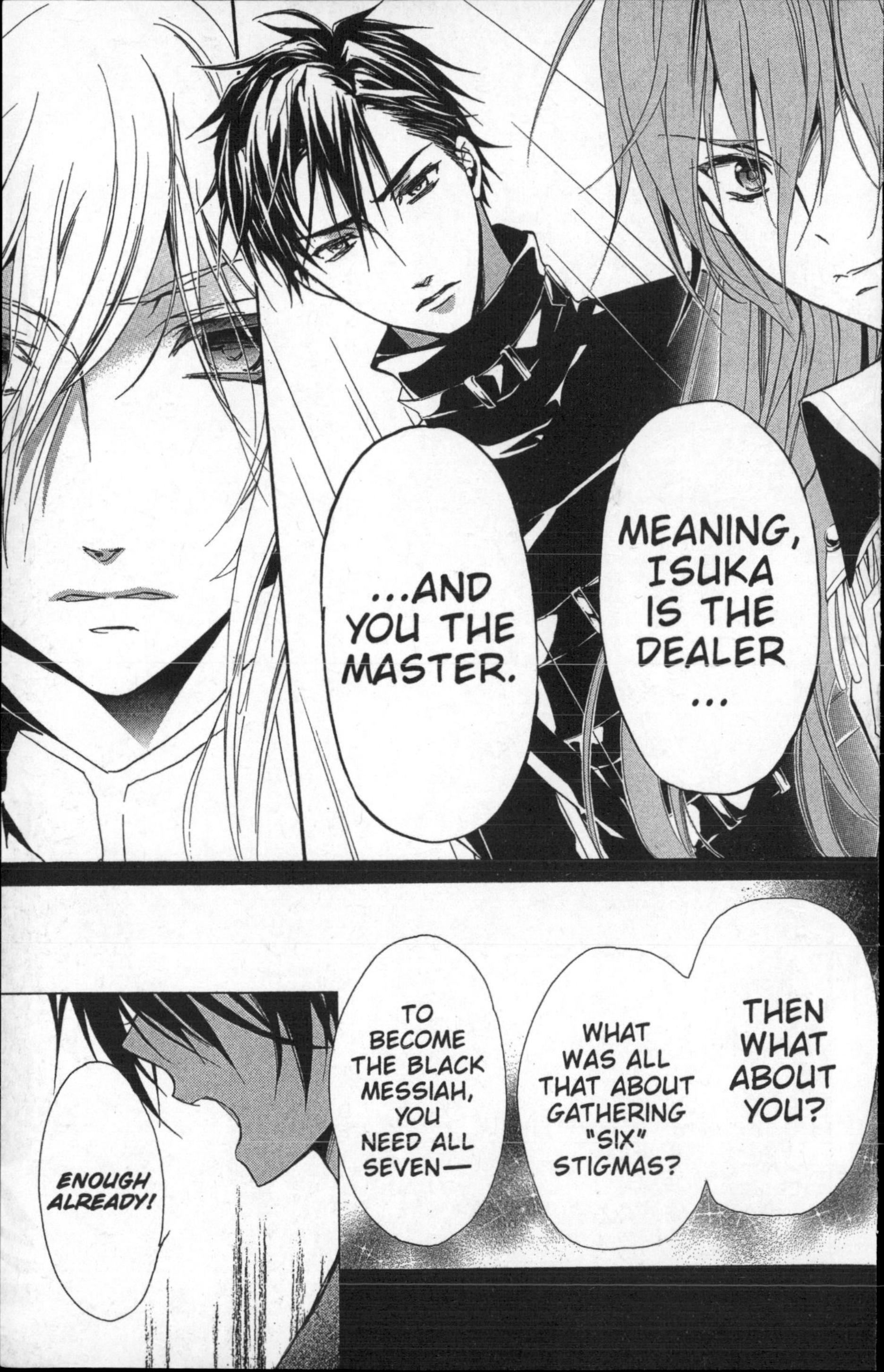
MEANING, ISUKA IS THE DEALER ...
...AND YOU THE MASTER.
THEN WHAT ABOUT YOU?
WHAT WAS ALL THAT ABOUT GATHERING "SIX" STIGMAS?
TO BECOME THE BLACK MESSIAH, YOU NEED ALL SEVEN—
ENOUGH ALREADY!

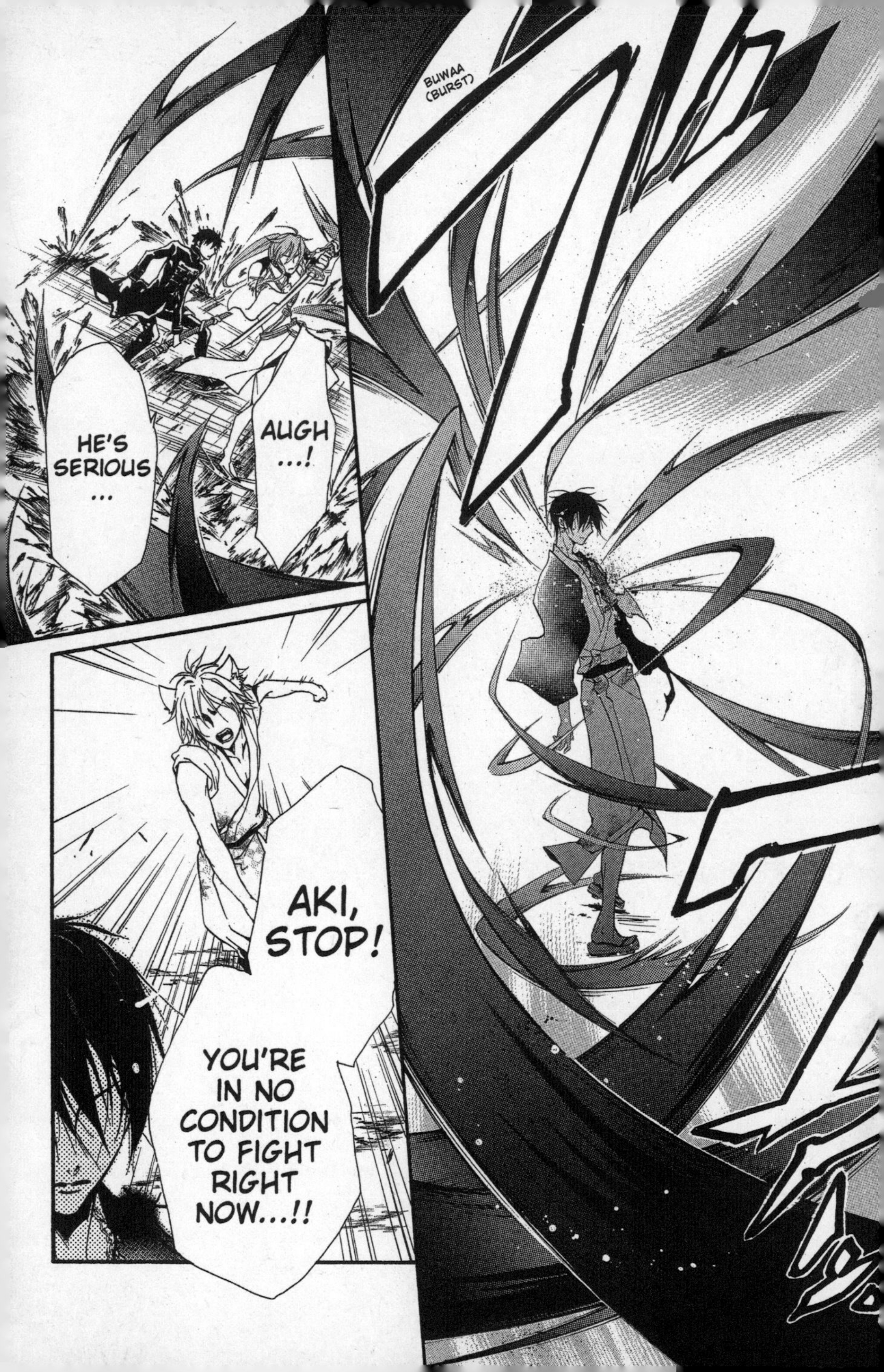
BUWAA (BURST)
AUGH ...!
HE'S SERIOUS ...
AKI, STOP!
YOU'RE IN NO CONDITION TO FIGHT RIGHT NOW...!!

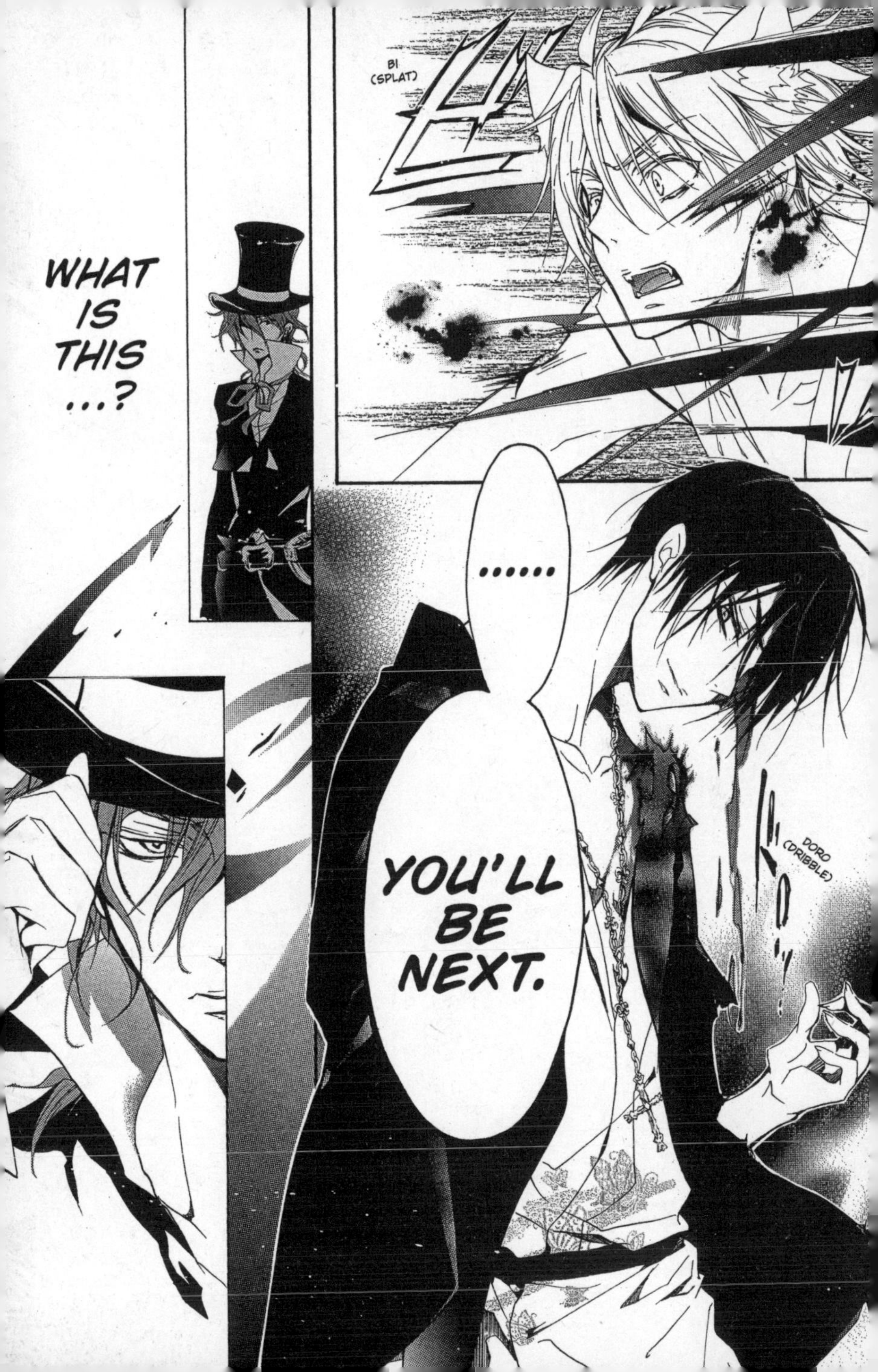
BI
(SPLAT)
WHAT IS THIS ...?
......
YOU'LL BE NEXT.
DORO
(DRIBBLE)

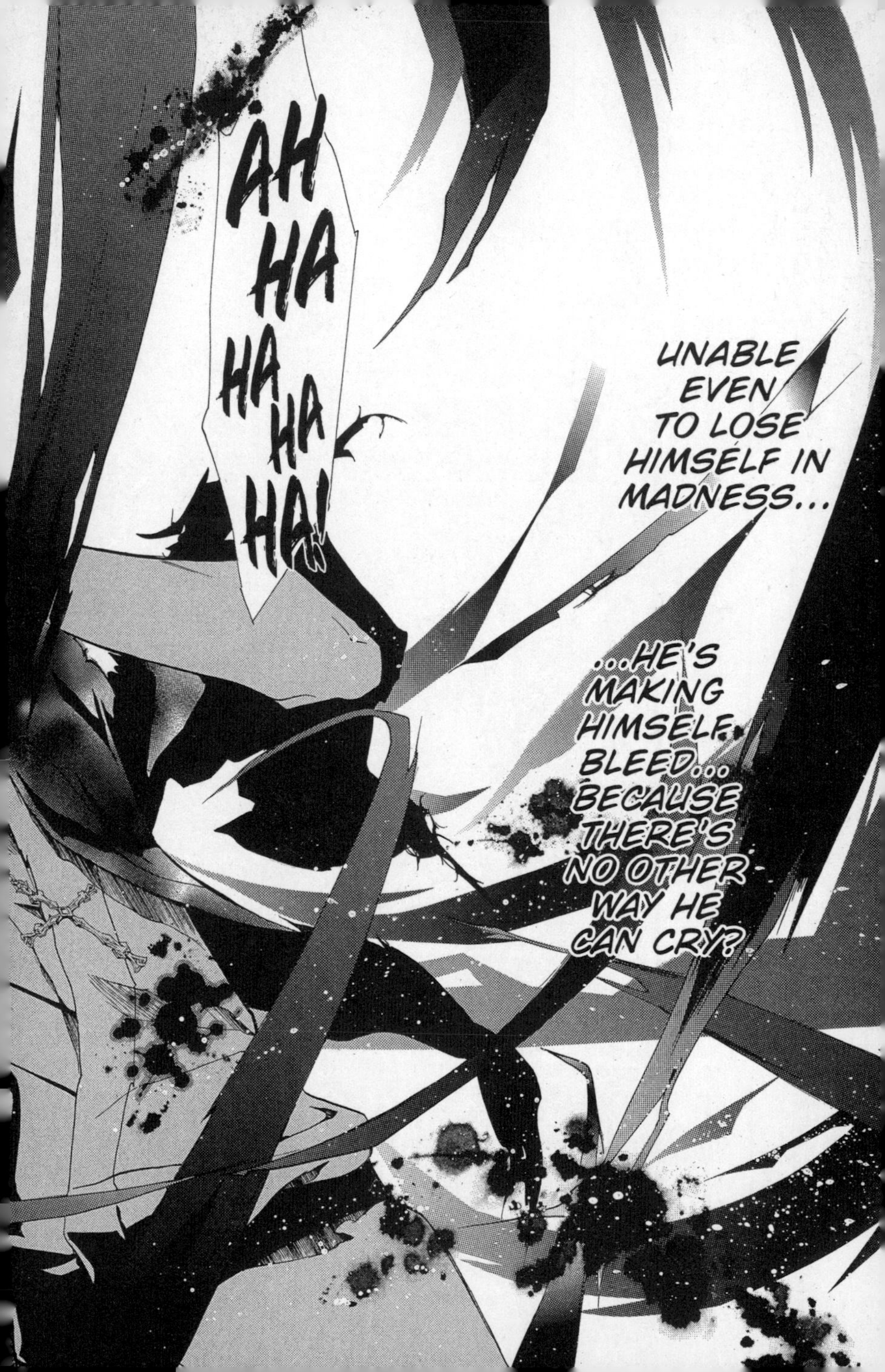
UNABLE EVEN TO LOSE HIMSELF IN MADNESS...
...HE'S MAKING HIMSELF BLEED... BECAUSE THERE'S NO OTHER WAY HE CAN CRY?
AH HA HA HA HA!

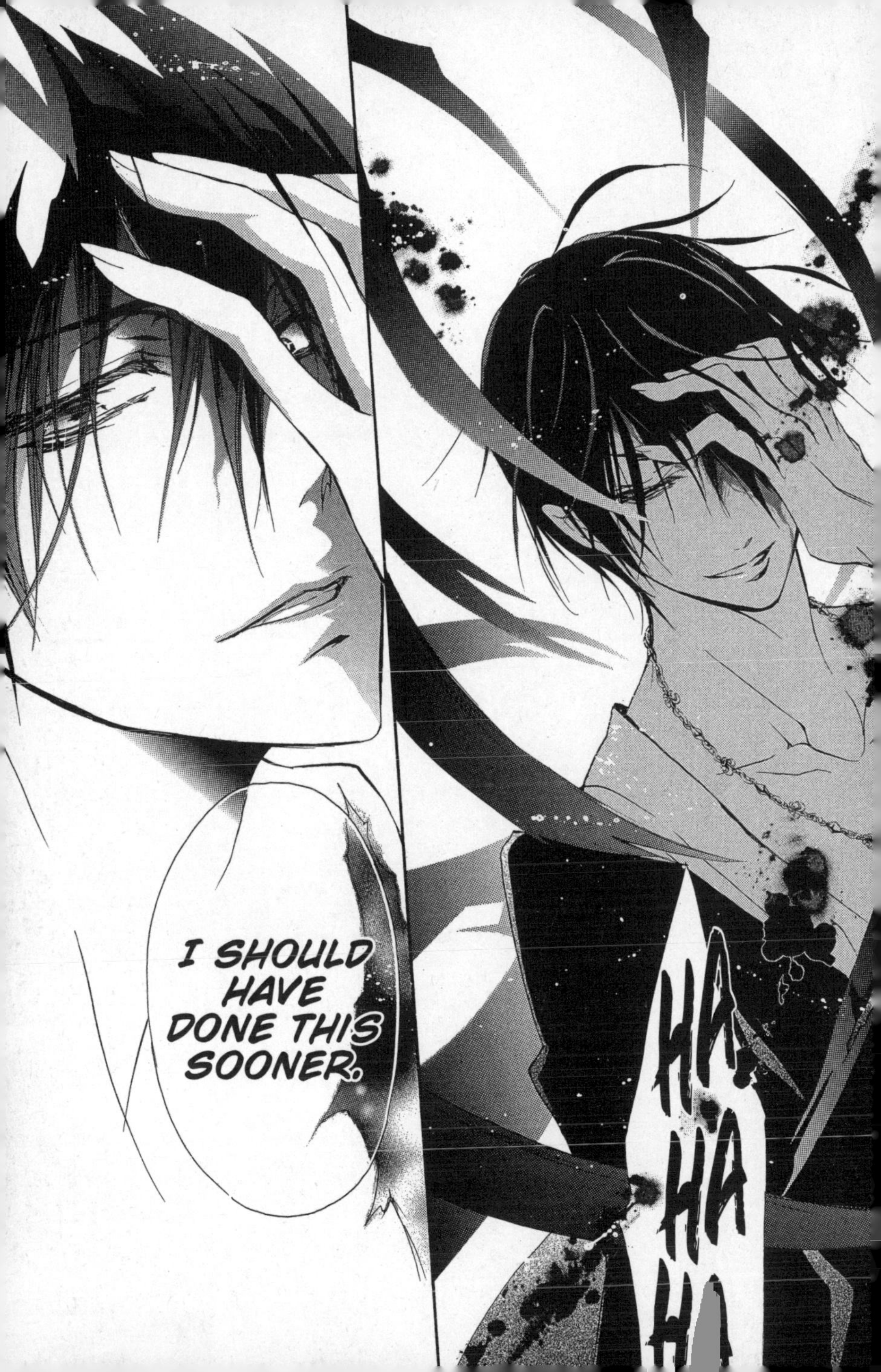
I SHOULD HAVE DONE THIS SOONER.
HA HA HA HA

He's my only vampire
Aya Shouoto

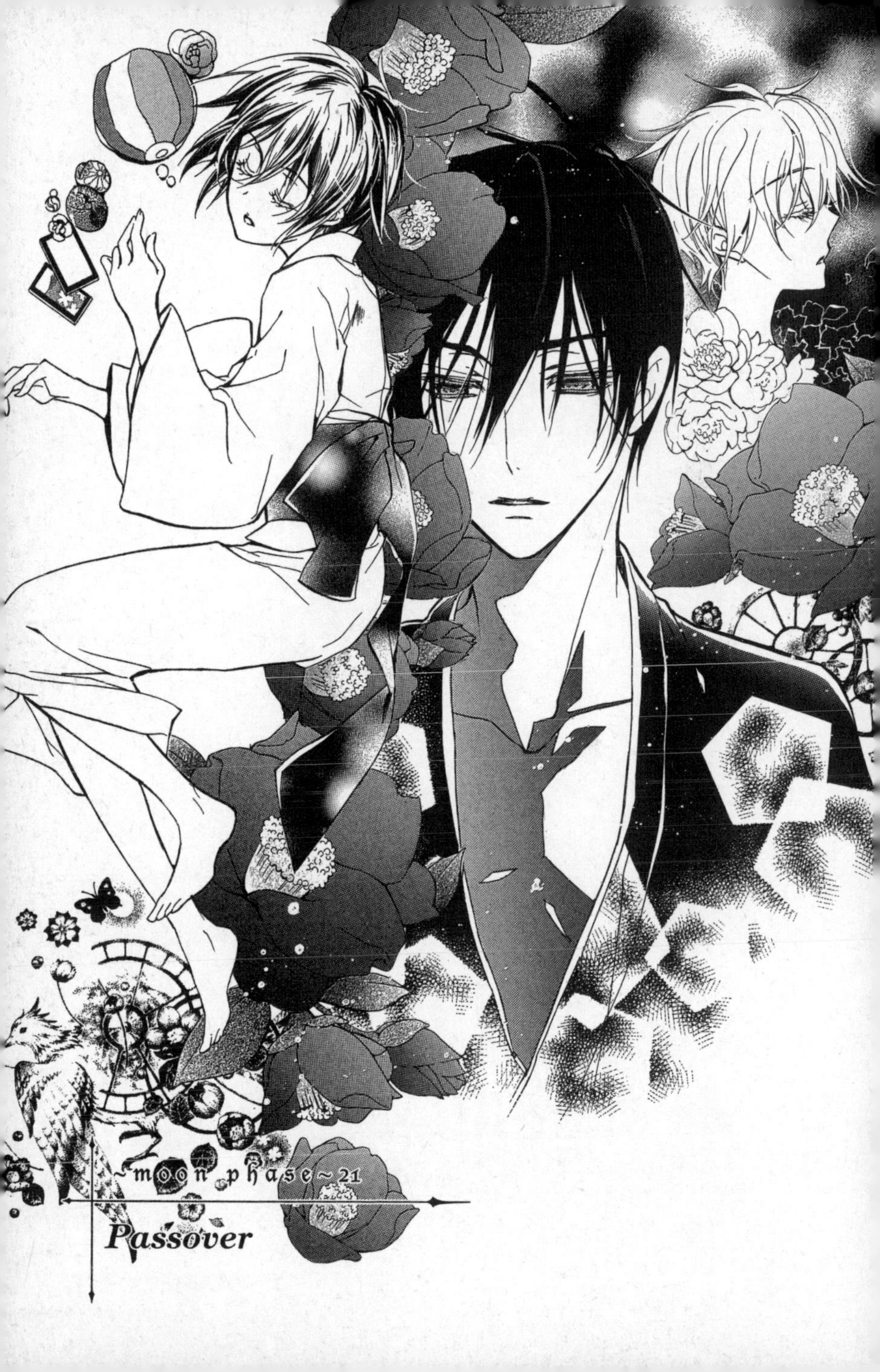
~moon phase~21
Passover

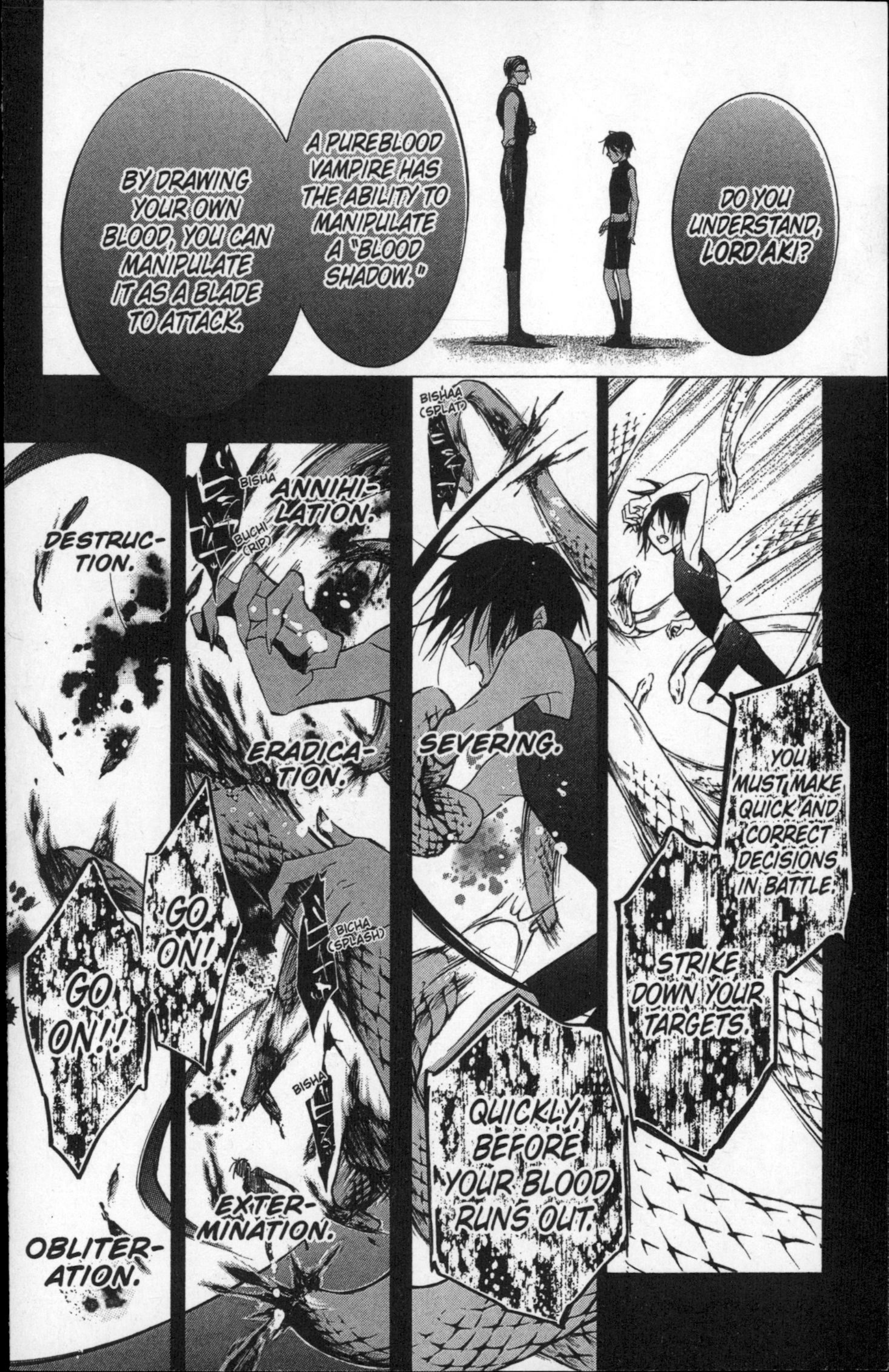
DO YOU UNDERSTAND, LORD AKI?
A PUREBLOOD VAMPIRE HAS THE ABILITY TO MANIPULATE A "BLOOD SHADOW."
BY DRAWING YOUR OWN BLOOD, YOU CAN MANIPULATE IT AS A BLADE TO ATTACK.
YOU MUST MAKE QUICK AND CORRECT DECISIONS IN BATTLE.
STRIKE DOWN YOUR TARGETS.
BISHAA (SPLAT)
SEVERING.
QUICKLY, BEFORE YOUR BLOOD RUNS OUT.
BISHA
ANNIHILATION.
BUCHI (RIP)
ERADICATION.
BICHA (SPLASH)
GO ON!
BISHA
EXTERMINATION.
DESTRUCTION.
GO ON!!
OBLITERATION.

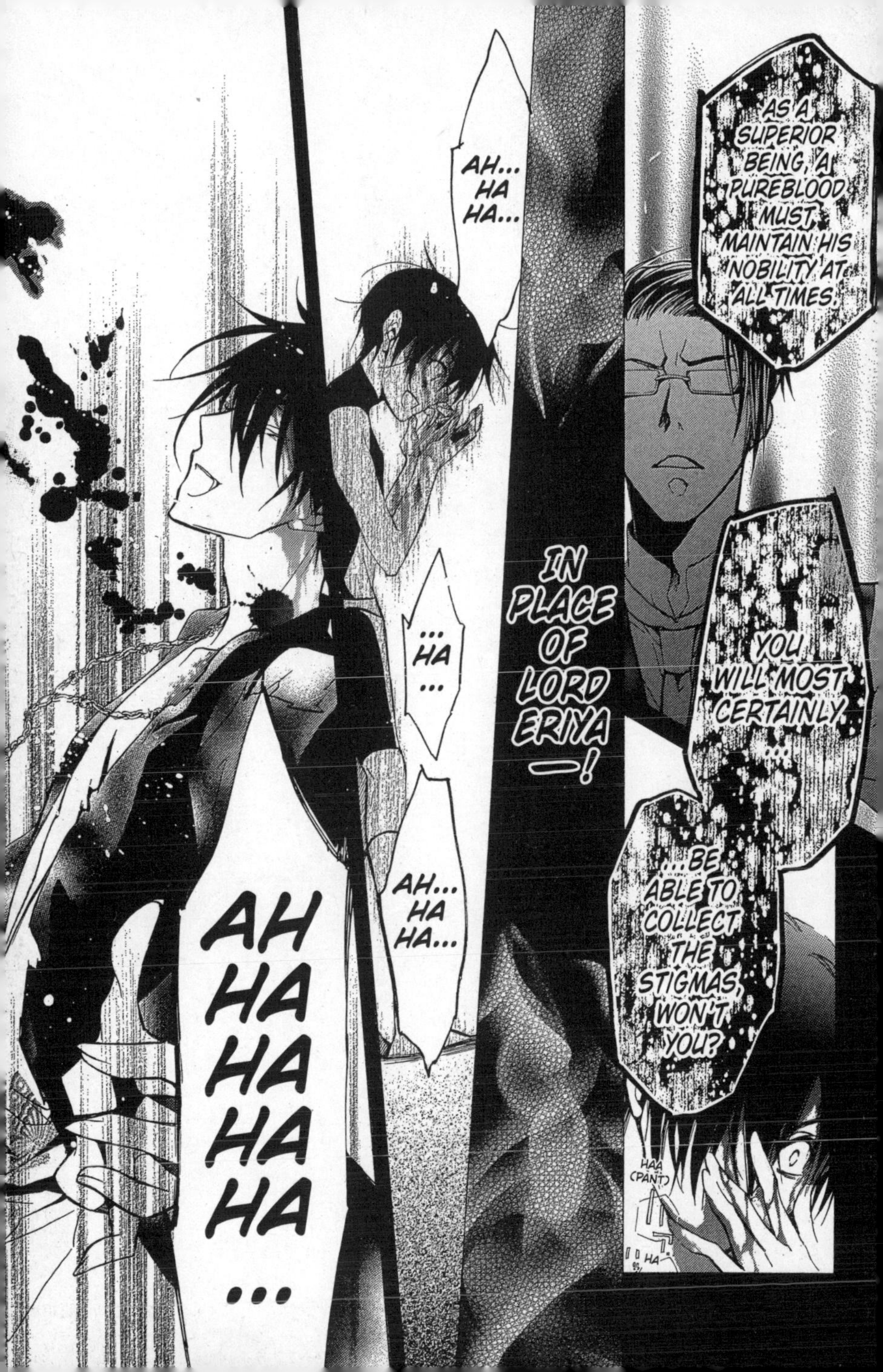
AS A SUPERIOR BEING, A PUREBLOOD MUST MAINTAIN HIS NOBILITY AT ALL TIMES.
IN PLACE OF LORD ERIYA—!
YOU WILL MOST CERTAINLY...
...BE ABLE TO COLLECT THE STIGMAS, WON'T YOU?
HAA (PANT)
HA
AH... HA HA...
...HA...
AH... HA HA...
AH HA HA HA HA HA...

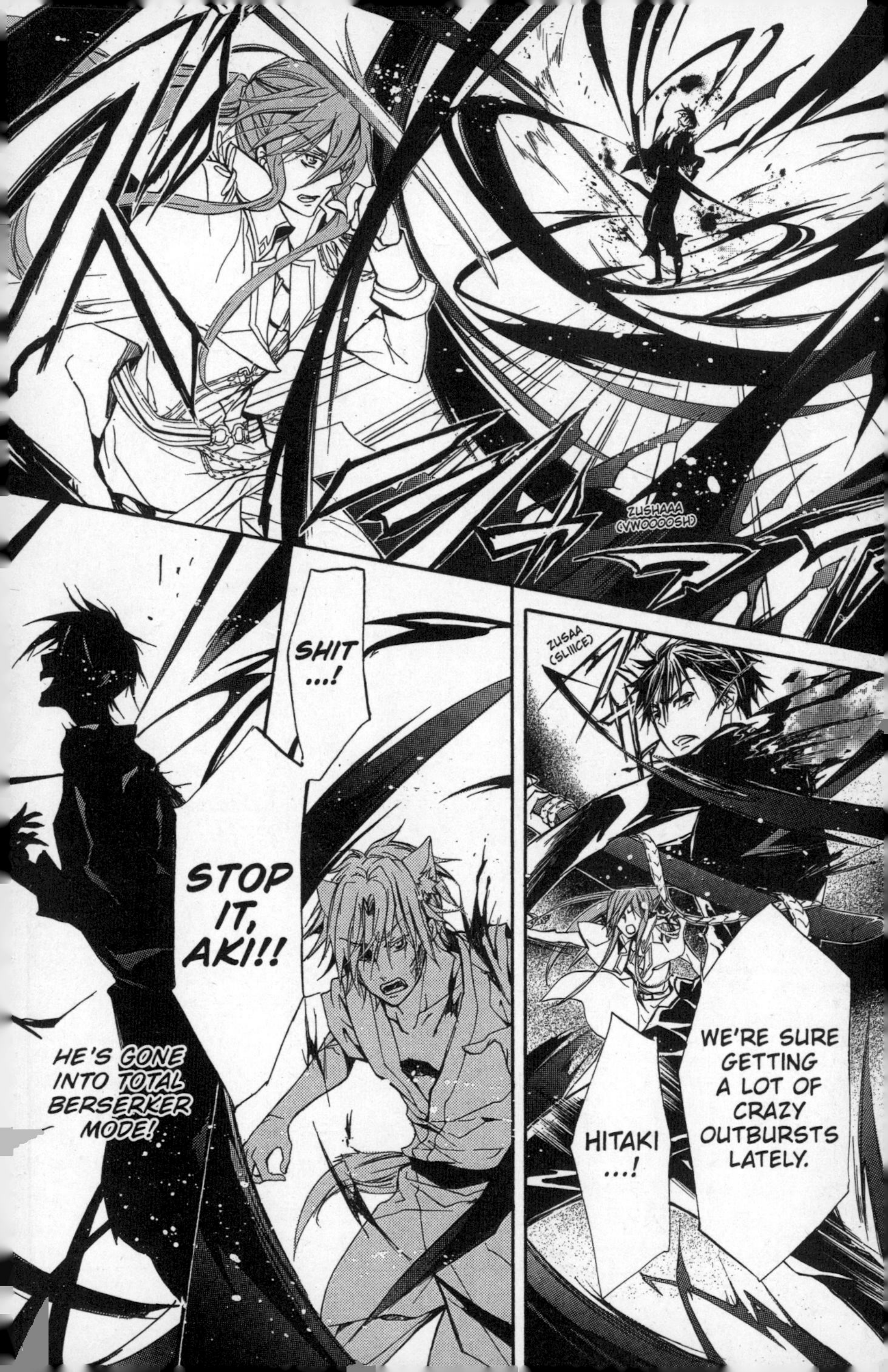
ZUSHAAA
(VWOOOOSH)
ZUSAA
(SLIICE)
WE'RE SURE GETTING A LOT OF CRAZY OUTBURSTS LATELY.
HITAKI ...!
SHIT ...!
STOP IT, AKI!!
HE'S GONE INTO TOTAL BERSERKER MODE!

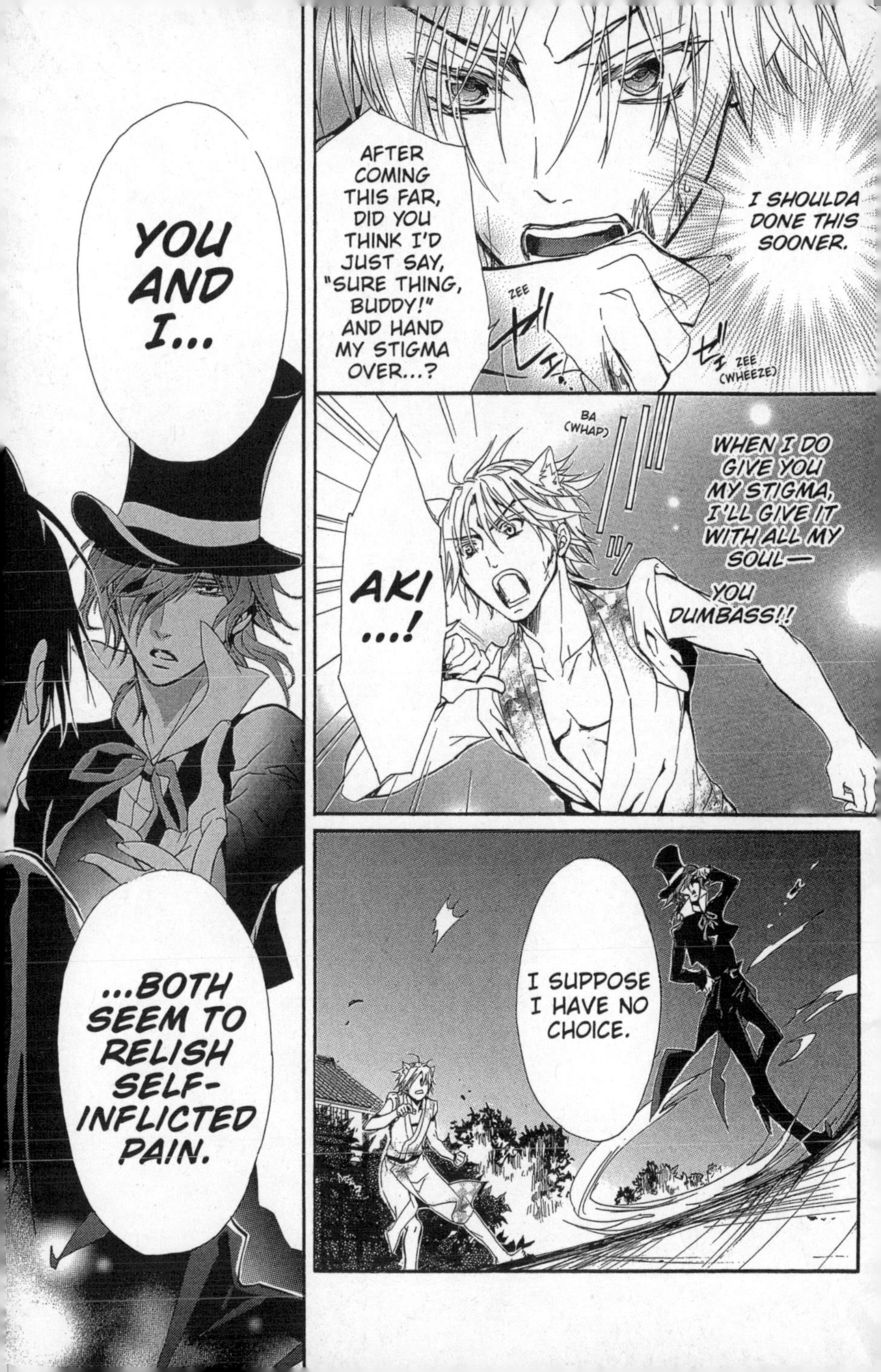
I SHOULDA DONE THIS SOONER.
AFTER COMING THIS FAR, DID YOU THINK I'D JUST SAY, "SURE THING, BUDDY!" AND HAND MY STIGMA OVER...?
ZEE (WHEEZE)
ZEE
BA (WHAP)
WHEN I DO GIVE YOU MY STIGMA, I'LL GIVE IT WITH ALL MY SOUL—
YOU DUMBASS!!
AKI ...!
I SUPPOSE I HAVE NO CHOICE.
YOU AND I...
...BOTH SEEM TO RELISH SELF-INFLICTED PAIN.

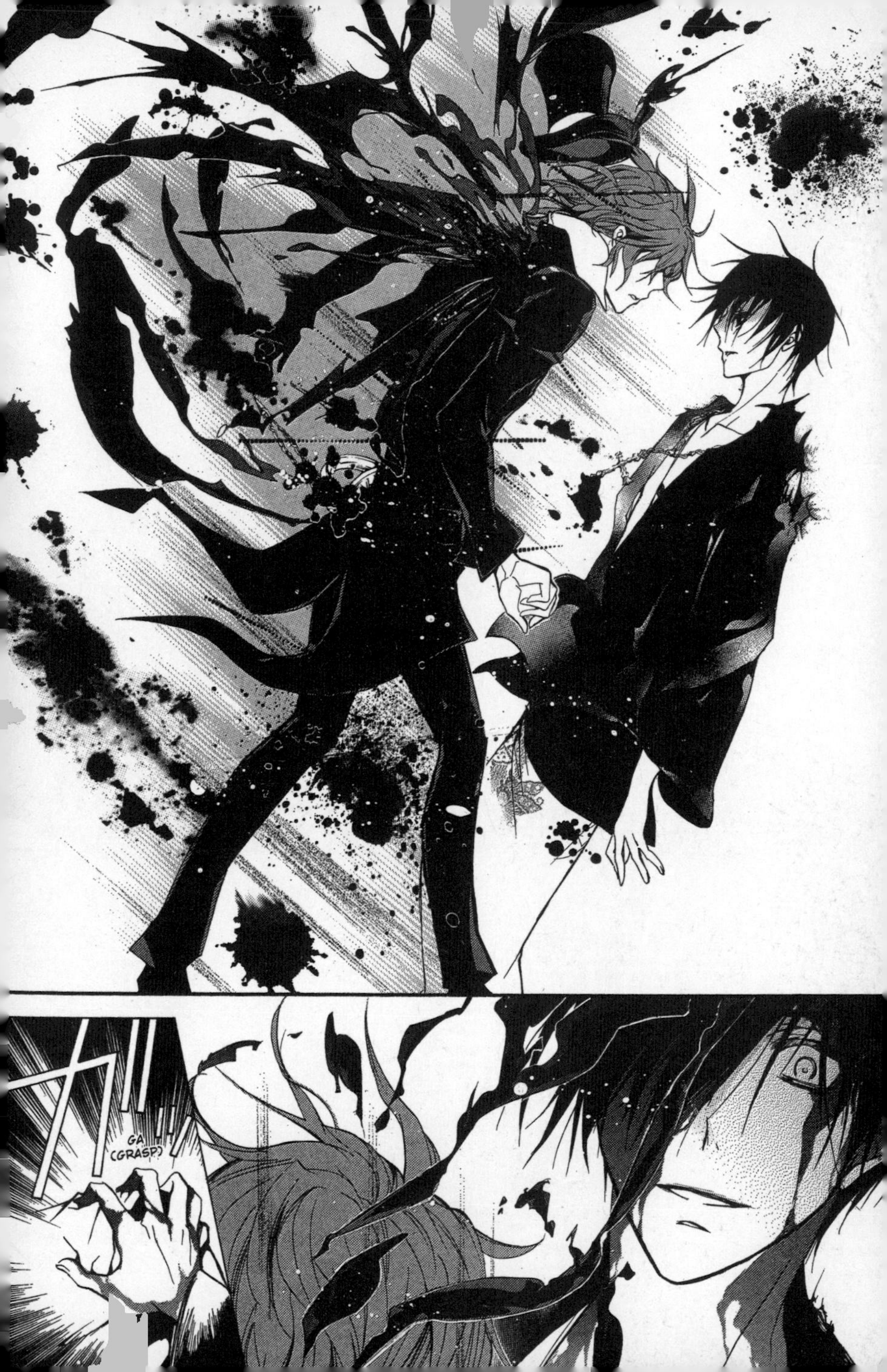
GA
(GRASP)

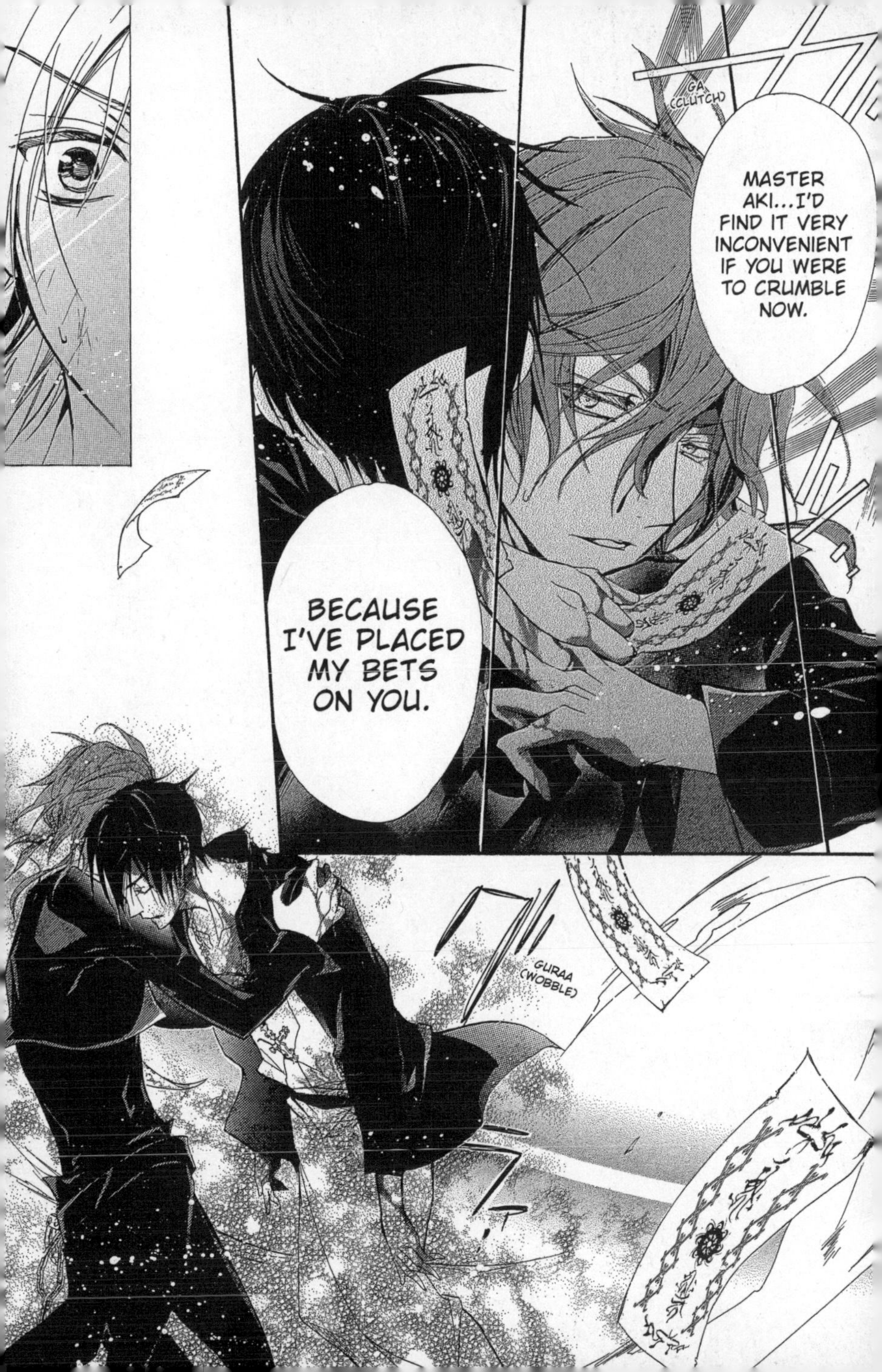
GA (CLUTCH)
MASTER AKI...I'D FIND IT VERY INCONVENIENT IF YOU WERE TO CRUMBLE NOW.
BECAUSE I'VE PLACED MY BETS ON YOU.
GURAA (WOBBLE)

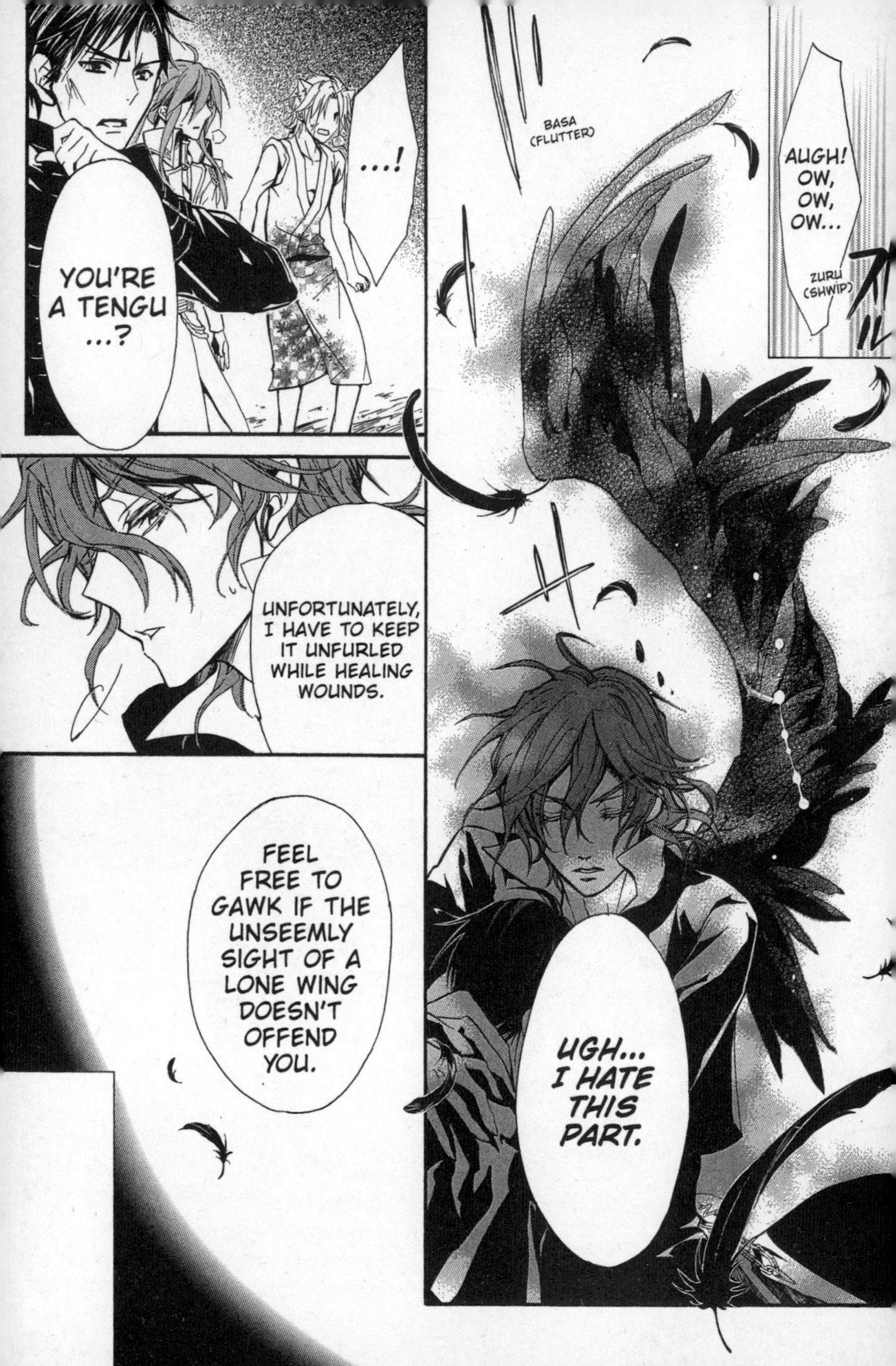
AUGH! OW, OW, OW...
ZURU (SHWIP)
BASA (FLUTTER)
UGH... I HATE THIS PART.
...!
YOU'RE A TENGU ...?
UNFORTUNATELY, I HAVE TO KEEP IT UNFURLED WHILE HEALING WOUNDS.
FEEL FREE TO GAWK IF THE UNSEEMLY SIGHT OF A LONE WING DOESN'T OFFEND YOU.

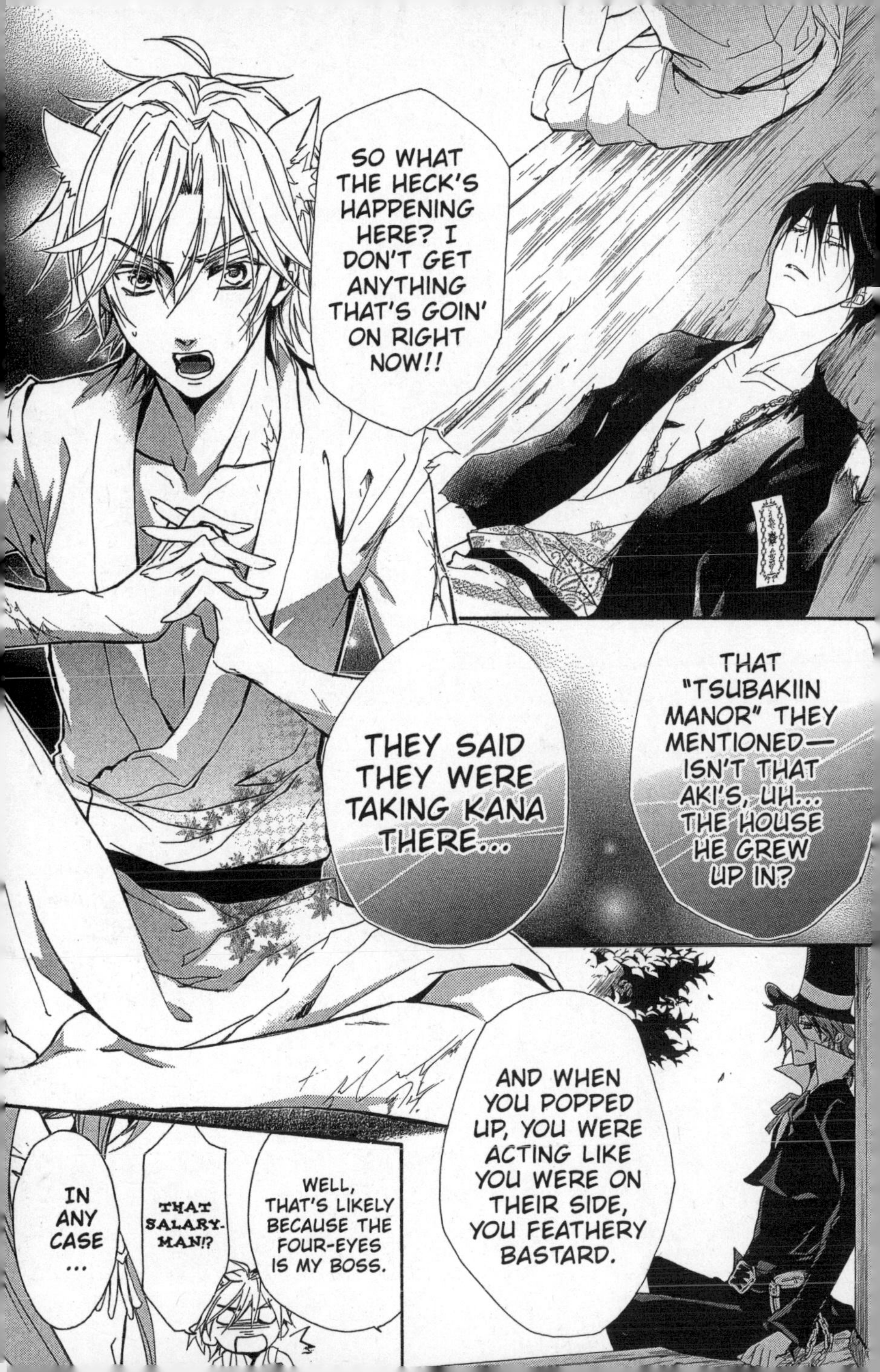
SO WHAT THE HECK'S HAPPENING HERE? I DON'T GET ANYTHING THAT'S GOIN' ON RIGHT NOW!!
THAT "TSUBAKIIN MANOR" THEY MENTIONED—ISN'T THAT AKI'S, UH... THE HOUSE HE GREW UP IN?
THEY SAID THEY WERE TAKING KANA THERE...
AND WHEN YOU POPPED UP, YOU WERE ACTING LIKE YOU WERE ON THEIR SIDE, YOU FEATHERY BASTARD.
WELL, THAT'S LIKELY BECAUSE THE FOUR-EYES IS MY BOSS.
THAT SALARY-MAN!?
IN ANY CASE ...

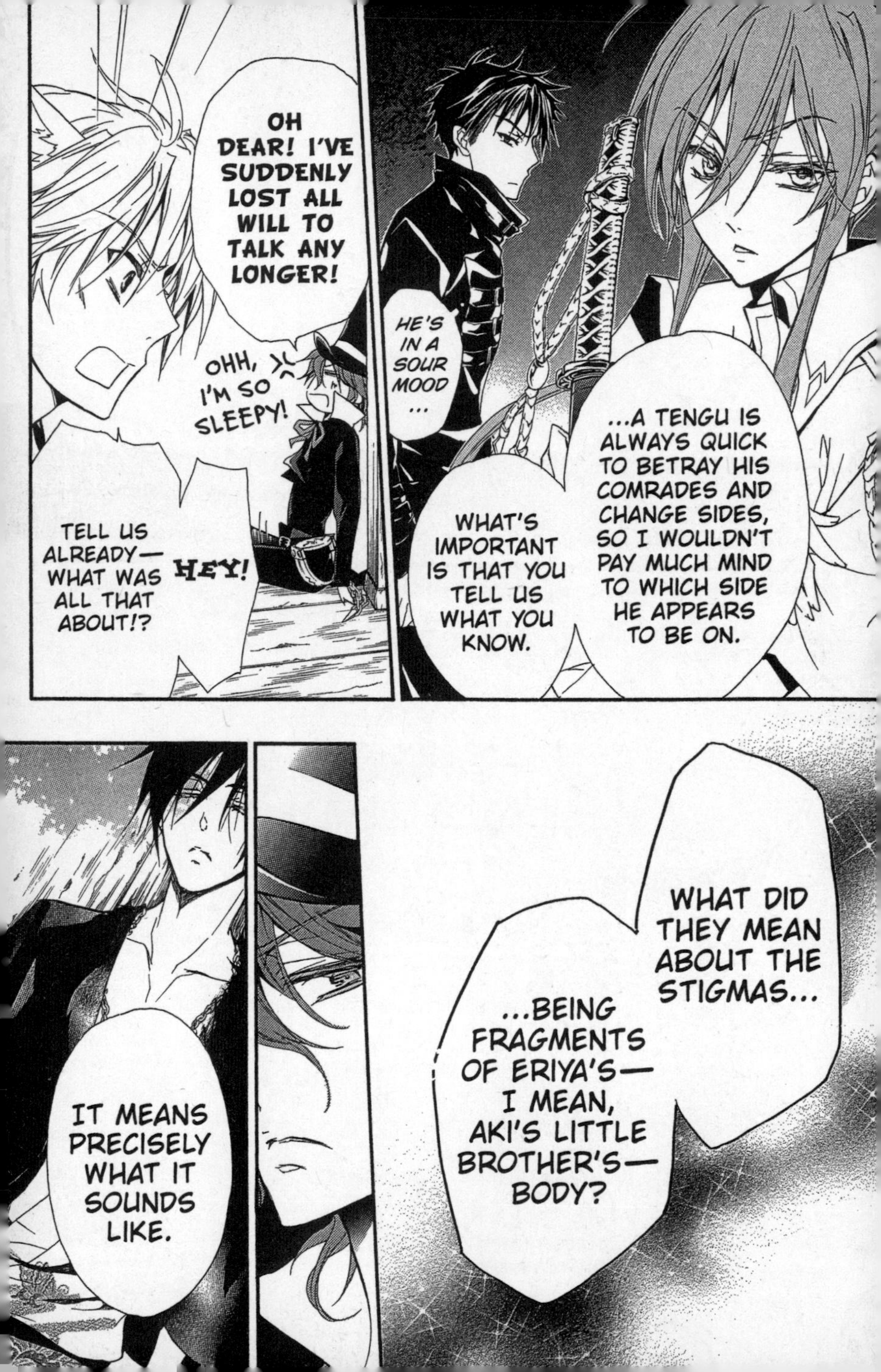
...A TENGU IS ALWAYS QUICK TO BETRAY HIS COMRADES AND CHANGE SIDES, SO I WOULDN'T PAY MUCH MIND TO WHICH SIDE HE APPEARS TO BE ON.
WHAT'S IMPORTANT IS THAT YOU TELL US WHAT YOU KNOW.
HE'S IN A SOUR MOOD ...
OH DEAR! I'VE SUDDENLY LOST ALL WILL TO TALK ANY LONGER!
OHH, I'M SO SLEEPY!
HEY!
TELL US ALREADY—WHAT WAS ALL THAT ABOUT!?
WHAT DID THEY MEAN ABOUT THE STIGMAS...
...BEING FRAGMENTS OF ERIYA'S—I MEAN, AKI'S LITTLE BROTHER'S—BODY?
IT MEANS PRECISELY WHAT IT SOUNDS LIKE.

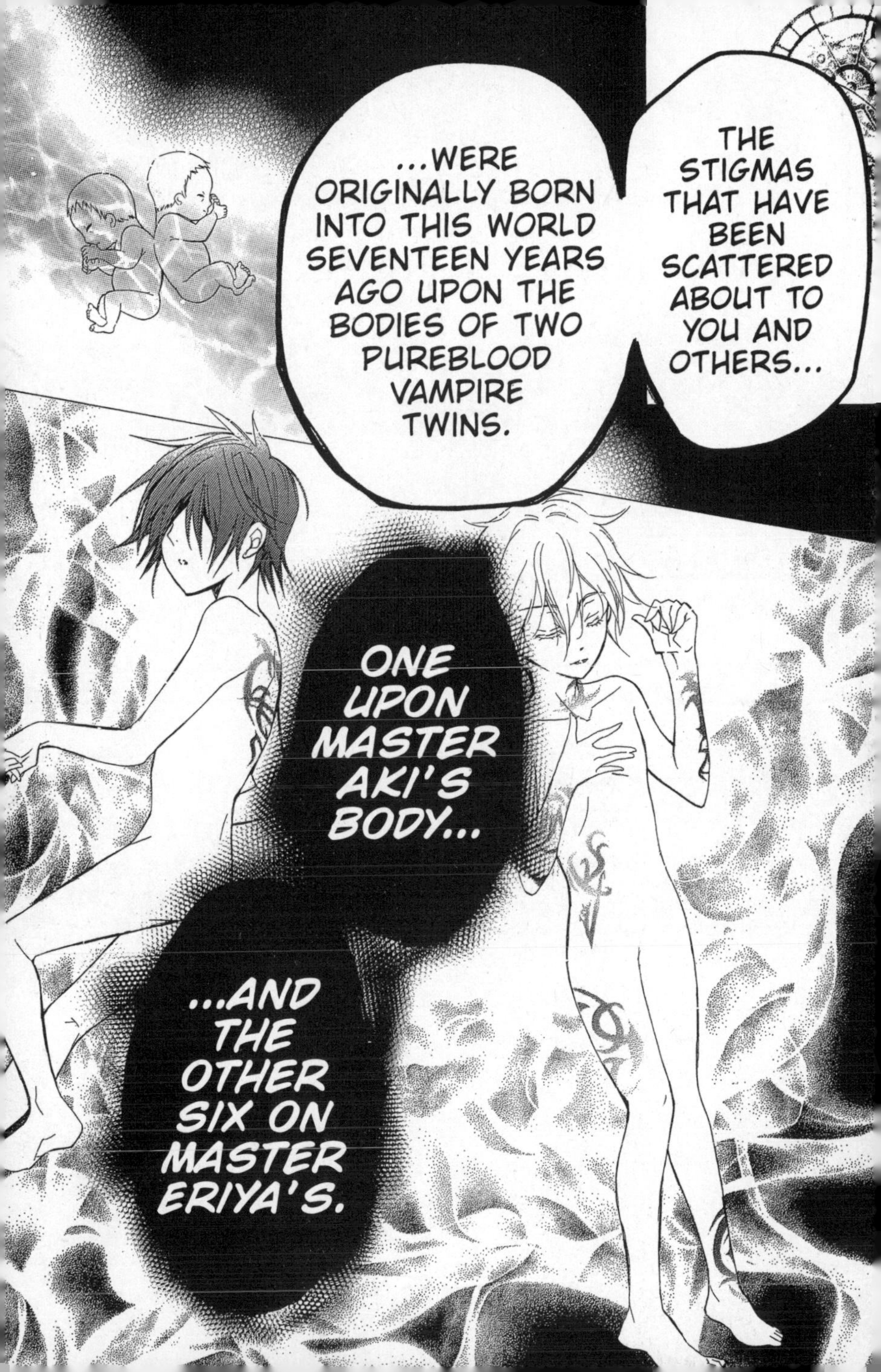
THE STIGMAS THAT HAVE BEEN SCATTERED ABOUT TO YOU AND OTHERS...
...WERE ORIGINALLY BORN INTO THIS WORLD SEVENTEEN YEARS AGO UPON THE BODIES OF TWO PUREBLOOD VAMPIRE TWINS.
ONE UPON MASTER AKI'S BODY...
...AND THE OTHER SIX ON MASTER ERIYA'S.

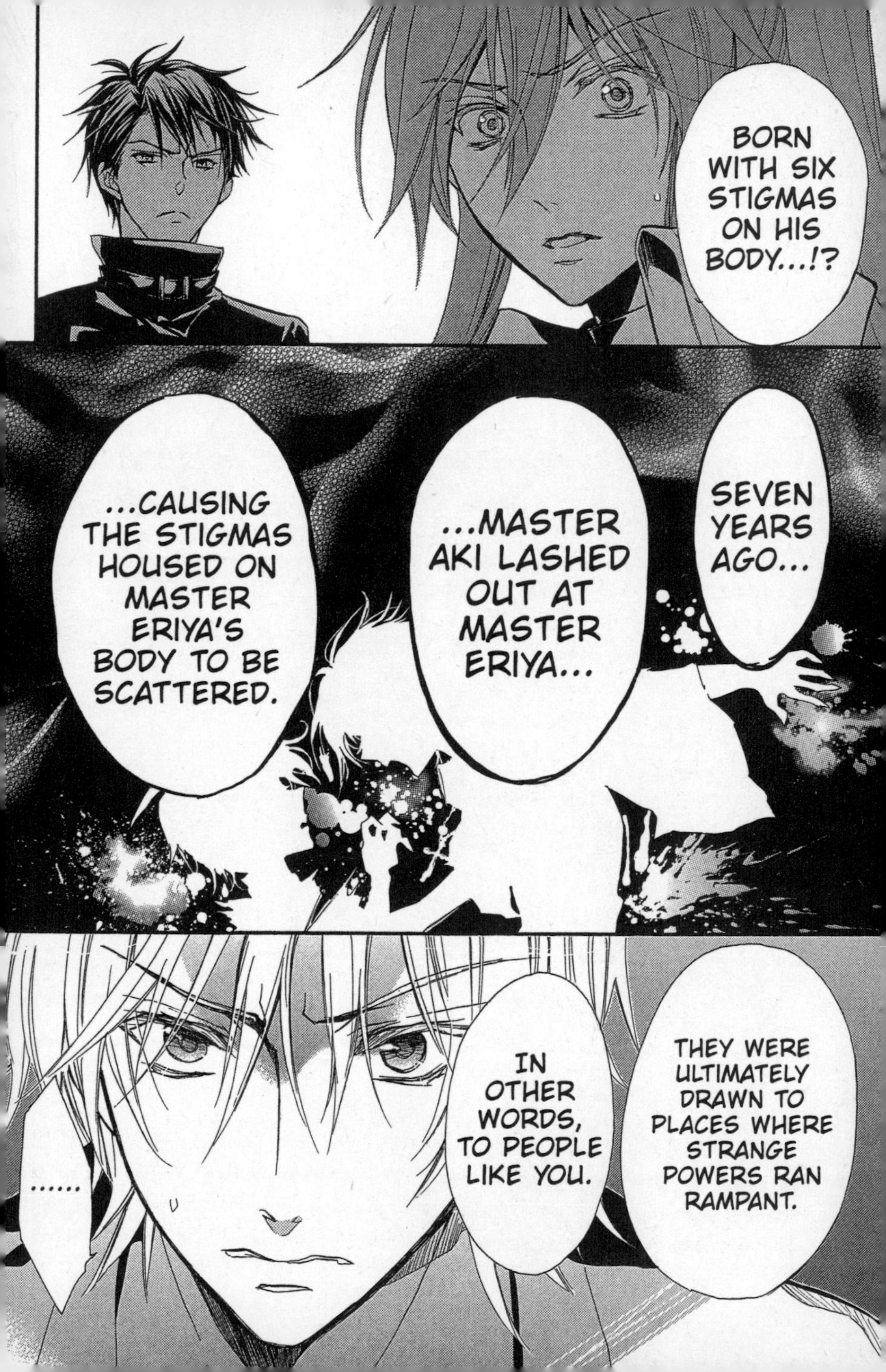
BORN WITH SIX STIGMAS ON HIS BODY...!?
SEVEN YEARS AGO...
...MASTER AKI LASHED OUT AT MASTER ERIYA...
...CAUSING THE STIGMAS HOUSED ON MASTER ERIYA'S BODY TO BE SCATTERED.
THEY WERE ULTIMATELY DRAWN TO PLACES WHERE STRANGE POWERS RAN RAMPANT.
IN OTHER WORDS, TO PEOPLE LIKE YOU.
......

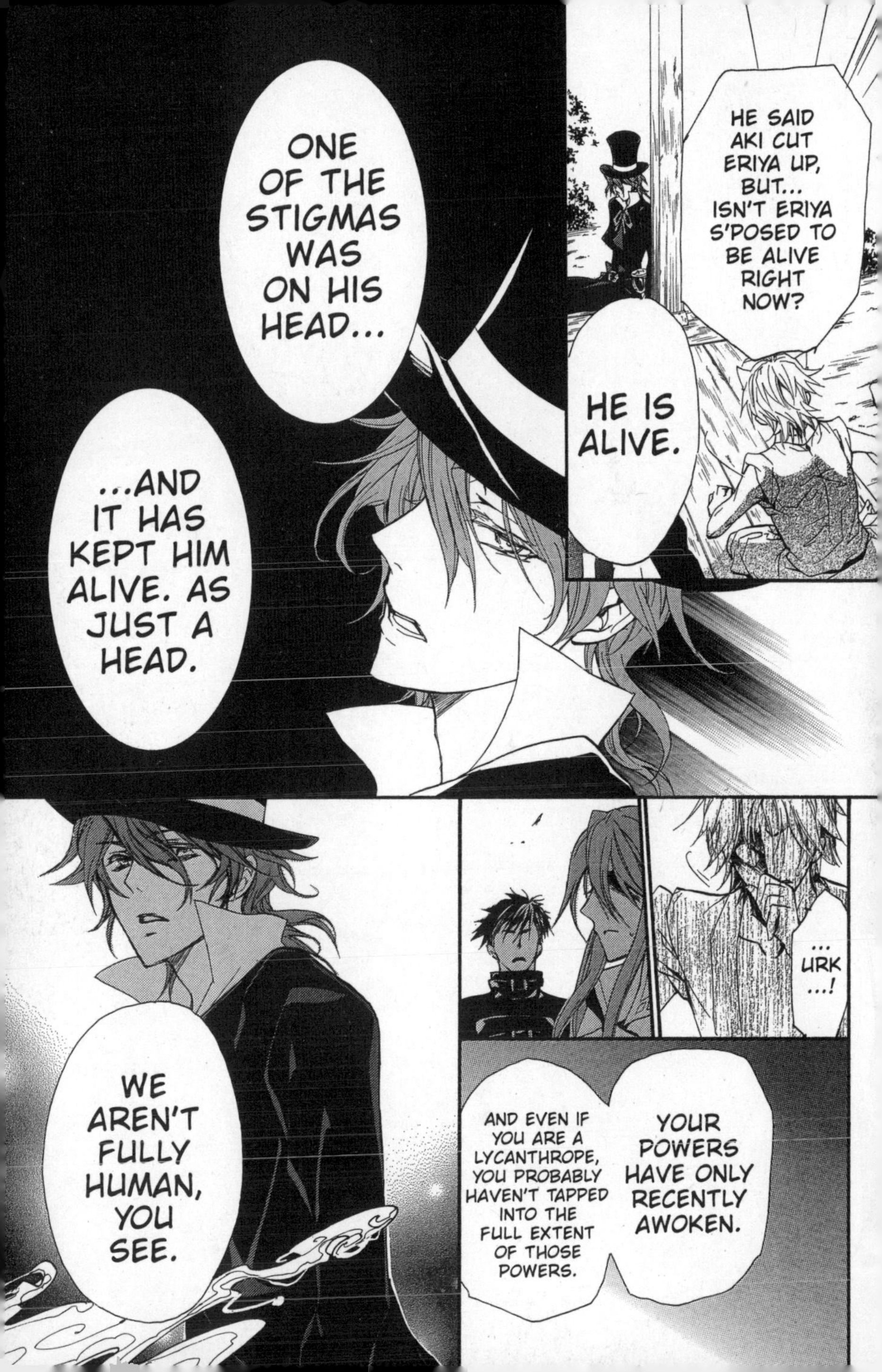
HE SAID AKI CUT ERIYA UP, BUT... ISN'T ERIYA S'POSED TO BE ALIVE RIGHT NOW?
HE IS ALIVE.
ONE OF THE STIGMAS WAS ON HIS HEAD...
...AND IT HAS KEPT HIM ALIVE. AS JUST A HEAD.
...URK...!
YOUR POWERS HAVE ONLY RECENTLY AWOKEN.
AND EVEN IF YOU ARE A LYCANTHROPE, YOU PROBABLY HAVEN'T TAPPED INTO THE FULL EXTENT OF THOSE POWERS.
WE AREN'T FULLY HUMAN, YOU SEE.

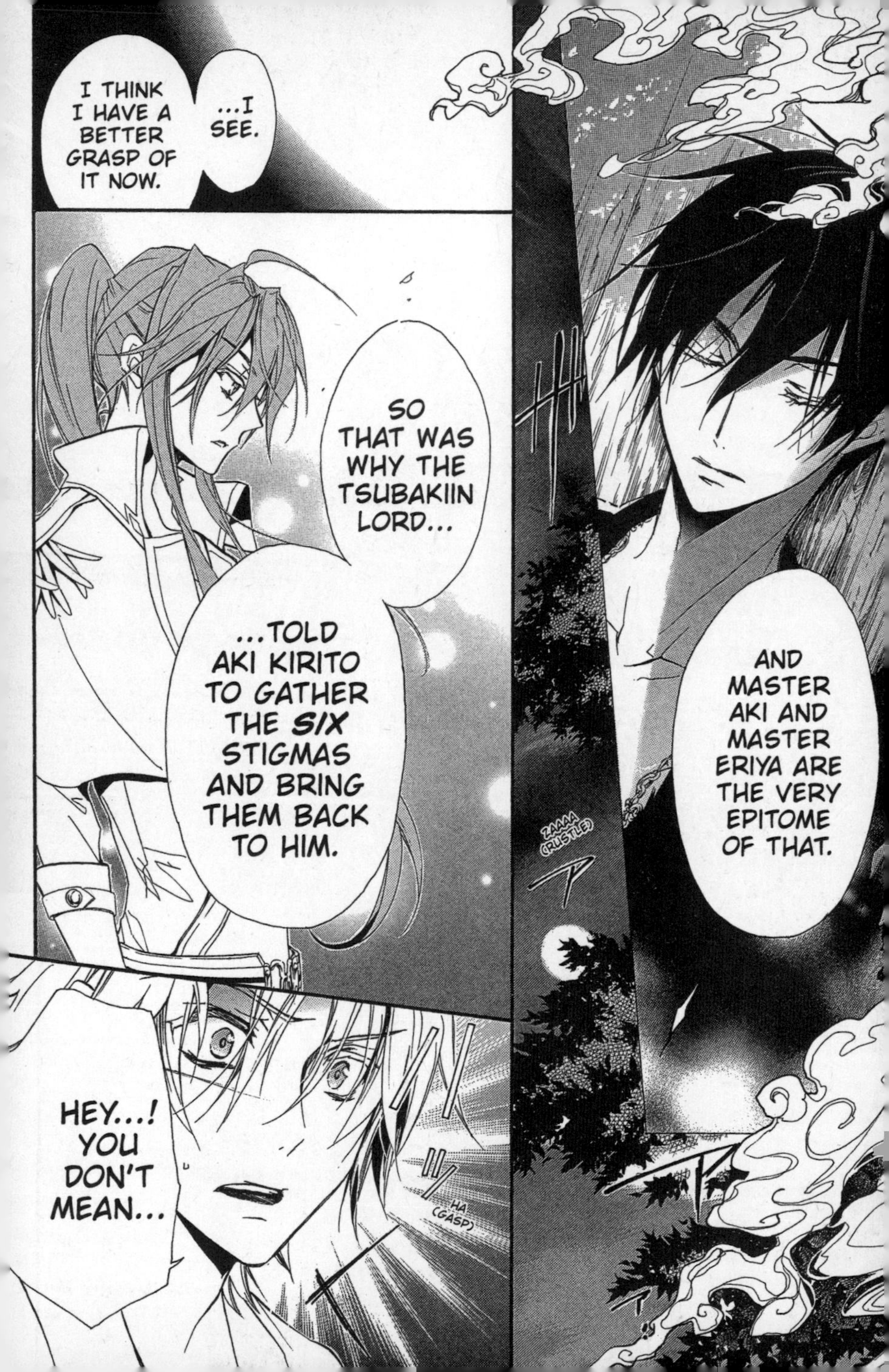
AND MASTER AKI AND MASTER ERIYA ARE THE VERY EPITOME OF THAT.
ZAAAA (RUSTLE)
...I SEE.
I THINK I HAVE A BETTER GRASP OF IT NOW.
SO THAT WAS WHY THE TSUBAKIIN LORD...
...TOLD AKI KIRITO TO GATHER THE *SIX* STIGMAS AND BRING THEM BACK TO HIM.
HA (GASP)
HEY...! YOU DON'T MEAN...

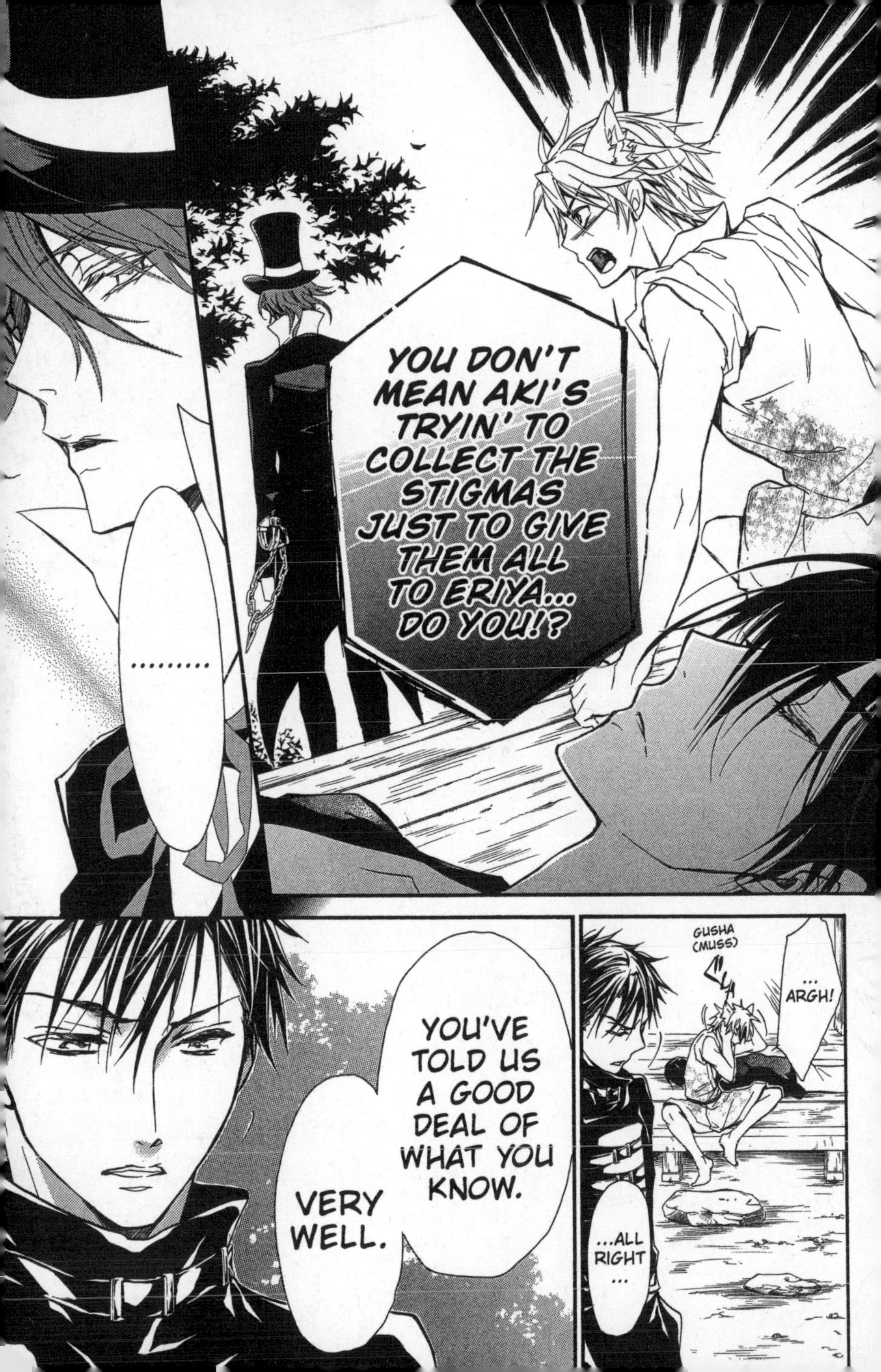
YOU DON'T MEAN AKI'S TRYIN' TO COLLECT THE STIGMAS JUST TO GIVE THEM ALL TO ERIYA... DO YOU!?
....
GUSHA (MUSS)
... ARGH!
...ALL RIGHT ...
YOU'VE TOLD US A GOOD DEAL OF WHAT YOU KNOW.
VERY WELL.

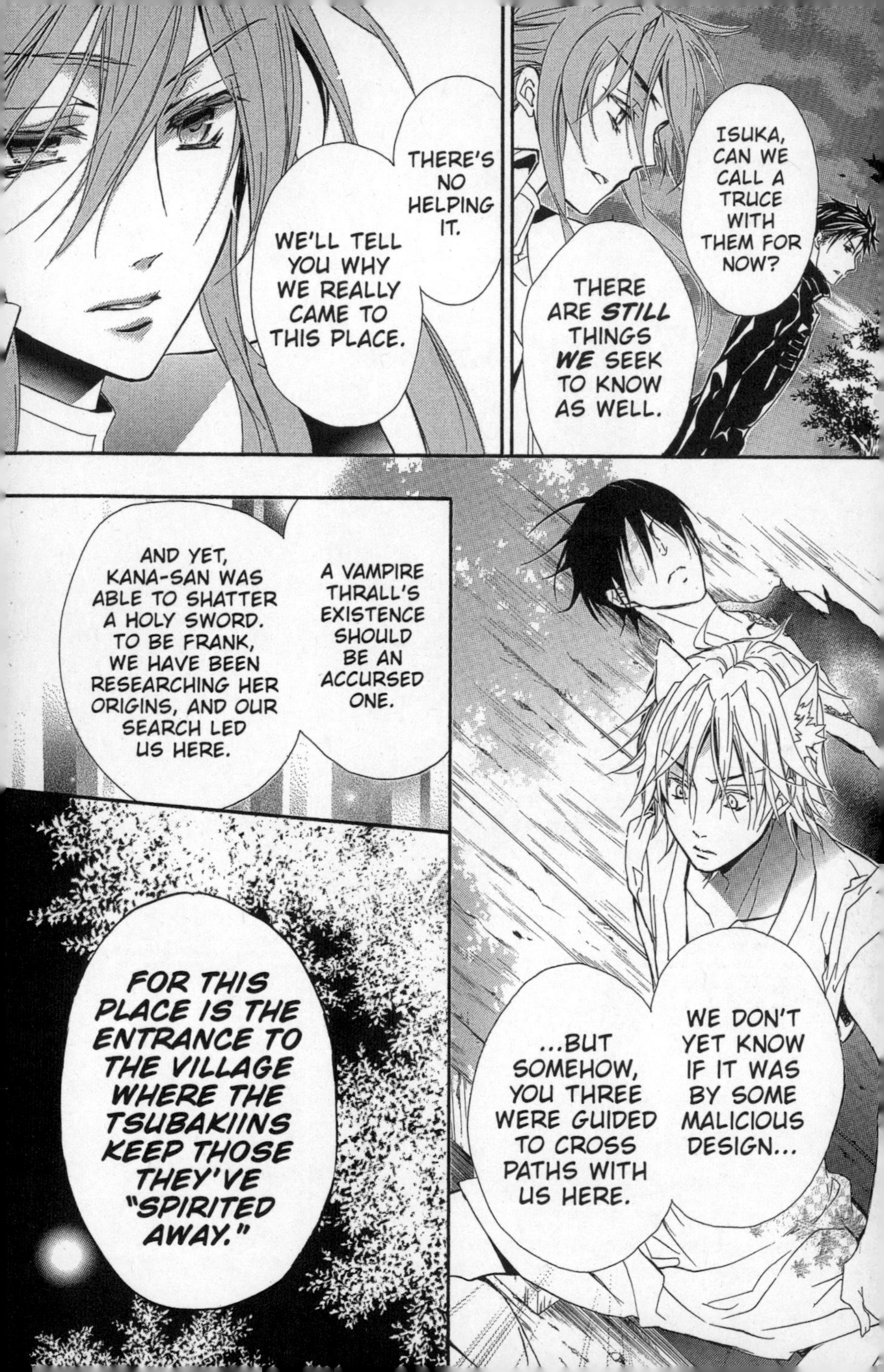
ISUKA, CAN WE CALL A TRUCE WITH THEM FOR NOW?
THERE ARE STILL THINGS WE SEEK TO KNOW AS WELL.
THERE'S NO HELPING IT.
WE'LL TELL YOU WHY WE REALLY CAME TO THIS PLACE.
WE DON'T YET KNOW IF IT WAS BY SOME MALICIOUS DESIGN...
...BUT SOMEHOW, YOU THREE WERE GUIDED TO CROSS PATHS WITH US HERE.
A VAMPIRE THRALL'S EXISTENCE SHOULD BE AN ACCURSED ONE.
AND YET, KANA-SAN WAS ABLE TO SHATTER A HOLY SWORD. TO BE FRANK, WE HAVE BEEN RESEARCHING HER ORIGINS, AND OUR SEARCH LED US HERE.
FOR THIS PLACE IS THE ENTRANCE TO THE VILLAGE WHERE THE TSUBAKIINS KEEP THOSE THEY'VE "SPIRITED AWAY."

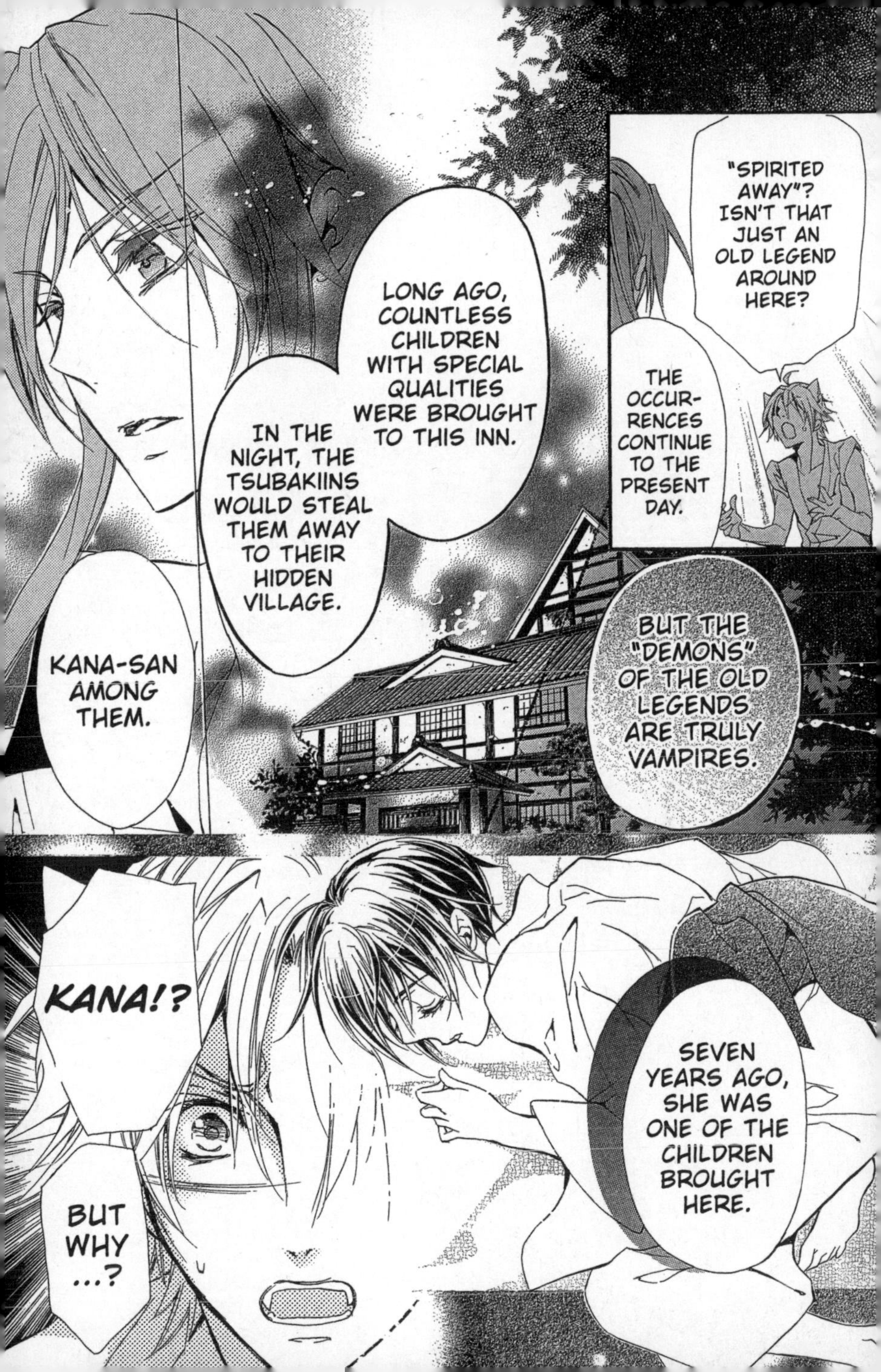
"SPIRITED AWAY"? ISN'T THAT JUST AN OLD LEGEND AROUND HERE?
THE OCCURRENCES CONTINUE TO THE PRESENT DAY.
LONG AGO, COUNTLESS CHILDREN WITH SPECIAL QUALITIES WERE BROUGHT TO THIS INN.
IN THE NIGHT, THE TSUBAKIINS WOULD STEAL THEM AWAY TO THEIR HIDDEN VILLAGE.
BUT THE "DEMONS" OF THE OLD LEGENDS ARE TRULY VAMPIRES.
KANA-SAN AMONG THEM.
SEVEN YEARS AGO, SHE WAS ONE OF THE CHILDREN BROUGHT HERE.
KANA!?
BUT WHY ...?

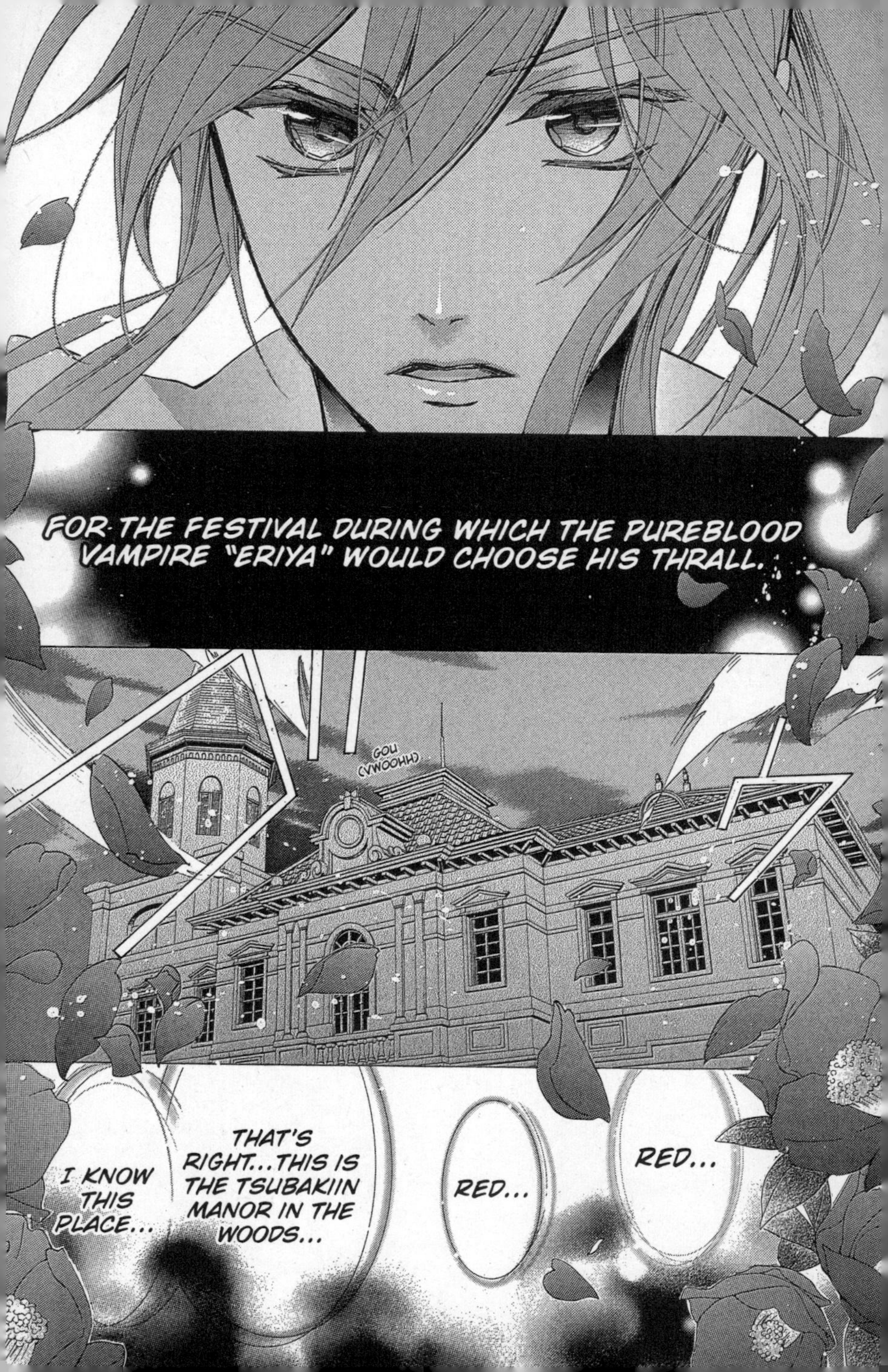
FOR THE FESTIVAL DURING WHICH THE PUREBLOOD VAMPIRE "ERIYA" WOULD CHOOSE HIS THRALL.
GOU (VWOOHH)
RED...
RED...
THAT'S RIGHT...THIS IS THE TSUBAKIIN MANOR IN THE WOODS...
I KNOW THIS PLACE...

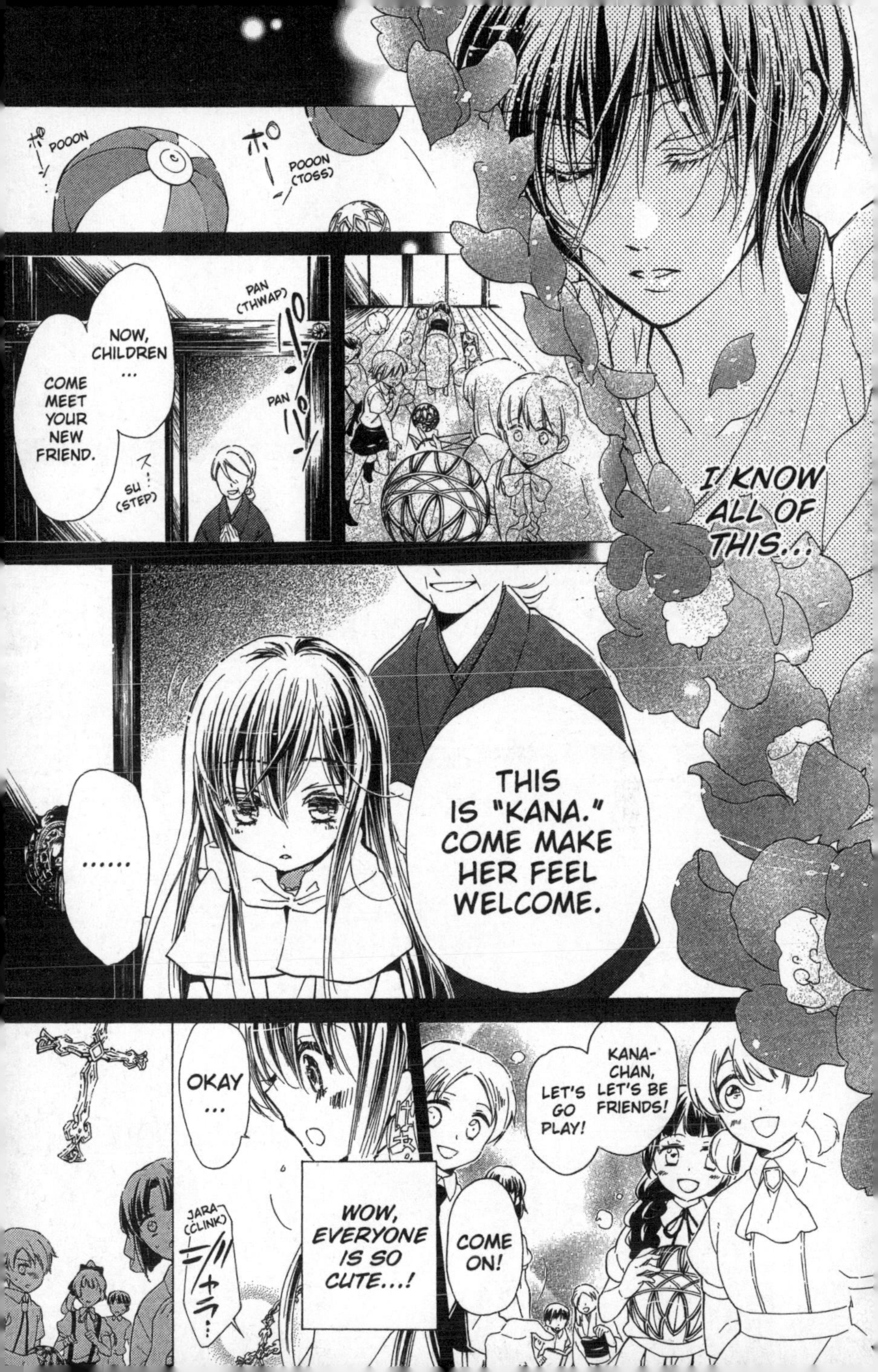
I KNOW ALL OF THIS...
POOON (TOSS)
POOON
PAN (THWAP)
PAN
NOW, CHILDREN ...
COME MEET YOUR NEW FRIEND.
SU (STEP)
THIS IS "KANA." COME MAKE HER FEEL WELCOME.
......
KANA-CHAN, LET'S BE FRIENDS!
LET'S GO PLAY!
COME ON!
WOW, EVERYONE IS SO CUTE...!
OKAY ...
JARA (CLINK)

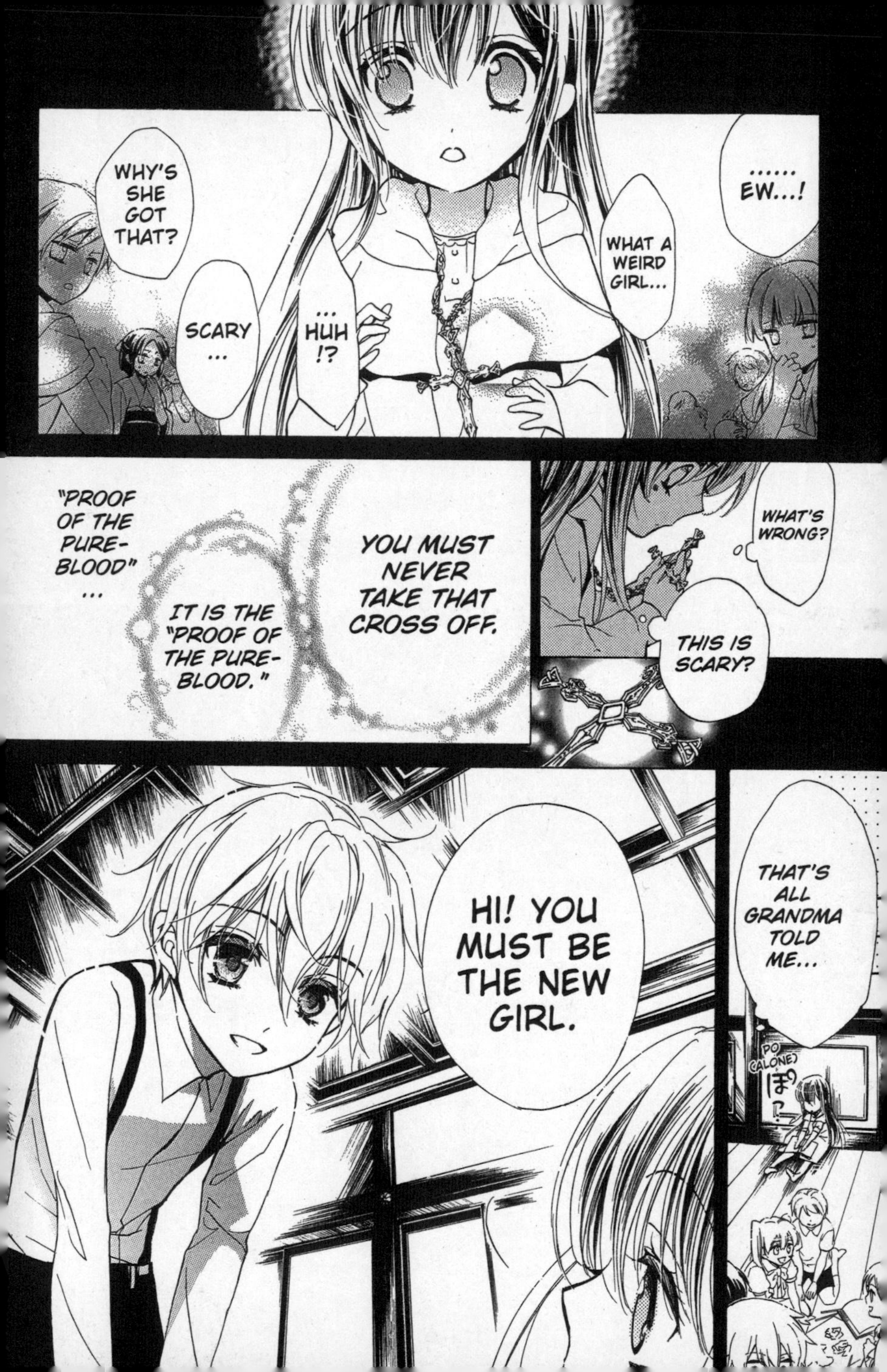

...... EW...!
WHAT A WEIRD GIRL...
... HUH!?
WHY'S SHE GOT THAT?
SCARY ...
WHAT'S WRONG?
THIS IS SCARY?
YOU MUST NEVER TAKE THAT CROSS OFF.
IT IS THE "PROOF OF THE PURE-BLOOD."
"PROOF OF THE PURE-BLOOD" ...
THAT'S ALL GRANDMA TOLD ME...
PO (ALONE)
HI! YOU MUST BE THE NEW GIRL.

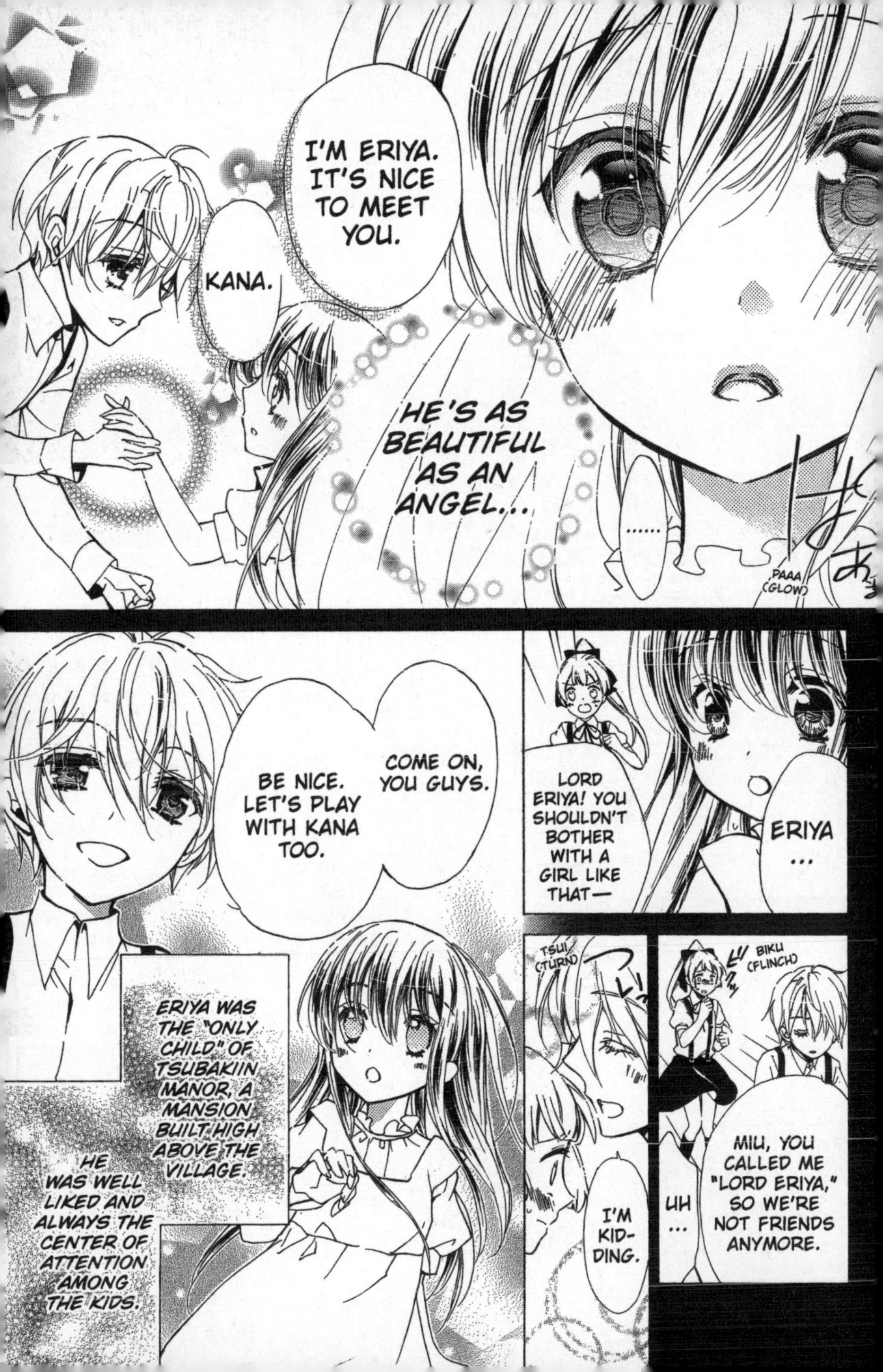
PAAA (GLOW)
......
HE'S AS BEAUTIFUL AS AN ANGEL...
I'M ERIYA. IT'S NICE TO MEET YOU.
KANA.
ERIYA ...
LORD ERIYA! YOU SHOULDN'T BOTHER WITH A GIRL LIKE THAT—
BIKU (FLINCH)
MIU, YOU CALLED ME "LORD ERIYA," SO WE'RE NOT FRIENDS ANYMORE.
UH ...
TSUI (TURN)
I'M KID-DING.
COME ON, YOU GUYS.
BE NICE. LET'S PLAY WITH KANA TOO.
ERIYA WAS THE "ONLY CHILD" OF TSUBAKIIN MANOR, A MANSION BUILT HIGH ABOVE THE VILLAGE.
HE WAS WELL LIKED AND ALWAYS THE CENTER OF ATTENTION AMONG THE KIDS.

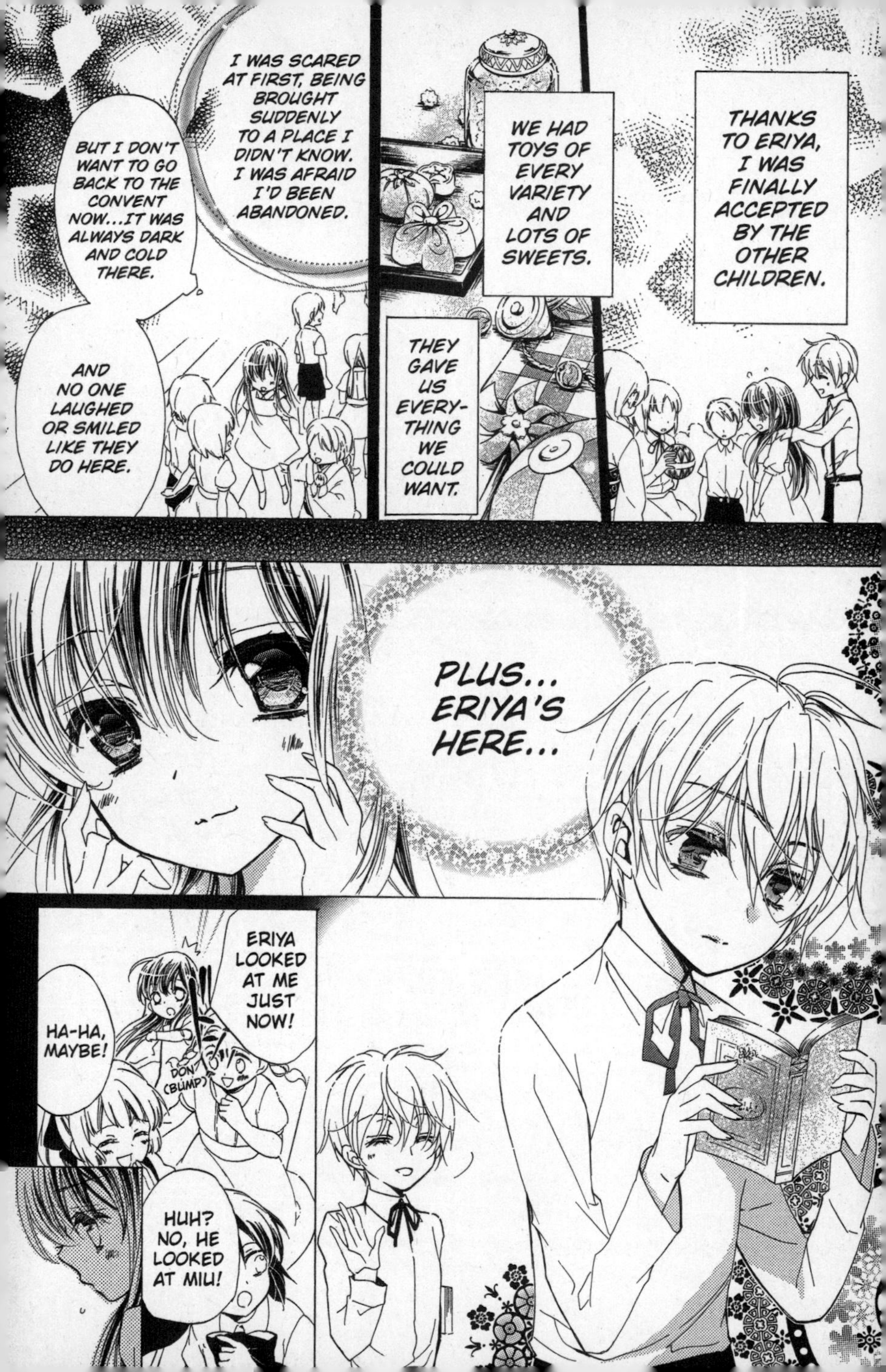
THANKS TO ERIYA, I WAS FINALLY ACCEPTED BY THE OTHER CHILDREN.
WE HAD TOYS OF EVERY VARIETY AND LOTS OF SWEETS.
THEY GAVE US EVERY-THING WE COULD WANT.
I WAS SCARED AT FIRST, BEING BROUGHT SUDDENLY TO A PLACE I DIDN'T KNOW. I WAS AFRAID I'D BEEN ABANDONED.
BUT I DON'T WANT TO GO BACK TO THE CONVENT NOW...IT WAS ALWAYS DARK AND COLD THERE.
AND NO ONE LAUGHED OR SMILED LIKE THEY DO HERE.
PLUS... ERIYA'S HERE...
ERIYA LOOKED AT ME JUST NOW!
HA-HA, MAYBE!
DON (BUMP)
HUH? NO, HE LOOKED AT MIU!

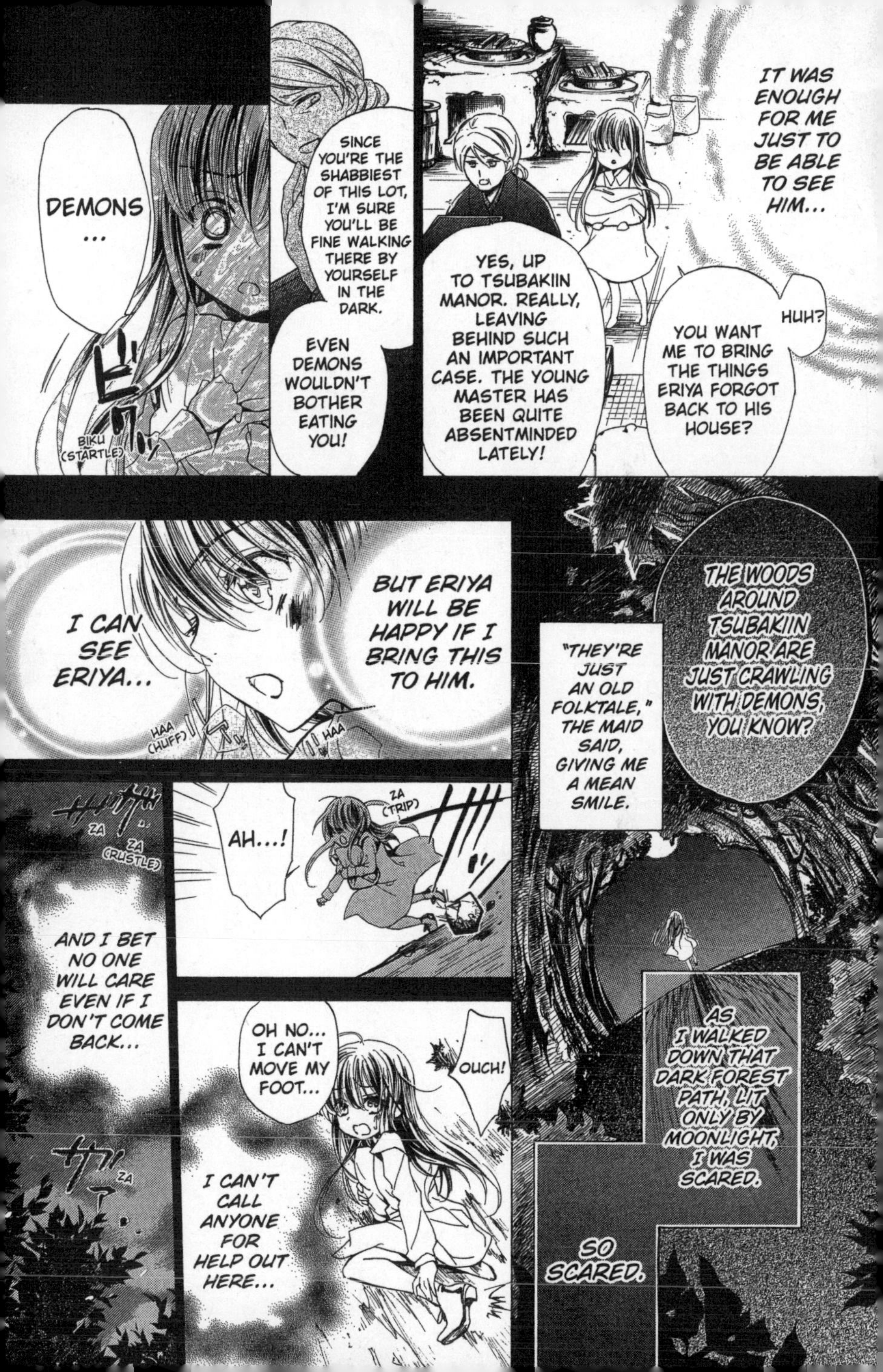
IT WAS ENOUGH FOR ME JUST TO BE ABLE TO SEE HIM...
HUH?
YOU WANT ME TO BRING THE THINGS ERIYA FORGOT BACK TO HIS HOUSE?
YES, UP TO TSUBAKIIN MANOR. REALLY, LEAVING BEHIND SUCH AN IMPORTANT CASE. THE YOUNG MASTER HAS BEEN QUITE ABSENTMINDED LATELY!
SINCE YOU'RE THE SHABBIEST OF THIS LOT, I'M SURE YOU'LL BE FINE WALKING THERE BY YOURSELF IN THE DARK.
EVEN DEMONS WOULDN'T BOTHER EATING YOU!
DEMONS ...
BIKU (STARTLE)
THE WOODS AROUND TSUBAKIIN MANOR ARE JUST CRAWLING WITH DEMONS, YOU KNOW?
"THEY'RE JUST AN OLD FOLKTALE," THE MAID SAID, GIVING ME A MEAN SMILE.
AS I WALKED DOWN THAT DARK FOREST PATH, LIT ONLY BY MOONLIGHT, I WAS SCARED.
SO SCARED.
BUT ERIYA WILL BE HAPPY IF I BRING THIS TO HIM.
I CAN SEE ERIYA...
HAA (HUFF)
HAA
ZA (TRIP)
AH...!
OUCH!
OH NO... I CAN'T MOVE MY FOOT...
I CAN'T CALL ANYONE FOR HELP OUT HERE...
ZA
ZA (RUSTLE)
AND I BET NO ONE WILL CARE EVEN IF I DON'T COME BACK...
ZA

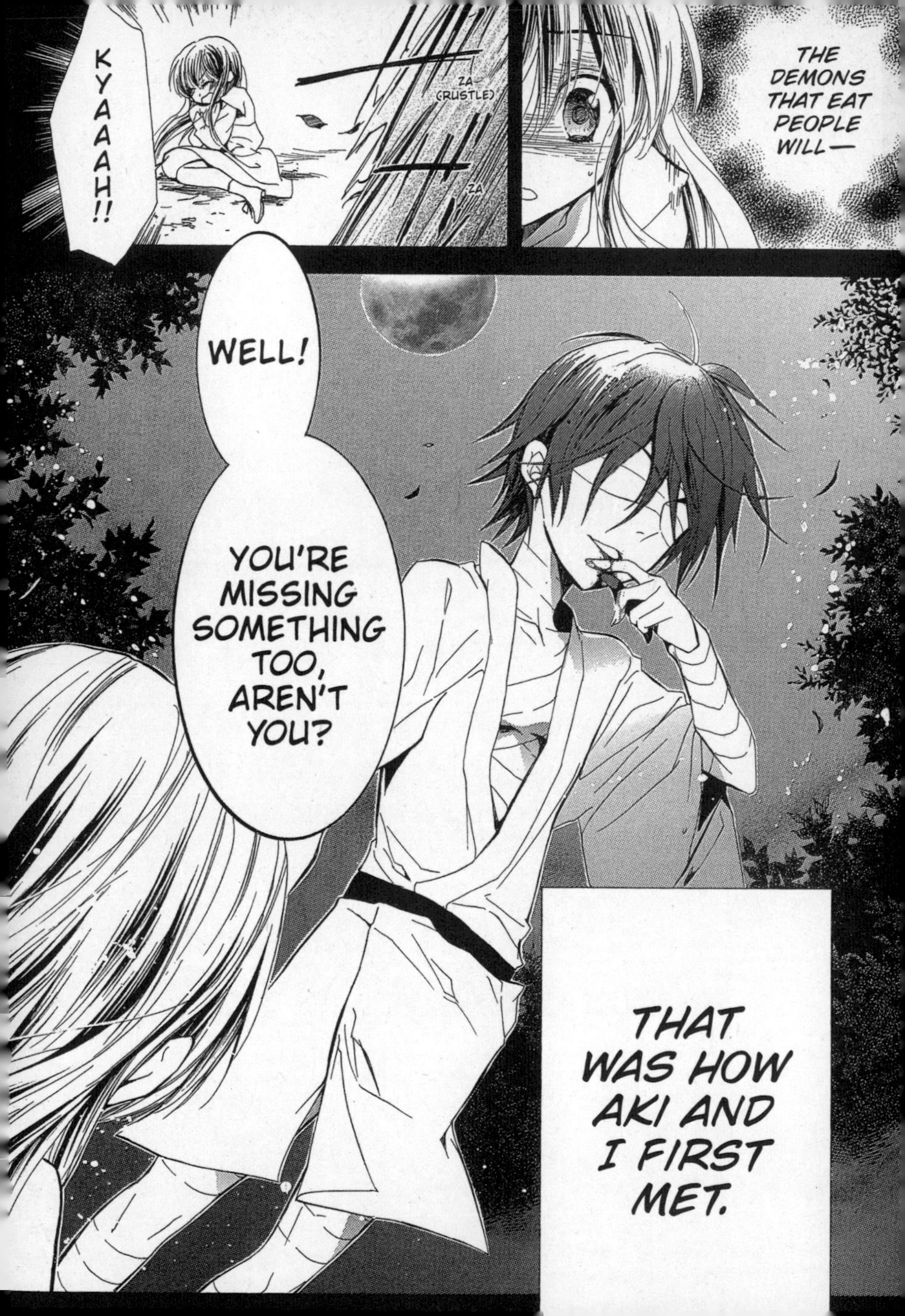
THE DEMONS THAT EAT PEOPLE WILL—
ZA (RUSTLE)
ZA
KYAAAH!!
WELL!
YOU'RE MISSING SOMETHING TOO, AREN'T YOU?
THAT WAS HOW AKI AND I FIRST MET.

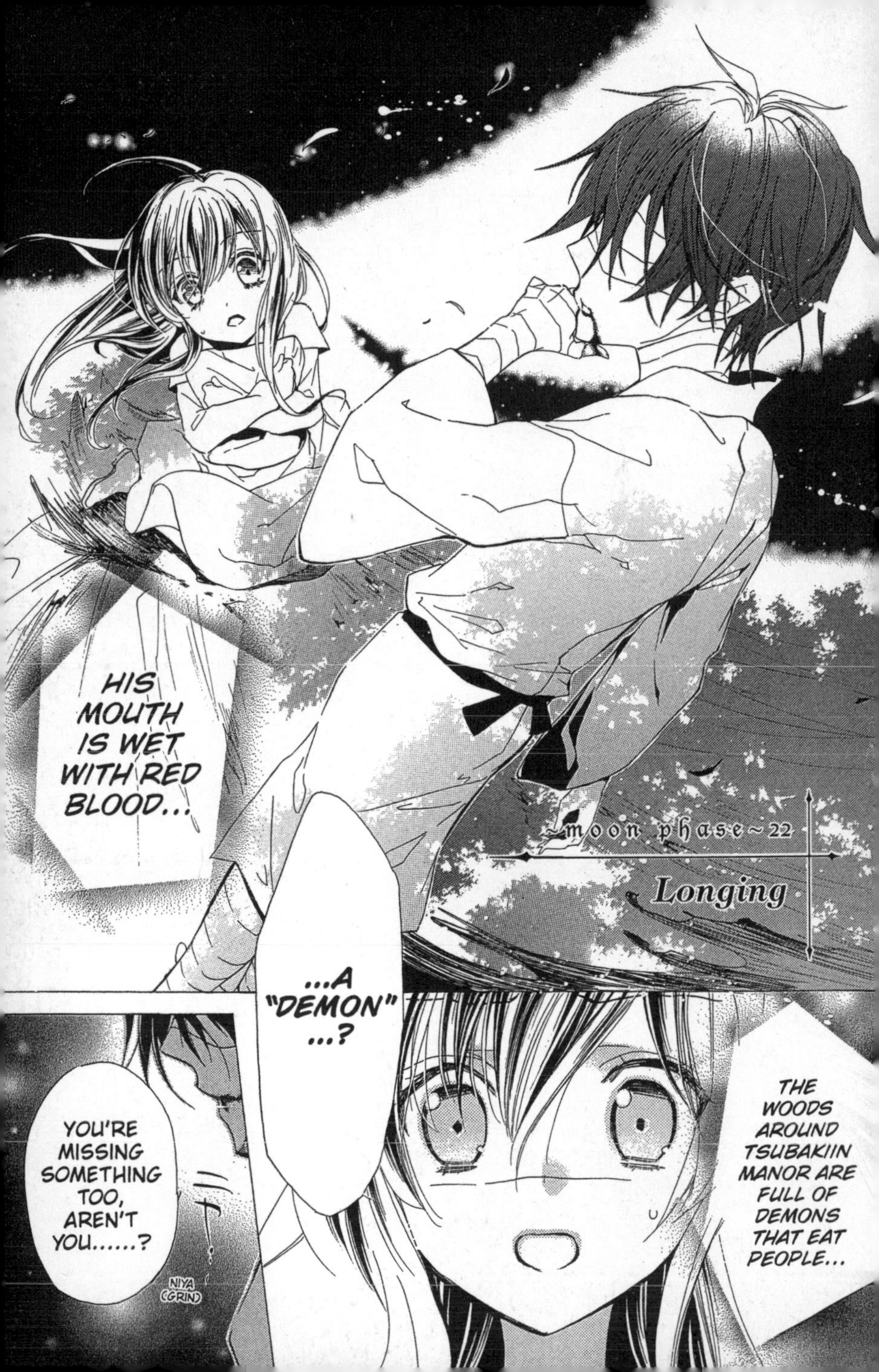
~moon phase~22
Longing
HIS MOUTH IS WET WITH RED BLOOD...
THE WOODS AROUND TSUBAKIIN MANOR ARE FULL OF DEMONS THAT EAT PEOPLE...
...A "DEMON" ...?
YOU'RE MISSING SOMETHING TOO, AREN'T YOU......?
NIYA (GRIN)

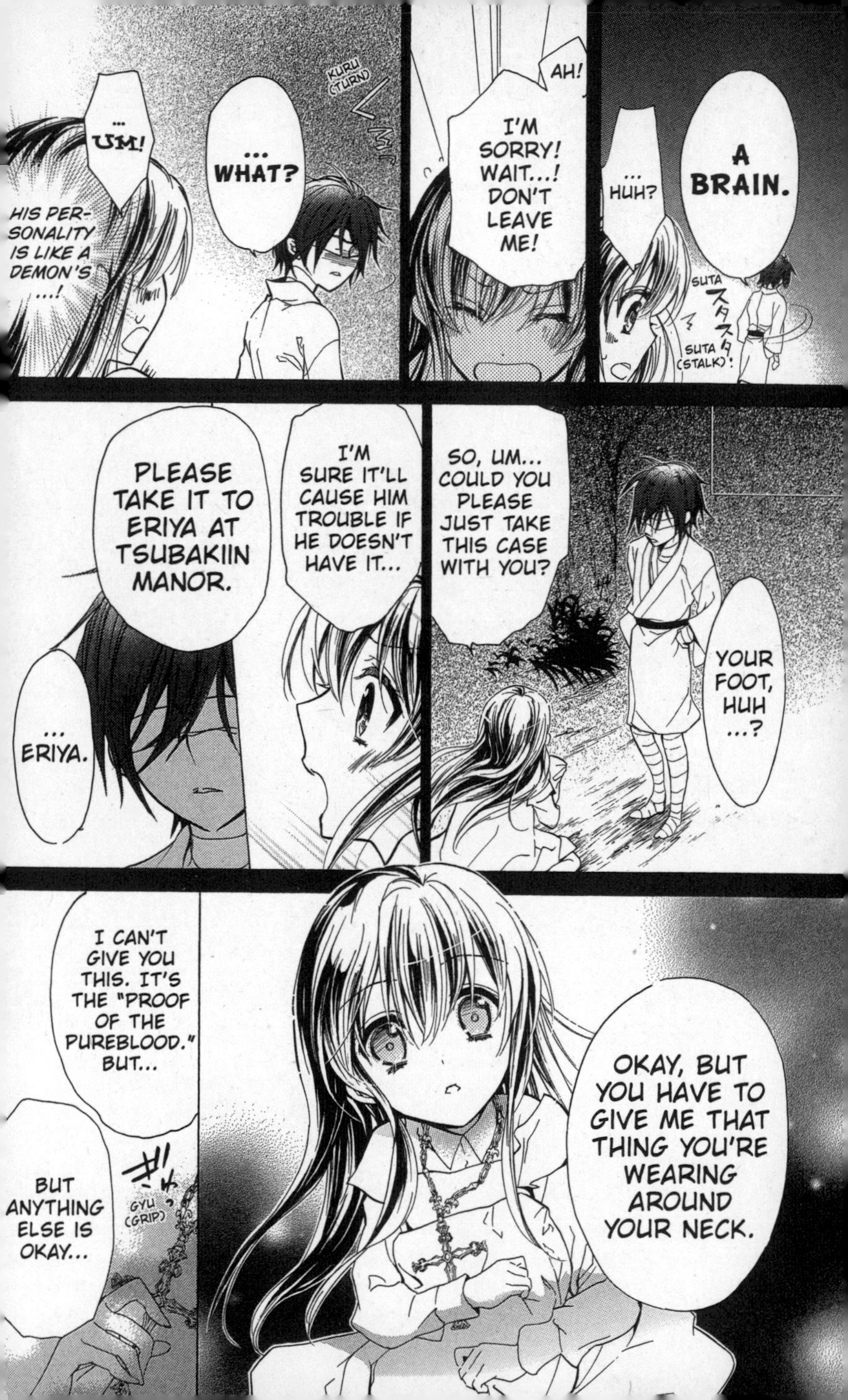
A BRAIN.
... HUH?
SUTA SUTA (STALK)
AH!
I'M SORRY! WAIT...! DON'T LEAVE ME!
KURU (TURN)
... WHAT?
... UM!
HIS PERSONALITY IS LIKE A DEMON'S ...!
SO, UM... COULD YOU PLEASE JUST TAKE THIS CASE WITH YOU?
YOUR FOOT, HUH ...?
I'M SURE IT'LL CAUSE HIM TROUBLE IF HE DOESN'T HAVE IT...
PLEASE TAKE IT TO ERIYA AT TSUBAKIIN MANOR.
... ERIYA.
OKAY, BUT YOU HAVE TO GIVE ME THAT THING YOU'RE WEARING AROUND YOUR NECK.
I CAN'T GIVE YOU THIS. IT'S THE "PROOF OF THE PUREBLOOD." BUT...
GYU (GRIP)
BUT ANYTHING ELSE IS OKAY...

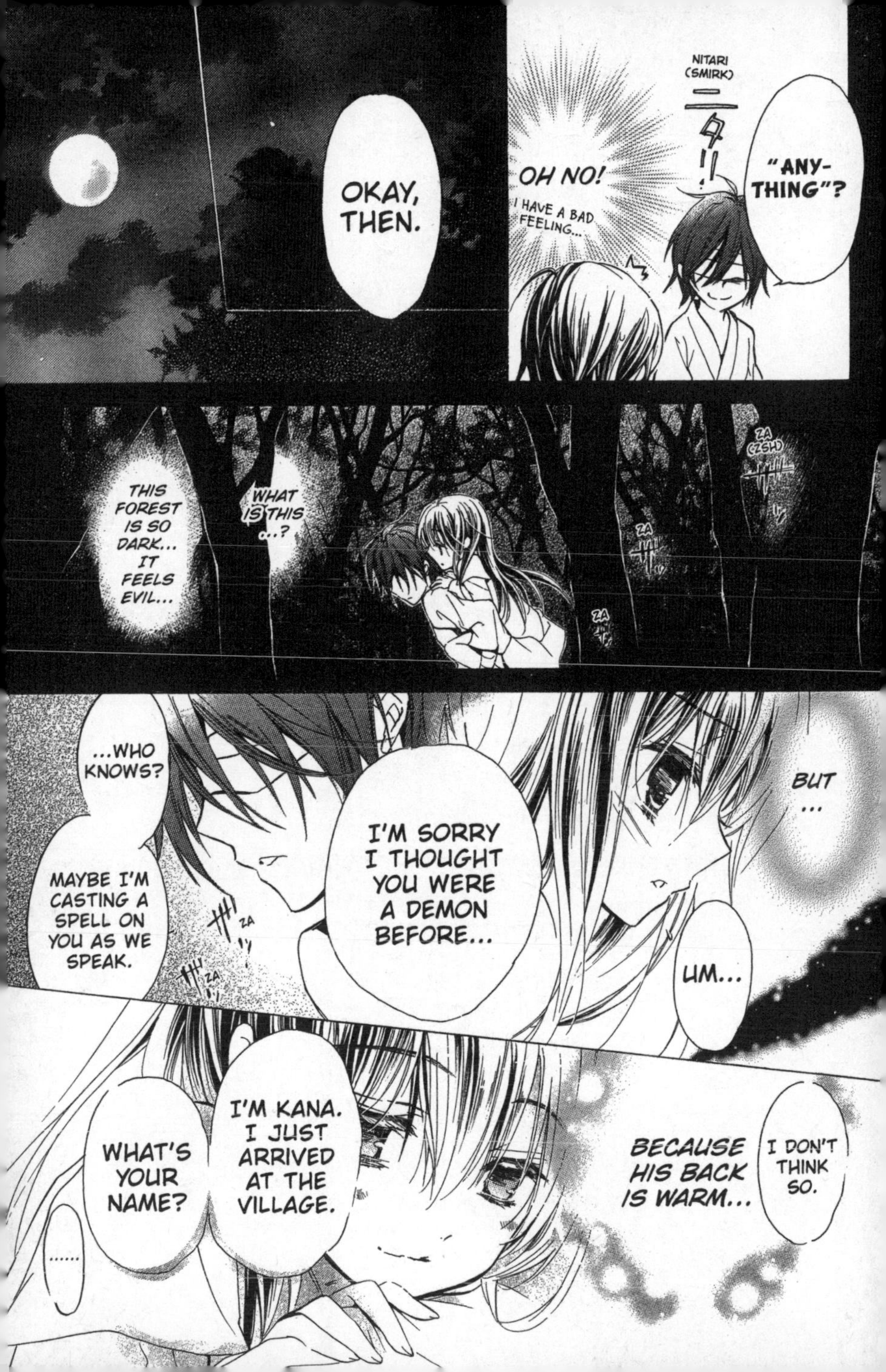
"ANY-THING"?
NITARI (SMIRK)
OH NO!
I HAVE A BAD FEELING...
OKAY, THEN.
ZA (ZSHD)
ZA
ZA
WHAT IS THIS ...?
THIS FOREST IS SO DARK... IT FEELS EVIL...
BUT ...
UM...
I'M SORRY I THOUGHT YOU WERE A DEMON BEFORE...
...WHO KNOWS?
MAYBE I'M CASTING A SPELL ON YOU AS WE SPEAK.
ZA
ZA
I DON'T THINK SO.
BECAUSE HIS BACK IS WARM...
I'M KANA. I JUST ARRIVED AT THE VILLAGE.
WHAT'S YOUR NAME?
......

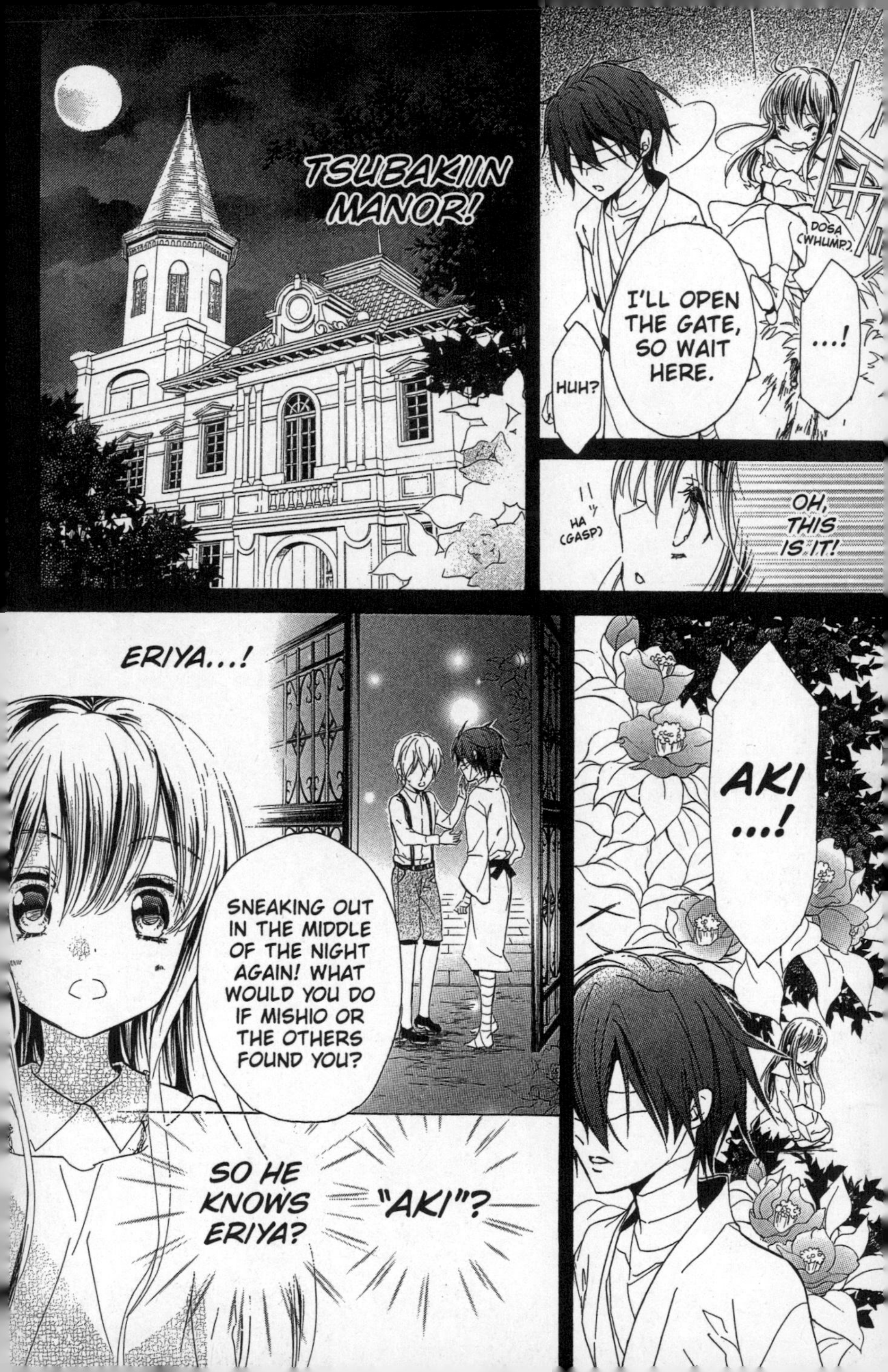
DOSA (WHUMP)
...!
I'LL OPEN THE GATE, SO WAIT HERE.
HUH?
OH, THIS IS IT!
HA (GASP)
TSUBAKIIN MANOR!
AKI ...!
ERIYA...!
SNEAKING OUT IN THE MIDDLE OF THE NIGHT AGAIN! WHAT WOULD YOU DO IF MISHIO OR THE OTHERS FOUND YOU?
"AKI"?
SO HE KNOWS ERIYA?

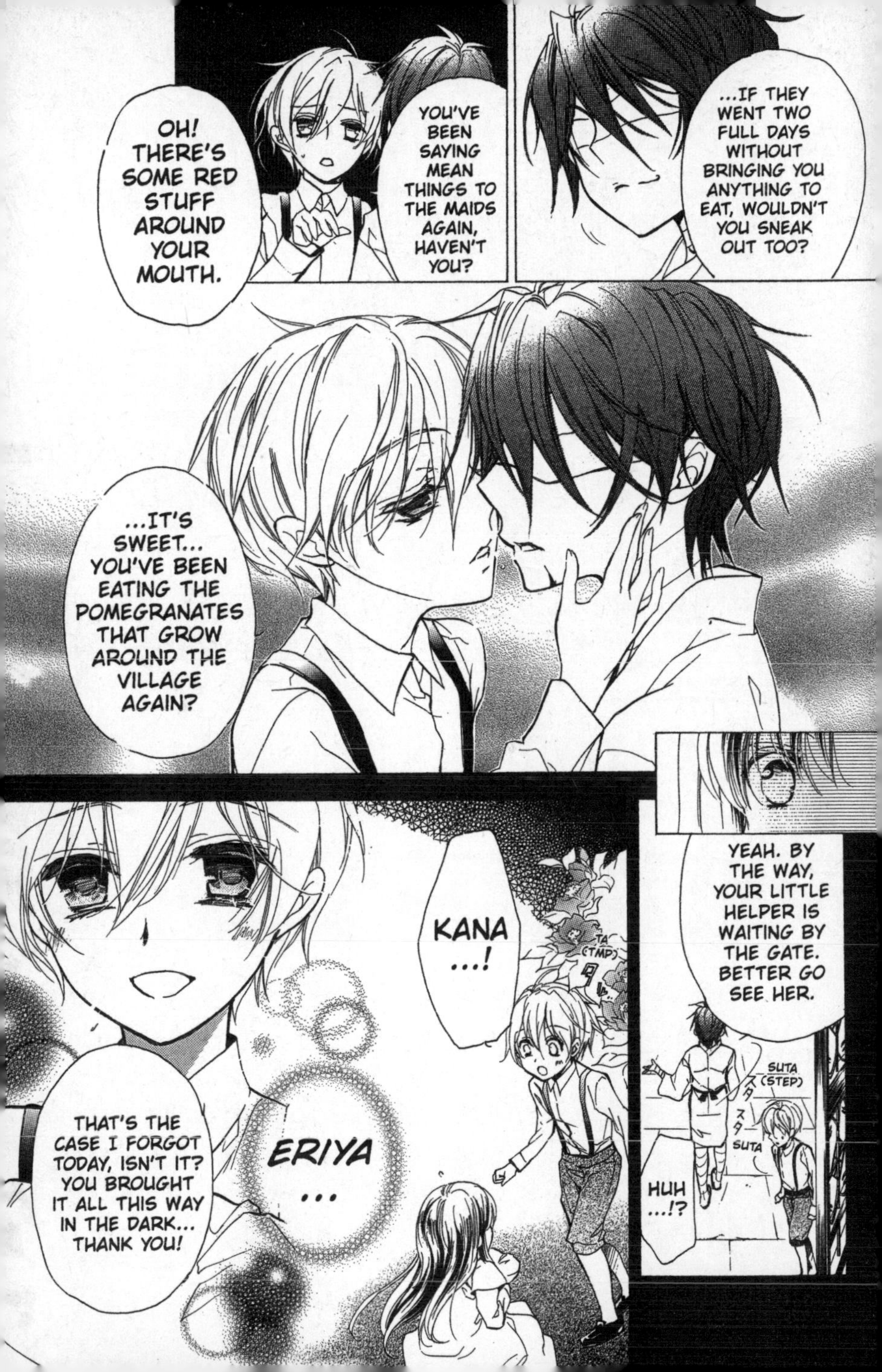
...IF THEY WENT TWO FULL DAYS WITHOUT BRINGING YOU ANYTHING TO EAT, WOULDN'T YOU SNEAK OUT TOO?
YOU'VE BEEN SAYING MEAN THINGS TO THE MAIDS AGAIN, HAVEN'T YOU?
OH! THERE'S SOME RED STUFF AROUND YOUR MOUTH.
...IT'S SWEET... YOU'VE BEEN EATING THE POMEGRANATES THAT GROW AROUND THE VILLAGE AGAIN?
YEAH. BY THE WAY, YOUR LITTLE HELPER IS WAITING BY THE GATE. BETTER GO SEE HER.
SUTA (STEP)
スタ
スタ
SUTA
HUH ...!?
TA (TMP)
KANA ...!
ERIYA ...
THAT'S THE CASE I FORGOT TODAY, ISN'T IT? YOU BROUGHT IT ALL THIS WAY IN THE DARK... THANK YOU!

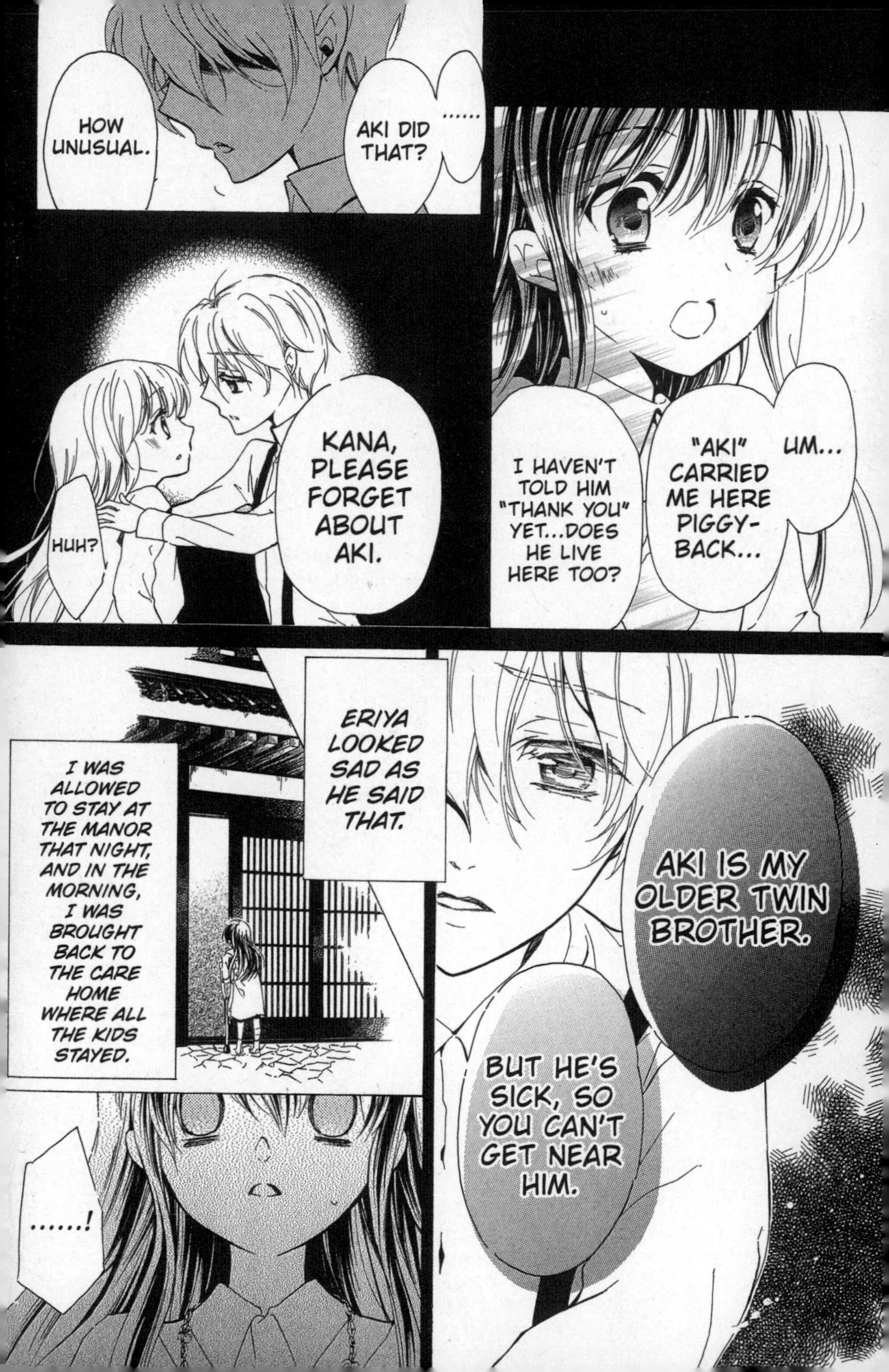
UM...
"AKI" CARRIED ME HERE PIGGY-BACK...
I HAVEN'T TOLD HIM "THANK YOU" YET...DOES HE LIVE HERE TOO?
......
AKI DID THAT?
HOW UNUSUAL.
KANA, PLEASE FORGET ABOUT AKI.
HUH?
AKI IS MY OLDER TWIN BROTHER.
BUT HE'S SICK, SO YOU CAN'T GET NEAR HIM.
ERIYA LOOKED SAD AS HE SAID THAT.
I WAS ALLOWED TO STAY AT THE MANOR THAT NIGHT, AND IN THE MORNING, I WAS BROUGHT BACK TO THE CARE HOME WHERE ALL THE KIDS STAYED.
......!

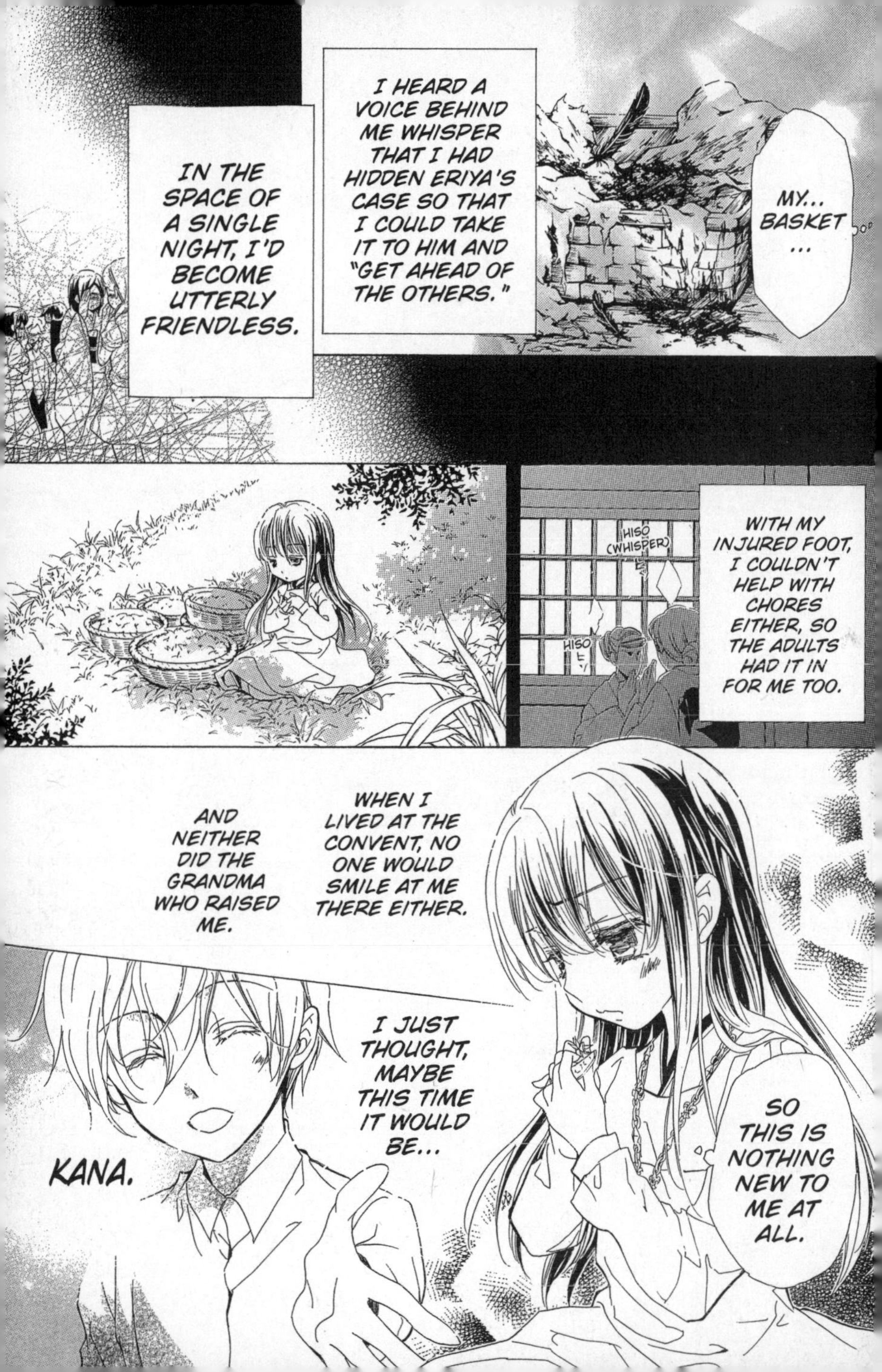

MY... BASKET...
I HEARD A VOICE BEHIND ME WHISPER THAT I HAD HIDDEN ERIYA'S CASE SO THAT I COULD TAKE IT TO HIM AND "GET AHEAD OF THE OTHERS."
IN THE SPACE OF A SINGLE NIGHT, I'D BECOME UTTERLY FRIENDLESS.
WITH MY INJURED FOOT, I COULDN'T HELP WITH CHORES EITHER, SO THE ADULTS HAD IT IN FOR ME TOO.
HISO (WHISPER)
HISO
WHEN I LIVED AT THE CONVENT, NO ONE WOULD SMILE AT ME THERE EITHER.
AND NEITHER DID THE GRANDMA WHO RAISED ME.
SO THIS IS NOTHING NEW TO ME AT ALL.
I JUST THOUGHT, MAYBE THIS TIME IT WOULD BE...
KANA.

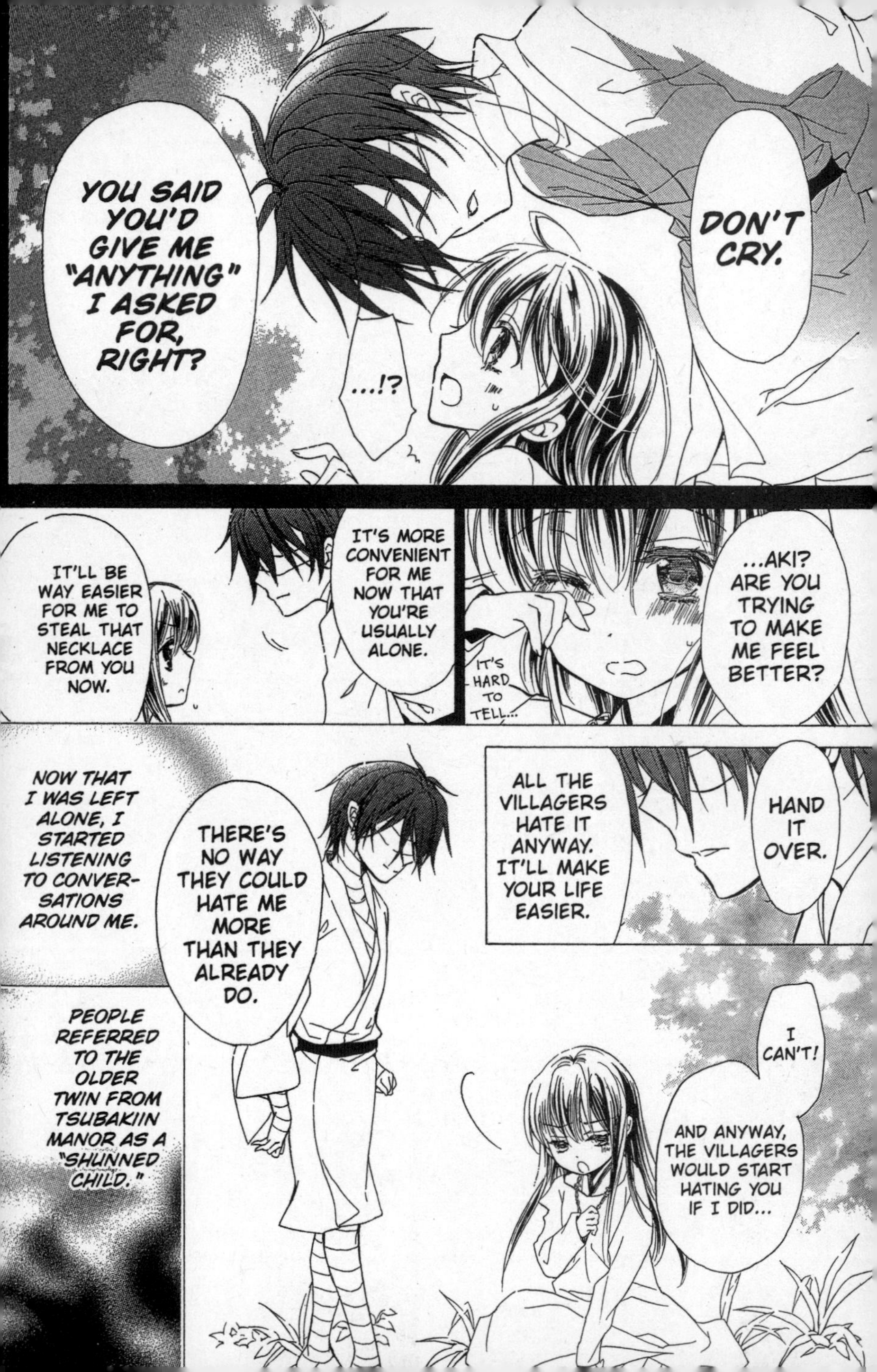
DON'T CRY.
...!?
YOU SAID YOU'D GIVE ME "ANYTHING" I ASKED FOR, RIGHT?
...AKI? ARE YOU TRYING TO MAKE ME FEEL BETTER?
IT'S HARD TO TELL...
IT'S MORE CONVENIENT FOR ME NOW THAT YOU'RE USUALLY ALONE.
IT'LL BE WAY EASIER FOR ME TO STEAL THAT NECKLACE FROM YOU NOW.
HAND IT OVER.
ALL THE VILLAGERS HATE IT ANYWAY. IT'LL MAKE YOUR LIFE EASIER.
I CAN'T!
AND ANYWAY, THE VILLAGERS WOULD START HATING YOU IF I DID...
THERE'S NO WAY THEY COULD HATE ME MORE THAN THEY ALREADY DO.
NOW THAT I WAS LEFT ALONE, I STARTED LISTENING TO CONVER-SATIONS AROUND ME.
PEOPLE REFERRED TO THE OLDER TWIN FROM TSUBAKIIN MANOR AS A "SHUNNED CHILD."

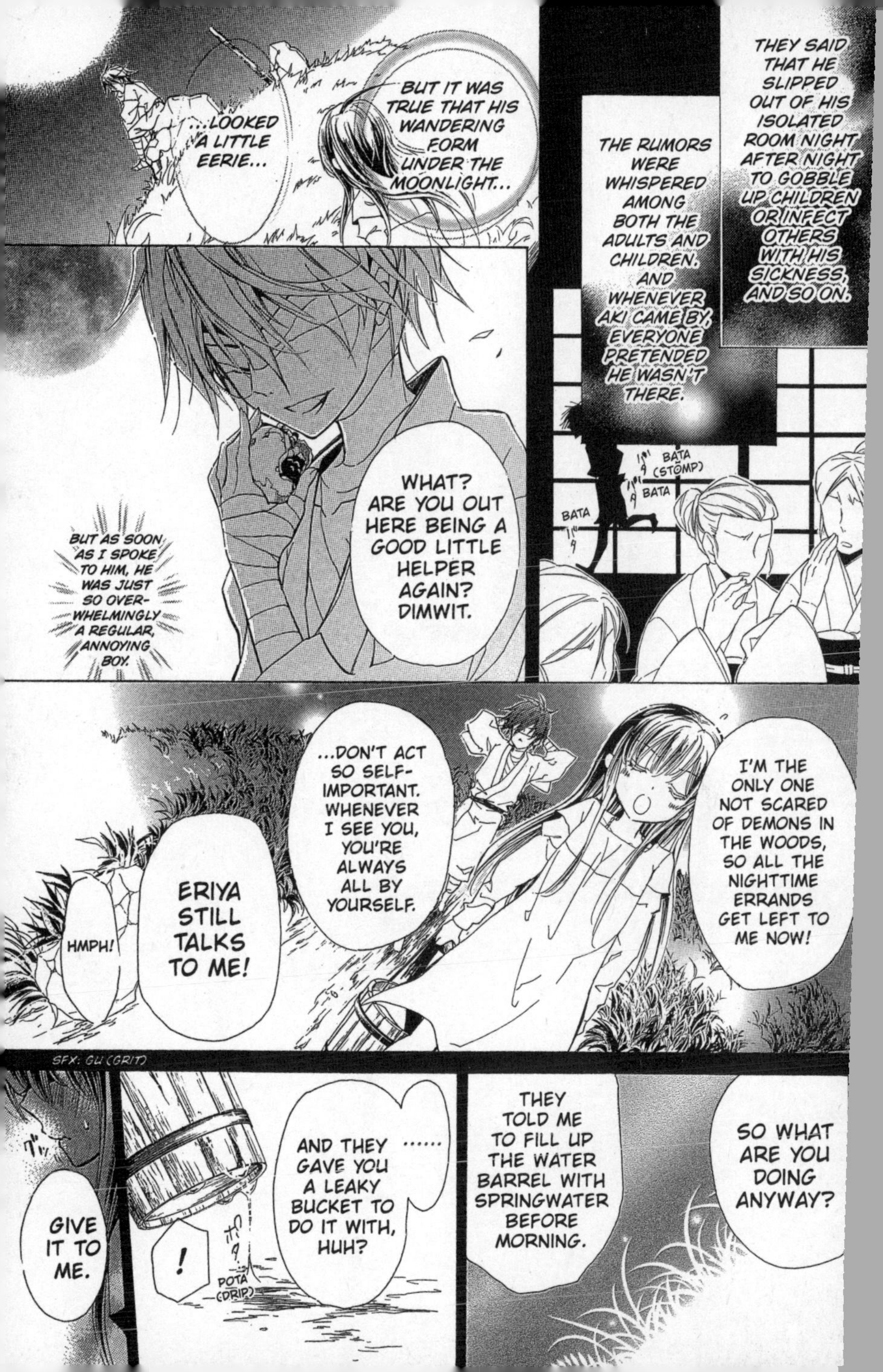
THEY SAID THAT HE SLIPPED OUT OF HIS ISOLATED ROOM NIGHT AFTER NIGHT TO GOBBLE UP CHILDREN OR INFECT OTHERS WITH HIS SICKNESS, AND SO ON.
THE RUMORS WERE WHISPERED AMONG BOTH THE ADULTS AND CHILDREN. AND WHENEVER AKI CAME BY, EVERYONE PRETENDED HE WASN'T THERE.
BATA (STOMP)
BATA
BATA
BUT IT WAS TRUE THAT HIS WANDERING FORM UNDER THE MOONLIGHT...
...LOOKED A LITTLE EERIE...
WHAT? ARE YOU OUT HERE BEING A GOOD LITTLE HELPER AGAIN? DIMWIT.
BUT AS SOON AS I SPOKE TO HIM, HE WAS JUST SO OVER-WHELMINGLY A REGULAR, ANNOYING BOY.
I'M THE ONLY ONE NOT SCARED OF DEMONS IN THE WOODS, SO ALL THE NIGHTTIME ERRANDS GET LEFT TO ME NOW!
...DON'T ACT SO SELF-IMPORTANT. WHENEVER I SEE YOU, YOU'RE ALWAYS ALL BY YOURSELF.
ERIYA STILL TALKS TO ME!
HMPH!
SFX: GU (GRIT)
SO WHAT ARE YOU DOING ANYWAY?
THEY TOLD ME TO FILL UP THE WATER BARREL WITH SPRINGWATER BEFORE MORNING.
......
AND THEY GAVE YOU A LEAKY BUCKET TO DO IT WITH, HUH?
POTA (DRIP)
!
GIVE IT TO ME.

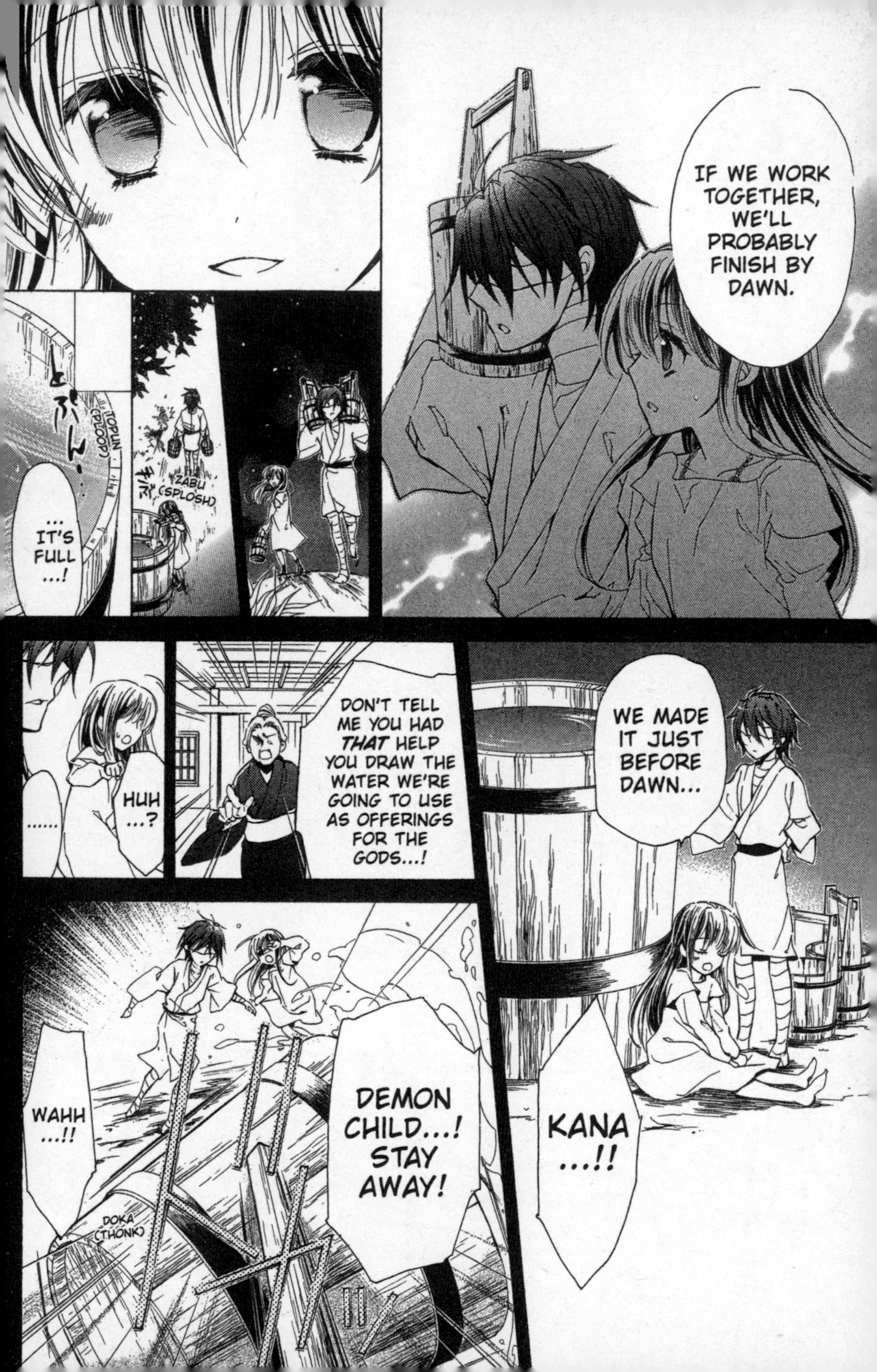
IF WE WORK TOGETHER, WE'LL PROBABLY FINISH BY DAWN.
ZABU (SPLOSH)
TOPUN (PLOOP)
... IT'S FULL ...!
WE MADE IT JUST BEFORE DAWN...
KANA ...!!
DON'T TELL ME YOU HAD *THAT* HELP YOU DRAW THE WATER WE'RE GOING TO USE AS OFFERINGS FOR THE GODS...!
HUH ...?
......
DEMON CHILD...! STAY AWAY!
WAHH ...!!
DOKA (THONK)

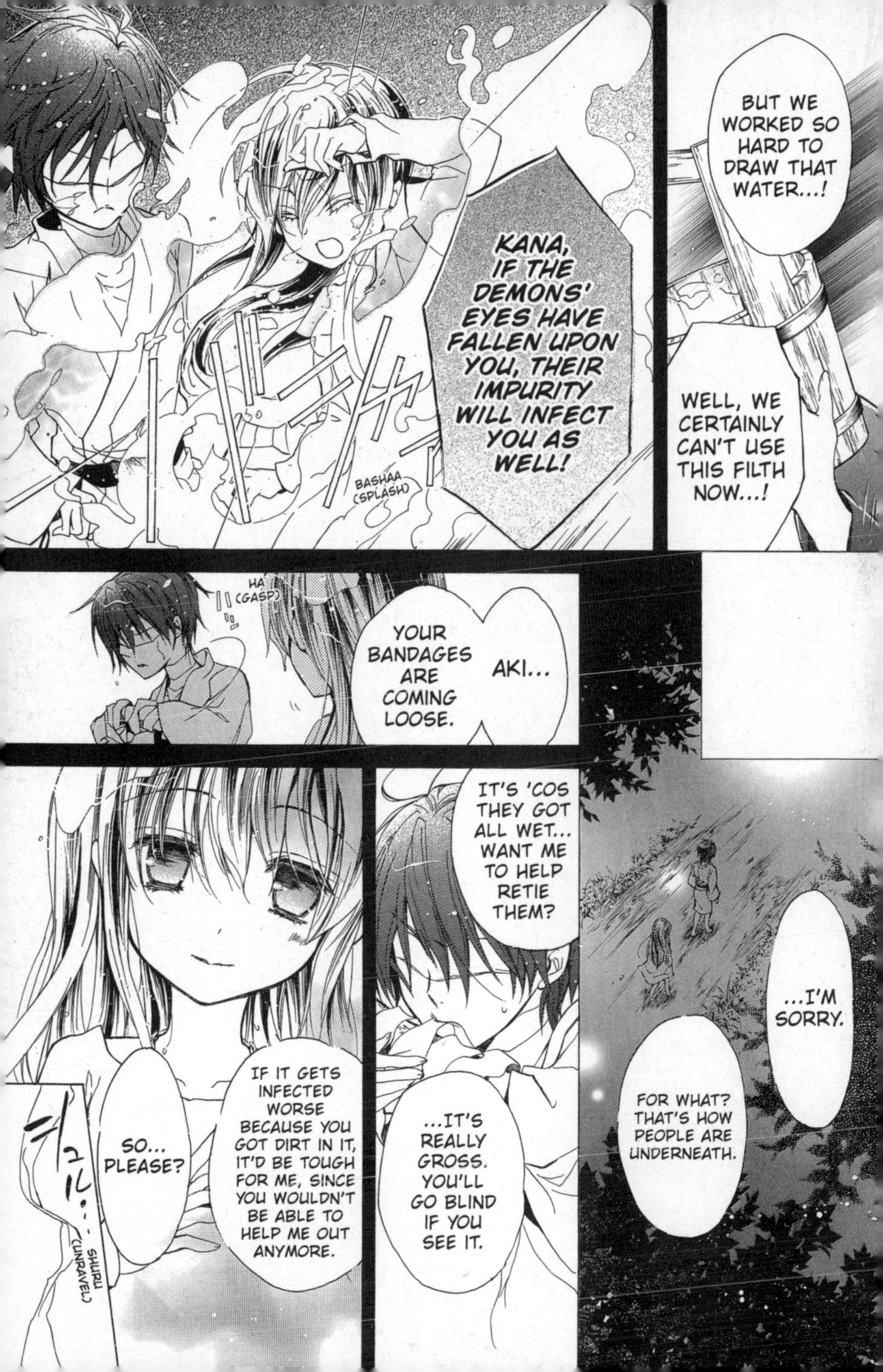
BUT WE WORKED SO HARD TO DRAW THAT WATER...!
WELL, WE CERTAINLY CAN'T USE THIS FILTH NOW...!
KANA, IF THE DEMONS' EYES HAVE FALLEN UPON YOU, THEIR IMPURITY WILL INFECT YOU AS WELL!
BASHAA (SPLASH)
...I'M SORRY.
FOR WHAT? THAT'S HOW PEOPLE ARE UNDERNEATH.
HA (GASP)
AKI...
YOUR BANDAGES ARE COMING LOOSE.
IT'S 'COS THEY GOT ALL WET... WANT ME TO HELP RETIE THEM?
...IT'S REALLY GROSS. YOU'LL GO BLIND IF YOU SEE IT.
IF IT GETS INFECTED WORSE BECAUSE YOU GOT DIRT IN IT, IT'D BE TOUGH FOR ME, SINCE YOU WOULDN'T BE ABLE TO HELP ME OUT ANYMORE.
SO... PLEASE?
SHURU (UNRAVEL)

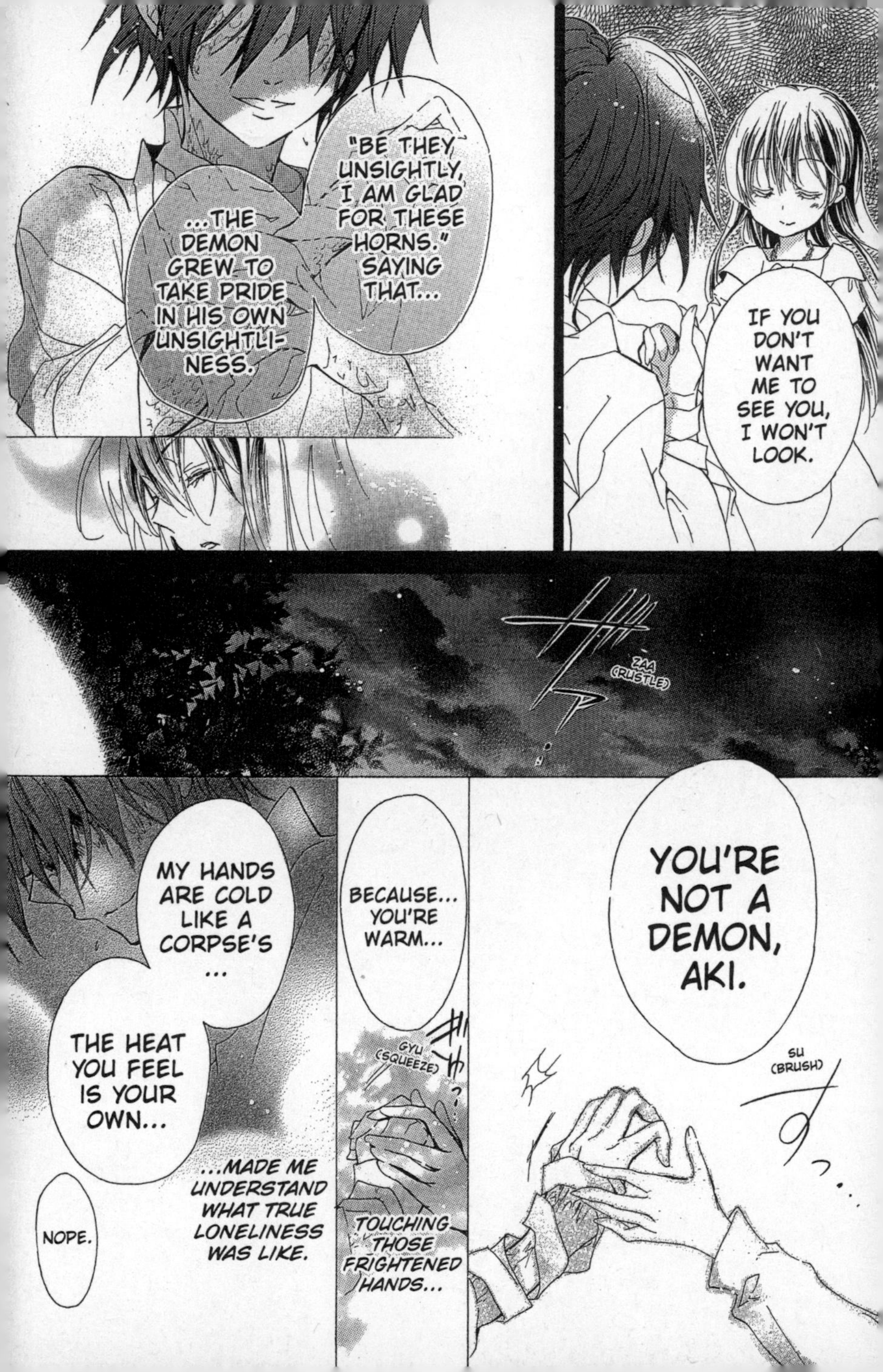
IF YOU DON'T WANT ME TO SEE YOU, I WON'T LOOK.
"BE THEY UNSIGHTLY, I AM GLAD FOR THESE HORNS." SAYING THAT...
...THE DEMON GREW TO TAKE PRIDE IN HIS OWN UNSIGHTLINESS.
ZAA (RUSTLE)
YOU'RE NOT A DEMON, AKI.
SU (BRUSH)
BECAUSE... YOU'RE WARM...
GYU (SQUEEZE)
TOUCHING THOSE FRIGHTENED HANDS...
MY HANDS ARE COLD LIKE A CORPSE'S...
THE HEAT YOU FEEL IS YOUR OWN...
...MADE ME UNDERSTAND WHAT TRUE LONELINESS WAS LIKE.
NOPE.

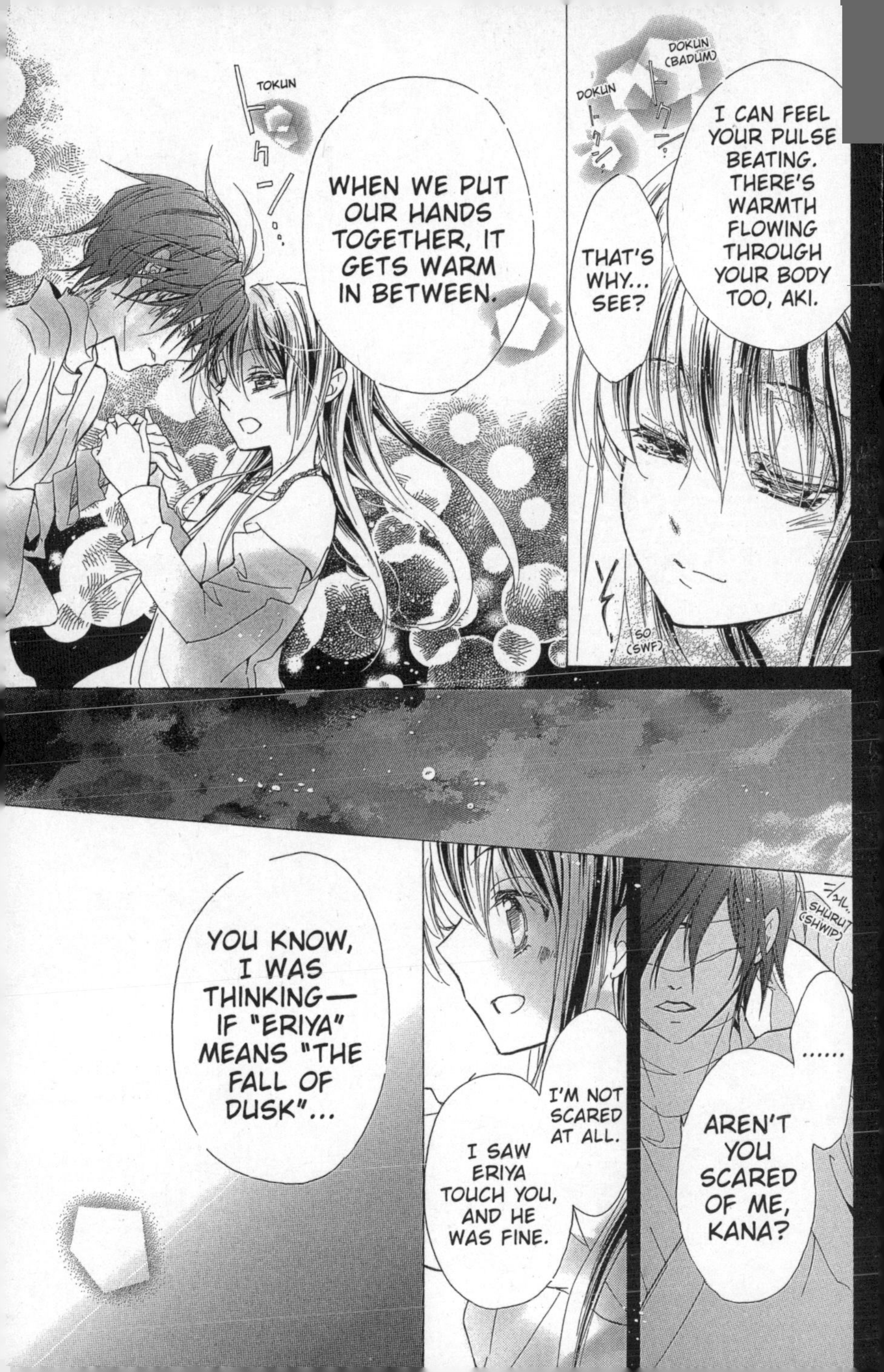
DOKUN (BADUM)
DOKUN
I CAN FEEL YOUR PULSE BEATING. THERE'S WARMTH FLOWING THROUGH YOUR BODY TOO, AKI.
THAT'S WHY... SEE?
SO (SWF)
TOKUN
WHEN WE PUT OUR HANDS TOGETHER, IT GETS WARM IN BETWEEN.
SHURUT (SHWIP)
......
AREN'T YOU SCARED OF ME, KANA?
I'M NOT SCARED AT ALL.
I SAW ERIYA TOUCH YOU, AND HE WAS FINE.
YOU KNOW, I WAS THINKING— IF "ERIYA" MEANS "THE FALL OF DUSK"...

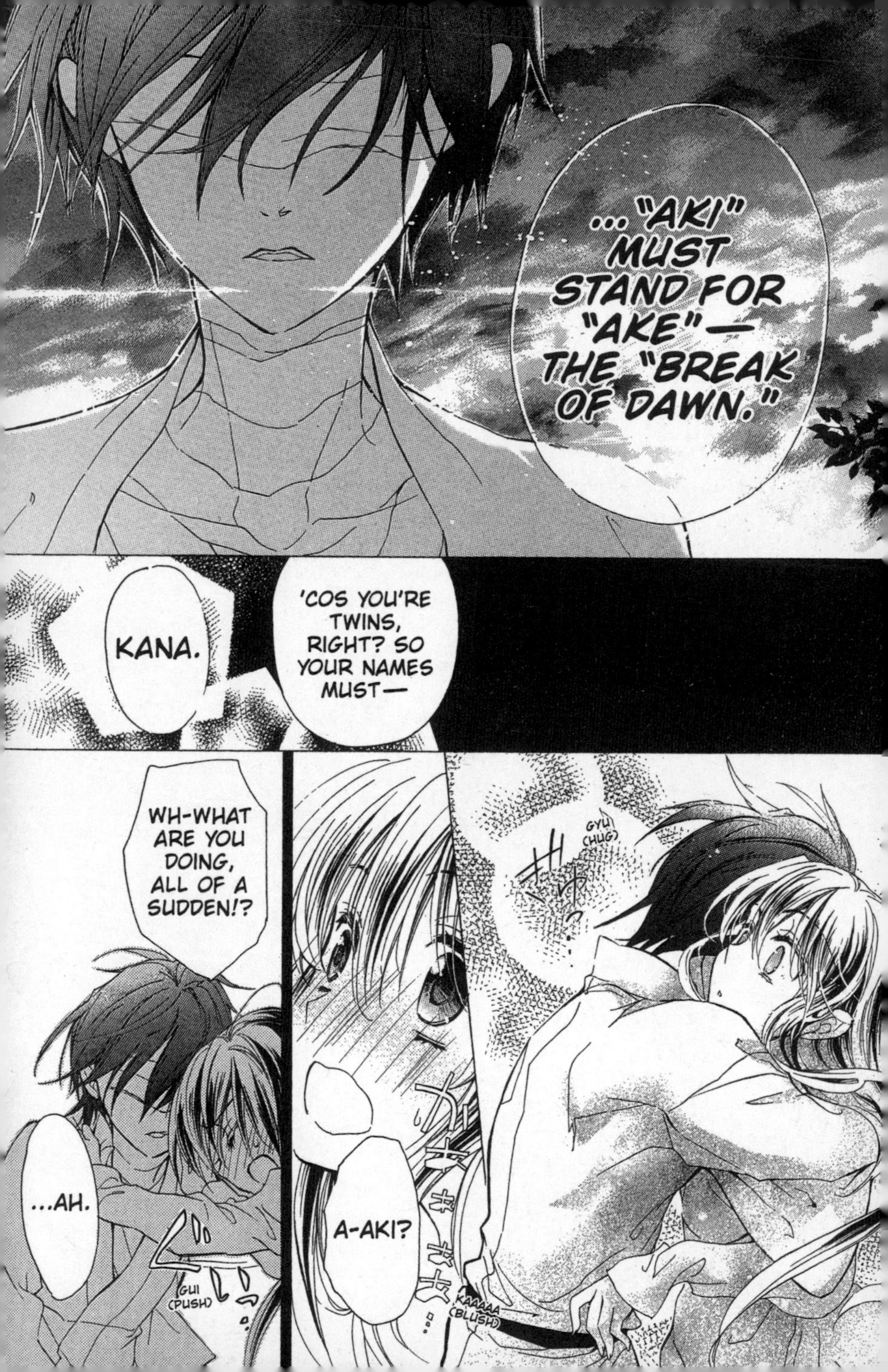

..."AKI" MUST STAND FOR "AKE"— THE "BREAK OF DAWN."
'COS YOU'RE TWINS, RIGHT? SO YOUR NAMES MUST—
KANA.
GYU (HUG)
A-AKI?
KAAAAA (BLUSH)
WH-WHAT ARE YOU DOING, ALL OF A SUDDEN!?
...AH.
GUI (PUSH)

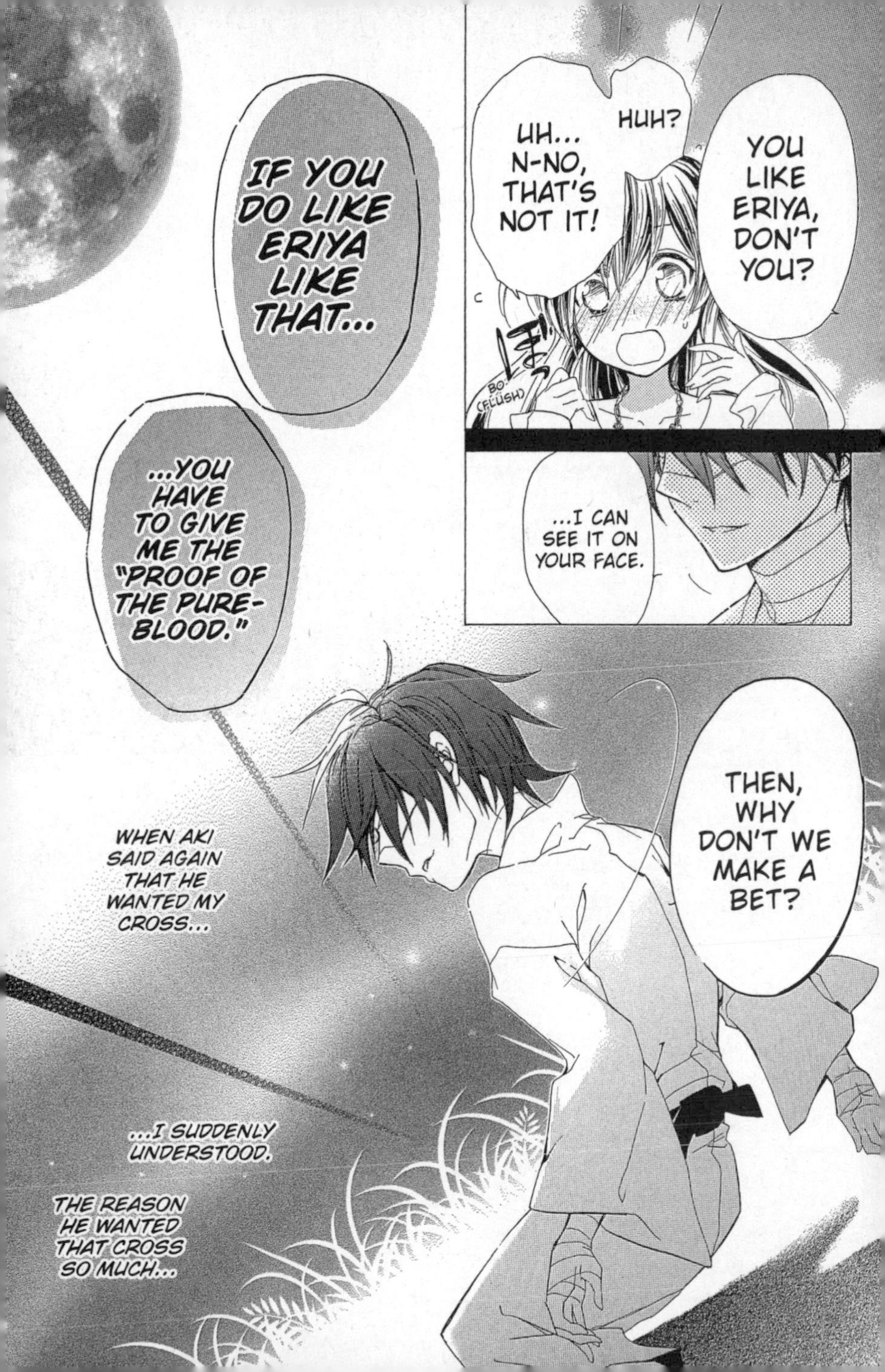
YOU LIKE ERIYA, DON'T YOU?
HUH?
UH... N-NO, THAT'S NOT IT!
BO (FLUSH)
...I CAN SEE IT ON YOUR FACE.
IF YOU DO LIKE ERIYA LIKE THAT...
...YOU HAVE TO GIVE ME THE "PROOF OF THE PURE-BLOOD."
THEN, WHY DON'T WE MAKE A BET?
WHEN AKI SAID AGAIN THAT HE WANTED MY CROSS...
...I SUDDENLY UNDERSTOOD.
THE REASON HE WANTED THAT CROSS SO MUCH...

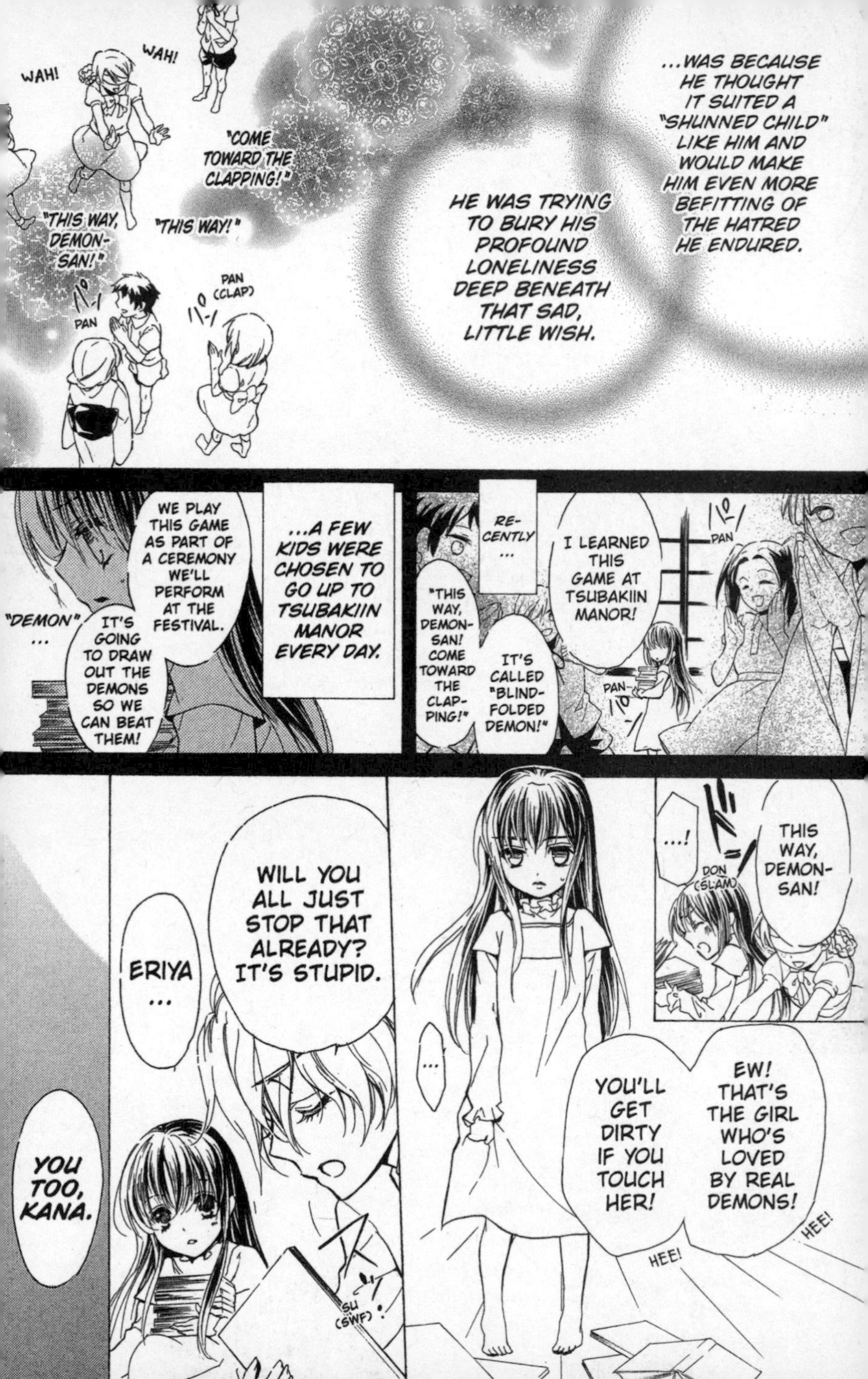
...WAS BECAUSE HE THOUGHT IT SUITED A "SHUNNED CHILD" LIKE HIM AND WOULD MAKE HIM EVEN MORE BEFITTING OF THE HATRED HE ENDURED.
HE WAS TRYING TO BURY HIS PROFOUND LONELINESS DEEP BENEATH THAT SAD, LITTLE WISH.
WAH!
WAH!
"COME TOWARD THE CLAPPING!"
"THIS WAY!"
"THIS WAY, DEMON-SAN!"
PAN (CLAP)
PAN
RE-CENTLY...
I LEARNED THIS GAME AT TSUBAKIIN MANOR!
PAN
"THIS WAY, DEMON-SAN! COME TOWARD THE CLAP-PING!"
IT'S CALLED "BLIND-FOLDED DEMON!"
PAN
...A FEW KIDS WERE CHOSEN TO GO UP TO TSUBAKIIN MANOR EVERY DAY.
WE PLAY THIS GAME AS PART OF A CEREMONY WE'LL PERFORM AT THE FESTIVAL.
IT'S GOING TO DRAW OUT THE DEMONS SO WE CAN BEAT THEM!
"DEMON"...
THIS WAY, DEMON-SAN!
DON (SLAM)
...!
EW! THAT'S THE GIRL WHO'S LOVED BY REAL DEMONS!
YOU'LL GET DIRTY IF YOU TOUCH HER!
HEE!
HEE!
...
WILL YOU ALL JUST STOP THAT ALREADY? IT'S STUPID.
ERIYA...
YOU TOO, KANA.
SU (SWF)

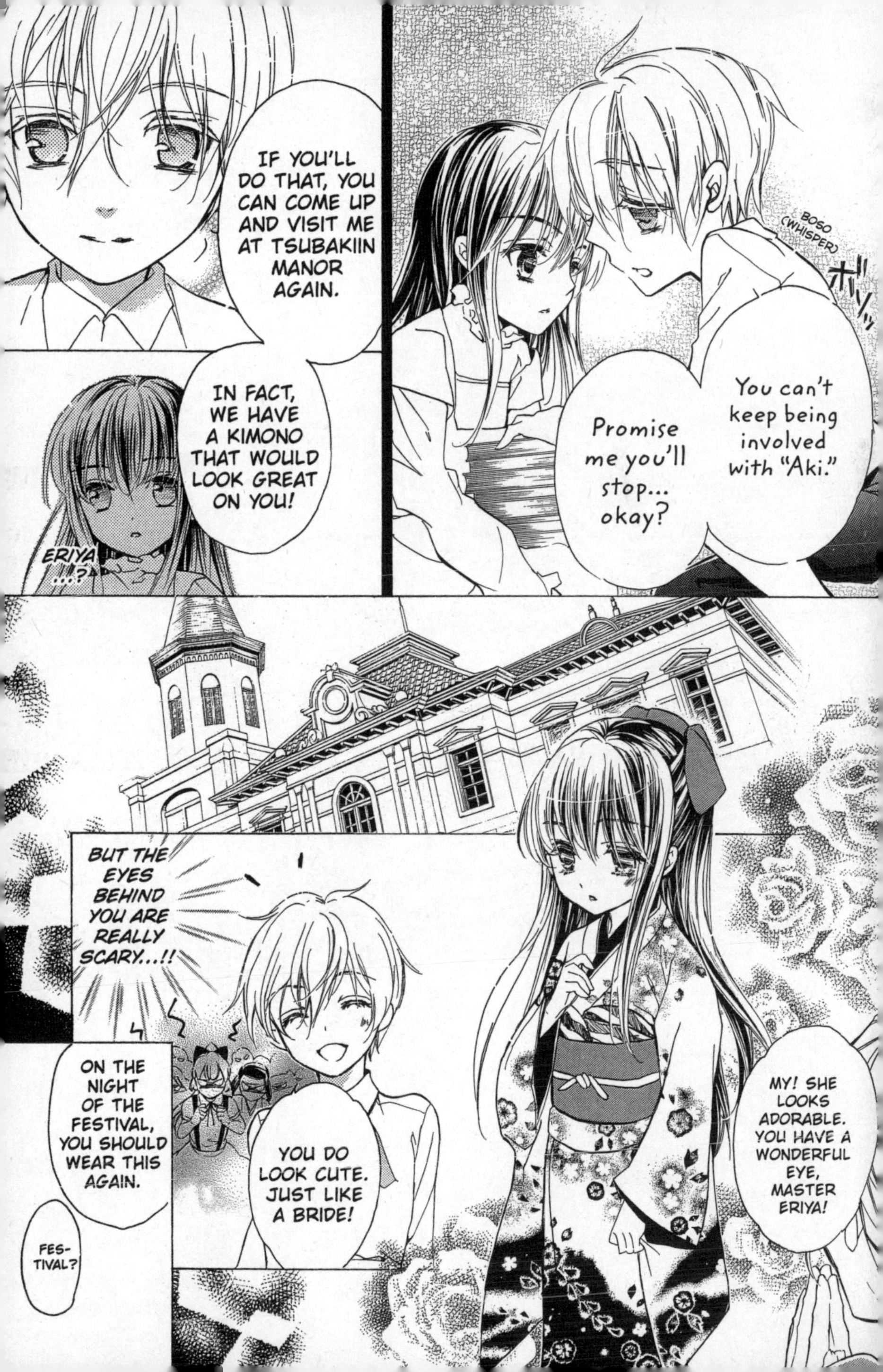
BOSO (WHISPER)
ボソッ
You can't keep being involved with "Aki."
Promise me you'll stop... okay?
IF YOU'LL DO THAT, YOU CAN COME UP AND VISIT ME AT TSUBAKIIN MANOR AGAIN.
IN FACT, WE HAVE A KIMONO THAT WOULD LOOK GREAT ON YOU!
ERIYA ...?
MY! SHE LOOKS ADORABLE. YOU HAVE A WONDERFUL EYE, MASTER ERIYA!
BUT THE EYES BEHIND YOU ARE REALLY SCARY...!!
YOU DO LOOK CUTE. JUST LIKE A BRIDE!
ON THE NIGHT OF THE FESTIVAL, YOU SHOULD WEAR THIS AGAIN.
FES-TIVAL?

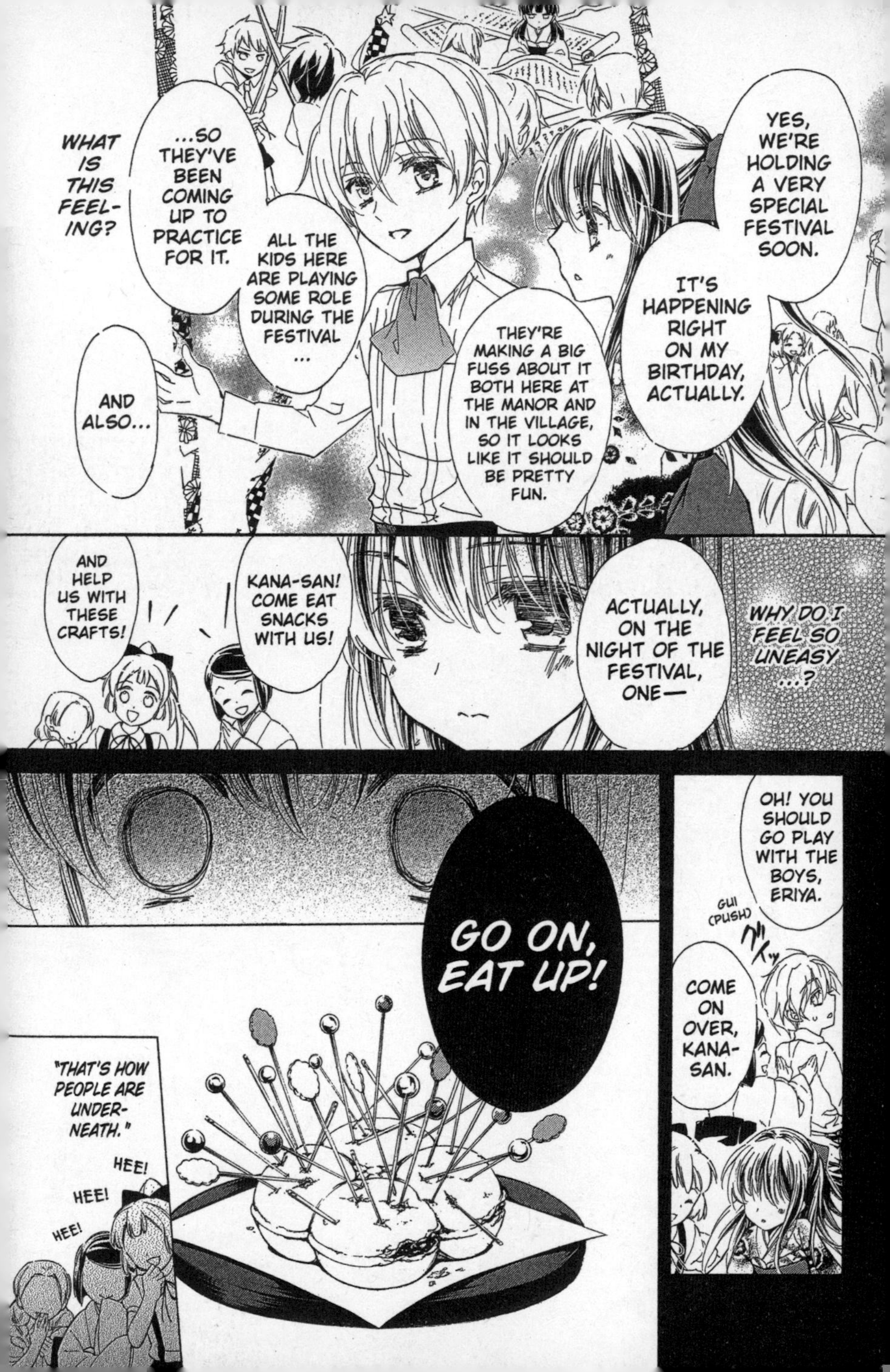
YES, WE'RE HOLDING A VERY SPECIAL FESTIVAL SOON.
IT'S HAPPENING RIGHT ON MY BIRTHDAY, ACTUALLY.
THEY'RE MAKING A BIG FUSS ABOUT IT BOTH HERE AT THE MANOR AND IN THE VILLAGE, SO IT LOOKS LIKE IT SHOULD BE PRETTY FUN.
ALL THE KIDS HERE ARE PLAYING SOME ROLE DURING THE FESTIVAL...
...SO THEY'VE BEEN COMING UP TO PRACTICE FOR IT.
WHAT IS THIS FEEL-ING?
AND ALSO...
WHY DO I FEEL SO UNEASY...?
ACTUALLY, ON THE NIGHT OF THE FESTIVAL, ONE—
KANA-SAN! COME EAT SNACKS WITH US!
AND HELP US WITH THESE CRAFTS!
OH! YOU SHOULD GO PLAY WITH THE BOYS, ERIYA.
GUI (PUSH)
COME ON OVER, KANA-SAN.
GO ON, EAT UP!
"THAT'S HOW PEOPLE ARE UNDER-NEATH."
HEE!
HEE!
HEE!

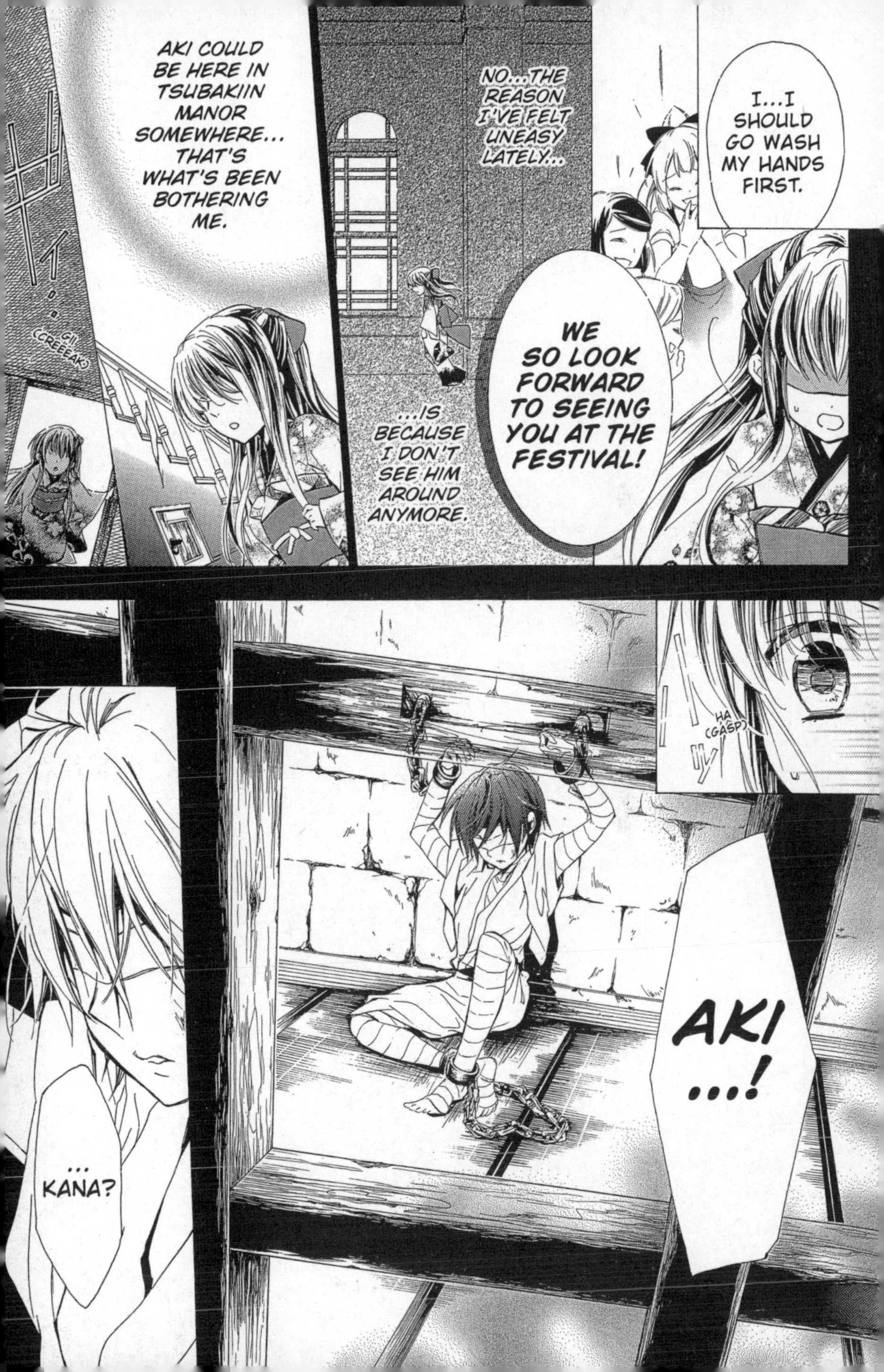
WE SO LOOK FORWARD TO SEEING YOU AT THE FESTIVAL!
I...I SHOULD GO WASH MY HANDS FIRST.
NO...THE REASON I'VE FELT UNEASY LATELY...
...IS BECAUSE I DON'T SEE HIM AROUND ANYMORE.
AKI COULD BE HERE IN TSUBAKIIN MANOR SOMEWHERE... THAT'S WHAT'S BEEN BOTHERING ME.
GI (CREEEAK)
HA (GASP)
AKI...!
...KANA?

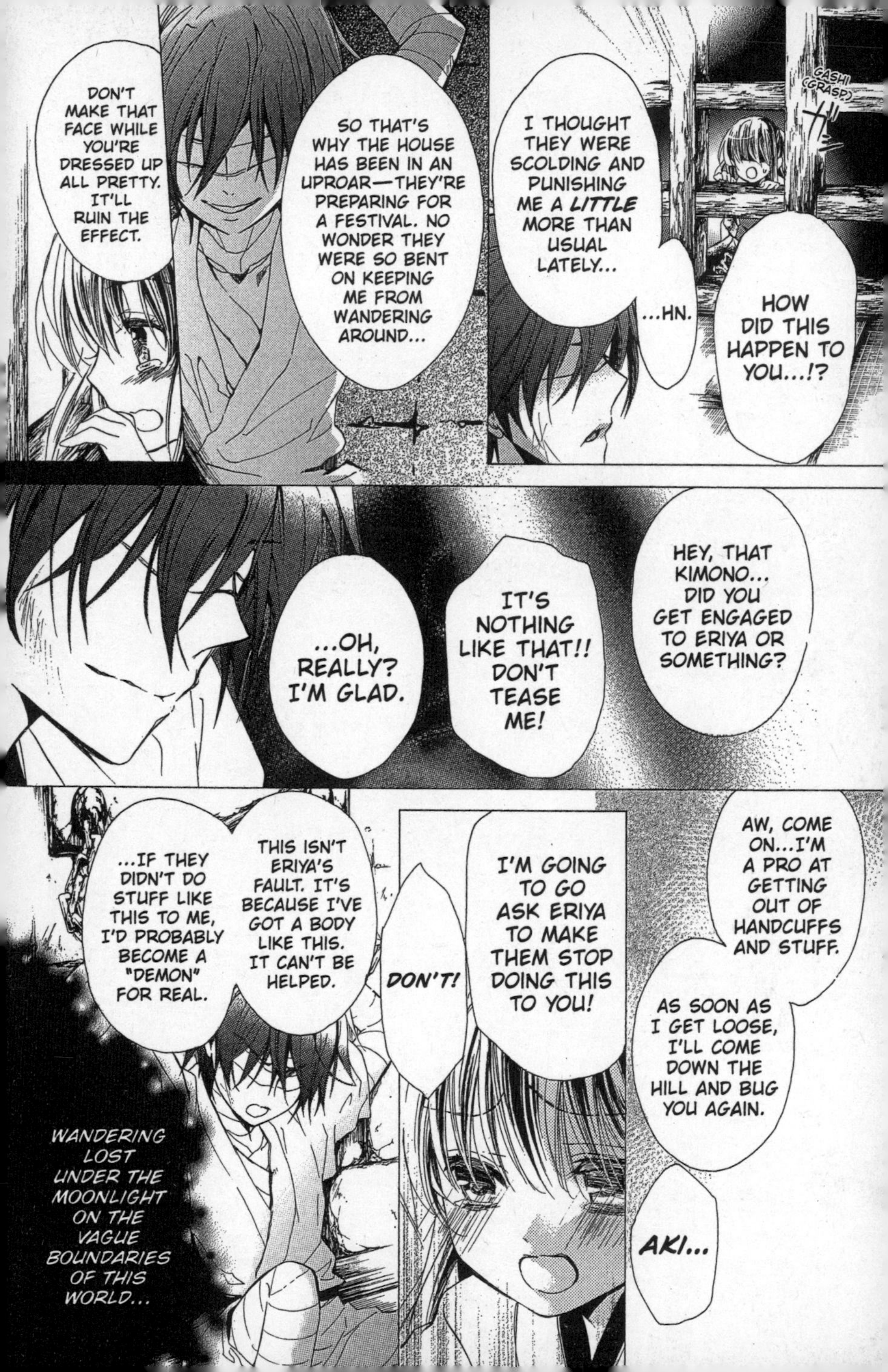
GASHI (GRASP)
HOW DID THIS HAPPEN TO YOU...!?
...HN.
I THOUGHT THEY WERE SCOLDING AND PUNISHING ME A *LITTLE* MORE THAN USUAL LATELY...
SO THAT'S WHY THE HOUSE HAS BEEN IN AN UPROAR—THEY'RE PREPARING FOR A FESTIVAL. NO WONDER THEY WERE SO BENT ON KEEPING ME FROM WANDERING AROUND...
DON'T MAKE THAT FACE WHILE YOU'RE DRESSED UP ALL PRETTY. IT'LL RUIN THE EFFECT.
HEY, THAT KIMONO... DID YOU GET ENGAGED TO ERIYA OR SOMETHING?
IT'S NOTHING LIKE THAT!! DON'T TEASE ME!
...OH, REALLY? I'M GLAD.
I'M GOING TO GO ASK ERIYA TO MAKE THEM STOP DOING THIS TO YOU!
DON'T!
THIS ISN'T ERIYA'S FAULT. IT'S BECAUSE I'VE GOT A BODY LIKE THIS. IT CAN'T BE HELPED.
...IF THEY DIDN'T DO STUFF LIKE THIS TO ME, I'D PROBABLY BECOME A "DEMON" FOR REAL.
AW, COME ON...I'M A PRO AT GETTING OUT OF HANDCUFFS AND STUFF.
AS SOON AS I GET LOOSE, I'LL COME DOWN THE HILL AND BUG YOU AGAIN.
AKI...
WANDERING LOST UNDER THE MOONLIGHT ON THE VAGUE BOUNDARIES OF THIS WORLD...

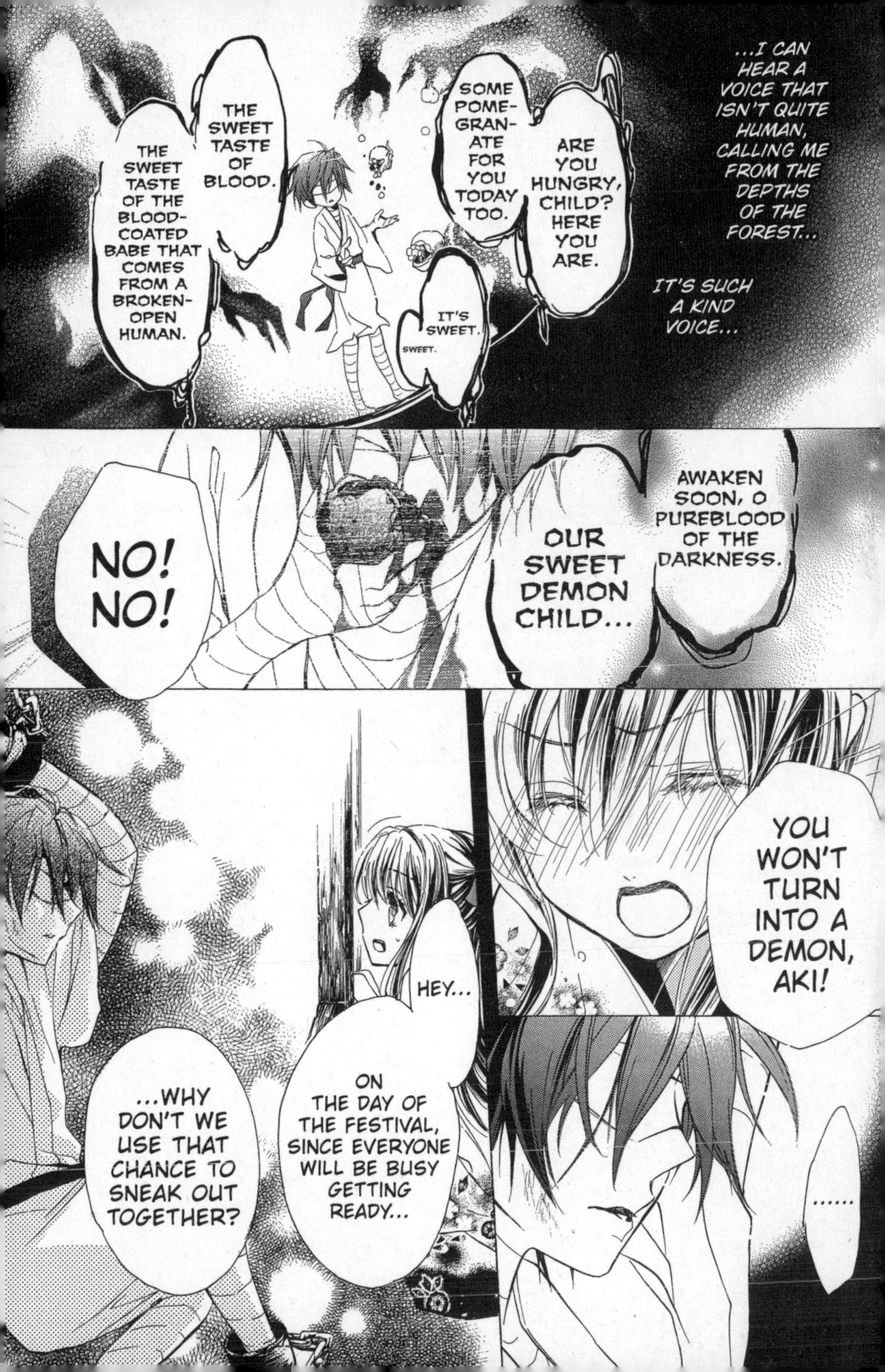
...I CAN HEAR A VOICE THAT ISN'T QUITE HUMAN, CALLING ME FROM THE DEPTHS OF THE FOREST...
IT'S SUCH A KIND VOICE...
ARE YOU HUNGRY, CHILD? HERE YOU ARE.
SOME POMEGRANATE FOR YOU TODAY TOO.
IT'S SWEET.
SWEET.
THE SWEET TASTE OF BLOOD.
THE SWEET TASTE OF THE BLOOD-COATED BABE THAT COMES FROM A BROKEN-OPEN HUMAN.
AWAKEN SOON, O PUREBLOOD OF THE DARKNESS.
OUR SWEET DEMON CHILD...
NO! NO!
YOU WON'T TURN INTO A DEMON, AKI!
......
HEY...
ON THE DAY OF THE FESTIVAL, SINCE EVERYONE WILL BE BUSY GETTING READY...
...WHY DON'T WE USE THAT CHANCE TO SNEAK OUT TOGETHER?

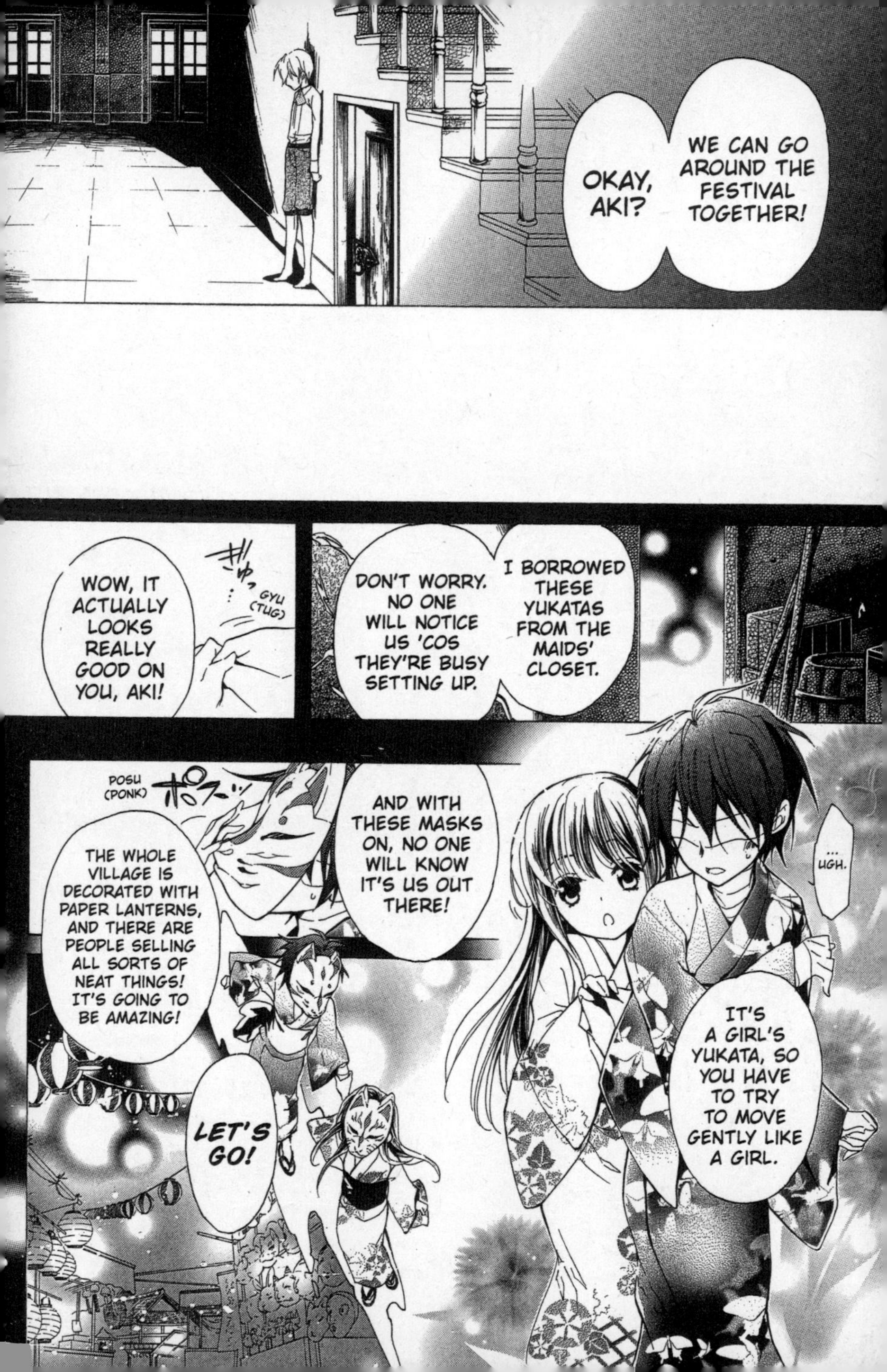
WE CAN GO AROUND THE FESTIVAL TOGETHER!
OKAY, AKI?
I BORROWED THESE YUKATAS FROM THE MAIDS' CLOSET.
DON'T WORRY. NO ONE WILL NOTICE US 'COS THEY'RE BUSY SETTING UP.
GYU (TUG)
WOW, IT ACTUALLY LOOKS REALLY GOOD ON YOU, AKI!
... UGH.
IT'S A GIRL'S YUKATA, SO YOU HAVE TO TRY TO MOVE GENTLY LIKE A GIRL.
AND WITH THESE MASKS ON, NO ONE WILL KNOW IT'S US OUT THERE!
POSU (PONK)
THE WHOLE VILLAGE IS DECORATED WITH PAPER LANTERNS, AND THERE ARE PEOPLE SELLING ALL SORTS OF NEAT THINGS! IT'S GOING TO BE AMAZING!
LET'S GO!

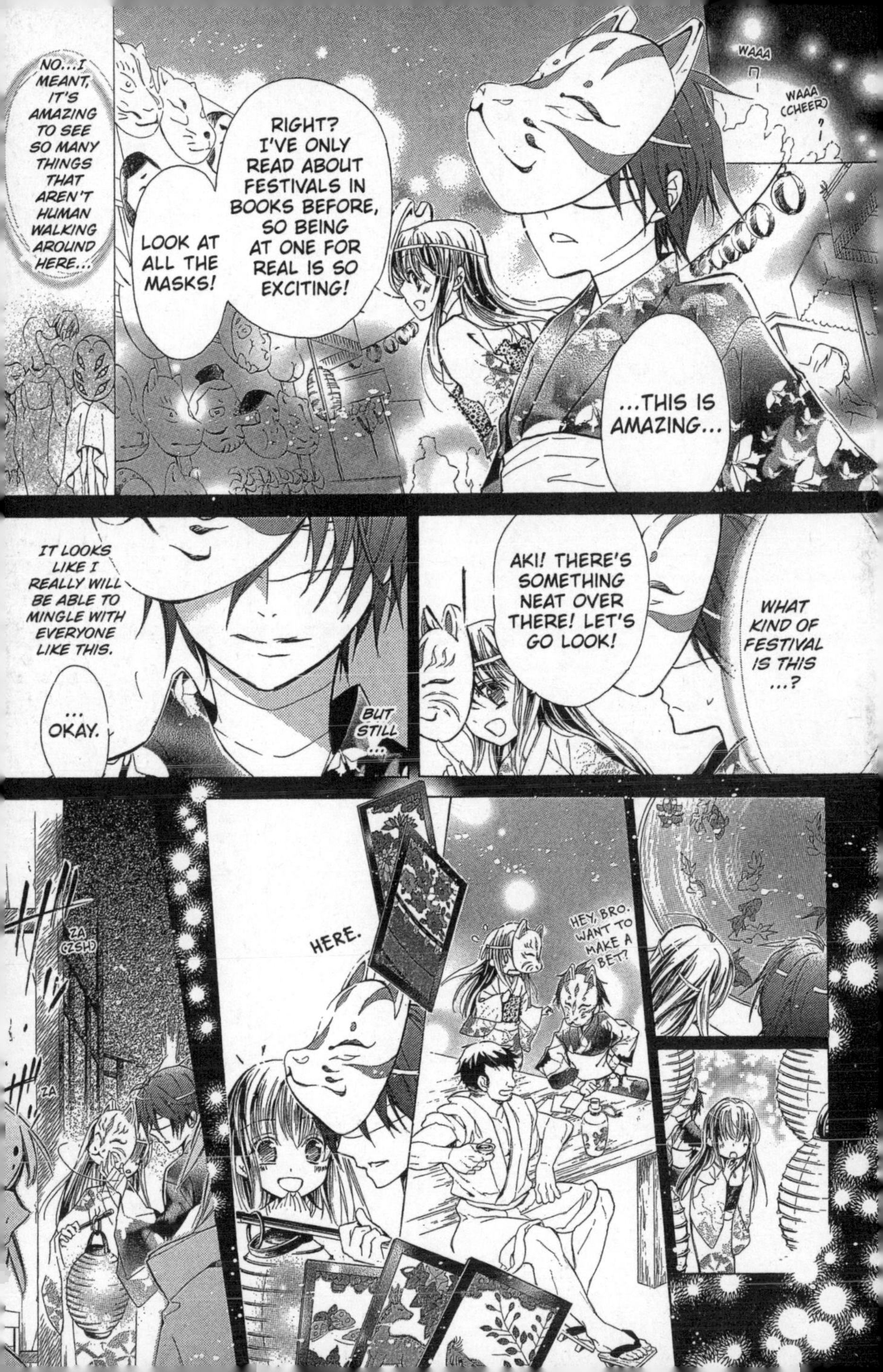
WAAA
WAAA (CHEER)
...THIS IS AMAZING...
RIGHT? I'VE ONLY READ ABOUT FESTIVALS IN BOOKS BEFORE, SO BEING AT ONE FOR REAL IS SO EXCITING!
LOOK AT ALL THE MASKS!
NO...I MEANT, IT'S AMAZING TO SEE SO MANY THINGS THAT AREN'T HUMAN WALKING AROUND HERE...
WHAT KIND OF FESTIVAL IS THIS ...?
AKI! THERE'S SOMETHING NEAT OVER THERE! LET'S GO LOOK!
... OKAY.
BUT STILL ...
IT LOOKS LIKE I REALLY WILL BE ABLE TO MINGLE WITH EVERYONE LIKE THIS.
HEY, BRO. WANT TO MAKE A BET?
HERE.
ZA (ZSH)
ZA

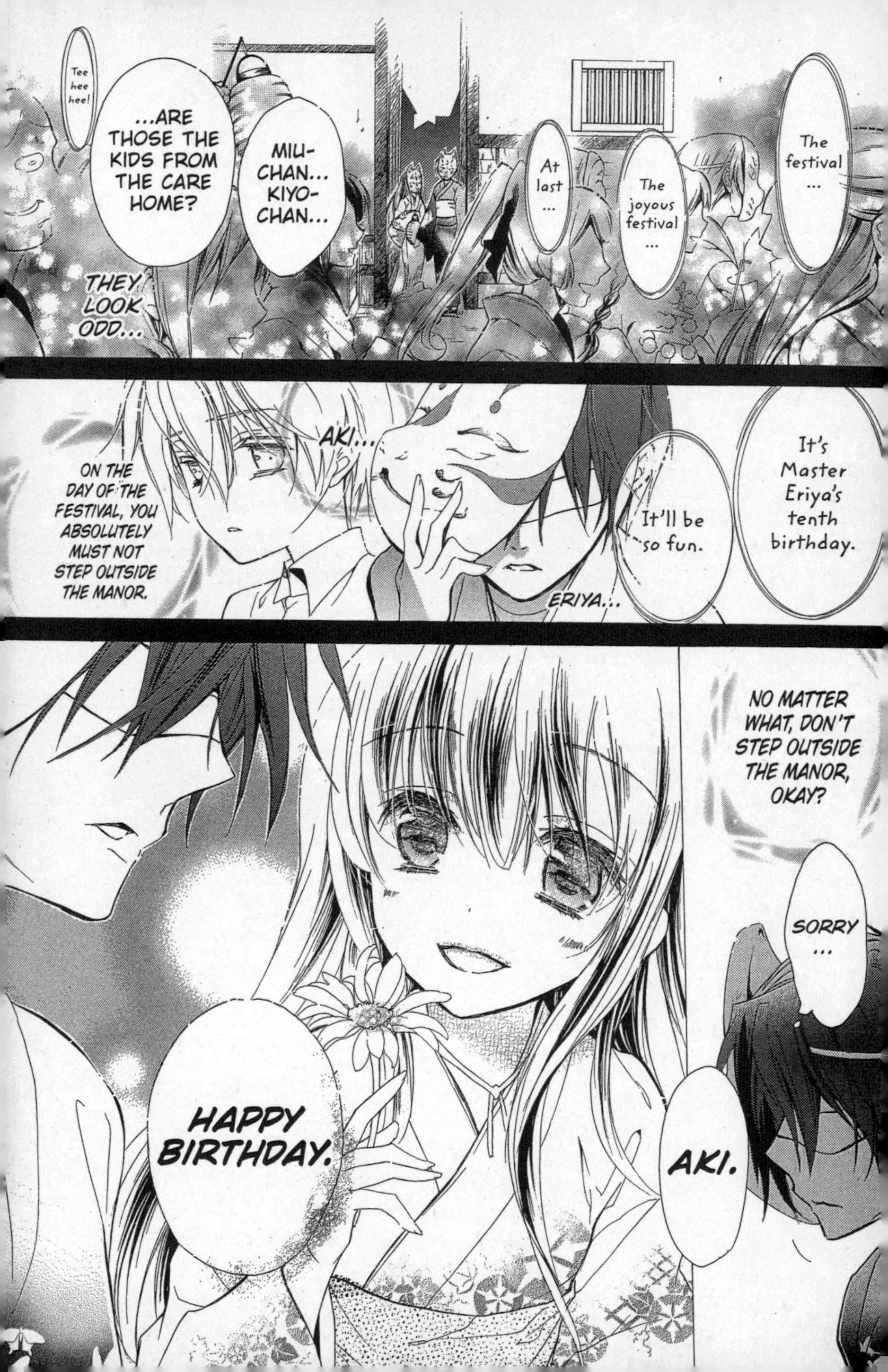
The festival ...
The joyous festival ...
At last ...
MIU-CHAN... KIYO-CHAN...
...ARE THOSE THE KIDS FROM THE CARE HOME?
Tee hee hee!
THEY LOOK ODD...
It's Master Eriya's tenth birthday.
It'll be so fun.
ERIYA...
AKI...
ON THE DAY OF THE FESTIVAL, YOU ABSOLUTELY MUST NOT STEP OUTSIDE THE MANOR.
NO MATTER WHAT, DON'T STEP OUTSIDE THE MANOR, OKAY?
SORRY ...
HAPPY BIRTHDAY.
AKI.

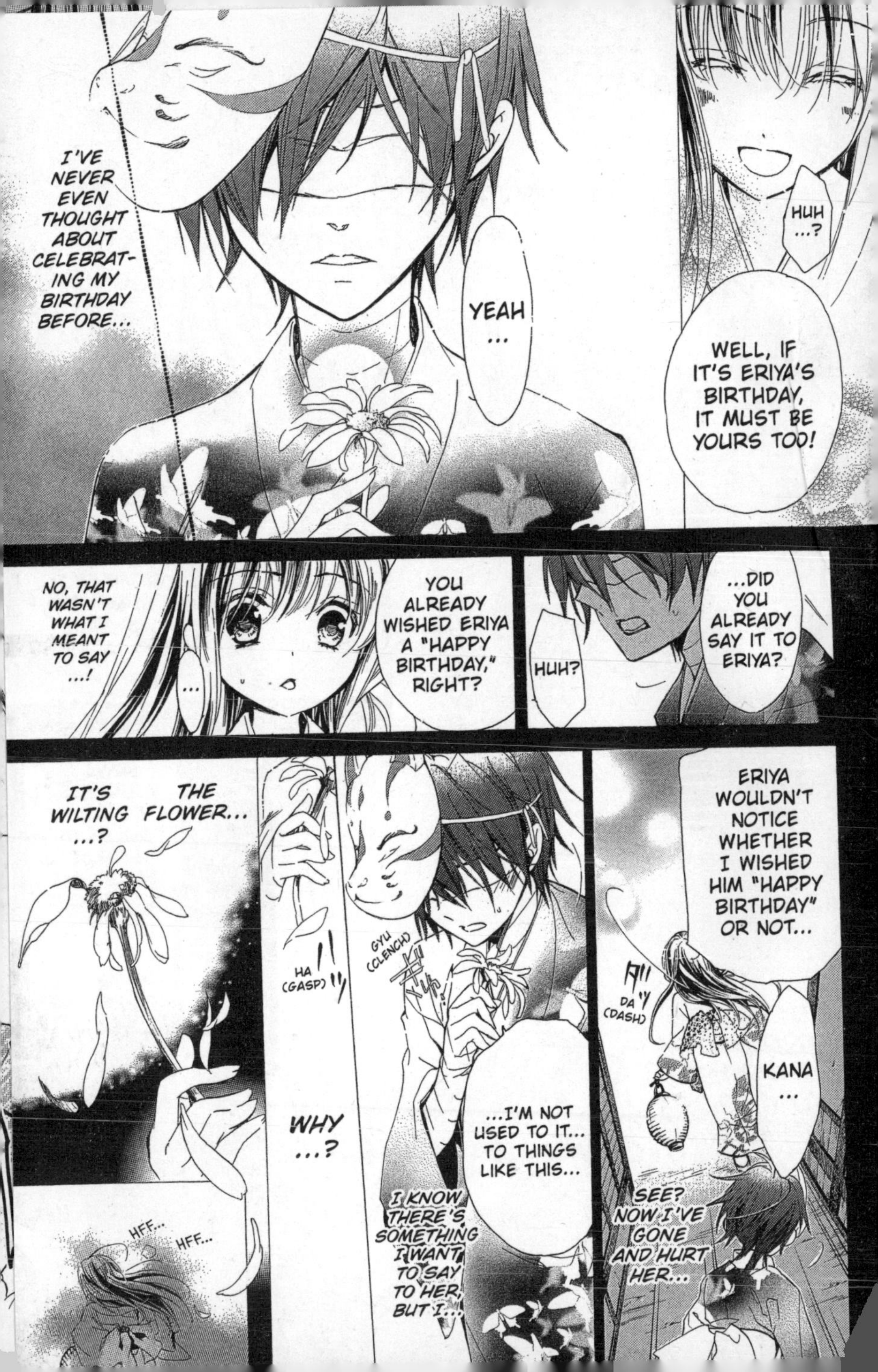
HUH ...?
WELL, IF IT'S ERIYA'S BIRTHDAY, IT MUST BE YOURS TOO!
YEAH ...
I'VE NEVER EVEN THOUGHT ABOUT CELEBRATING MY BIRTHDAY BEFORE...
...DID YOU ALREADY SAY IT TO ERIYA?
HUH?
YOU ALREADY WISHED ERIYA A "HAPPY BIRTHDAY," RIGHT?
...
NO, THAT WASN'T WHAT I MEANT TO SAY ...!
ERIYA WOULDN'T NOTICE WHETHER I WISHED HIM "HAPPY BIRTHDAY" OR NOT...
DA (DASH)
KANA ...
SEE? NOW I'VE GONE AND HURT HER...
GYU (CLENCH)
HA (GASP)
...I'M NOT USED TO IT... TO THINGS LIKE THIS...
I KNOW THERE'S SOMETHING I WANT TO SAY TO HER, BUT I...
WHY ...?
IT'S THE WILTING FLOWER... ...?
HFF... HFF...

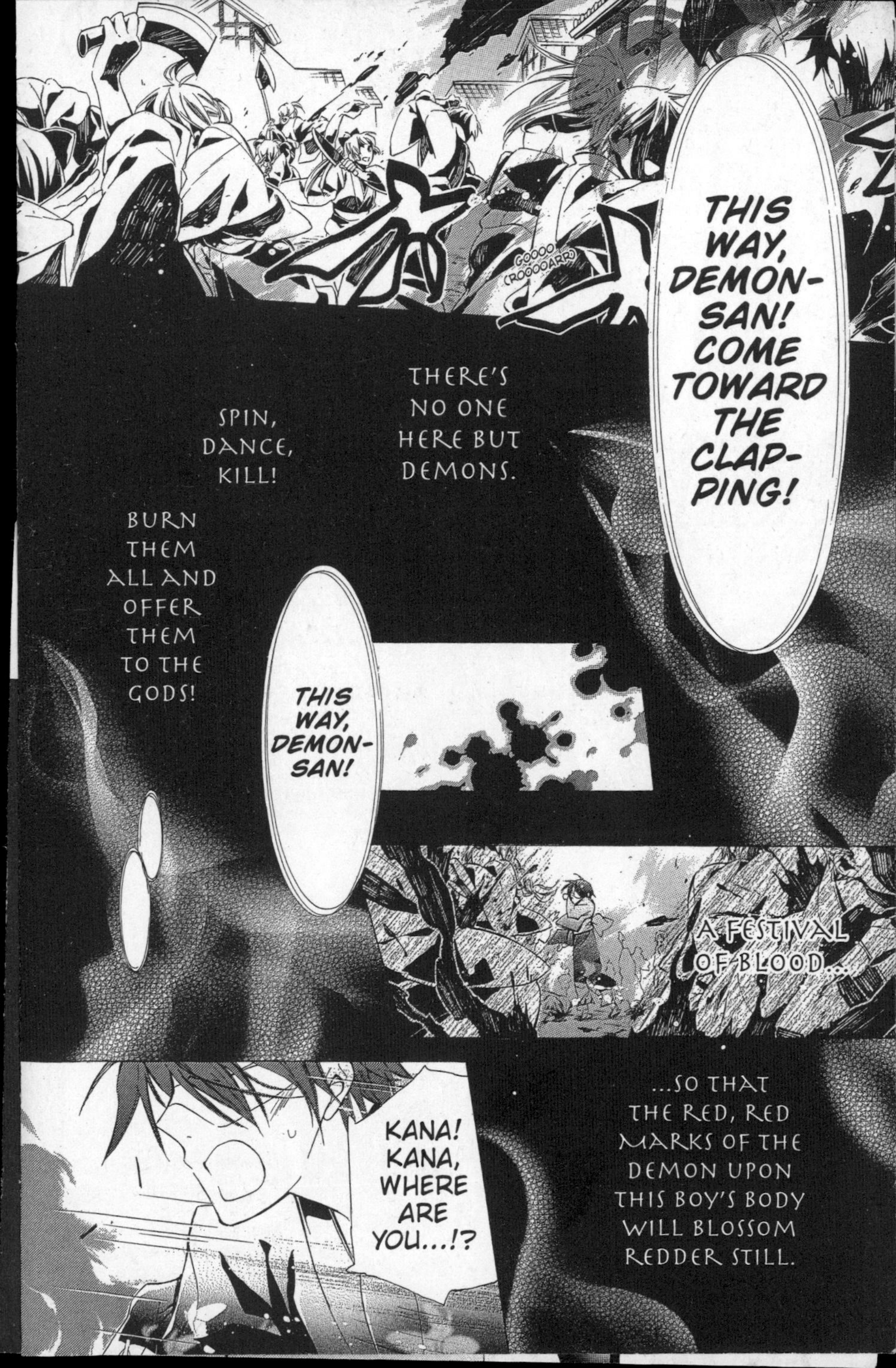
THIS WAY, DEMON-SAN! COME TOWARD THE CLAP-PING!
GOOOO (ROOOOARR)
THERE'S NO ONE HERE BUT DEMONS.
SPIN, DANCE, KILL!
BURN THEM ALL AND OFFER THEM TO THE GODS!
THIS WAY, DEMON-SAN!
A FESTIVAL OF BLOOD...
...SO THAT THE RED, RED MARKS OF THE DEMON UPON THIS BOY'S BODY WILL BLOSSOM REDDER STILL.
KANA! KANA, WHERE ARE YOU...!?

THIS DAY IS JOYOUS.
KANA ...!
FOR IT MARKS THE BIRTH OF THE DEMON CHILD.
... AKI.
HERE, I'LL GIVE THIS TO YOU.
I DO LOVE ERIYA.

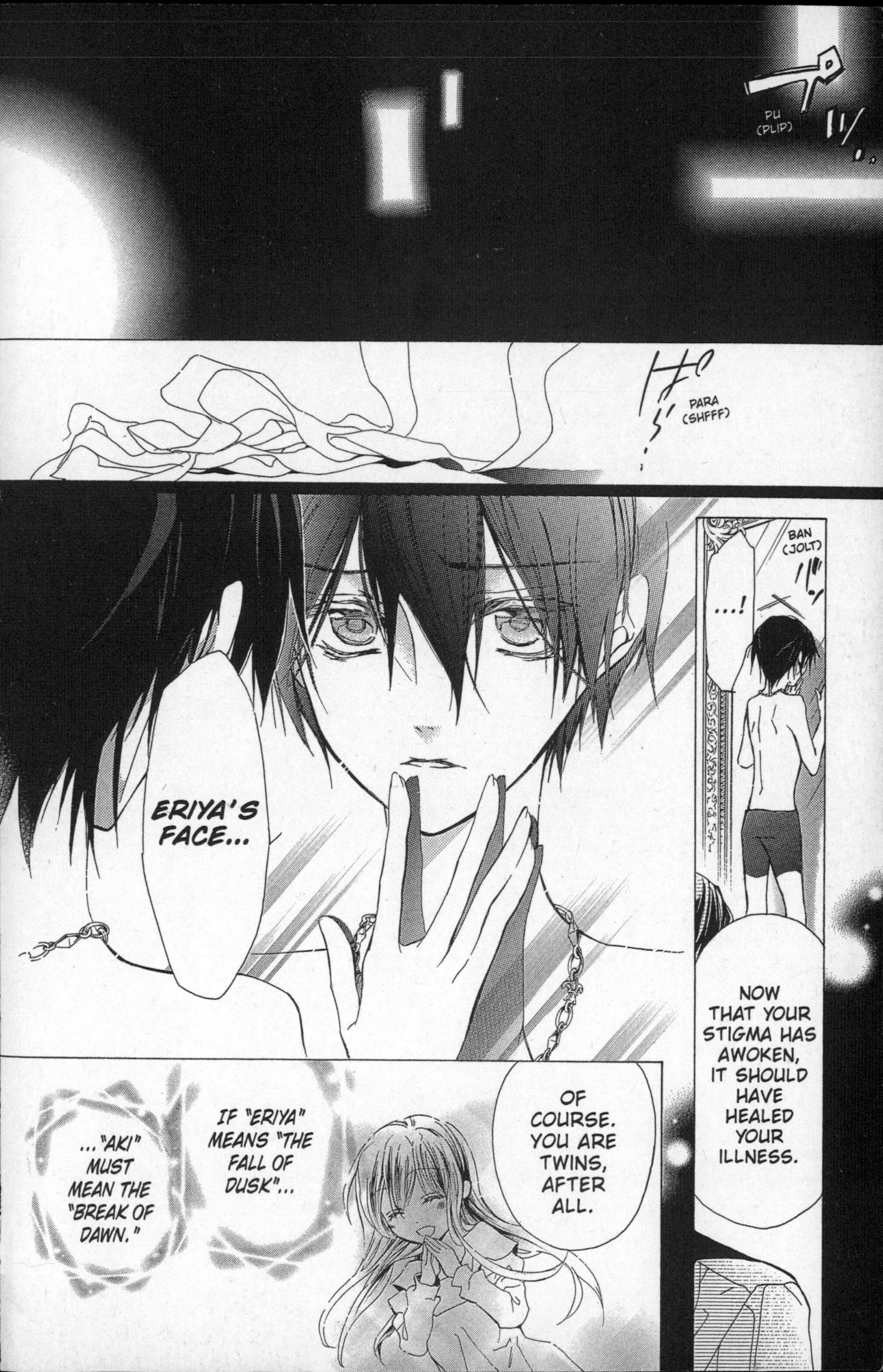
PU
(PLIP)
PARA
(SHFFF)
BAN
(JOLT)
...!
ERIYA'S FACE...
NOW THAT YOUR STIGMA HAS AWOKEN, IT SHOULD HAVE HEALED YOUR ILLNESS.
OF COURSE. YOU ARE TWINS, AFTER ALL.
IF "ERIYA" MEANS "THE FALL OF DUSK"...
..."AKI" MUST MEAN THE "BREAK OF DAWN."

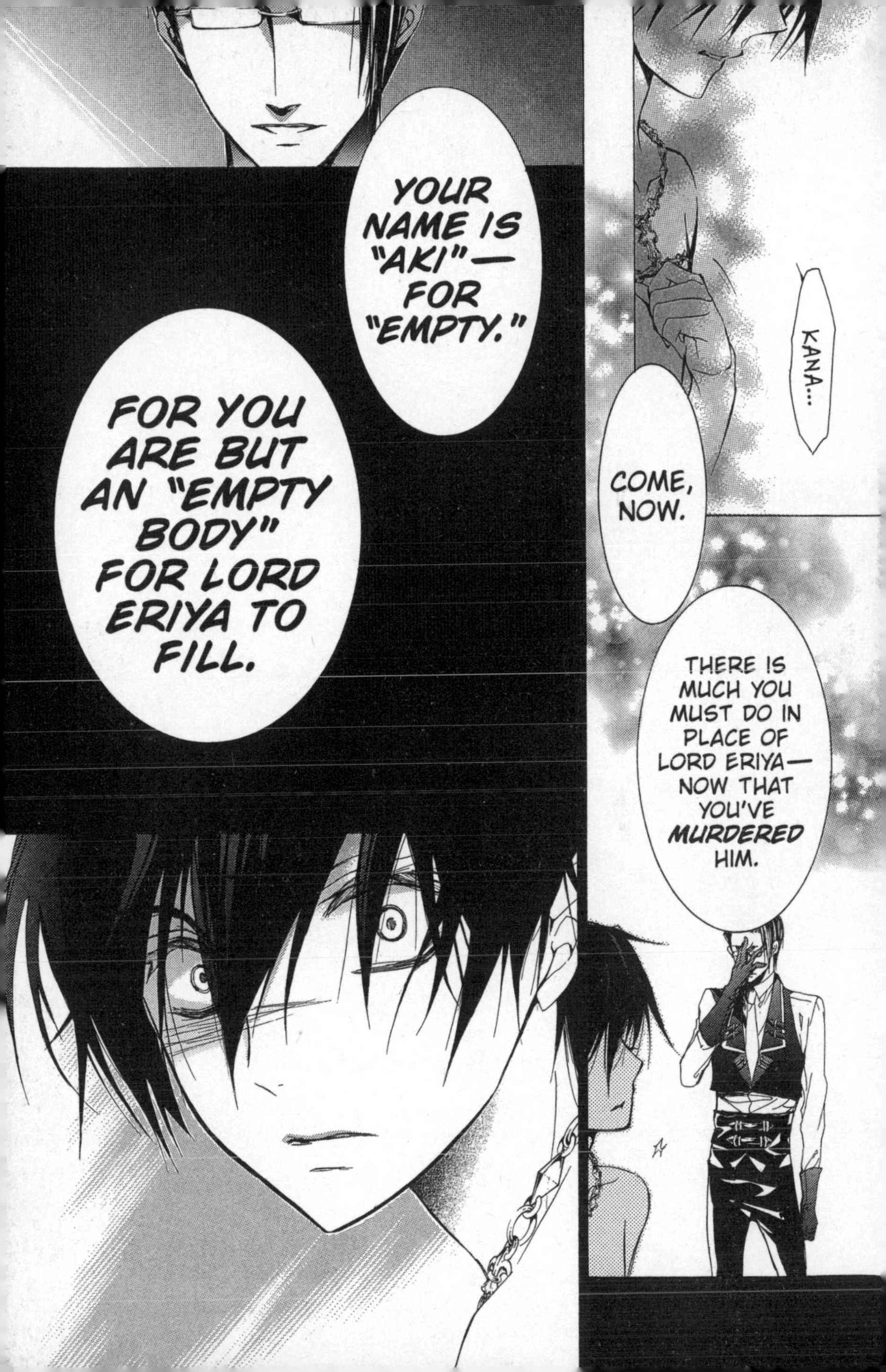
KANA...
COME, NOW.
THERE IS MUCH YOU MUST DO IN PLACE OF LORD ERIYA—NOW THAT YOU'VE *MURDERED* HIM.
YOUR NAME IS "AKI"—FOR "EMPTY."
FOR YOU ARE BUT AN "EMPTY BODY" FOR LORD ERIYA TO FILL.

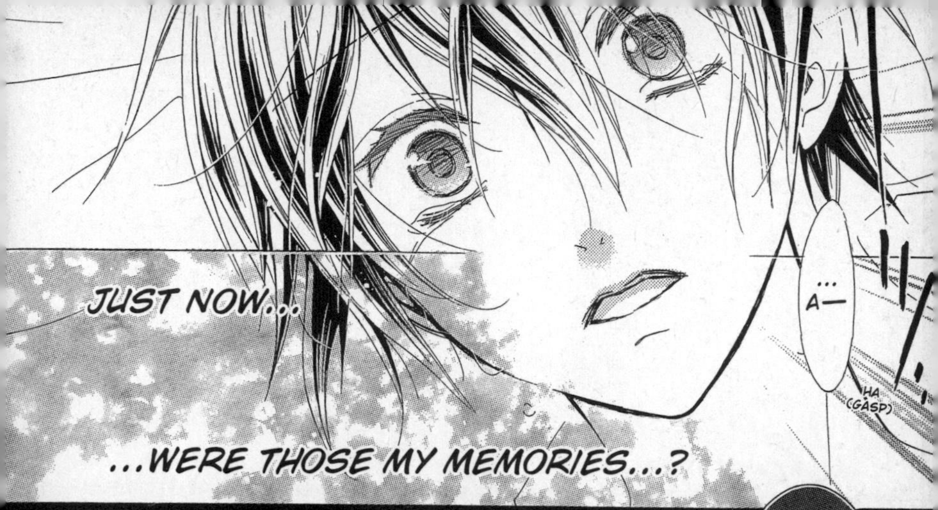
...A—
HA (GASP)
JUST NOW...
...WERE THOSE MY MEMORIES...?
WELL! FINALLY AWAKE, ARE YOU?
PRINCESS THRALL...
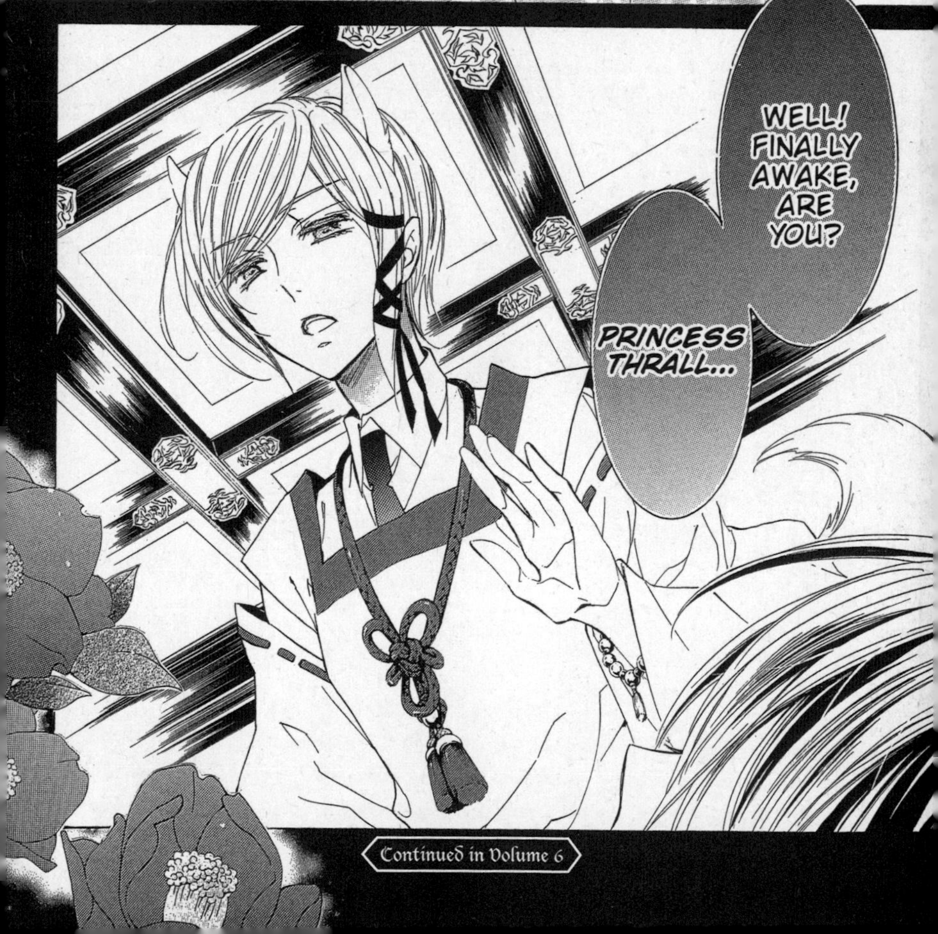
Continued in Volume 6

He's my only vampire

Aya Shouoto

The Words of *He's My Only Vampire*

Unlock the keywords of the dangerous yet beautiful world of *He's My Only Vampire*!

[Angel]
The true form of St. Agatha Academy's student council president, Isuka Bernstein, and vice president, Hitaki Miyajima, is that of angels. As beings aligned with the "Light," they are suspicious of Aki, who, as a being of Darkness, is their opposite.

[Curious Events Club]
A school club started by Kana in order to facilitate the gathering of information about STIGMAs. The CE Club will help resolve any type of trouble and is composed of Kana, Aki, and Jin.

[Dealer]
The title given to the judges of the Game. One is assigned to watch over every participant of the Game and has the power to punish any rule violations with an execution of the player. Aki's Dealer is Swallow.

[Electra]
A new drug that is spreading among the public. It is actually made from Aki's pure vampire blood and can turn humans into Lunatics.

[Emperor]
An elderly man with countless secrets, the Emperor is the absolute ruler of the Tsubakiins and the one who pulls all the strings from the shadows. He is referred to as the head of the Tsubakiins. It was he who educated the pureblood lord, Aki. He is also Eve's guardian. His true identity remains unknown and shrouded in mystery.

[Game]
The Game is a contest to gather the Seven STIGMAs and is centered around the city of Yagai, where Kana lives. The person who gathers all seven will be endowed with immense power and become the "Black Messiah." Aki is participating in this contest in order to gain the power to wake Eriya from his slumber.

[Lunatics]
When exposed to the scent of a pureblood vampire's blood, humans with darkness in their hearts transform into Lunatics under strong moonlight. Lunatics temporarily lose any sense of self and revert to beings of base instinct.

[Pureblood]
Pureblood have special powers even greater than that of a regular vampire. Their blood causes humans to go mad. They are beings both revered and feared. It is said that only a handful of them (including Aki) still exist.

[Soiree]
A private party the Tsubakiin clan hosts behind closed doors. It is ostensibly held to give leaders of certain industries a chance to mingle in an opulent setting, but in actuality, it is an opportunity for the Dark Nobility, who revere Aki's pure vampiric blood, to gather and worship during depraved "ceremonies."

[STIGMA]
STIGMAs are the embodiments of the Demonic Powers.

Anyone who can gather them all will gain enough power to rule the entire world should they choose. There are seven in total: Pride, Greed, Lust, Envy, Wrath, Gluttony, and Sloth.

[Thrall]
Thralls are special followers of purebloods vampires. Each purebloods may have only one thrall and cannot drink blood from any being but their own thrall. In short, a thrall is a purebloods's only possible prey. Thralls' bodies are almost invincible, though they may be injured by certain holy instruments. The relationship between a purebloods and thrall is so intimate that if a thrall dies, its purebloods will die as well.

[Tsubakiin]
Tsubakiin is the name of the household that Aki and Eriya grew up in. It is a very old and respected name. The head of the Tsubakiins (who also controls many other great families in all but name) resides at the Tsubakiin manor, along with a large number of other members of the Tsubakiin clan, who possess a variety of special powers. The clan has long revered the purebloods vampire lord and reigns over the country's underworld.

[Woods]
The place Kana, Aki, and Eriya lived when they were children. The three were separated due to the great fire that occurred there seven years ago.

Pure Blood Boyfriend In The House

IT'S FINALLY VOLUME 5! HURRAY!! THIS IS THE VOLUME THAT FINALLY BRINGS US INTO THE TRUE HEART OF HE'S MY ONLY VAMPIRE. THOUGH WE'VE HAD LITTLE GLIMPSES OF THIS PIVOTAL TIME IN KANA'S PAST SINCE VOLUME 1, WE FINALLY UNRAVEL ONE PART OF THE MYSTERY IN THIS VOLUME...WHAT DID YOU THINK?

SINCE I FIRST STARTED THINKING UP THIS STORY, I HAD THE SENSE THAT, "VAMPIRES ARE AN UTTERLY WESTERN MONSTER...BUT WHAT WOULD JAPANESE VAMPIRES BE LIKE? ESPECIALLY THE PUREBLOOD ONES STEEPED IN TRADITION?" FOLLOWING THAT TRAIN OF THOUGHT IS WHAT ULTIMATELY GOT ME TO START THIS SERIES.

AFTER THIS, MORE TROUBLES LIE AHEAD FOR OUR HEROES...I'M A BIT AFRAID FOR THEM, AS THEIR CREATOR.

LET'S MEET AGAIN IN VOLUME 6!

OH! BY THE WAY, I'M WORKING HARD TO PROVIDE COLOR PAGES FOR THE SERIALIZATION IN *ARIA* MAGAZINE, SO PLEASE READ HMOV IN MAGAZINE FORM TOO!

硝音あや
AYA SHOUOTO
xxx

SPECIAL THANX

NORIE OGAWA
MAIKO YOSHISE
AYA MAEDA
RIKA KASAHARA
KANAE SAITOU
YURIKA HONDA
YOSHIKO OTA
JYURI KODAMA
KOU HIYOCO

and YOU

http://www.kashi.jpn.org/w/

THAT REMINDS ME...
WHEN AKI WAS YOUNG, HE WAS PRETTY MISCHIEVOUS.
HRM. HRMMM.
HMPH!
BUCHI (SNAP)
HIS IMAGE HAS KIND OF CHANGED NOW.
YEAH, I'M THE REAL DELINQUENT~!
CAN'T TOUCH ALL THIS WILD~!
THAT'S NOT AN EDIBLE PLANT! THESE ONES ARE EDIBLE!
AH... NOW MY IMAGE OF HIM HAS TOTALLY CHANGED
IT'S SHATTERED...

A VAMPIRE WITH TOO MANY WORRIES

Aya Shouoto

Next Story

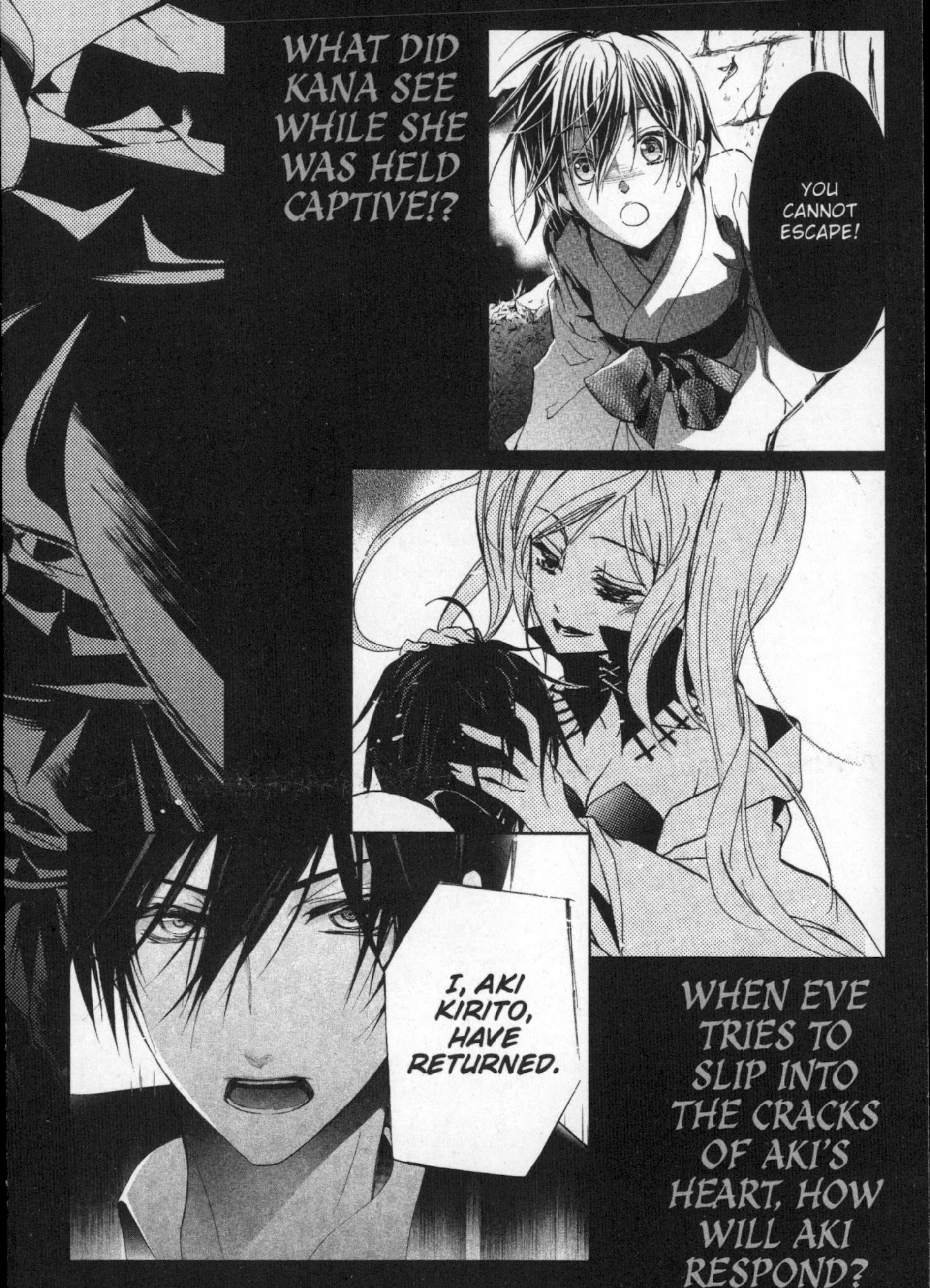
YOU CANNOT ESCAPE!
WHAT DID KANA SEE WHILE SHE WAS HELD CAPTIVE!?
WHEN EVE TRIES TO SLIP INTO THE CRACKS OF AKI'S HEART, HOW WILL AKI RESPOND?
I, AKI KIRITO, HAVE RETURNED.